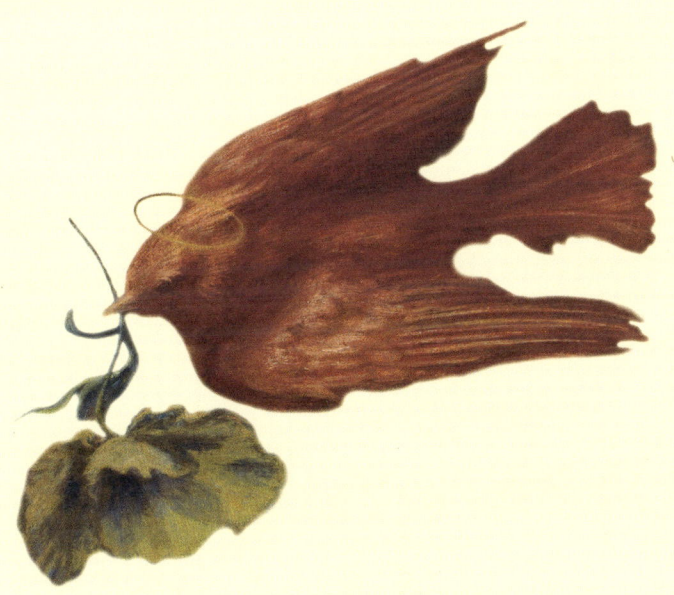

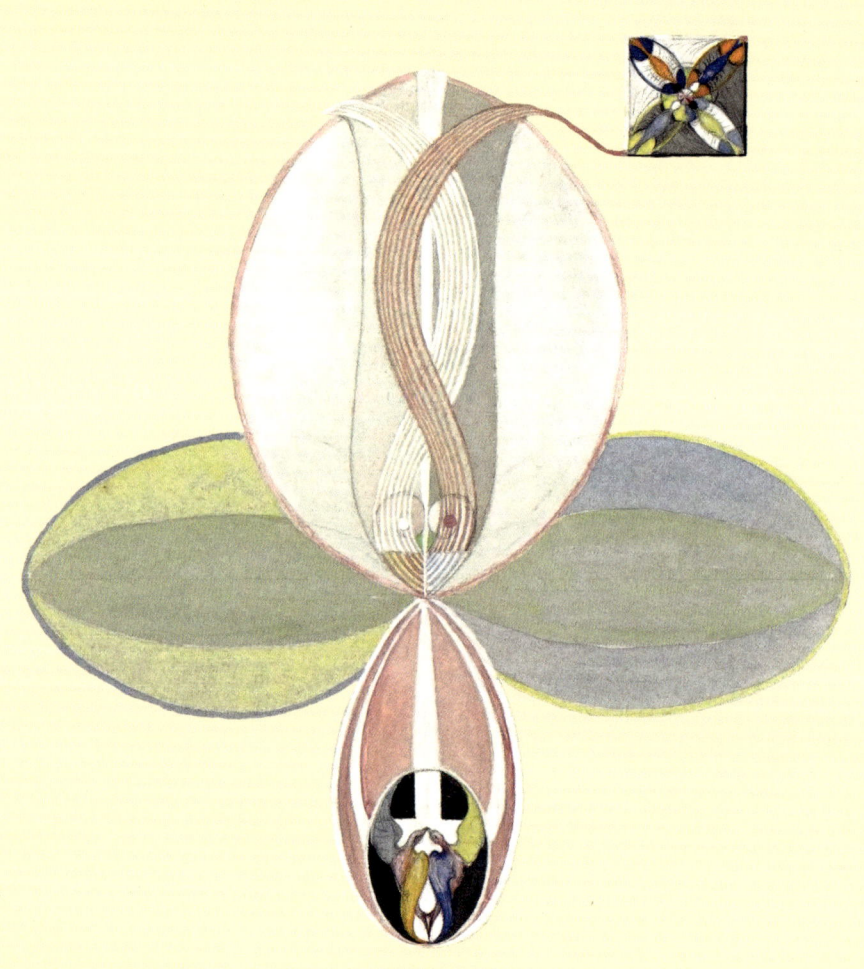

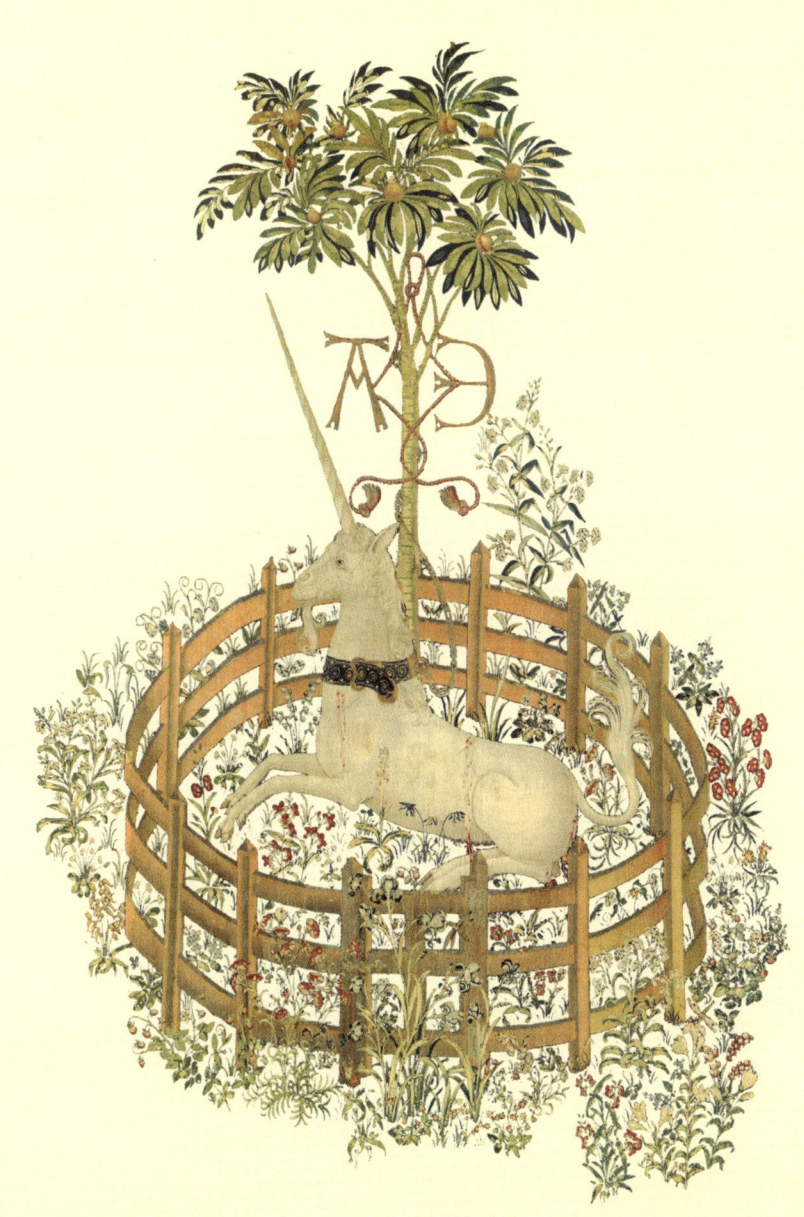

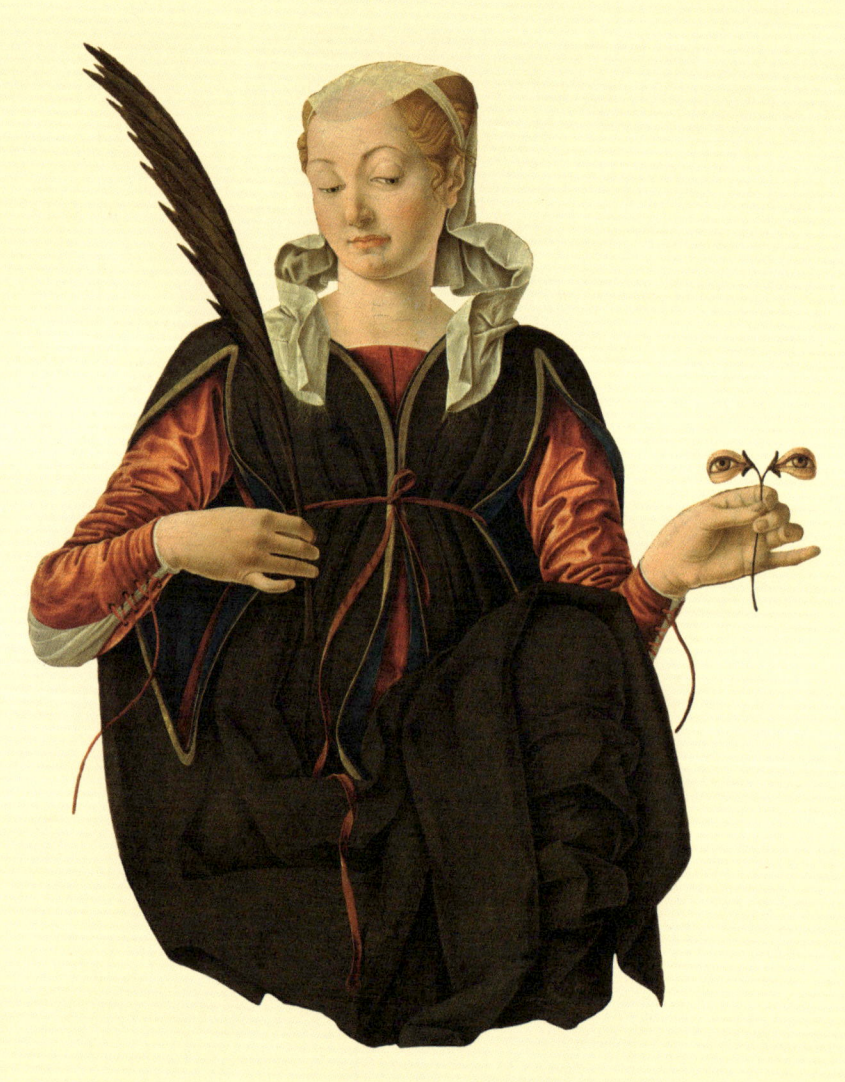

HOPE B. WERNESS

FLORA

THE SECRET LANGUAGE
OF PLANTS IN ART

Timber Press | Portland, Oregon

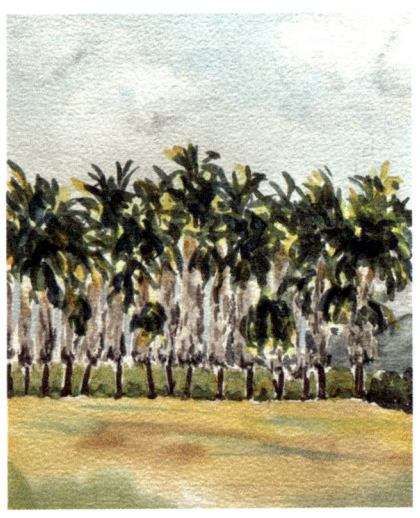

This volume is dedicated to my mother:

JOANNE HILL BENEDICT
(1920–2014)

An artist and prize-winning quiltmaker,
she loved nature and incorporated many plants
and flowers into her work. She also provided
an environment in which my sister and
I could flourish.

It is also dedicated to the new twig on the family
tree, Charles Severn ('Sev') Werness-Rude.
May he grow and prosper.

And to my husband, George, who died as this
book was being prepared. His enthusiasm,
support and love are greatly missed.

CONTENTS

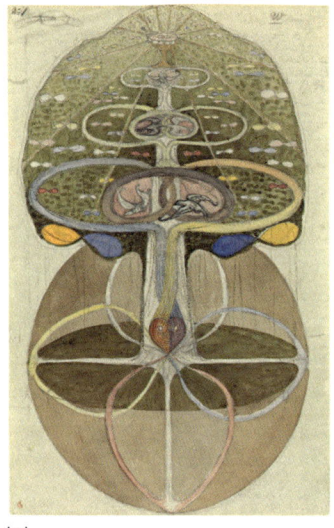

Confucius wrote: 'If you think in terms of a year, plant a seed; if in terms of ten years, plant trees; if in terms of 100 years, teach the people.' But artists and botanists think in millennia or even longer.

According to a list compiled by Botanic Gardens Conservation International using data from its 500 member organizations, there are approximately 400,000 flower species and 60,065 tree species. Of course, not all of them carry symbolic meaning; if they did, this book could never be completed or even begun. Symbolic plants vary from culture to culture, time to time and place to place. Many provide sustenance and shelter and, beyond significance and usefulness, their awesome beauty and abundant life force are sources of endless wonder.[1] Their perceived meanings provide insights that would otherwise go unnoticed, and add to our sum of knowledge.

This book attempts to review and discuss the cultural and art-historical treatment of plants.[2] A new perspective is developing among scholars and artists, stemming from the sweeping ecological changes the world is undergoing. In *Why Look at Plants?* (2018), Giovanni Aloi suggests that John Berger's *Why Look at Animals?* (2009) can be used as a model for current plant studies. Aloi suggests that we must take a different approach, one that does not involve distancing ourselves from and objectifying plants:

> *The hope is that like human-animal studies, the field of plant studies will enrich our perspectives on plants, thus leading to different modalities in what right now constitutes a mostly unacknowledged critical node in the survival of life on the planet...[Instead of counterproductive approaches] contemporary art has the ability to complement, unhinge, problematize, and challenge philosophical concepts – the synergy between the two can constitute a powerful tool just as long as it is put to work to achieve actual change.*

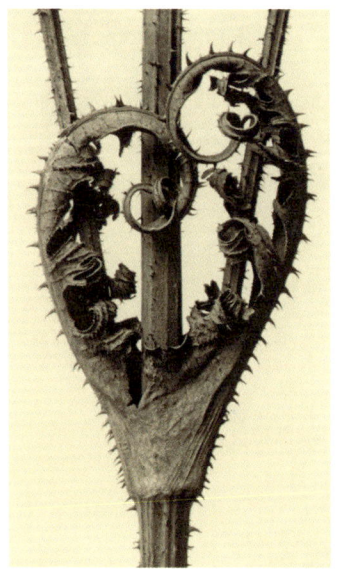

The field of plant studies has grown and changed since the turn of the millennium, resulting in a new, wide-ranging literature that is often international in scope.[3] Not just scientific and environmental in nature, it examines aesthetic, literary, philosophical and spiritual issues. A central theme regards the sentience of plants, replacing the common, long-held idea that they are immobile and unfeeling. Recent fiction, such as Richard Powers's *The Overstory: A Novel* (2018) and Brian Selznick's *Big Tree* (2023), also addresses this subject, drawing attention to the complexity of plant interaction. Contemporary art exemplifies the new approaches, such as the work of John Grade (see 'Cedar', p. 38), Precious Okoyomon (see 'Kudzu', p. 216) and Mark Dion (see 'Hemlock', p. 44). Artists also concern themselves with extinction – not just that of plants, but also that of animals and entire environments.[4] As Dion puts it:

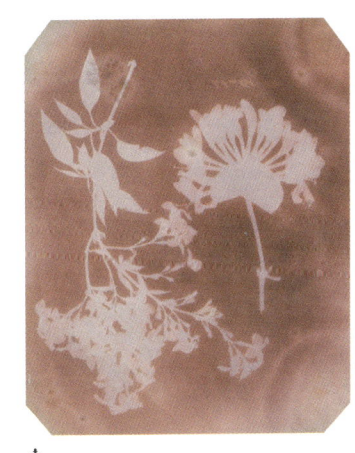

> *Certainly for the things I care about – oceans, forests, wild places and wild things, there is little good news. This is a serious role for the arts – bearing witness and mourning. After all, mourning is a legitimate mode of thinking.*

When I began this book, I thought I'd be doing the 'acorn = strength, fertility' and so on. And I have done that. I have found, however, that plants are being re-evaluated. Artists, art historians, philosophers, scientists and others are looking anew at plants – at their beauty, sentience and life force. Most maintain that we must change our ideas about and relationships with plants. To do so, they believe, could be a crucial step towards making changes that might eventually impact the environmental disasters now occurring.

Readers wishing to find information about specific plants should consult the Plant Index in the following pages.

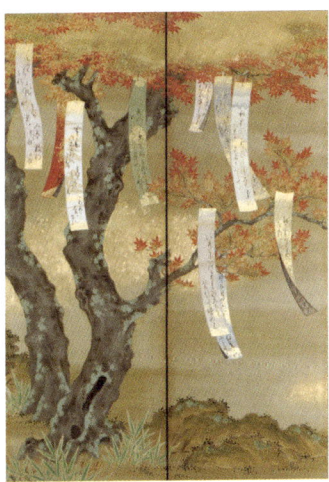

⊗ Hilma af Klint, *Tree of Knowledge, no. 1*, 1913, watercolour on paper. Potomac, MA: Glenstone Museum.

✳ Karl Blossfeldt, *Dipsacus laciniatus* (*cutleaf teasel*), 1928, gelatin silver print. Los Angeles, CA: J. Paul Getty Museum.

✳ William Henry Fox Talbot, *Two Plant Specimens*, 1839, photogenic drawing. Chicago, IL: Art Institute of Chicago.

✳ Tosa Mitsuoki, *Autumn Maples with Poem Slips* (detail), 1670–80, ink, colours, gold leaf and gold powder on silk. Chicago, IL: Art Institute of Chicago.

32

30

28

34

36

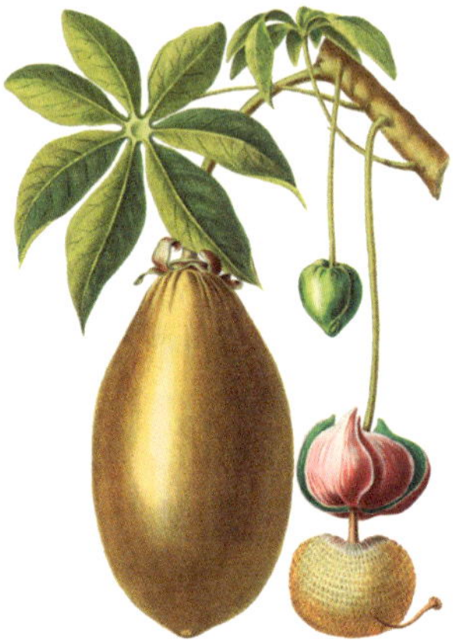

38

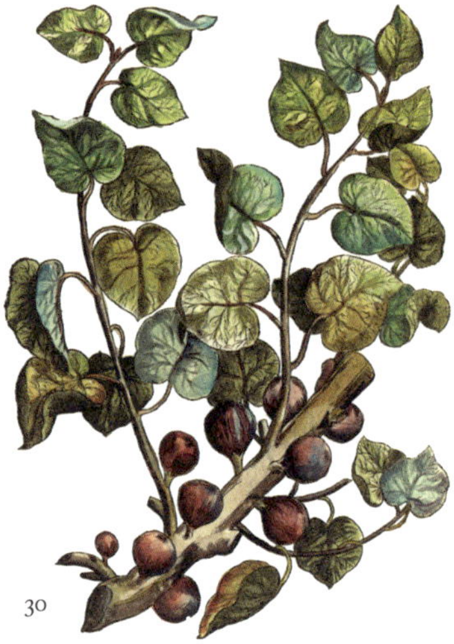

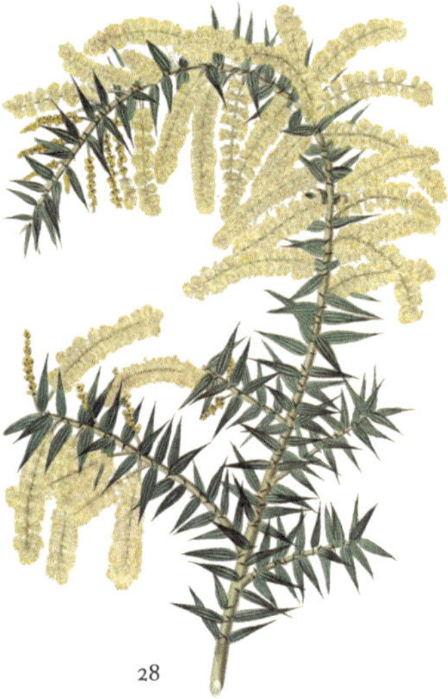

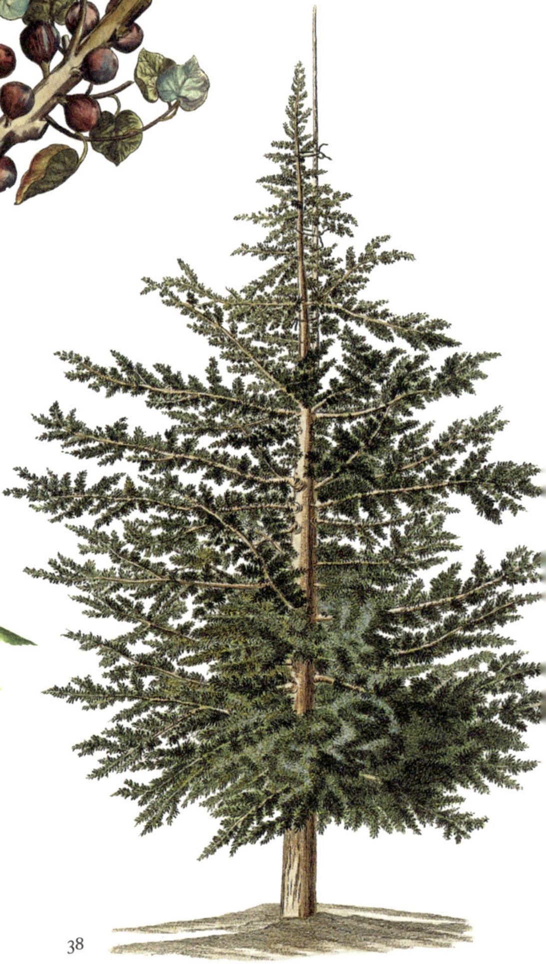

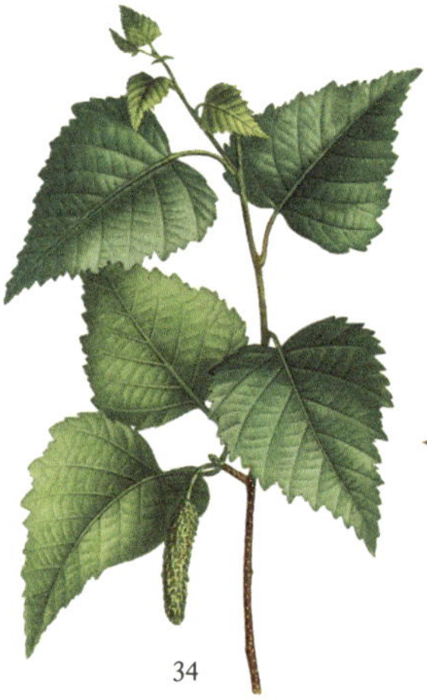

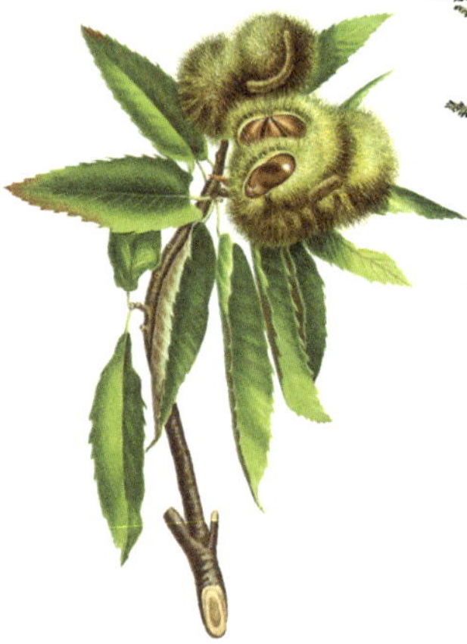

TREES

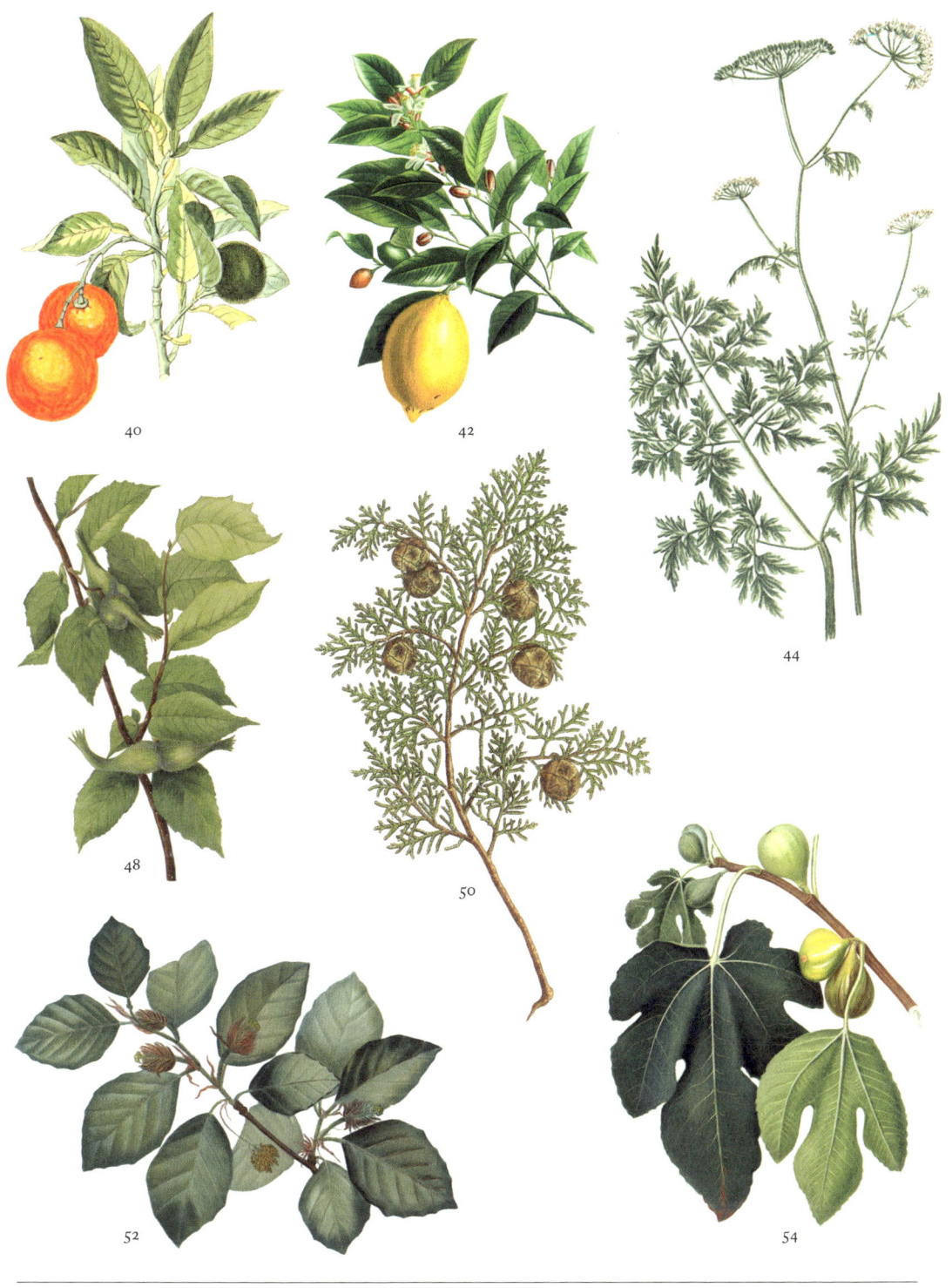

40 . . . . ORANGE	44 . . . . HEMLOCK	50 . . . . CYPRESS	54 . . . . FIG
42 . . . . LEMON	48 . . . . HAZEL	52 . . . . BEECH	

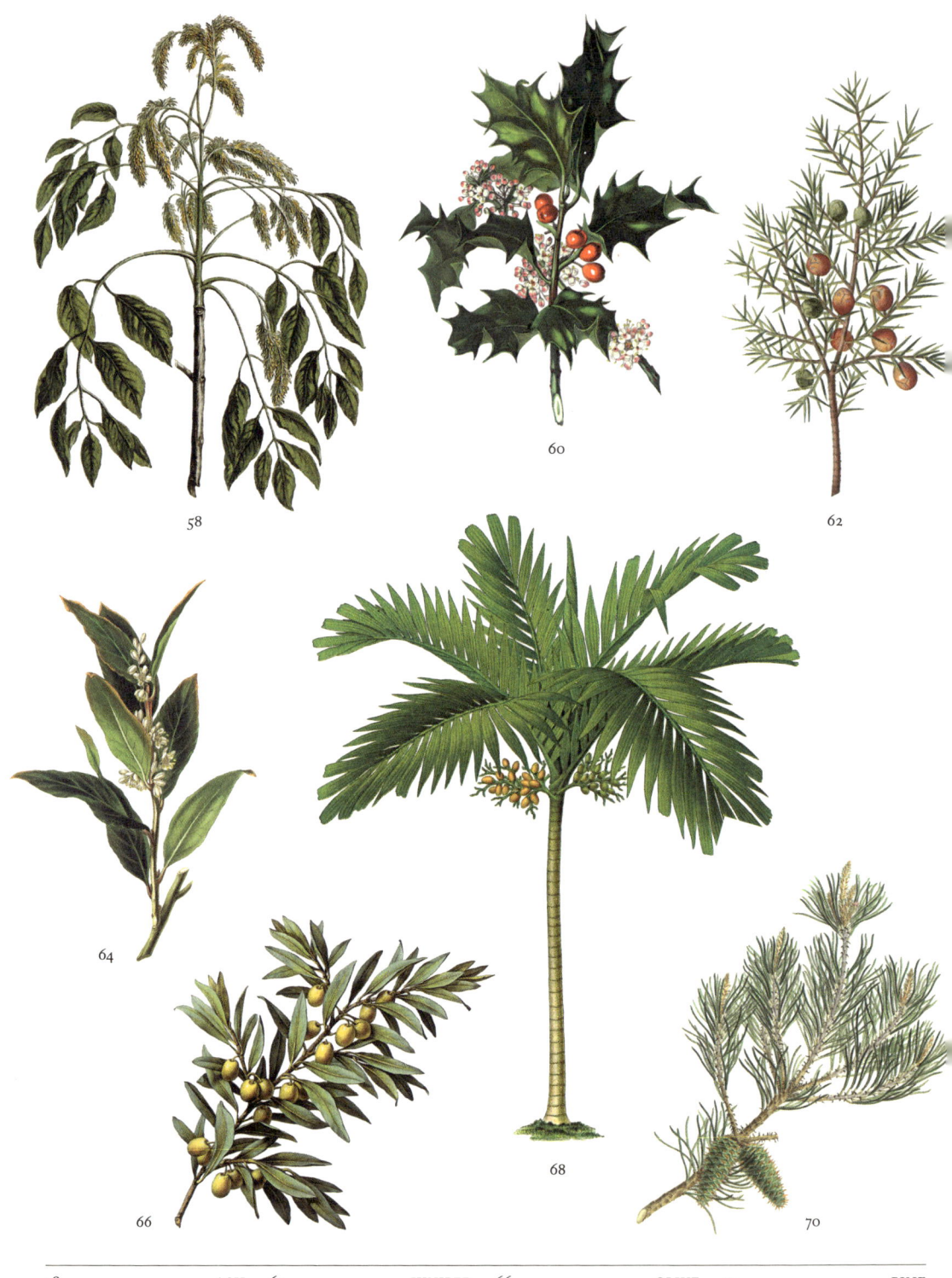

58

60

62

64

66

68

70

58 . . . . ASH   62 . . . . JUNIPER   66 . . . . OLIVE   70 . . . . PINE

60 . . . . HOLLY   64 . . . . LAUREL   68 . . . . PALM

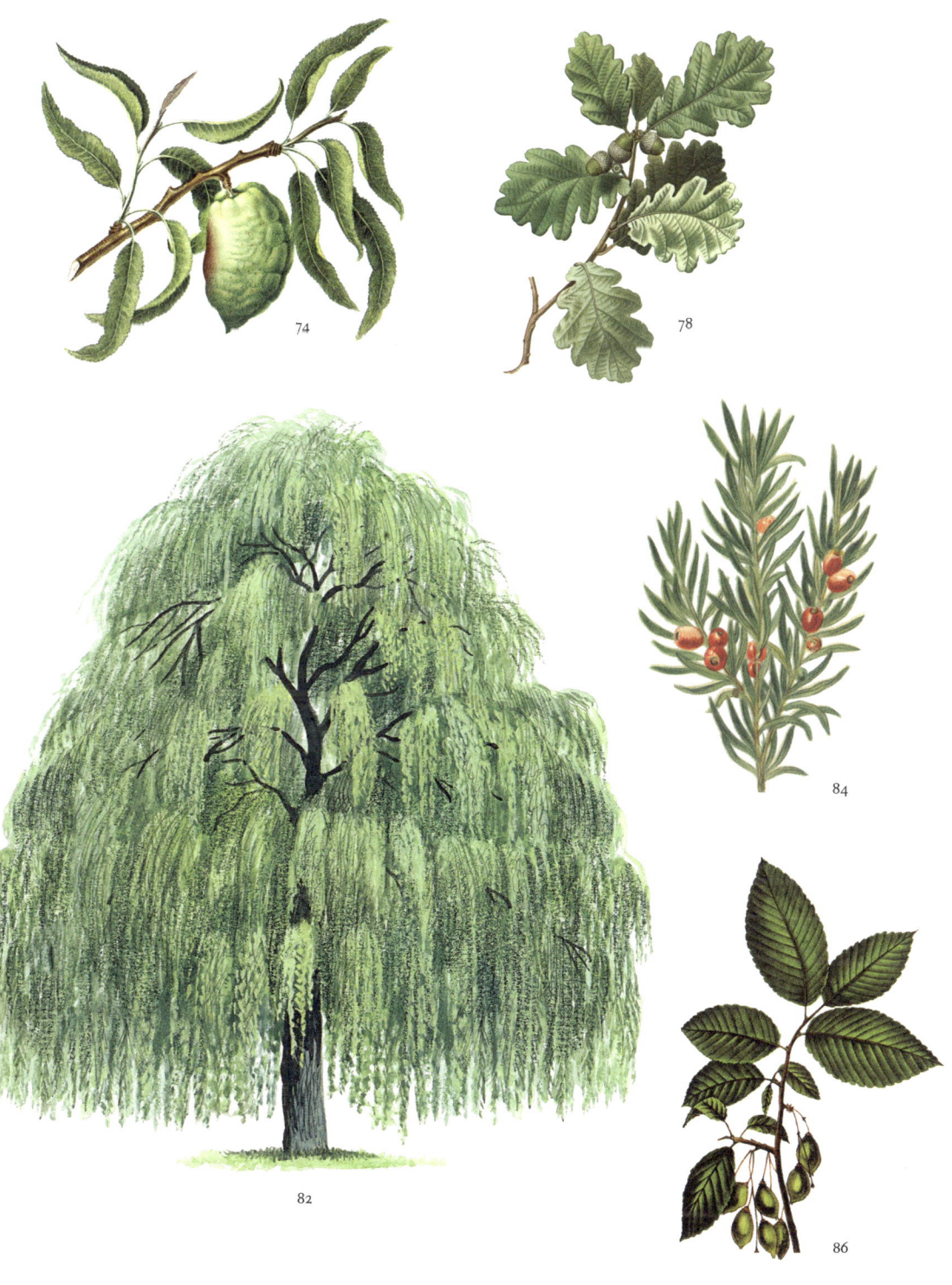

74 . . . . ALMOND   82 . . . . WILLOW   86 . . . . ELM
78 . . . . OAK   84 . . . . YEW

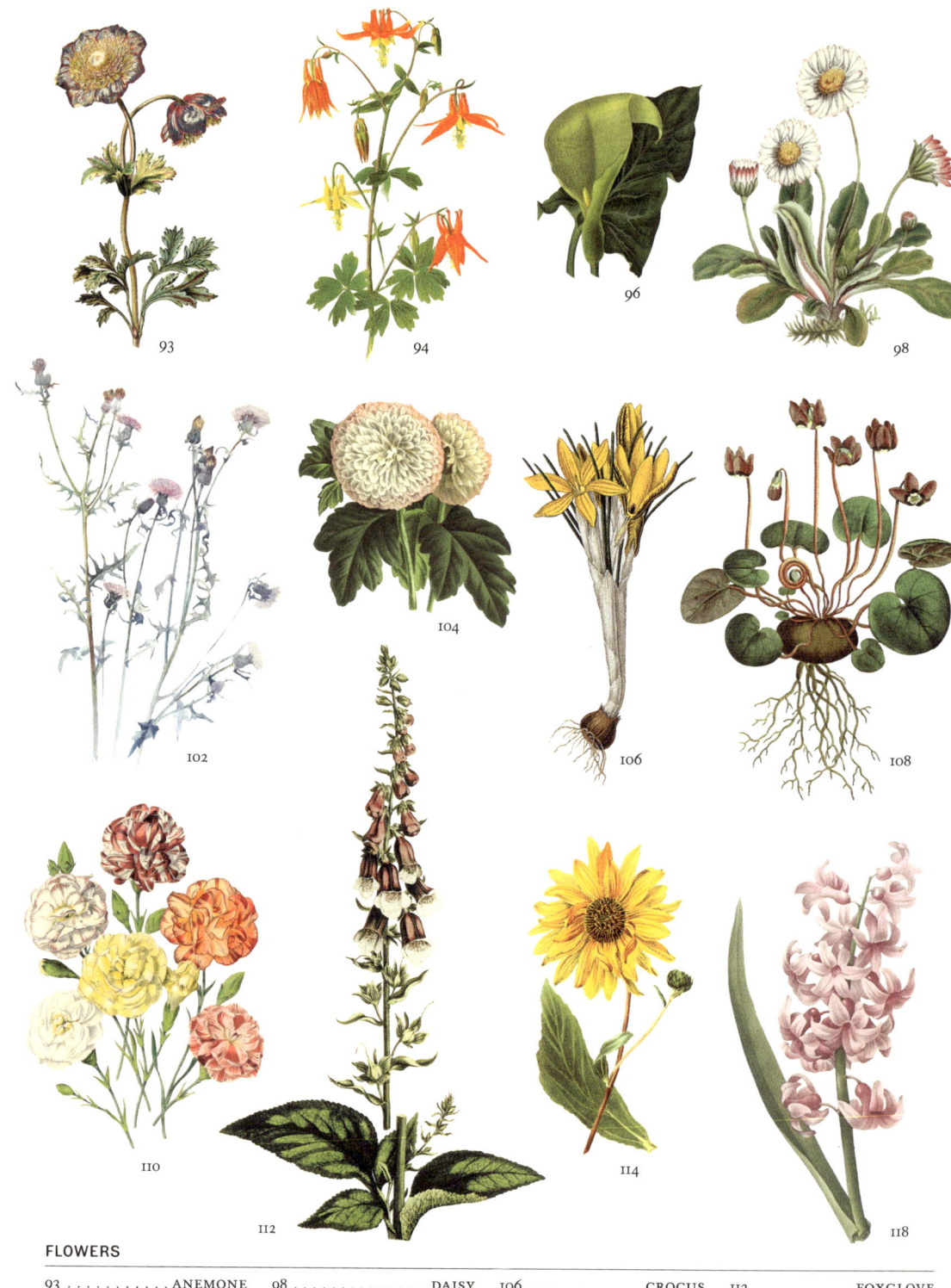

FLOWERS

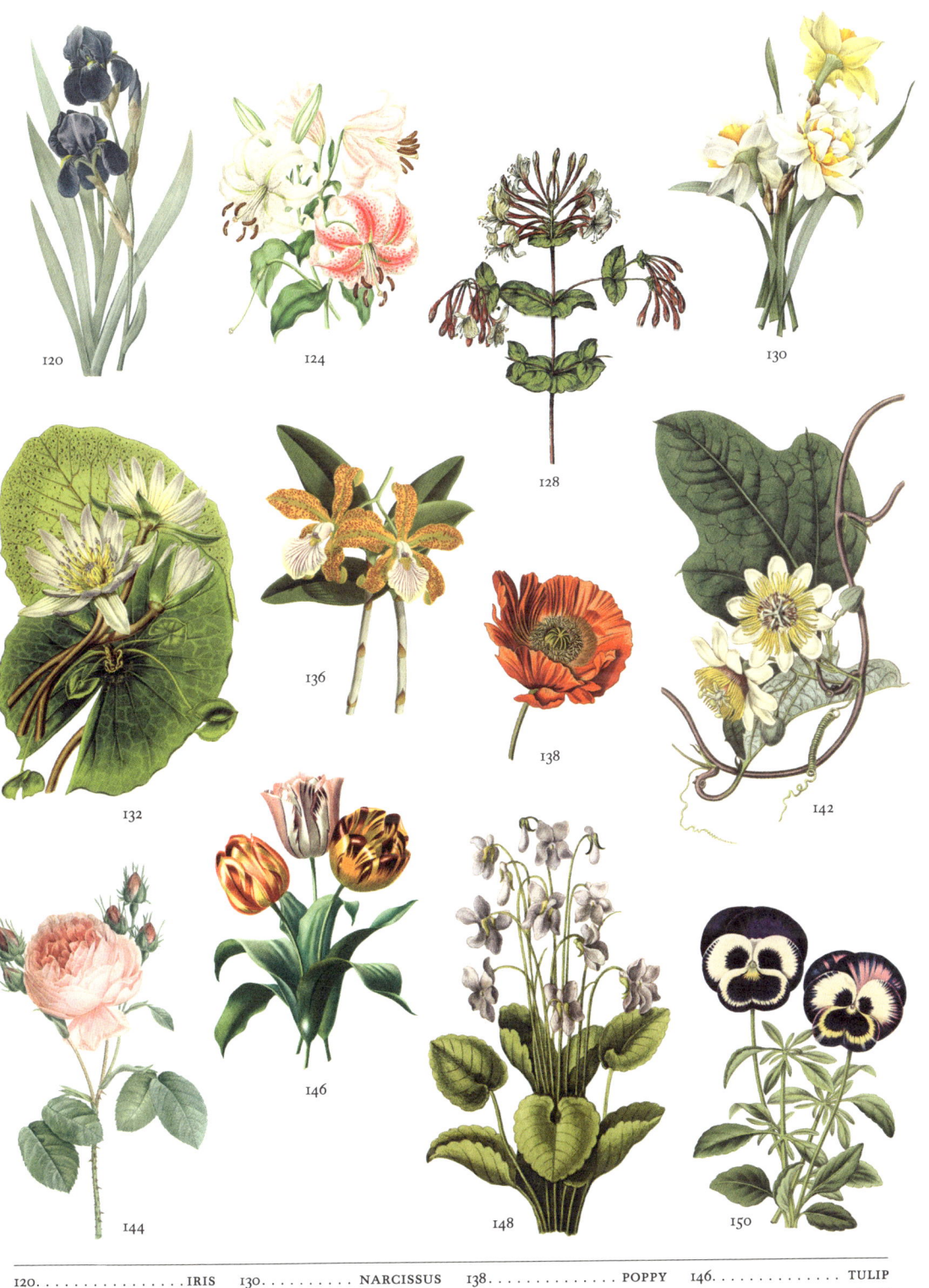

120 ⋯⋯⋯⋯⋯⋯IRIS 130 ⋯⋯⋯⋯NARCISSUS 138 ⋯⋯⋯⋯⋯POPPY 146 ⋯⋯⋯⋯⋯TULIP
124 ⋯⋯⋯⋯⋯⋯LILY 132 ⋯⋯⋯WATER LILY 142 ⋯⋯PASSIONFLOWER 148 ⋯⋯⋯⋯VIOLET
128 ⋯⋯HONEYSUCKLE 136 ⋯⋯⋯⋯ORCHID 144 ⋯⋯⋯⋯⋯ROSE 150 ⋯⋯⋯⋯⋯PANSY

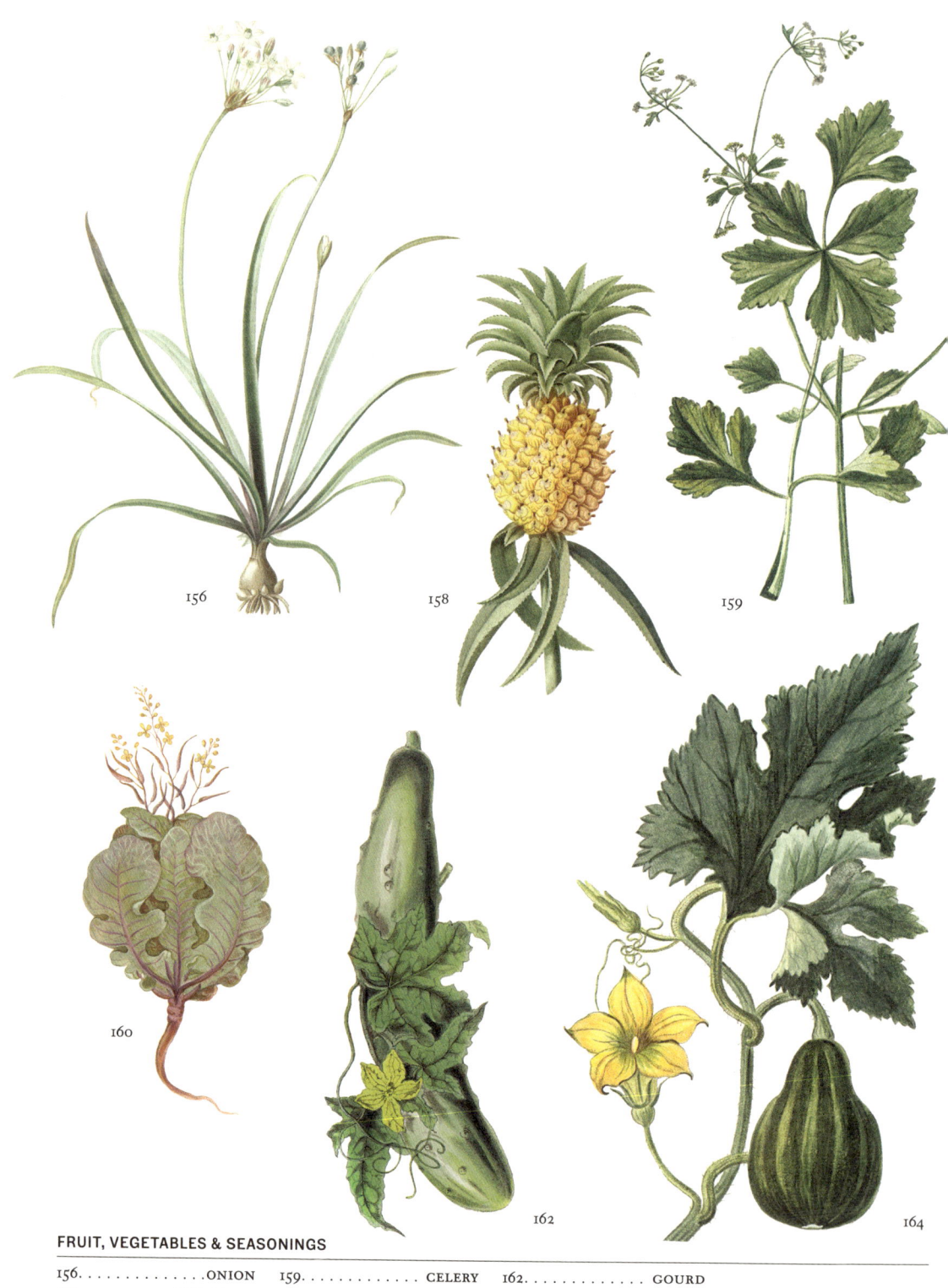

FRUIT, VEGETABLES & SEASONINGS

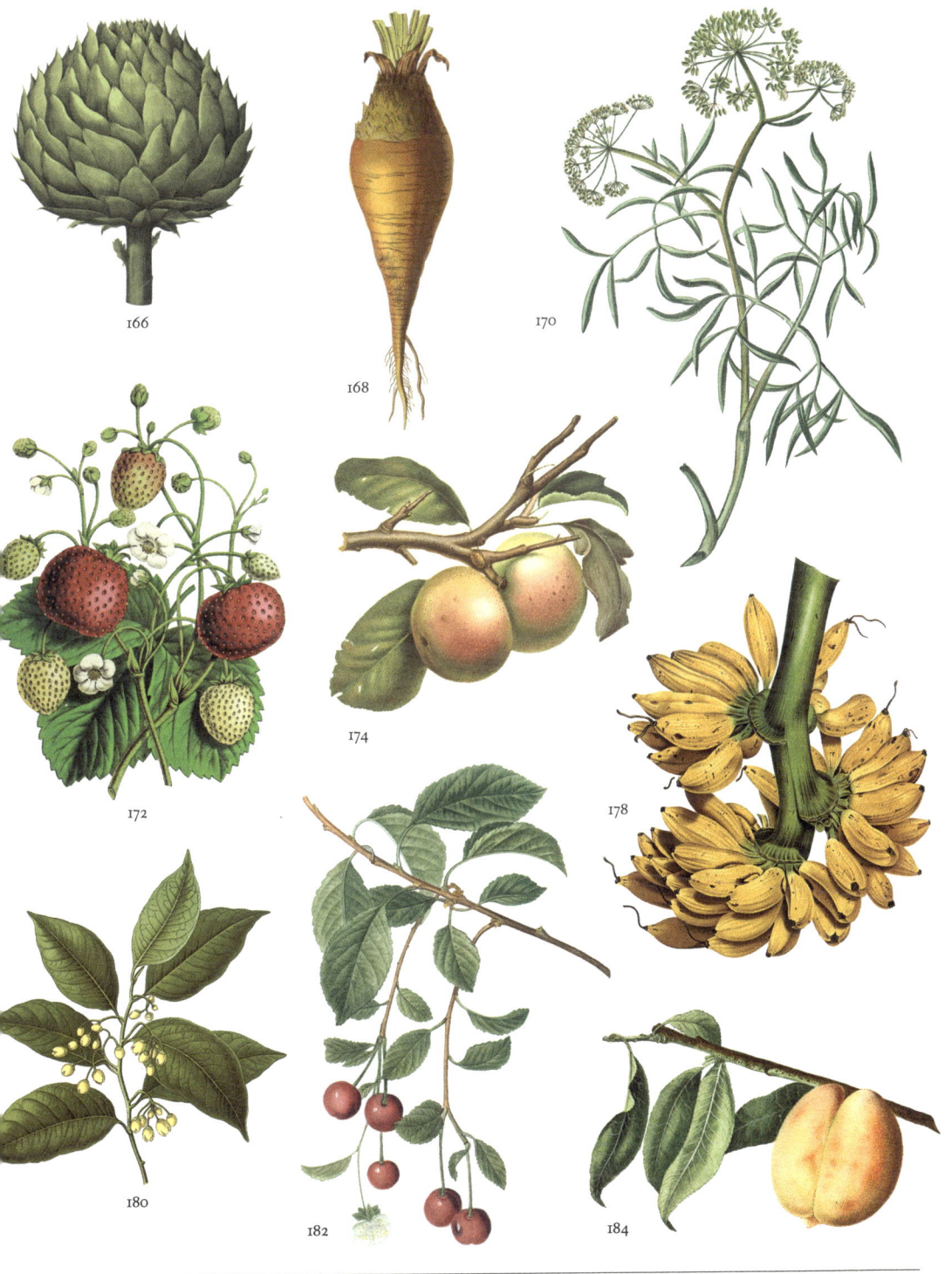

166 . . . . ARTICHOKE   172 . . . . STRAWBERRY   180 . . . . NUTMEG
168 . . . . CARROT   174 . . . . APPLE   182 . . . . CHERRY
170 . . . . FENNEL   178 . . . . BANANA   184 . . . . PEACH

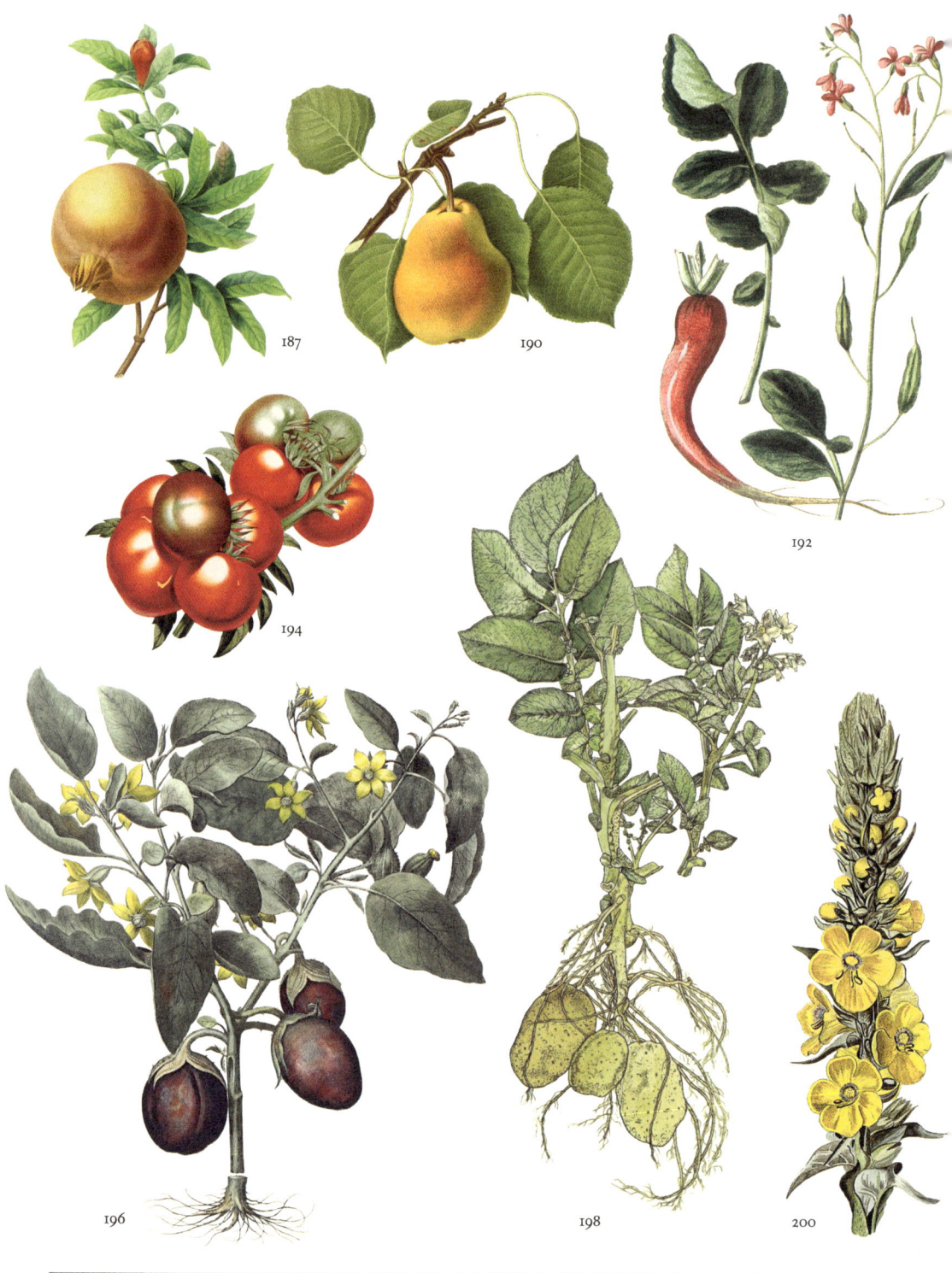

187 . . . . POMEGRANATE   192 . . . . RADISH   196 . . . . AUBERGINE   200 . . . . MULLEIN
190 . . . . PEAR   194 . . . . TOMATO   198 . . . . POTATO

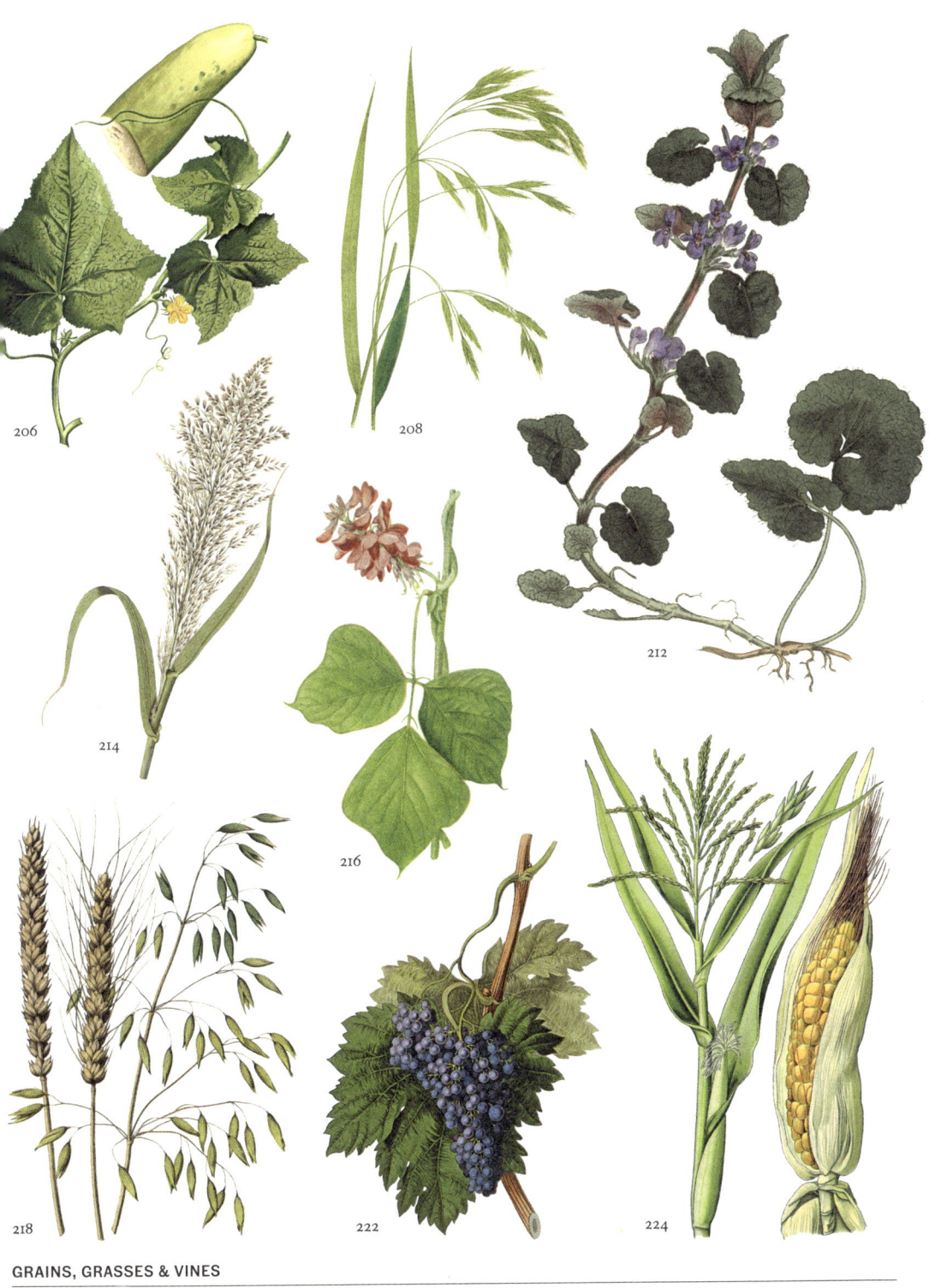

GRAINS, GRASSES & VINES

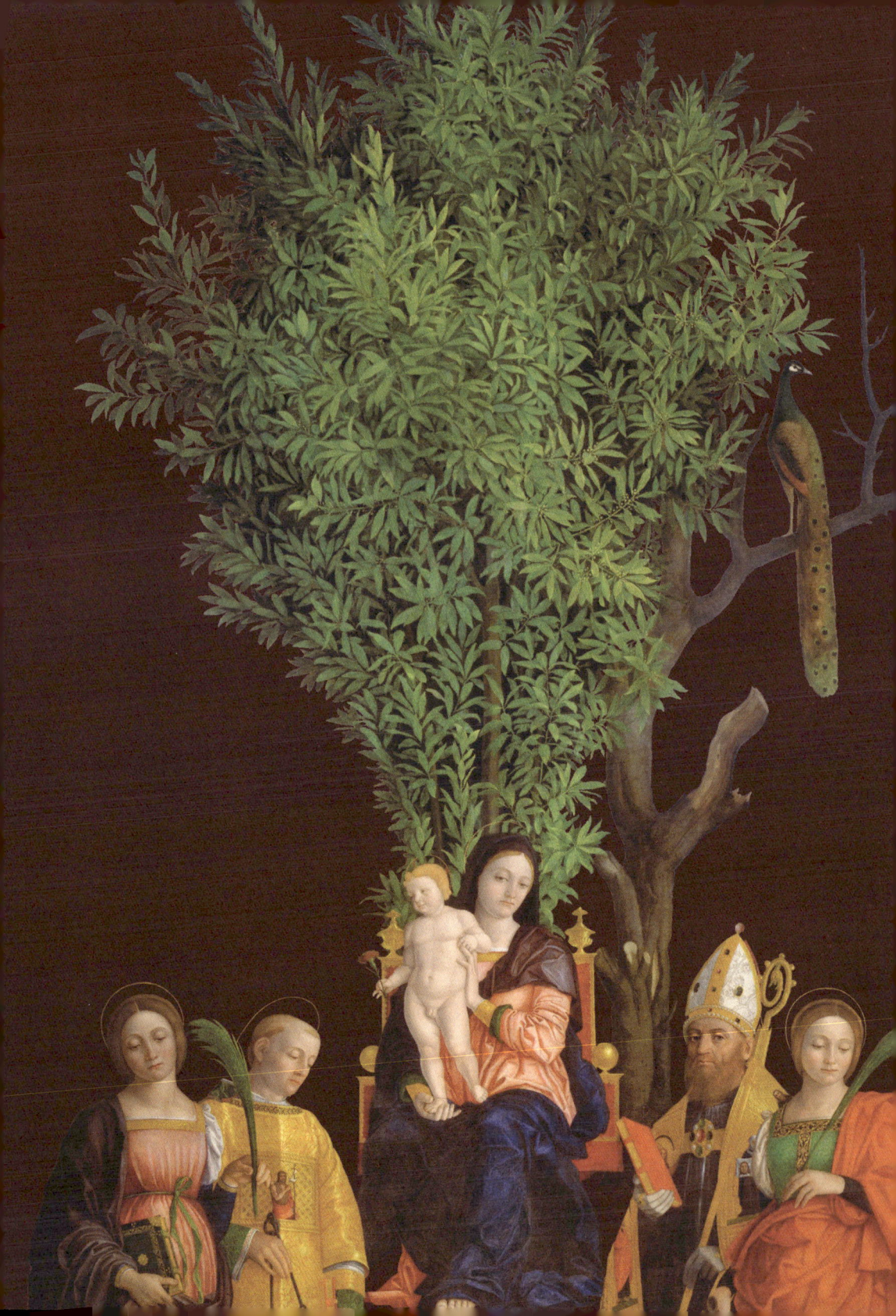

TREES

There are more than 60,000 species of tree – fewer than flower species, but perhaps of greater importance. Trees are larger than humans, outlive us by aeons and have been on earth far longer than us; indeed, many might seem to us to be immortal. They provide shelter – shade and building materials – and flowering trees provide sustenance and nurture in the form of medicine, fruit and nuts. We often refer to our family line as a tree, and use similar words to describe trees and our own bodies: crown, trunk and limbs.

The importance of trees in the environment cannot be overstated. They stabilize the soil and prevent erosion. They breathe, absorbing carbon dioxide and replenishing oxygen. They are abidingly strange and beautiful. We may have been expelled from Eden, but Paradise lives on in national parks, botanical gardens, nature reserves and seed banks, and in the critical work of artists and environmentalists.[5]

Some depictions of trees convey more general meanings. Allison Meier delineated several of these 'types' in the catalogue of an exhibition at the Courtauld Gallery in London in 2014, 'A Dialogue with Nature: Romantic Landscapes from Britain and Germany':

> *The Blasted Tree: a wounded but still living tree –*
> *the cycle of nature, disruption of pastoral peace.*
> *The Lone Tree: a sometimes damaged but surviving lone*
> *tree – subtext man lives and dies, but trees continue*
> *in a longer life; in a Christian context, Resurrection.*
> *Dead Trees: memento mori.*
> *Reaching to the Sky: spiritual symbols connecting earth*
> *and sky, often with rainbows.*
> *Trees Entwined: in connection with family portraits,*
> *entwined lives of people.*
> *Gnarled Giants: often anthropomorphic depictions*
> *of rooted strength.*

In the following pages, all aspects of each tree are considered: the tree itself, its blossom and its fruit or nuts. For separate discussions of fruit, please see the plant index.

H. J. Ruprecht, Trunk and roots of a pine tree cut to show growth rings; microscopic views of wood cells in longitudinal and transverse section and of a root tip, chromolithograph, 1877. London: Wellcome Collection.

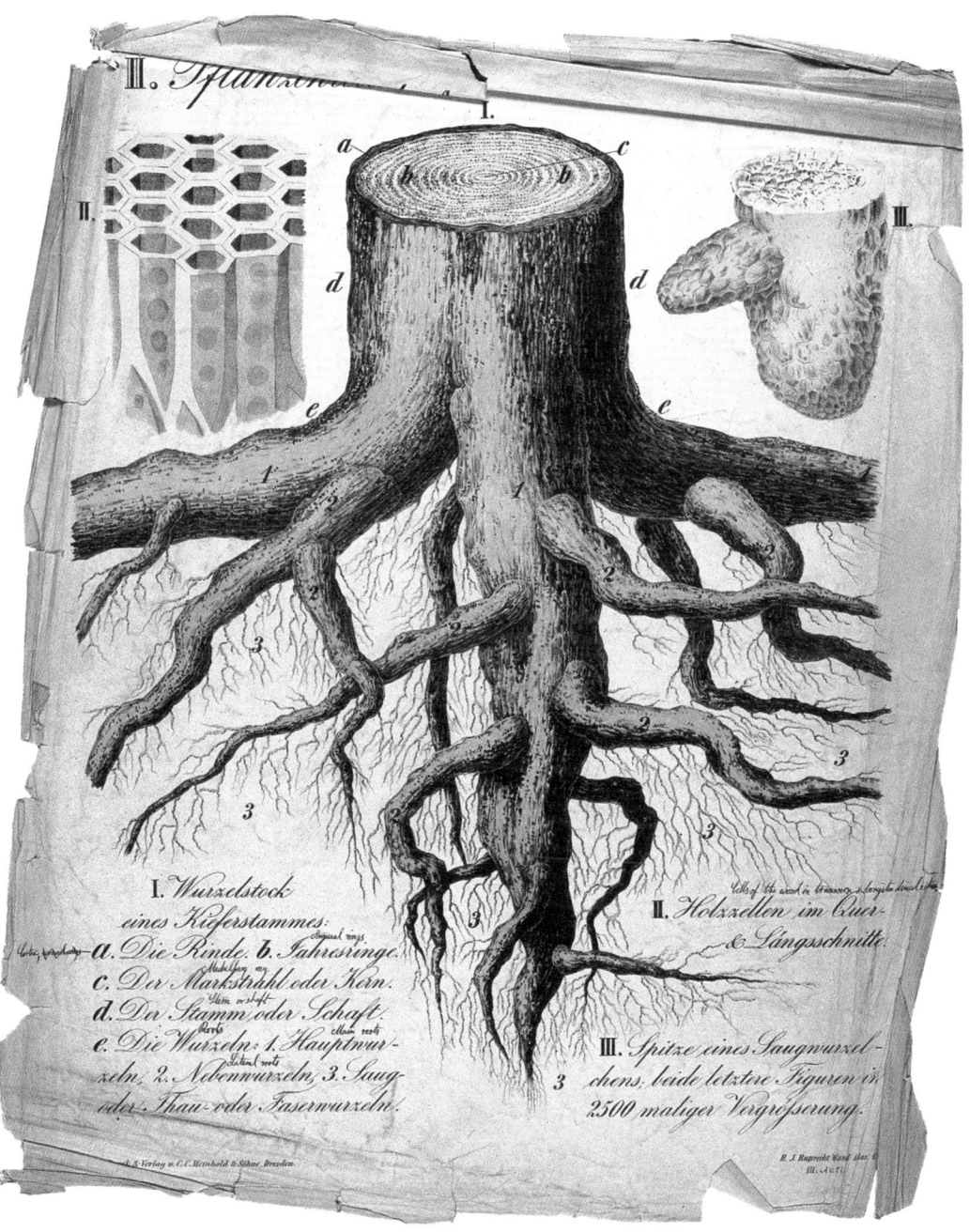

I. Wurzelstock
eines Kieferstammes:
a. Die Rinde. b. Jahresringe.
c. Der Markstrahl oder Kern.
d. Der Stamm oder Schaft:
e. Die Wurzeln: 1. Hauptwur-
zeln, 2. Nebenwurzeln, 3. Saug-
oder Thau- oder Faserwurzeln.

II. Holzzellen im Quer-
& Längsschnitte.

III. Spitze eines Saugwurzel-
chens; beide letztere Figuren in
2500 maliger Vergröfserung.

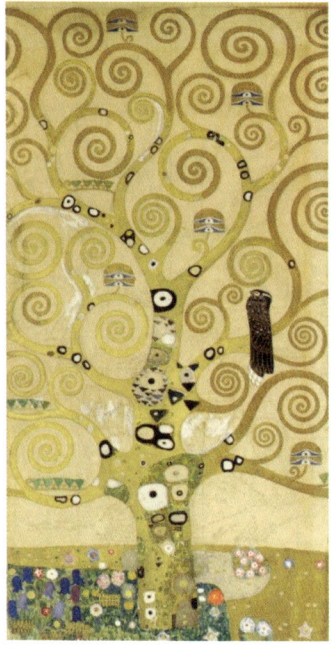

The concept of the Tree of Life is ancient and widespread; perhaps unsurprisingly, since trees are among the most obvious things in the landscape. The Tree of Life is one of the two trees described in the Biblical book of Genesis, the other being the Tree of Knowledge:

> *And out of the ground the Lord God made every tree grow that is pleasant to the sight and good for food. The tree of life was also in the midst of the garden, and the tree of the knowledge of good and evil (2:9, 16–17)*

Since Genesis does not mention a particular species, many candidates have been suggested: acacia, apple, cedar, cherry, dragon tree, elm, fig, palm, persea, pomegranate, quince and sycamore. The tree is seen in Christian images of Paradise, for instance in Albrecht Dürer's *Adam and Eve* (1504). In Eastern Orthodox art, Christ often sits in or hangs crucified from the tree.

The most ancient images of the Tree of Life appear in Egyptian tomb paintings and low-relief carvings from Mesopotamia. In the twelfth-century Jewish mystical tradition the Kabbalah, the Tree is depicted as a diagram called the Sefirot (or Sephirot), a word meaning 'emanations'. In Kabbalist theory, ten creative forces, or emanations, exist between Ein Sof (the infinite, unknowable divine) and the created world.

Gustav Klimt's *Tree of Life* mosaic, one of three commissioned for the dining room of a palace in Brussels, depicts the concept with swirling branches, climbing plants and fragile threads, indicating the energy and complexity of life. Flowers, symbols and glittering surfaces magically convey vitality and immortality.

A 2021 image by the San Francisco artist David Maxim is a poignant example of the Tree of Life. Some years ago Maxim created images of himself hugging trees in the Sierras. In 2021 he was diagnosed with a terminal disease. He writes of a visit to Golden Gate Park:

Gustav Klimt, *Tree of Life*, Stoclet Frieze (detail), 1909, working drawing of a mosaic frieze. Vienna: Museum of Applied Arts.

Sefirotic tree, *The Great Parchment*, copied by James Hepburn, 1606. Oxford: The Bodleian Library.

David Maxim, *Old Man with Young Tree*, 2021, watercolour on paper. Courtesy of the artist.

*With my diagnosis fresh in my mind I decided this was
a good day for a park visit...I was drawn to the hopeful,
promising vision of young trees.*

*After I set up my camera to capture the right position,
I had to get on my knees to find space free of limbs to put
my arms around the slender trunk. My body will never
hug the mature tree. I whispered to the tree as I would
to a small child. With my pose in a prayerful attitude,
I imagined an exchange of energy, in my body's touch
of the tree, and the tree to me.*

*I will die very soon compared to this tree with its whole
life before it. Yet it seems kindred, family, insofar that
our lives may intersect while we are both on the planet
at the same time. Man to tree and tree to man. It accepted
my connection to it and to the earth deep below. In my
embrace of the tree, I engage all of life around me. And
its life will all go on and on. I embrace it – a welcome,
a farewell, a meditation, a prayer. For now we live together
on the planet. The tree is rooted; I am grounded, and at
ease with the world around me.*

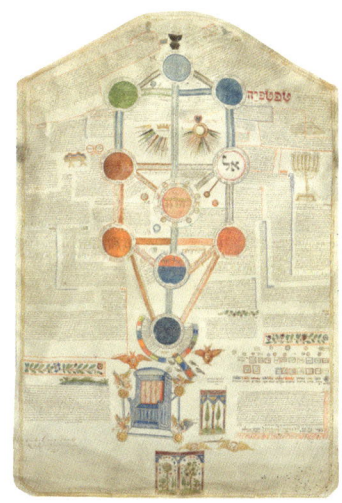

This apparently simple image evokes not only the Tree of Life
but other complex themes: life and death, the idiosyncrasies of
time and the enormity and endurance of life. The tenderness
of the artist's embrace conveys hope, humility, an abiding
gratitude and acceptance, and love. The fragile young tree
stands at the centre, uniting and connecting all.

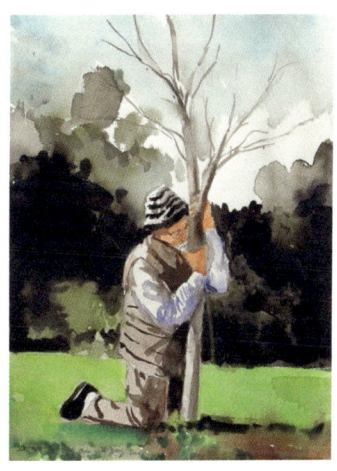

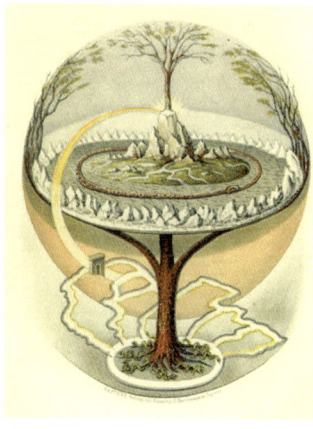

Although not entirely universal, the concept of a primordial tree that grew at the centre of the universe and connected the heavens, earth and the underworld is widespread. Symbolism is attributed to its branches, trunk, leaves and roots. Stars crown it in the heavens, animals and birds inhabit its branches, and serpents lie at its roots. It is aligned to the cardinal points and springs forth from sacred fountains that sustain it.

Yggdrasil is the World Tree in Scandinavia. Similar trees or pillars occur in ancient Egypt, Persia, India (both Hindu and Buddhist) and Greece (under Alexander the Great), as well as in Islamic and Teutonic traditions. Siberia and Russia also have mythical trees, as does Oceania (Papua New Guinea, Maori Aotearoa New Zealand, Hawai'i, Samoa). Mesoamerica, Maya and some Native North Americans (the Hopi, Navajo and Plains people) also have dramatic World Trees. Various species are candidates for the World Tree: apple, ash, bo/bodhi (pipal), oak, pine and yew.

FOREST

A forest is a mysterious place; in legends and fairy tales, it is the haunt of shadowy and dangerous creatures. It is a place of testing, a realm of death holding the secrets of nature, which must be penetrated to find meaning.

The forest contrasts with various human environments – city, town and village – and that contrast implies the difference between irrationality and rationality, unconscious and conscious, and feminine and masculine. A dramatic instance of this is the wilderness versus the planned and organized garden. The untamed nature of the forest differs dramatically from the controlled safety of the places in which humans live. In his *Dictionary of Symbols* (first published in 1958), Juan Eduardo Cirlot writes:

The forest is the place where vegetable life thrives and luxuriates, free from any control or cultivation.

⊠ Oluf Olufsen Bagge, *Yggdrasil, The Mundane Tree*, 1847, engraving.

✳ William Blake, *The Wood of the Self-Murderers: The Harpies and the Suicides*, 1824–27, graphite, ink and watercolour on paper. London: Tate.

✤ Max Ernst, *The Forest*, 1927–28, oil on canvas. New York: Guggenheim Museum.

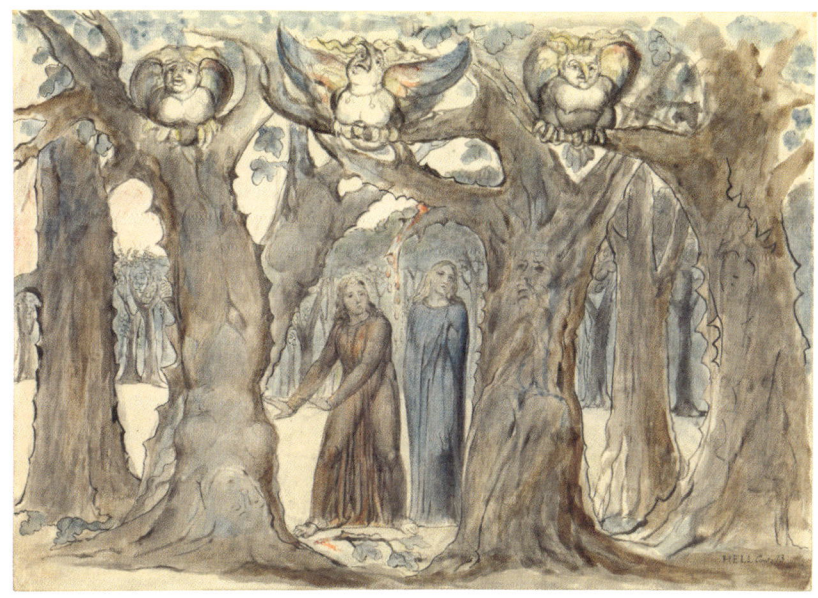

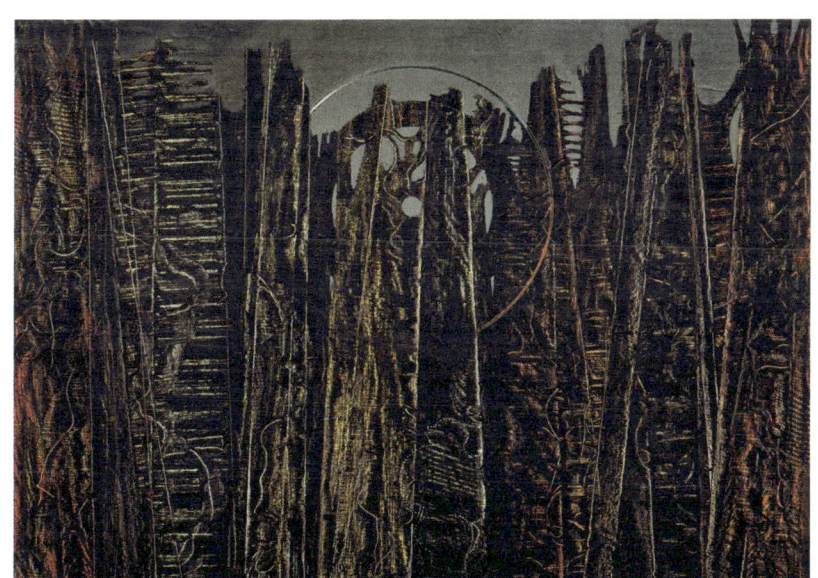

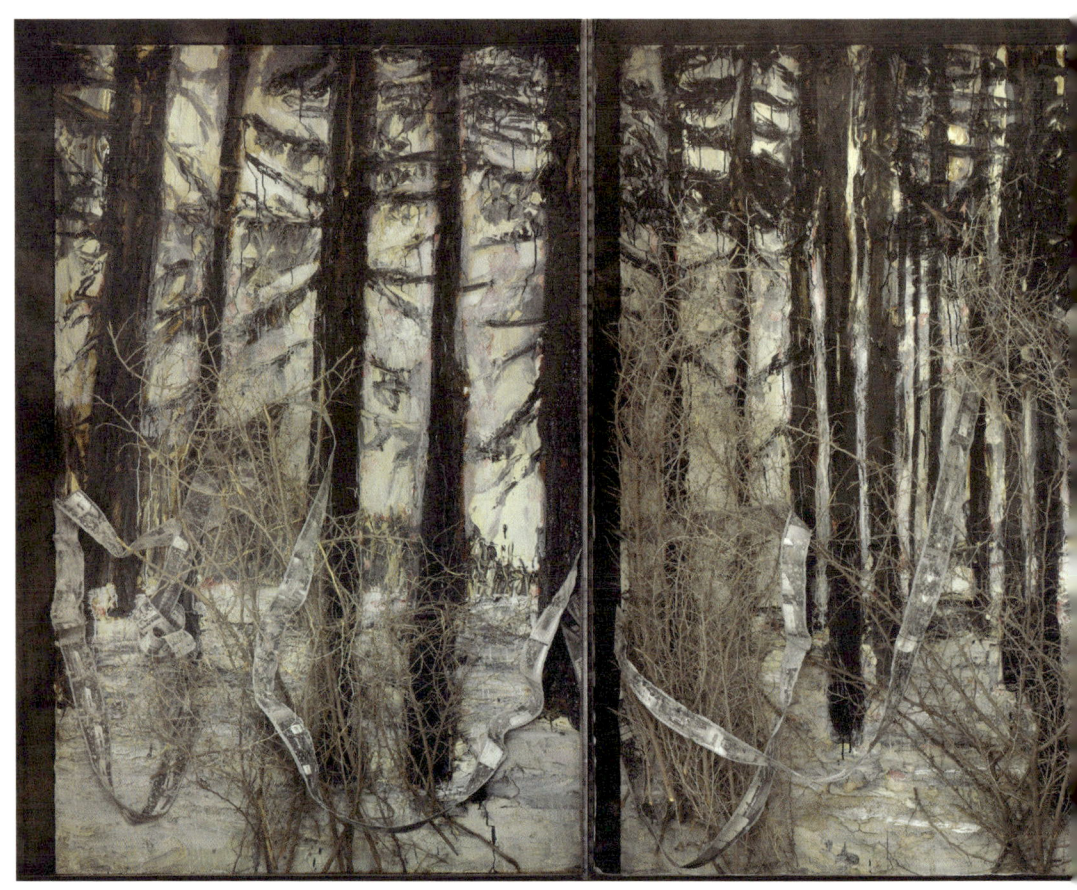

*

And since its foliage obscures the light of the sun, it is therefore regarded as opposed to the sun's power and as a symbol of the earth...Since the female principle is identified with the unconscious in Man, it follows that the forest is also a symbol of the unconscious.

Emphasizing the forest as a source of knowledge, in *The Forest in Folklore and Mythology* (1928) Alexander Porteous writes: 'It has been said that the forest knows all and is able to teach all, and there is a French proverb to the effect that the forest, which always listens, has the secret of every mystery'. Udo Becker notes the forest's ambiguous character, suggesting

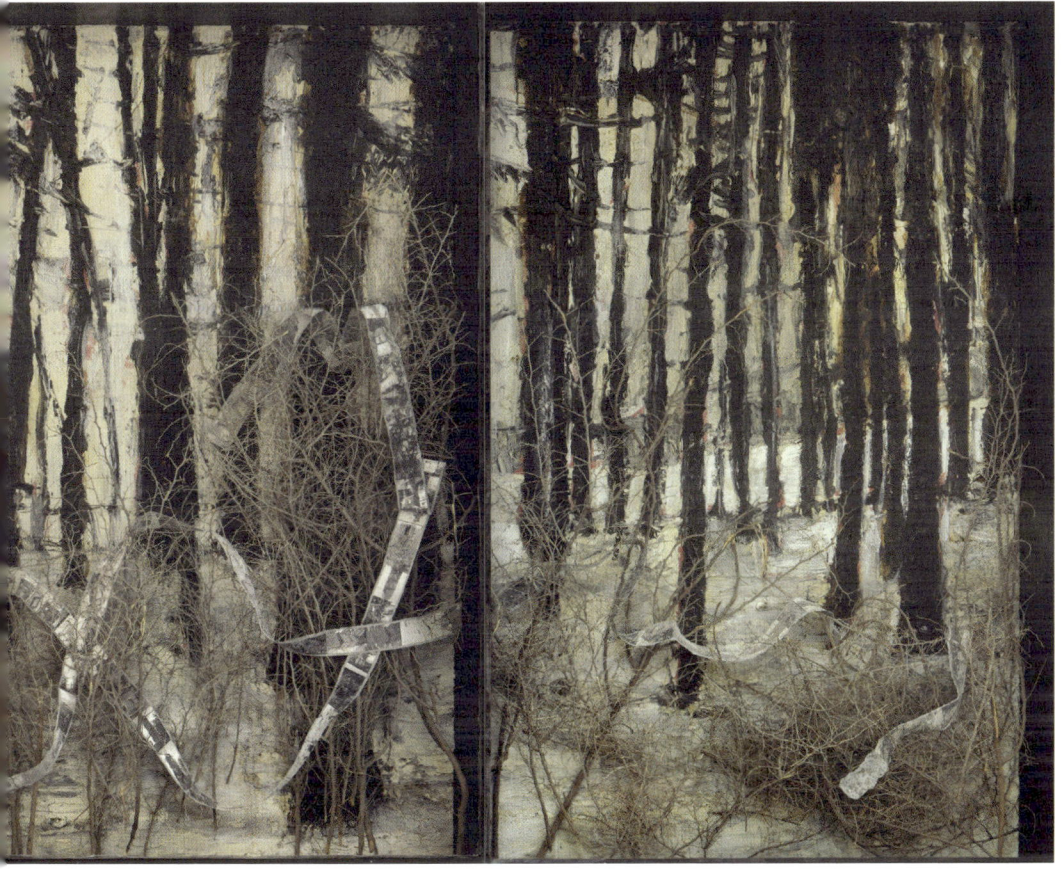

that, as a favoured dwelling place of hermits and ascetics, the forest represents sanctuary and provides a safe abode for concentration and contemplation.

Beginning in 1824, the English visionary artist William Blake created 102 watercolour images to illustrate an edition of Dante Alighieri's *Divine Comedy*. One of the most memorable is 'The Wood of the Self-Murderers: The Harpies and the Suicides'. Dante and Virgil enter a forest before exploring the levels of the Inferno. In the seventh circle of hell, murderers and suicides (suicide was then considered an immoral act) have been turned into nasty-looking trees and are fed on by harpies.

＊ Anselm Kiefer, *Entrance to Paradise*, 2010, mixed media. Los Angeles, CA: The Broad.

FAMILY Fabaceae

The acacia, native to Africa and Australia, grows throughout the temperate regions of the world. All species bear seed pods and spiny thorns. It has a number of medicinal uses and, combined with other plants, is often an ingredient in incense.

Acacia often serves as a divine attribute linked with male solar gods. Because of its hard wood, it can symbolize victory over death. It was sacred to the ancient Egyptians because of its colour, and some scholars suggest that it functioned as their Tree of Life. The creator goddess Neith resided in the tree; worshipped as early as Pre-Dynastic times, she was mother of Ra and goddess of war, weaving and hunting. The acacia's thorns were thought to repel evil.

In Judeo-Christian thought, the almost incorruptible acacia, with its sharp thorns and white or blood-red blossoms (although some species have yellow flowers), served as a solar symbol of rebirth and immortality. The Ark of the Covenant was made of gold-plated acacia (Exodus 37:1–4). It may have been the burning bush described in Exodus 3:2 and 25:10, 23; the bush instructed Moses to build the Tabernacle of acacia wood. Christ's Crown of Thorns was said to be woven from acacia. The crown has been linked with the marriage of heaven and earth – interpreted as the wedding ring of the Word (Christ) and the earth, virgin and as yet unfertile.

Acacia can be found in coats of arms, and its leaf figures in Masonic symbolism (for more information, see Hans Biedermann).

'Netting Birds, Tomb of Khnumhotep' (detail), Middle Kingdom, *c.* 1897–1878 BCE. Facsimile by Nina de Garis Davies of painting in Tomb 3, Beni Hasan, Egypt. New York: Metropolitan Museum of Art.

James Watts, after E. D. Smith, *Acacia oxycedrus* (sharp-pointed acacia), 1827.

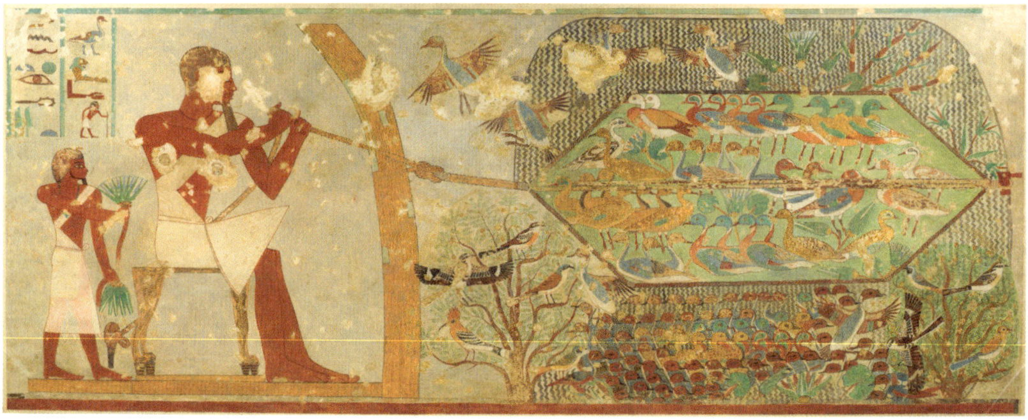

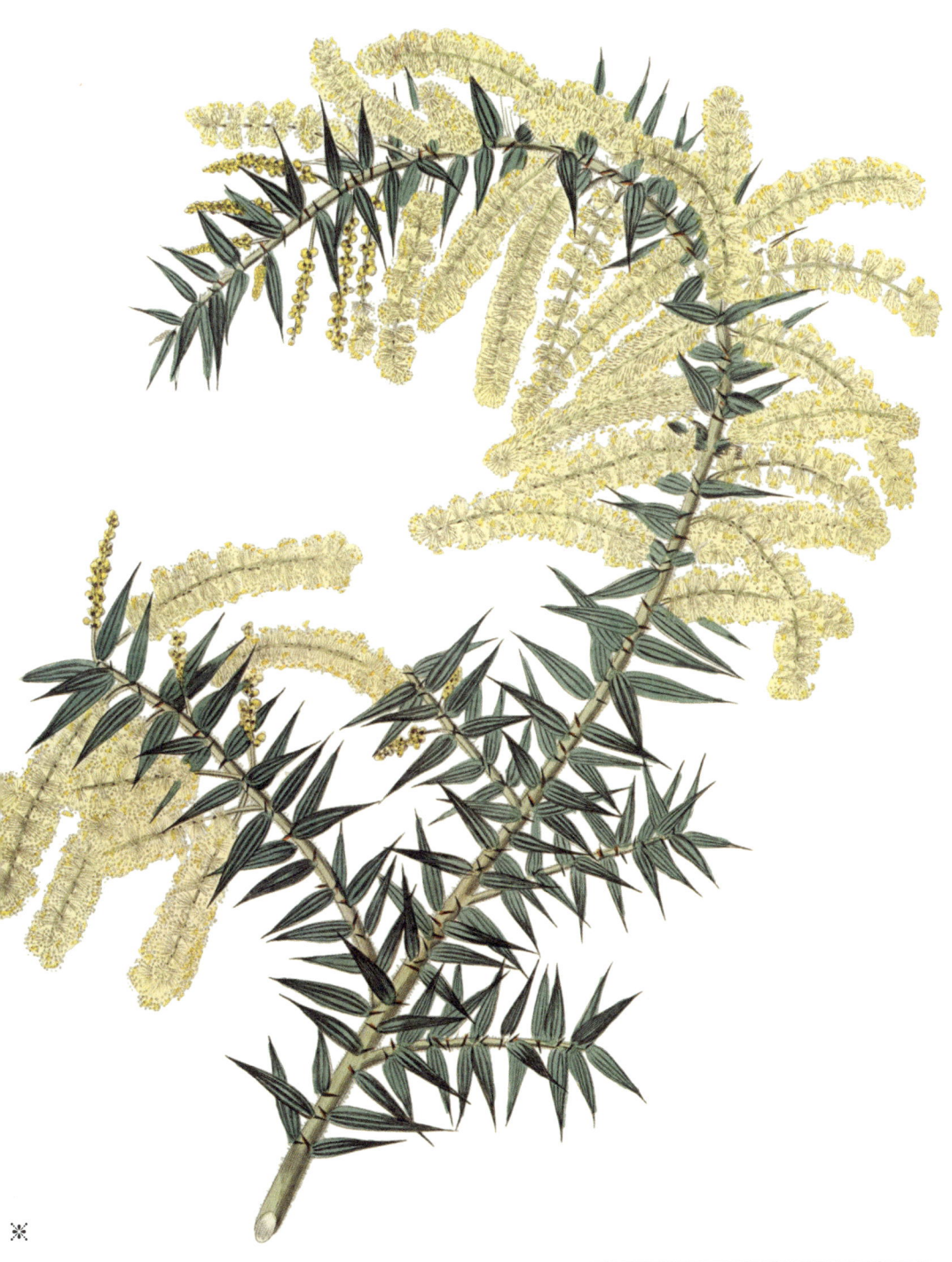

FAMILY Sapindaceae / Moraceae

The sycamore, sometimes sycamore fig or fig-mulberry – because its leaves resemble those of the mulberry – grows in West Asia and in southern parts of Africa.

In Europe and sometimes the United States, the name refers to a type of maple (*Acer pseudoplatanus*). In the United States, a type of plane tree (*Platanus occidentalis*) is also commonly referred to as sycamore. A relative of the sycamore fig, the Moreton Bay fig (*Ficus macrophylla*), native to Australia, often reaches very large sizes.

The sycamore fig, along with the persea, served as the ancient Egyptians' Tree of Life. Since it was the only tree of any size to which they had access, they also used it to build mummy cases. The tomb of the artisan Sennedjem contains many fine paintings; in one, the regenerated Sennedjem (as indicated

by his green flesh) participates in the rebirth of the sun. The calf represents the rising sun, and the god Ra-Horakhty-Atum embodies the risen sun's future triumph. The greenish-blue colour of the trees relates to the turquoise mines of the Arabian and Sinai deserts.

The sycamore was sacred to the goddesses Isis, Hathor and Nut, all of whom are depicted in tomb paintings rising out of trees and reaching out to offer sustenance to the deceased. Since some coffins were made of sycamore wood, the mummy might be thought of as being placed in the womb of a goddess. The souls of the dead,

⊗   Wolfgang Meyerpick, after Giorgio Liberale, *Ficus sycomorus* (Sycamore fig), 1568.

✳   Brian Selznick, 'Merwin (left) and Louise (right)', from *Big Tree*, 2023.

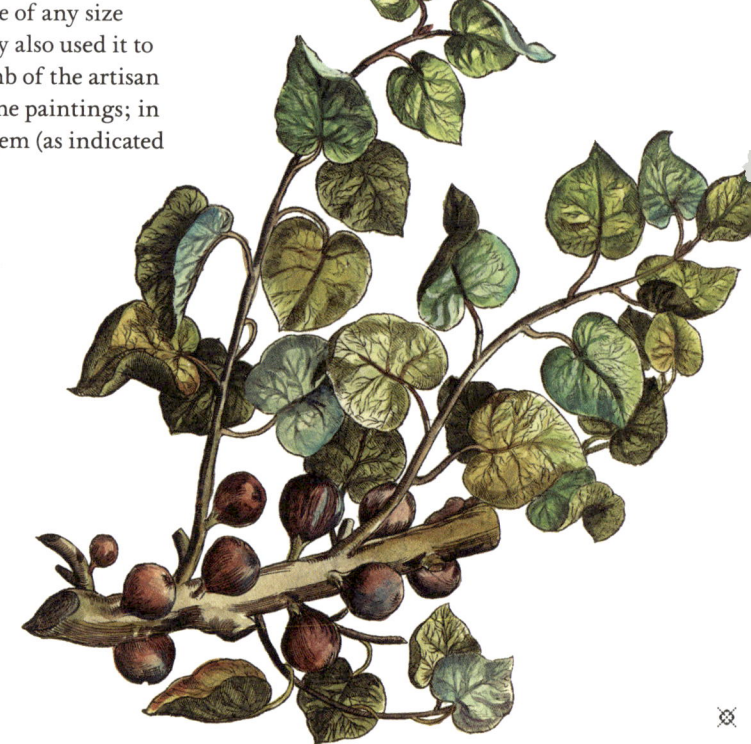

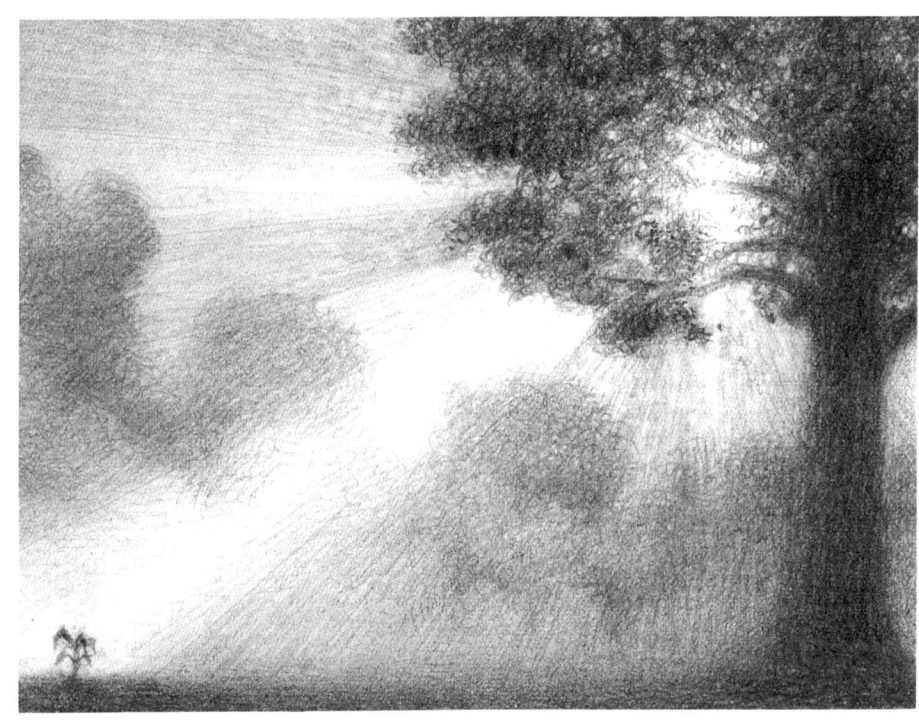

which take the shape of birds (*ba*), rest in the trees just as the living enjoyed the shade and security of the trees. The sycamore fig is now endangered in Egypt.

In Luke (19:1–10), Zacchaeus – a wealthy and detested Jericho tax collector – wished to see Jesus as he passed through the town on the way to Jerusalem. Being short in stature, Zacchaeus was unable to see over the crowd, so he ran ahead and climbed a sycamore tree. As he passed the tree, Jesus looked up and said: 'Zacchaeus, make haste and come down, for today I must stay at your house.' Although the story has been interpreted in various ways, it can be understood as an example of Christ's mission to bring salvation to all.

Big Tree, written and illustrated by Brian Selznick, is an epic saga of cosmic history. His afterword cites the ecologist Suzanne Simard's discovery of the interconnectedness of plant life, called the 'wood-wide web'. Selznick summarizes: 'the forest in real life is not a place where individual trees grow. Rather it's an interdependent community with members that help one another survive'. Selznick notes that sycamore fossils from the Cretaceous Period (65–146 million years ago) exist, but he chose to describe and picture modern sycamores. His main characters are Merwin and Louise, who begin the book as two tiny sycamore seeds.

FAMILY Malvaceae

The baobab tree, which is native to Madagascar, mainland Africa and Australia, can grow up to 30 m (100 ft) tall, with a circumference of 50 m (165 ft).

Baobabs are sometimes nicknamed 'upside down trees' for their canopy, which resembles a root system. They can live for over 1,000 years, and as a result, have become symbols of resilience and endurance. In the 2010s and 2020s, South African baobabs began to die off rapidly, possibly because of dehydration caused by global heating.

Antoine de Saint-Exupéry published *The Little Prince* in 1943, the year before he died. In the story, a pilot crash-lands in the Sahara Desert and meets the little prince, who comes from an asteroid known as B-612, where there grows a rose bush beloved by the prince, and baobab trees, which threaten to take over his planet. The pilot sees the danger of the baobabs and draws three huge, magnificent, entwined trees to warn the prince. They are said to represent fears, problems or habits that, if unchecked, grow ever larger; like the trees, they must be rooted out in a timely way to avoid disaster.

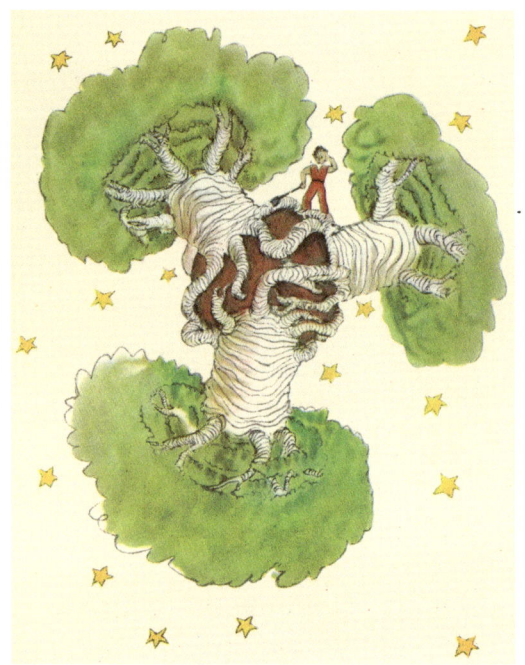

⊗

⊗ Antoine de Saint-Exupéry, *The Baobabs*, from *The Little Prince*, 1943.

✳ Mme E. Panckoucke and P. J. F. Turpin, *Baobab*, 1833.

✤ Lith Vayron, Baobab (*Adansonia digitata*), 1843–46.

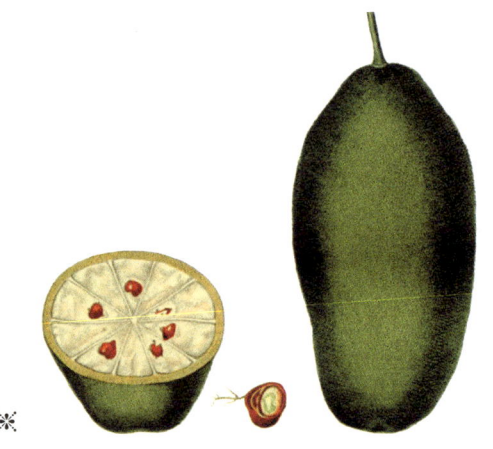

✳

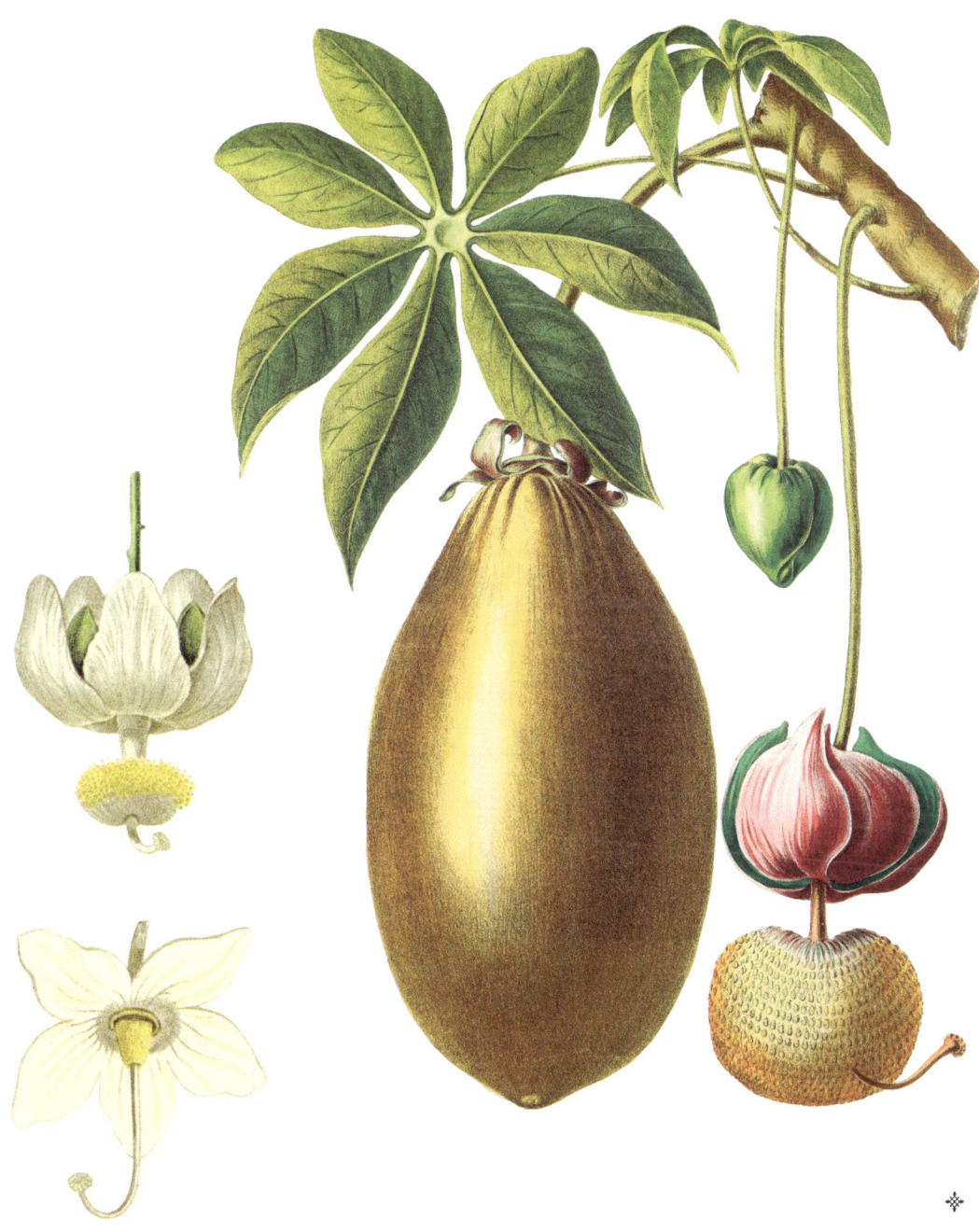

FAMILY Betulaceae

A deciduous hardwood tree, the birch belongs to
the same family as alders, hazels and hornbeams.
It serves as an ornamental tree and also has uses
in folk medicine.

Birch trees are, perhaps most notably, a source
of paper. The bark can be peeled and written
on directly, or it can be pulped. The oldest birch-
bark manuscripts date back to first-century CE
India. In Germany, the inventor Johannes

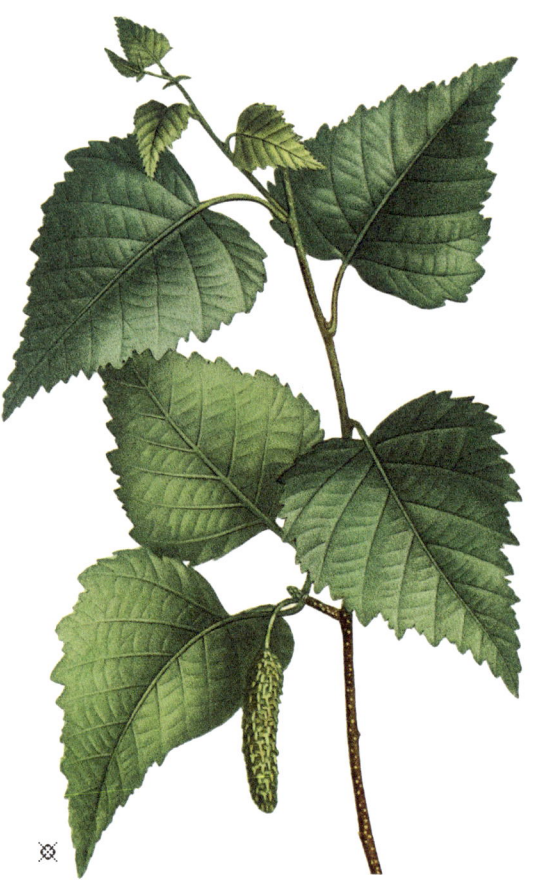

Gutenberg carved letters out of birch bark and
wrapped them in paper while still damp; upon
unwrapping them, he observed an impression
on the paper. From this discovery, the art of
printing evolved in Europe.

The birch tree was sacred in Russia and
Siberia, as well as among the ancient Celts.
Associating it with the sun and moon, the
Celts believed it to be a conduit between the
heavens and earth – spiritual energy descends
and human aspirations ascend. Pliny described
its applications in the ancient world, including
for switches used by magistrates as punishment;
its more positive attributes linked the tree to
wedding torches and guardianship.

Gustav Klimt spent summers in Litzlberg,
Austria, where he was surrounded by trees and
depicted them with a powerful combination
of detail and abstraction. He has been called a
Waldschrat, a solitary wood-dweller. Seen close
up in ranks in *Birch Forest*, the trees mostly block
out the sky, but with no sense of claustrophobia.
Instead, flickering patterns, colour and light
fill the pictorial space from side to side and
top to bottom in a way that is reminiscent
of Byzantine mosaics.

⊗   Pancrace Bessa, White Birch
     (*Betula populifolia*), 1819.

✳   Gustav Klimt, *Birch Forest*,
     1903, oil on canvas. Private
     collection.

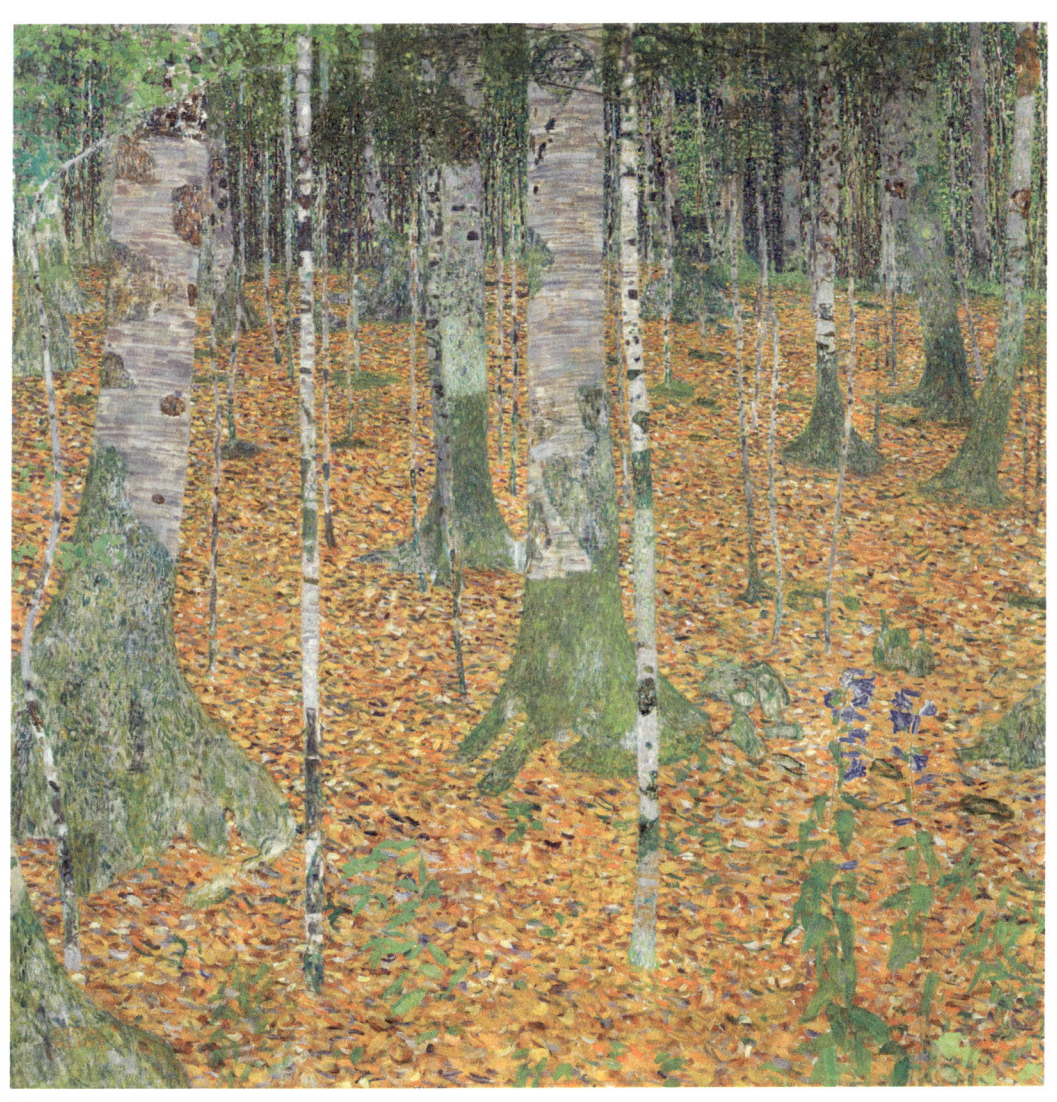

※

FAMILY Fagaceae

The chestnut tree is a member of the beech family, as is the oak (pp. 78–81). It is native to temperate zones of the northern hemisphere.

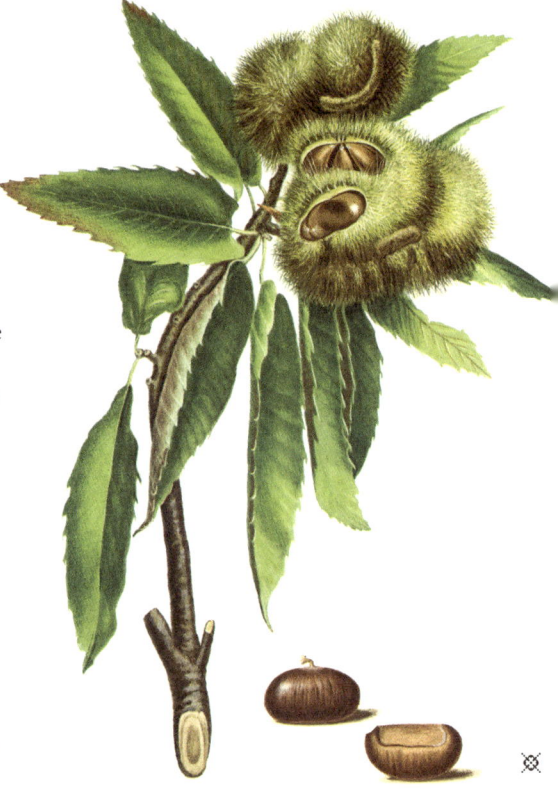

The horse chestnut is unrelated (genus: *Aesculus*), and is so named because it produces similar-looking but toxic and inedible nuts. The true chestnut produces nuts covered with spiny husks. The trees have been cultivated since 2000 BCE and were at one time an important food source; later they fell out of favour because they came to be regarded as food for the poor. Chestnut blight has decimated about a billion American chestnuts since the beginning of the twentieth century.

One of the most fabled chestnuts is the Tree of One Hundred Horses on Mt Etna, Sicily. It is believed to be between 2,000 and 4,000 years old, despite being only 8 km (5 miles) from the volcano's crater. The name stems from a legend that a large group of horsemen, caught in a storm, was able to shelter under the canopy of the tree. In 1780, the trunk measured 58 m (190 ft) in circumference, which Guinness World Records has recorded as the 'greatest tree girth ever', although the tree has since split into multiple trunks.

Probably the most famous literary use of this genus is Henry Wadsworth Longfellow's poem 'The Village Blacksmith', which begins 'Under the spreading chestnut-tree. . .' In Christian art, the chestnut husk has evoked Christ's suffering. The nut itself symbolizes the Immaculate Conception; like the nut within the spiny husk, the Virgin was without thorns, surrounded – but unaffected – by Original Sin. Mary's chastity and purity were also associated with the nut, protected by the husk. The remarkable ability of the tree to regenerate after it is cut led to its association with Christ's Crucifixion and Resurrection.

Charles E. Burchfield's *Summer Solstice* was inspired in part by Julia Ellen Roger's *The Tree Book*, first published in 1905, in which he read about the Tree of One Hundred Horses. He drew and painted chestnuts as early as 1916 and even then was surely aware of their disease and death. Here, the heat of the solstice sun falls on the glowing, mysterious tree, giving it an iconic, visionary quality – alive and safe in memory.

⊗ Giorgio Gallesio, Spanish chestnut (*Castanea sativa*), 1817–39.

※ Charles E. Burchfield, *Summer Solstice* (*In Memory of the American Chestnut Tree*), 1961–66, watercolour on paper. Buffalo, NY: Burchfield Penney Art Center at SUNY Buffalo State.

OTHER CHESTNUT IMAGES
• Samuel Palmer, *A Hilly Scene*, c. 1826–28, watercolour on paper. London: Tate (see p. 220).

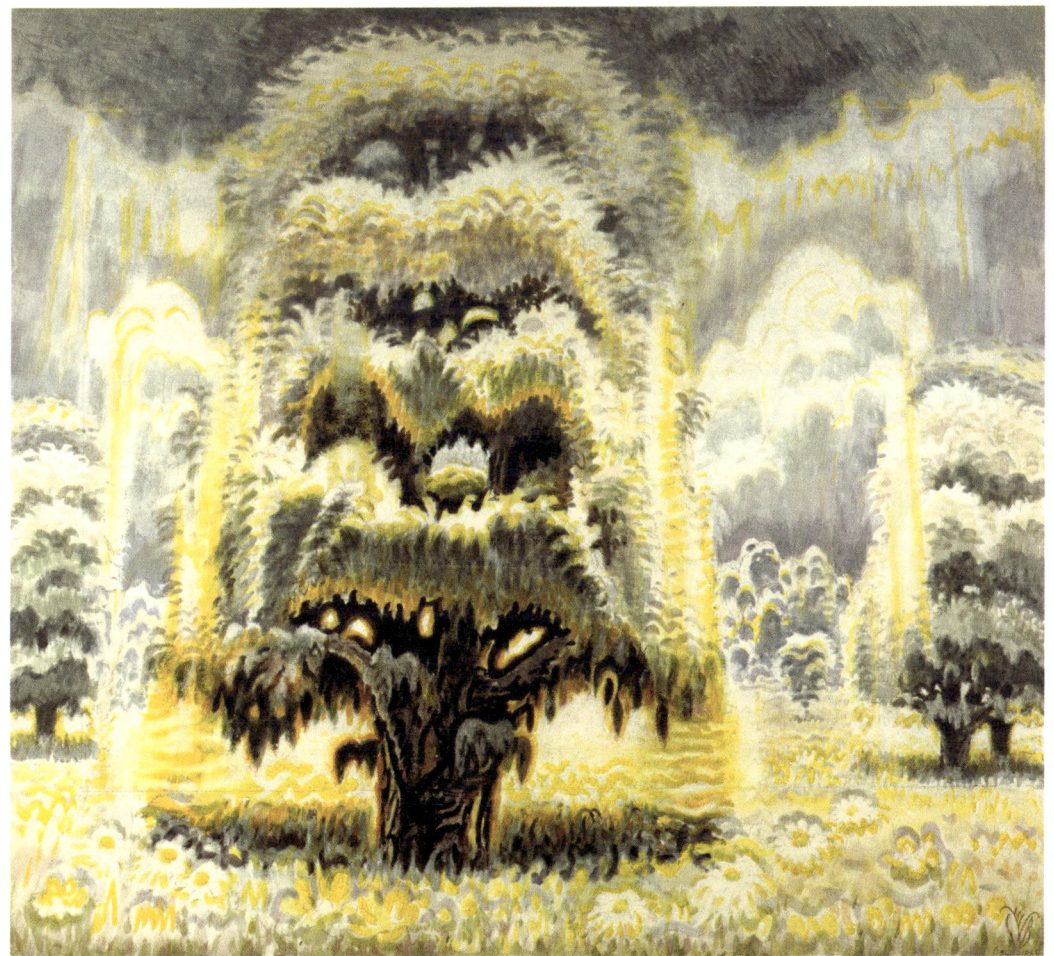

※

FAMILY Pinaceae

Cedar trees comprise four species of evergreen conifer, most of them native to the Mediterranean region, where they functioned as the Tree of Life for some ancient cultures.

The tree is particularly associated with the mountains of Lebanon, where it once grew plentifully. The wood is insect-repellent and resistant to decay, and therefore very useful for building houses, fence posts and furniture, and for use in a variety of folk remedies. Its name comes from a Hebrew word meaning 'to be firm', and the tree's natural properties also made it a symbol of incorruptibility and immortality.

The ancient Egyptians used cedar wood to build ships and coffins, and for sculptures. The wooden parts of Tutankhamun's sarcophagus were carved from cedar, and this and other cedar objects were in remarkable condition when they were excavated in the early twentieth century. Cedar resin was used in mummification and to preserve papyrus documents.

In ancient Judaea, cedar wood was also used for shipbuilding, and Solomon is said to have constructed his Temple at Jerusalem of cedar. Cedar is mentioned often in the Old Testament, as when Noah is reported to have built his ark from a variety of cedars.

Greco-Roman sculptures of immortal gods and ancestors were often made from cedarwood. In Christian art, Christ has been depicted emerging from a cedar tree. The cedar is one of the four trees said to have been used to make Christ's Cross, the other three being cypress, olive and palm.

The contemporary American sculptor John Grade works in wood on a monumental scale. *Treeline* was made primarily of yellow cedar

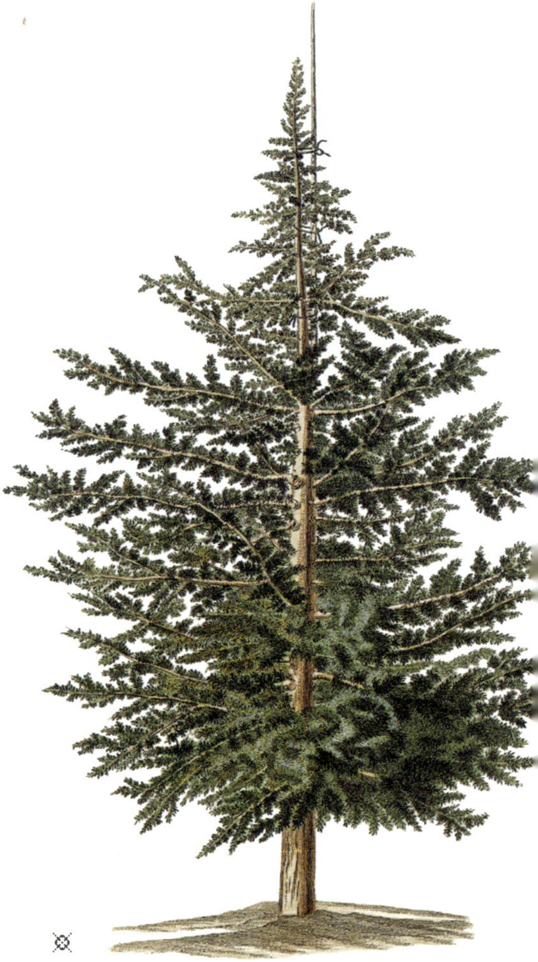

J. J. or J. E. Haid, after Georg Dionysius Ehret, *Cedrus*, *c.* 1750.

John Grade, *Treeline*, 2017, Alaskan yellow cedar and Metasequoia wood. Portland, OR: Karl Miller Center atrium, Portland State University.

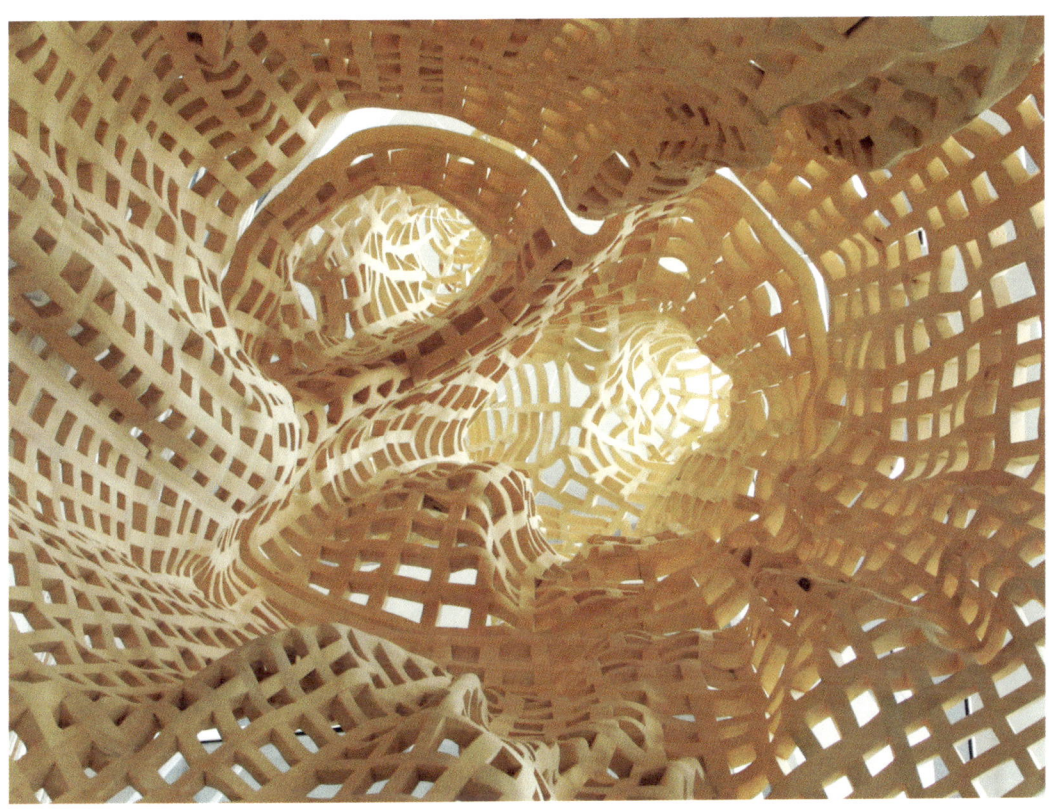

✳

salvaged from the building site of a new art gallery at Portland State University. Grade, who worked with PSU students on the sculpture, said: 'We had this beautiful little unusual tree standing where the new building was going to be sited, which inspired thoughts about salvaging it as material and more broadly about trees in general, longevity and legacy.' Displayed at the grand opening of the gallery, the sculpture hangs 3 m (10 ft) above the ground and is 9.5 m high, 3.5 m wide and 3 m deep (31 × 12 × 10 ft). By recycling cedar and other woods, Grade dramatizes the plight of trees and can be said to be recreating and rejuvenating trees that would otherwise die.

FAMILY Rutaceae

Oranges are the fruit of various citrus species, a hybrid between pomelo and mandarin. They originated in Asia, and are first mentioned in Chinese literature in 314 BCE.

The sweet orange accounts for about 70 per cent of citrus production worldwide and includes Valencia, navel and blood oranges. Oranges are of great economic importance, supplying fruit, juice, oils, jams/jellies and orange peel, all rich sources of vitamin C and other nutrients.

It is possible that the golden apples of the Hesperides were oranges (see 'Apple', p. 174).

Images of the Virgin and her retinue sometimes contain orange trees, their white blossom symbolizing purity. In Cosmè Tura's *Madonna and Child in a Garden* (*c.* 1455), two orange trees can be seen behind Mary, signifying her virginity. The oranges are green, possibly because the Christ Child is still an infant. Other flowers adorn the foreground, probably also symbols of the Virgin. Botticelli's *Primavera* (p. 90) contains some of the most

beautiful orange trees in art, linked with the Virgin Mary as well as with marriage, since it was probably commissioned to celebrate a Medici wedding.

In *The Orchard*, an Art Nouveau tapestry by the designer John Henry Dearle of Morris & Co., female figures and plants symbolize the seasons: summer, at the far left, has fully laden orange trees and assorted flowers. A poem composed by William Morris appears on a banner that unfurls across the tapestry. Here, the orange trees seem to have been chosen to demonstrate the bounty of nature.

The custom of using orange blossom in weddings dates from the Crusades, when

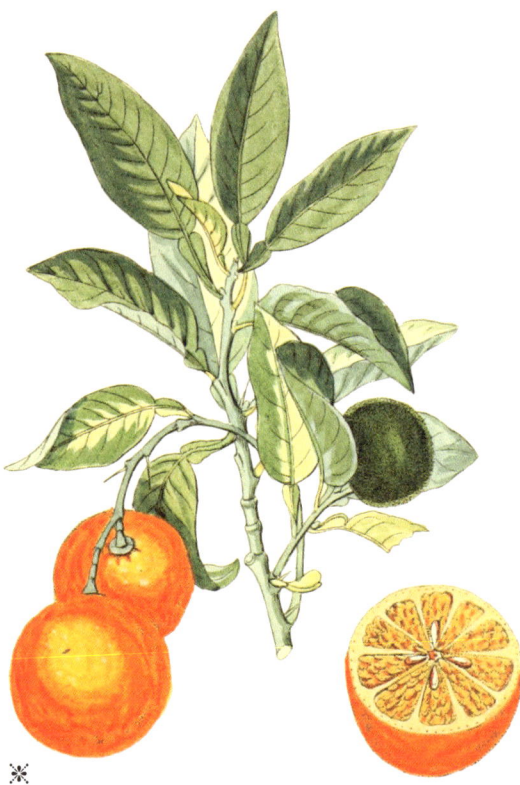

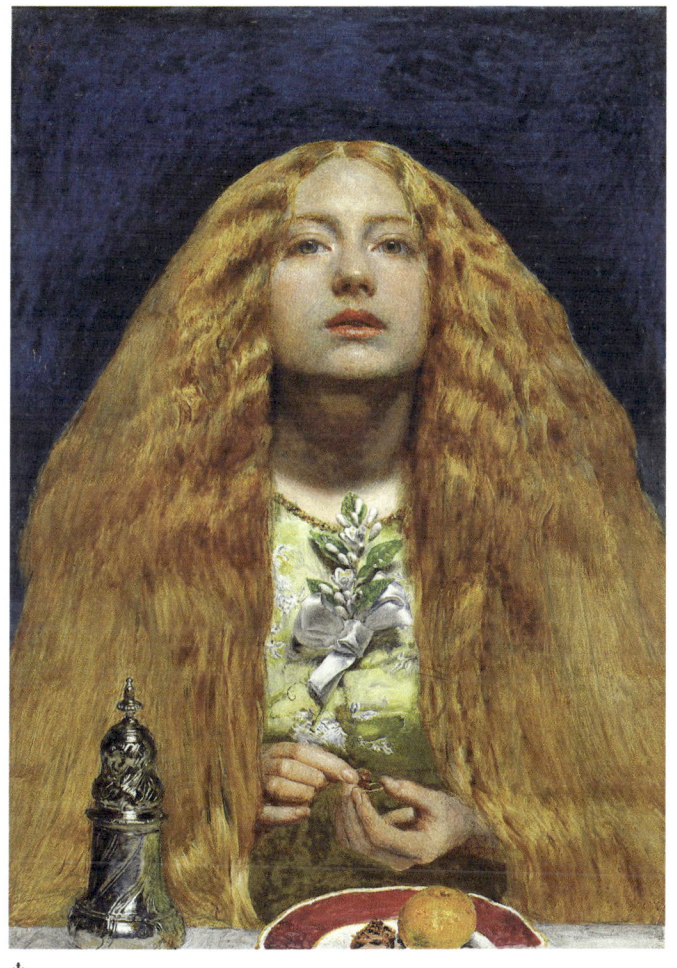

William Morris and John Henry Dearle, 'Summer' (detail) from *The Orchard*, also called *The Seasons*, 1890, tapestry. London: Victoria and Albert Museum.

Citrus x Aurantium, 1831.

John Everett Millais, *The Bridesmaid*, 1851, oil on panel. Cambridge, UK: Fitzwilliam Museum.

OTHER ORANGE IMAGES
- Cosmè Tura, *Madonna and Child in a Garden*, *c.* 1455, tempera on panel. Washington, DC: National Gallery of Art.

Europeans saw Arab brides wearing orange blossom as a double symbol of virginity and fecundity, since both flowers and fruit can appear on the tree at the same time. Eventually, the practice spread throughout Europe and to North America. Both brides and bridal attendants wore these fragrant flowers. But the fruit of the orange was also linked with marriage and fertility. In John Everett Millais's *The Bridesmaid*, a plate at the bottom of the painting holds an orange and a piece of wedding cake. Having been served the cake, according to folk tradition, the bridesmaid will pass a morsel through a ring and place it under her pillow in the hope of dreaming of her future spouse.

FAMILY Rutaceae

The lemon is a small evergreen tree native to Asia and northeastern India. Its fruit is used in cooking and baking, and the juice is an effective cleaning agent.

According to some sources, Alexander the Great brought lemons to Greece; they arrived in Europe no later than the second century CE, and the first substantial cultivation occurred in Genoa in the fifteenth century. The fruit was believed to have healing properties, to act as a disinfectant and to work as an antidote to poison.

The Greeks believed that lemon trees celebrated the marriage of Zeus and Hera. The Romans certainly knew the plant, since it appeared in Pompeiian frescoes, but it probably wasn't widespread at that point. By the Italian Renaissance, lemons appear in paintings of the Garden of Eden, symbolizing redemption and immortality. A trellis supporting a lemon shrub forms the background of Antonio da Correggio's *Virgin and Child with the Young St John the Baptist*. Expanding on his treatment of the shift towards realism as a celebration of God's creation, Giovanni Aloi notes that the lemon fruit's brilliant yellow colour linked it to the sun. Lemons were also associated with the Virgin Mary.

In the eighteenth and nineteenth-century Netherlands, lemons were linked with fidelity

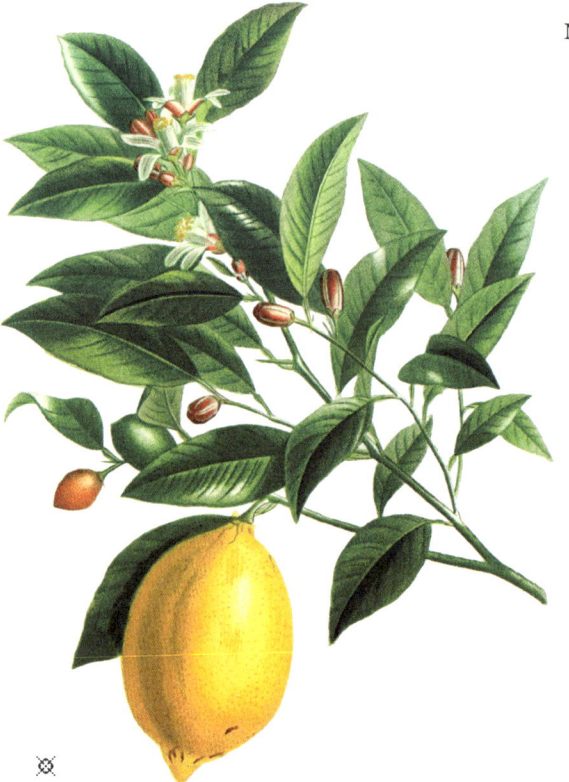

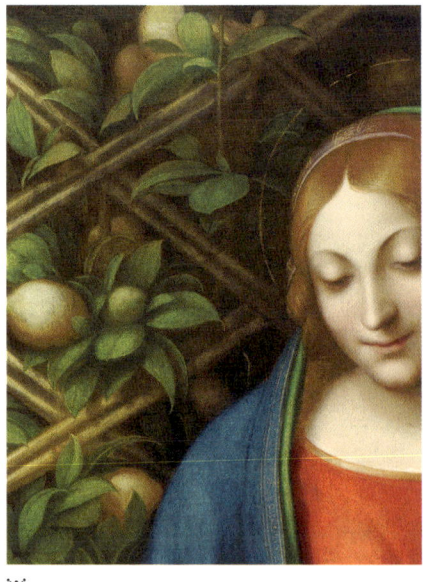

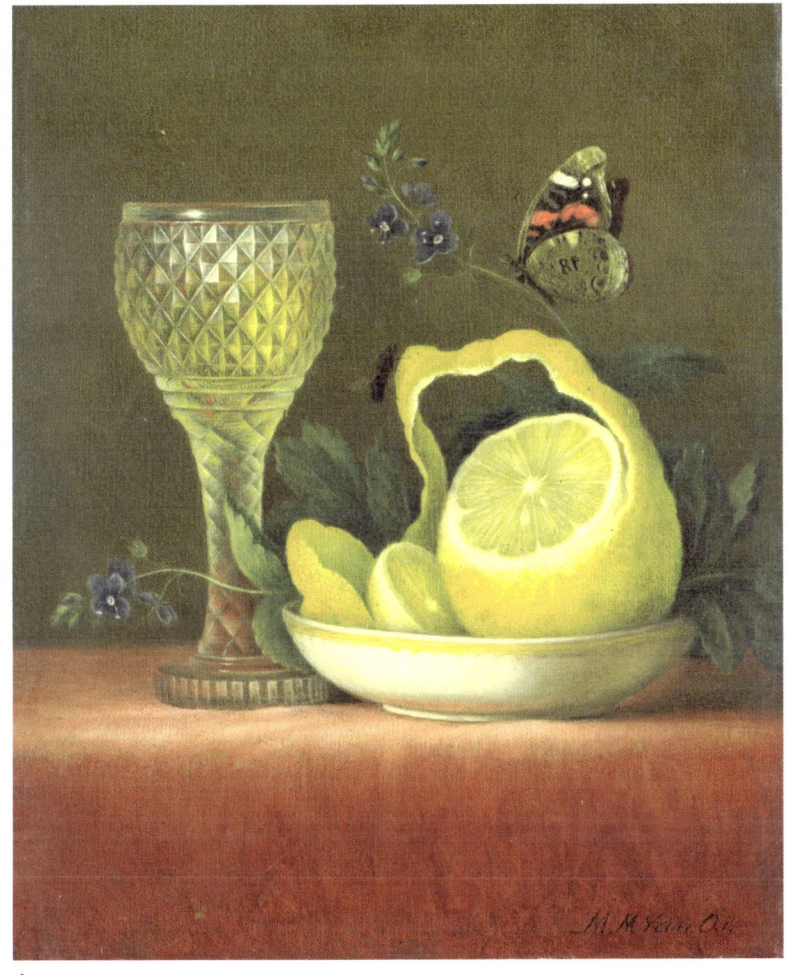

❈

Charles Dessalines D'Orbigny, *Citrus Limonium*, 1892.

Antonio da Correggio, *Virgin and Child with the Young St John the Baptist* (detail), c. 1515, oil on panel. Chicago, IL: Art Institute of Chicago.

Maria Margaretha van Os, *Still Life with Lemon and Cut Glass*, 1823–26, oil on panel. Amsterdam: Rijksmuseum.

and may also have symbolized the passage of time. They show up in still-life paintings, often with a long curl of peel that allowed the artist to display their skill for the admiration of their patrons. The art historian Mariët Westermann suggests that the lemon indicated that one had arrived in society.

OTHER LEMON IMAGES
- Domenico Ghirlandaio, *The Last Supper*, 1480, fresco. Florence: refectory of the Convent of the Ognissanti.
- Willem Claesz. Heda, *Still Life with a Gilt Cup*, 1635, oil on panel. Amsterdam: Rijksmuseum.

FAMILY Apiaceae | Pinaceae

Hemlock refers to both a flowering plant of the carrot family and a tree of the pine family. Native to Europe and North Africa, the plant – which is famously poisonous – can reach heights of up to 3.5 m (12 ft).

Wild carrot, a plant from the same family, is less tall and has hairy stems without hemlock's purple blotches; giant hogweed and cow parsley, which has paler, weaker stems and tiny green leaves, are other plants in the genus.

Hemlock's deadliness has led to it symbolizing treason and death. In ancient Greece, it was used to poison condemned prisoners, the most famous being the philosopher Socrates.

The name also refers to several species in a genus of conifers found in North America and East Asia, so-called because the crushed foliage – which is harmless – smells like poison hemlock. The North American hemlock is seriously threatened by a sap-sucking insect and, in many places, has died out.

In a famous legend of the Northwest Coast Native American people, a great chief was the only one with light, which he kept hidden in a treasure box, causing great suffering for humanity. The trickster Raven disguised himself as a hemlock needle; when the chief's daughter swallowed the needle, she became pregnant, and Raven was born as a human child. The child cried until he was given the box.

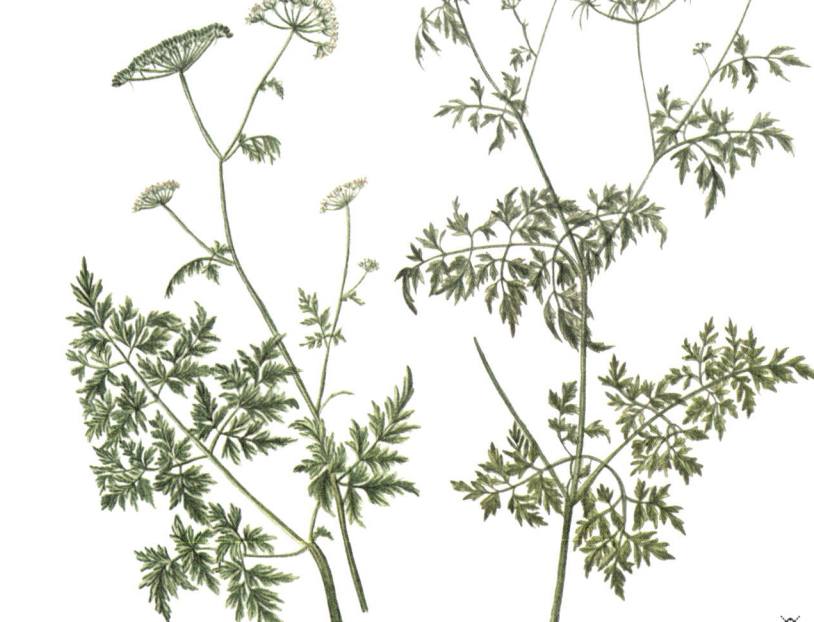

⊗ Hemlock (left) and fine-leaved water hemlock (right), 1772–93.

⊗ Jacques-Louis David, *The Death of Socrates* (detail), 1787, oil on canvas. New York: Metropolitan Museum of Art.

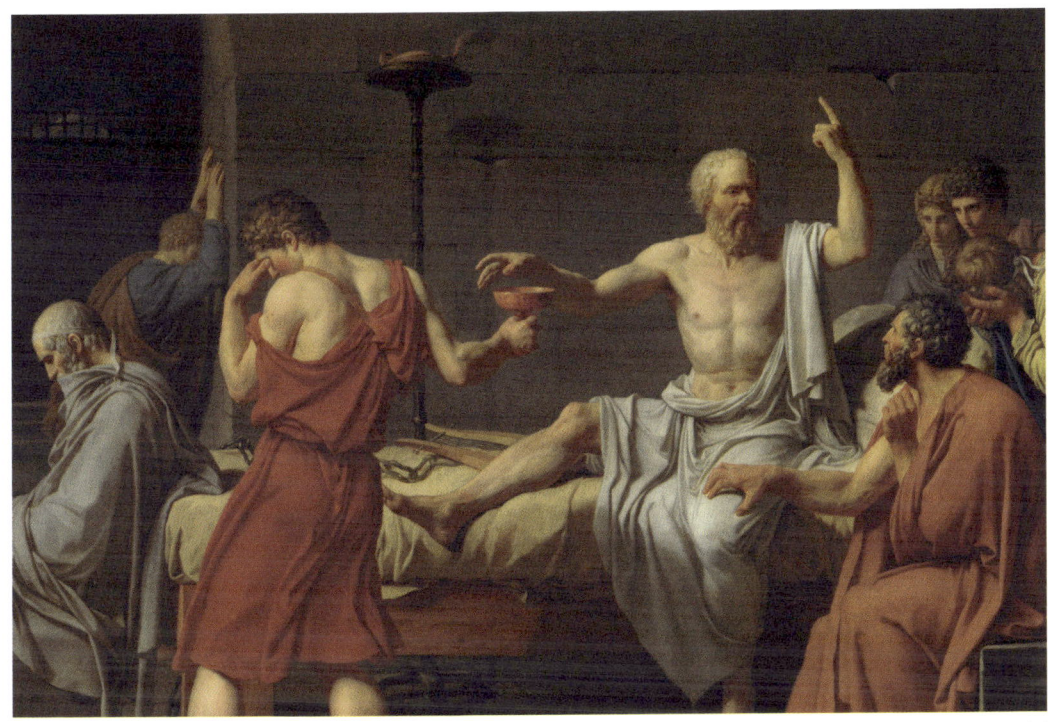

※

Raven, reverting to bird form, opened the box, bringing into the open the light of the sun (shown as a mask in George Hunt Jr's print, overleaf), the moon and the stars, thus illuminating the world.

In 2006, the contemporary conceptual and installation artist Mark Dion completed *Neukom Vivarium*, a large work focused on ecosystems and extinction. With extensive help from donors, he installed an 18.3 m (60 ft) fallen Western hemlock in a purpose-built greenhouse. The tree acts as a nurse log for bacteria, fungi, insects, lichen and plants. Visitors can enter this 'art system' and study it with magnifying glasses and tiles that identify its features. Dion states:

I think that one of the important things about this work is that it's really not an intensely positive, back-to-nature kind of experience. In some ways, this project is an abomination. We're taking a tree that is an ecosystem – a dead tree, but a living system – and we are re-contextualizing it and taking it to another site. We're putting it in a sort of Sleeping Beauty coffin, a greenhouse we're building around it. And we're pumping it up with a life support system – an incredibly complex system of air, humidity, water, and soil enhancement –

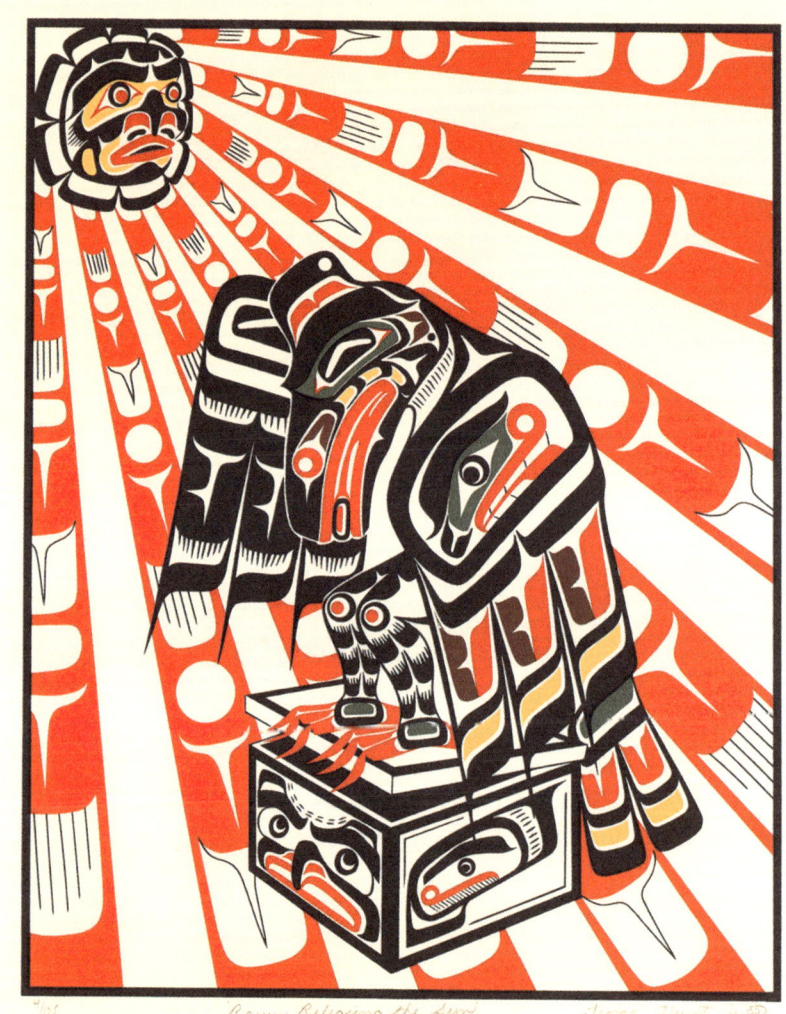

⊗ George Hunt Jr., *Raven Releasing the Sun*, 1985, silkscreen on paper. Seattle, WA: Seattle Art Museum.

※ Mark Dion, *Seattle Vivarium*, 2002, coloured pencil on paper.

❉ Mark Dion, *Neukom Vivarium*, 2006, mixed-media installation. Seattle, WA: Olympic Sculpture Park.

to keep it going. All those things are substituting what nature does, emphasizing how, once that's gone, it's incredibly difficult, expensive, and technological to approximate that system – to take this tree and to build the next generation of forests on it. So, this piece is in some way perverse.

It shows that, despite all of our technology and money, when we destroy a natural system, it's virtually impossible to get it back. In a sense, we're building a failure.

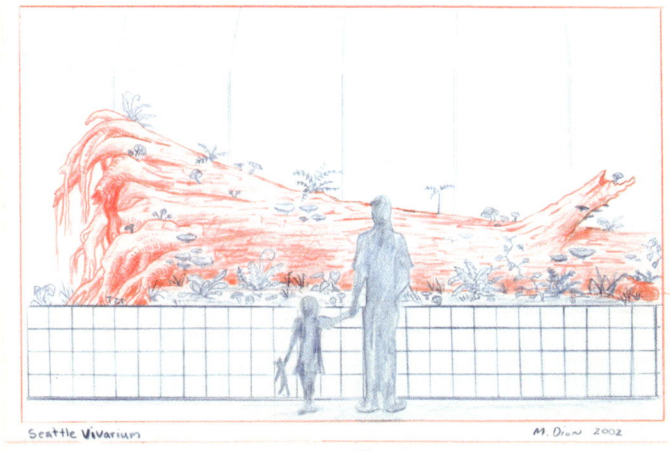

Seattle Vivarium   M. Dion 2002

❊

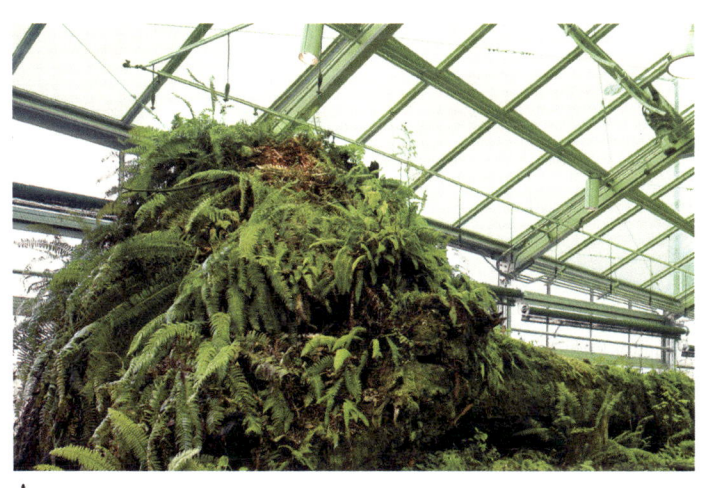

❊

OTHER HEMLOCK IMAGES
- William Holman Hunt, *The Light of the World*, 1853–54, oil on canvas. Oxford, UK: side chapel, Keble College. Two other versions exist: a smaller one in Manchester and a copy painted in 1900–4 in St Paul's Cathedral, London.
- Joan Mitchell, *Hemlock*, 1956, oil on canvas. New York: Whitney Museum of American Art.
- David Buckley Borden and Aaron M. Ellison, *Hemlock Hospice*, 2017–18, art–science installation and exhibition. Petersham, MA: Harvard Forest.

FAMILY Betulaceae

The hazel, a member of the birch family, is a genus of deciduous trees and large shrubs native to the temperate northern hemisphere. The fruit is called the hazelnut, or sometimes (erroneously) the filbert.[6]

In Greek mythology, the sons of Zeus, Apollo (god of music and harmony) and Hermes (the messenger god), received gifts intended to better the human condition. Apollo's was the lyre and Hermes's a hazel wand that promoted the exchange of ideas. The wand, the so-called *caduceus*, with wings and two entwined serpents, today symbolizes communication, commerce, writing and eloquence.

A Y-shaped branch of hazel was believed to have supernatural properties, especially divination. The rod of Asclepius, god of healing, has only one snake and no wings, and the use of Hermes's *caduceus* to represent the medical profession is inaccurate.

In ancient Germanic and Nordic cultures, the hazel was sacred to Thor, god of thunder, war and strength, and Idun, goddess of life and fertility. Loki freed Idun from captivity by changing himself into a falcon and carrying her off in the shape of a hazelnut.

The hazel was sacred to the ancient Celts, who associated it with wisdom and inspiration. The tree's protective properties explain why its leaves and nuts are found in ancient burials and why it appears so often in Celtic myths.

The hazel tree appears in the Unicorn Tapestries, a series of Netherlandish tapestries made around the turn of the sixteenth century and now in the Metropolitan Museum of Art. Its presence here may offer protection from evil and even death. The unicorn, symbolizing Christ, dies, but is resurrected in the final image, appearing whole and very much alive.

According to apocryphal Christian tradition, after the expulsion from Eden, God gave Adam a hazel rod that enabled him to create any animal he wished by striking the sea. Adam first created sheep. Eve followed this by creating the wolf, which immediately devoured the sheep. In turn, Adam created the dog, thus saving his sheep and balancing out the wild and the tame. In another Christian legend, the Virgin left the sleeping Christ Child to pick strawberries for him. A viper emerged from the grass and pursued her until she sought refuge in a hazelnut bush. She declared that henceforth the hazelnut would have the power to drive off evil. This may be why Mantegna included hazelnuts in the centre panel of the San Zeno altarpiece. Hazelnuts in their husks appear on a swag of fruit above the Madonna, backed by a relief of *putti* holding a cornucopia.

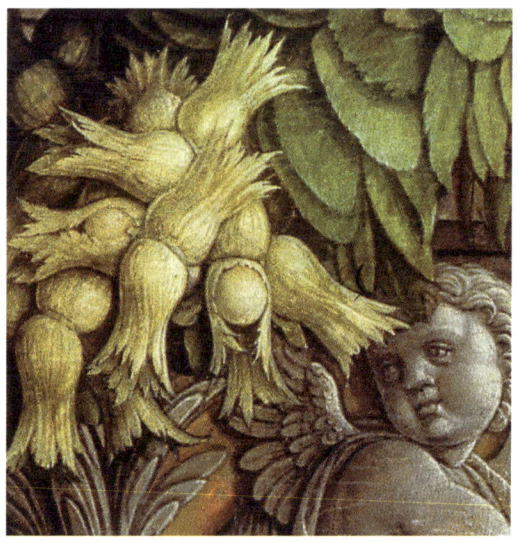

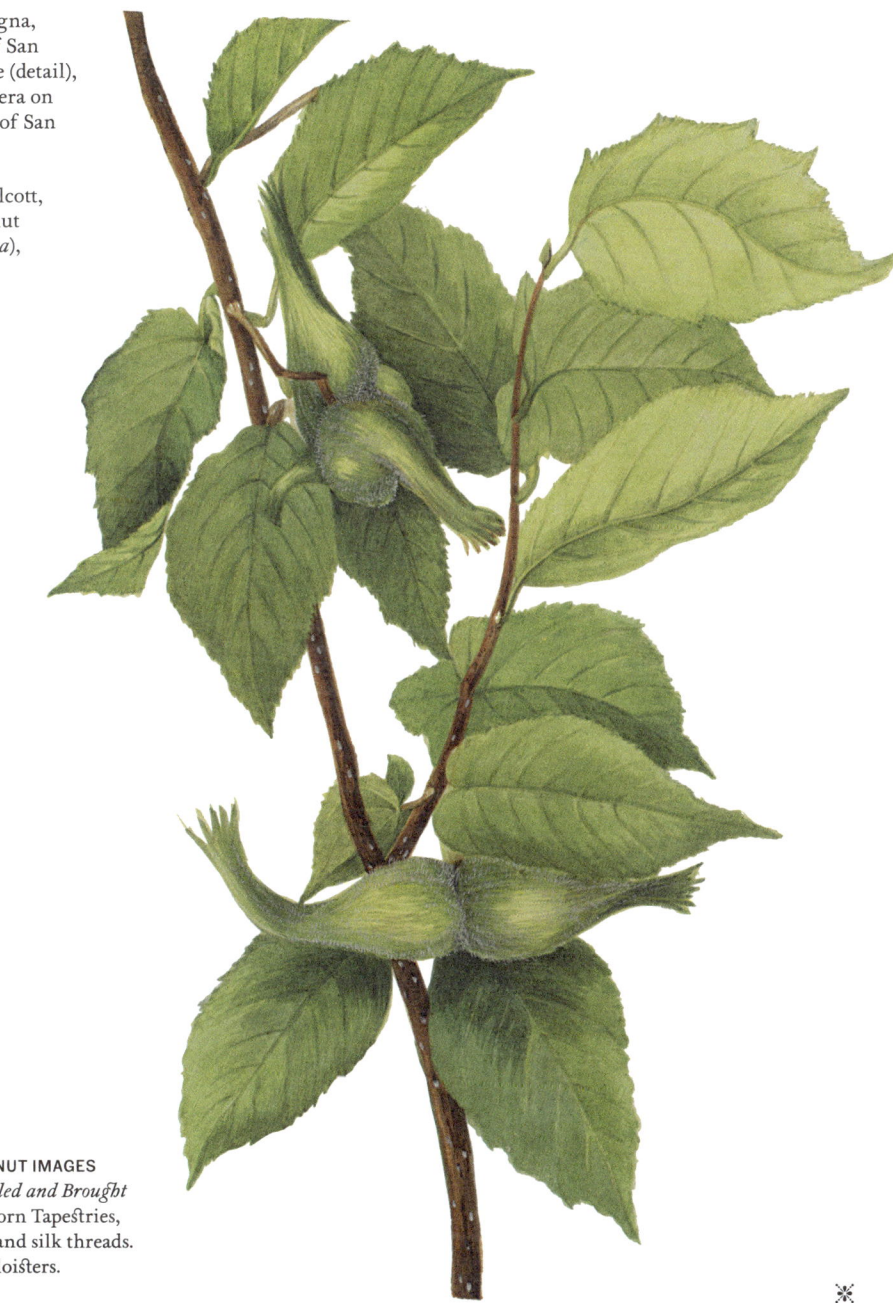

⊗ Andrea Mantegna, centre panel of San Zeno altarpiece (detail), 1457–60, tempera on panel. Basilica of San Zeno, Verona.

※ Mary Vaux Walcott, Beaked Hazelnut (*Corylus rostrata*), 1932.

OTHER HAZEL/HAZELNUT IMAGES
- *The Unicorn Is Killed and Brought to the Castle*, Unicorn Tapestries, 1495–1505, wool and silk threads. New York: The Cloisters.

※

FAMILY Cupressaceae

Native to the Himalayas, the cypress was introduced into the Mediterranean by the Phoenicians, who colonized the island of Cyprus, from which the tree derived its name. It has been cultivated for ornamental use and for its strong, durable timber.

The Roman poet Ovid tells of a legendary island youth named Cyparissus (a favourite of Apollo), who was accidentally killed by a large stag. Apollo was so grief-stricken that he begged the gods to let his sorrow last forever, and so they turned the youth into a cypress tree, which became a symbol of the immortal soul. In Greco-Roman myth, the tree was related to the gods of the Underworld, Hades, the Fates and the Furies. Cypress wood, believed

to preserve bodies, provided the timber for some ancient Egyptian mummy cases, and the ancient Greeks built coffins of it; the tree was also planted in cemeteries.

As do all evergreens, the cypress signifies incorruptibility and immortality. Other deities associated with it include Cronos, Asclepius, Aphrodite, Athena, Artemis, Cybele, Hera and Persephone. Because Orpheus descended into the Underworld and was able to return from it, Orphic initiates believed that, upon entering

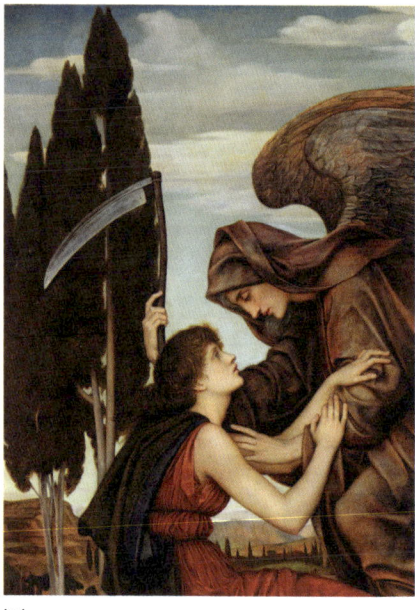

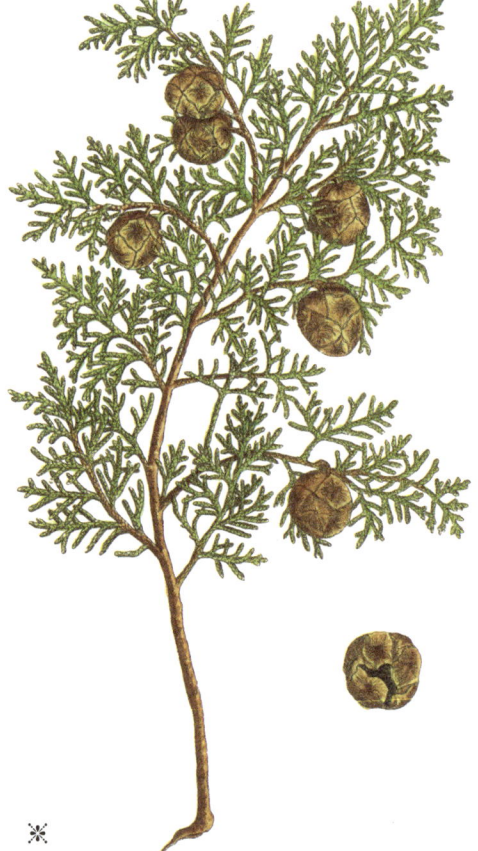

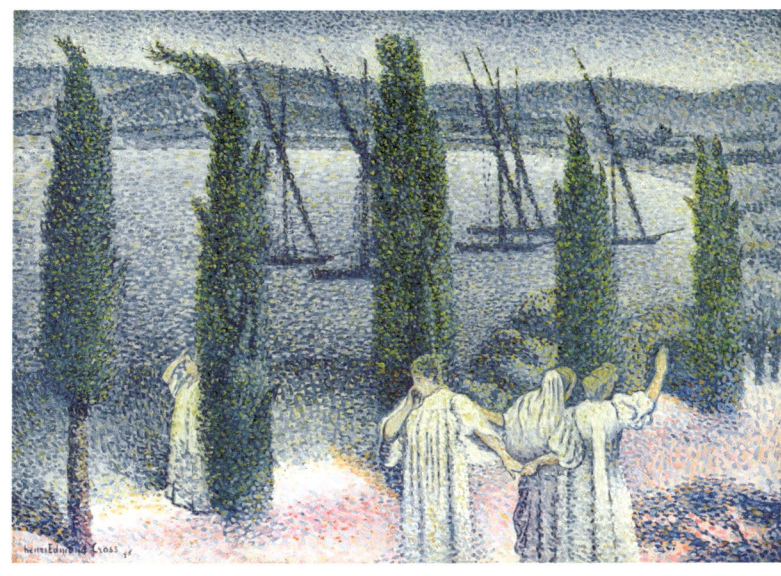

Hades, they would encounter a cypress leaning over a fountain. They were warned not to drink from the Fountain of Lethe (oblivion) but could retain the memory of their past by imbibing from the Fountain of Mnemosyne (memory). The tree's association with death arose because the cypress, once cut, does not grow back.

In Christian art, the cypress sometimes appears in images of martyred saints. Because of its vertical thrust to the heavens, it is also linked with the Virgin Mary, Christ and the Church. Cypress trees appear in Annunciation scenes, and it was thought to have been one of the four trees used to create Christ's Cross, along with the cedar, olive and palm.

Van Gogh painted many images of the cypress, a tree that he considered characteristic of Provence. The flame-like cypress in *The Starry Night* connects the celestial heaven filled with swirling stars and an earthly village with a few lighted windows. The painting may embody an old belief that the souls of the dead travel to the stars, and the cypress provides the bridge.

OTHER CYPRESS IMAGES
- Arnold Böcklin, *Island of the Dead*, 1886, oil on wood. Leipzig: Museum der bildenden Künste.
- John Singer Sargent, *Cypress Trees at San Vigilio*, 1912, oil on canvas. Andover, MA: Addison Gallery, Phillips Academy.

FAMILY Fagaceae

Beech trees, native to the temperate regions of the world, have between ten and thirteen species. Beechwood can be used in construction, but has traditionally been preferred as firewood.

The ancient Greek oracle at Dodona, while primarily sacred to the oak, sometimes used beech leaves in prophecy. The Roman writer and naturalist Pliny wrote of beech groves sacred to Diana and Juno. The beech was apparently favoured for carving lovers' names, as in Shakespeare's *As You Like It*, and has also been connected with study and knowledge because its smooth, pale bark can be written on.

Paul Nash painted trees frequently, including beeches, as well as other plants. For him, they were a mysterious part of the living world, as he wrote in 1912:

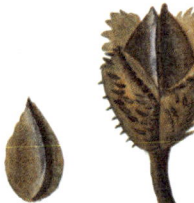

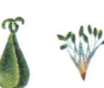

⊗ Pierre-Joseph Redouté, *Fagus silvatica*, 1801–19.

✳ Paul Nash, *The Wood on the Hill (Wittenham Clumps)*, 1912, pen-and-ink drawing. Oxford: Ashmolean Museum.

True, I have tried to paint trees as tho they were human beings. . .because I sincerely love & worship trees & know that they are people & wonderfully beautiful people. . .Do you realise the full significance of 'tree' or what it would try to mean to you: A shelter, a shade, a consoling old thing, a strong kind friend to come to.

Wittenham Clumps in Berkshire are said to be the oldest human-planted beech trees in England, at more than 280 years old. The chalky Sinodun Hills on which they stand were late

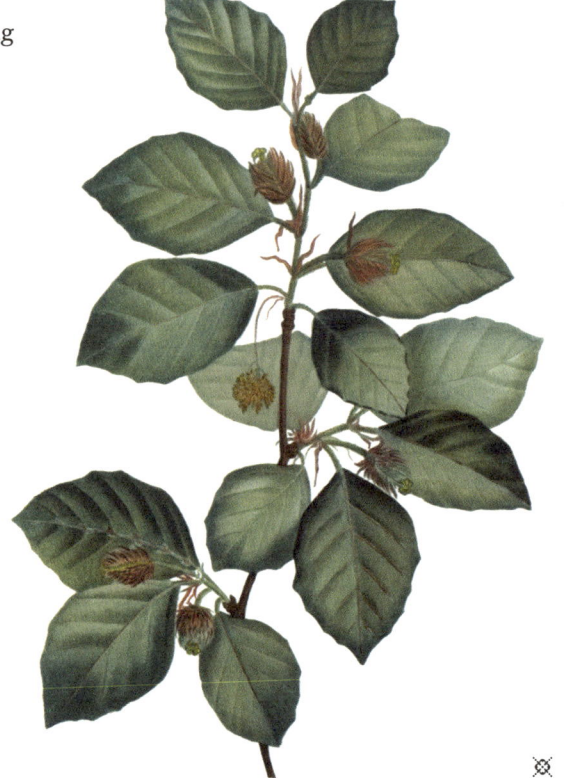

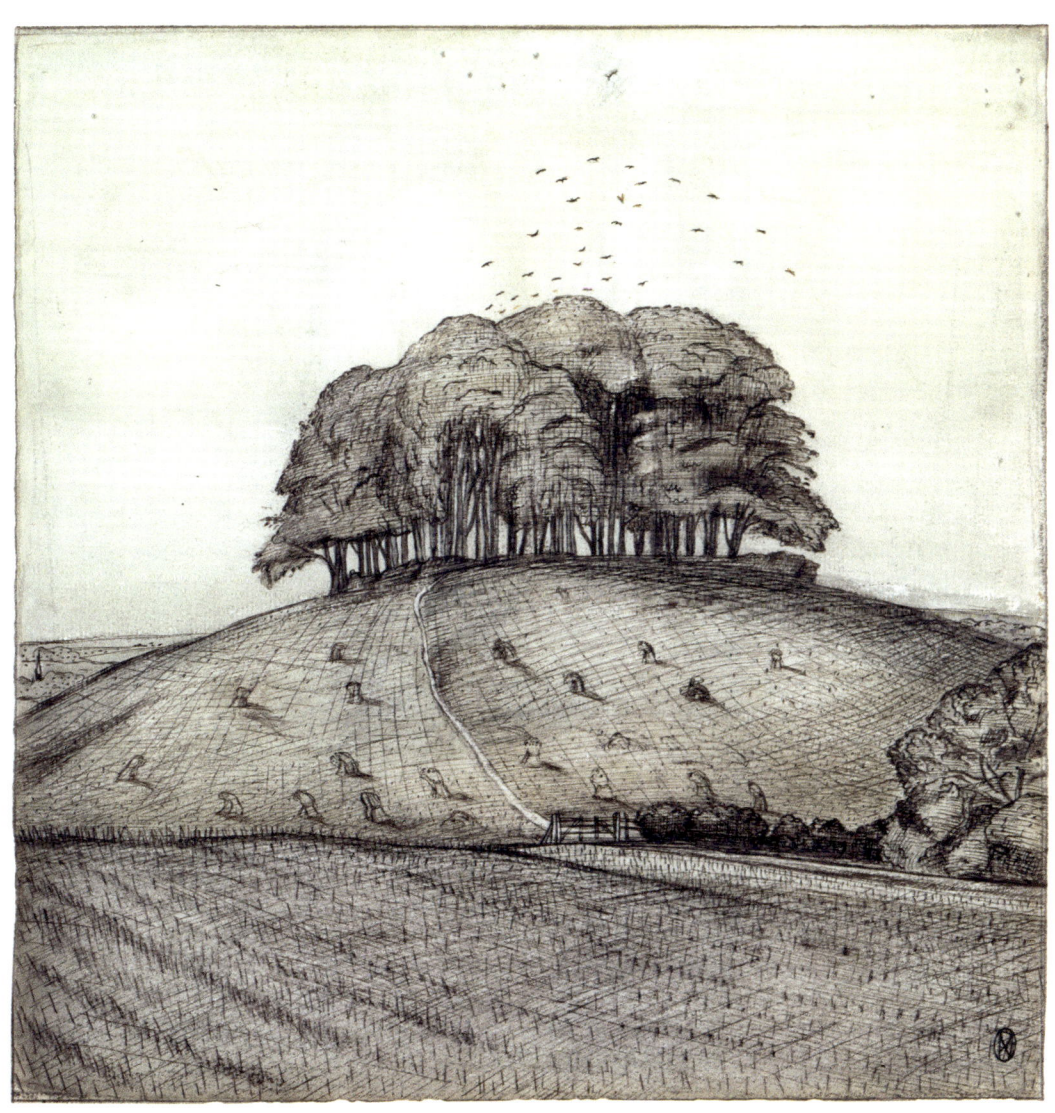

Bronze Age hill forts, inhabited by people who herded animals and farmed wheat and barley, and the site, abandoned around 300 BCE, was later used by the Romans. Nash powerfully captured the connection between trees and landforms. His image of Wittenham Clumps conveys the continuity of life – a path, probably the remains of a Roman road, follows the contour of the hill – in both human lives and nature. Nash was only twenty-three when he made this drawing, but he produced several images of the trees, hills and path.

FAMILY Moraceae

The common fig is a flowering plant in the mulberry family and has been known since ancient times. Native to the Mediterranean region and Asia, it is now also grown widely in North America and Europe. It is one of the earliest plants to have been cultivated by humans.

In the Greco-Roman world, the earth goddess Gaia ordered a fig tree to protect her son, the Titan Sykeus, from Zeus' thunderbolts. It is for this reason that the fig is said to be impervious to lightning strikes. The tree was also associated with the founding of Rome, since Romulus and Remus, abandoned on the Tiber River, providentially stopped beneath a fig tree.

Most garden images in the destroyed city of Pompeii are found in reception rooms, but those in the House of the Orchard occupy two smaller rooms that served for relaxation. The central painting of one room depicts a snake winding around the trunk of a fig tree, said to be a symbol of prosperity.

In Genesis, when Adam and Eve understood that they were naked, 'they sewed fig leaves together and made themselves coverings' (Genesis 3:7). Fig trees are sometimes included in depictions of the infant Jesus, where they recall the Tree of Knowledge and Adam and Eve's Fall, remedied by Christ's Crucifixion and Resurrection. This explains why Grünewald included the tree in his *Birth of Jesus*. The setting is a *hortus conclusus* (secluded garden) and the Virgin's red rose appears on the right.

The gesture known as the 'sign of the fig' – the fist with the thumb protruding between the index and middle finger – is believed to ward off the evil eye. Amulets representing the sign are made in a variety of materials, a favourite being red coral. The gesture can also be obscene, meaning sexual intercourse or contempt.

In 2022, the art historian Giovanni Aloi curated an exhibition entitled 'Lucian Freud: Plant Portraits' at the Garden Museum in London. Aloi points out that Freud painted his own potted plants – some of which embodied his family history – and gardens. Freud excluded traditional symbolism, often choosing plants that have no meaning in European traditions. He focused instead on details, creating images that treated the plants as individuals, capturing their essence. The plants move beyond the Christian symbolism of seventeenth-century art and the objectifying, legislated realism of eighteenth-century botanical illustration. As in all his art, Freud eschewed beauty, here creating small-scale, silent images that engage the viewer.

A large fig leaf conceals most of the girl's face except for her wide-open, unblinking left eye.[7] Although most of the artist's plant images lack symbolic meaning, this work may be an exception. The fig leaf's long history, from Adam and Eve's 'coverings' to concealing genitals in Renaissance images, implies sin and shame. Here the leaf covers her right eye and mouth, giving the print an enigmatic character, partially blocking vision and speech. The staring left eye may signify Freud's intense and silent study of the figures and plants.

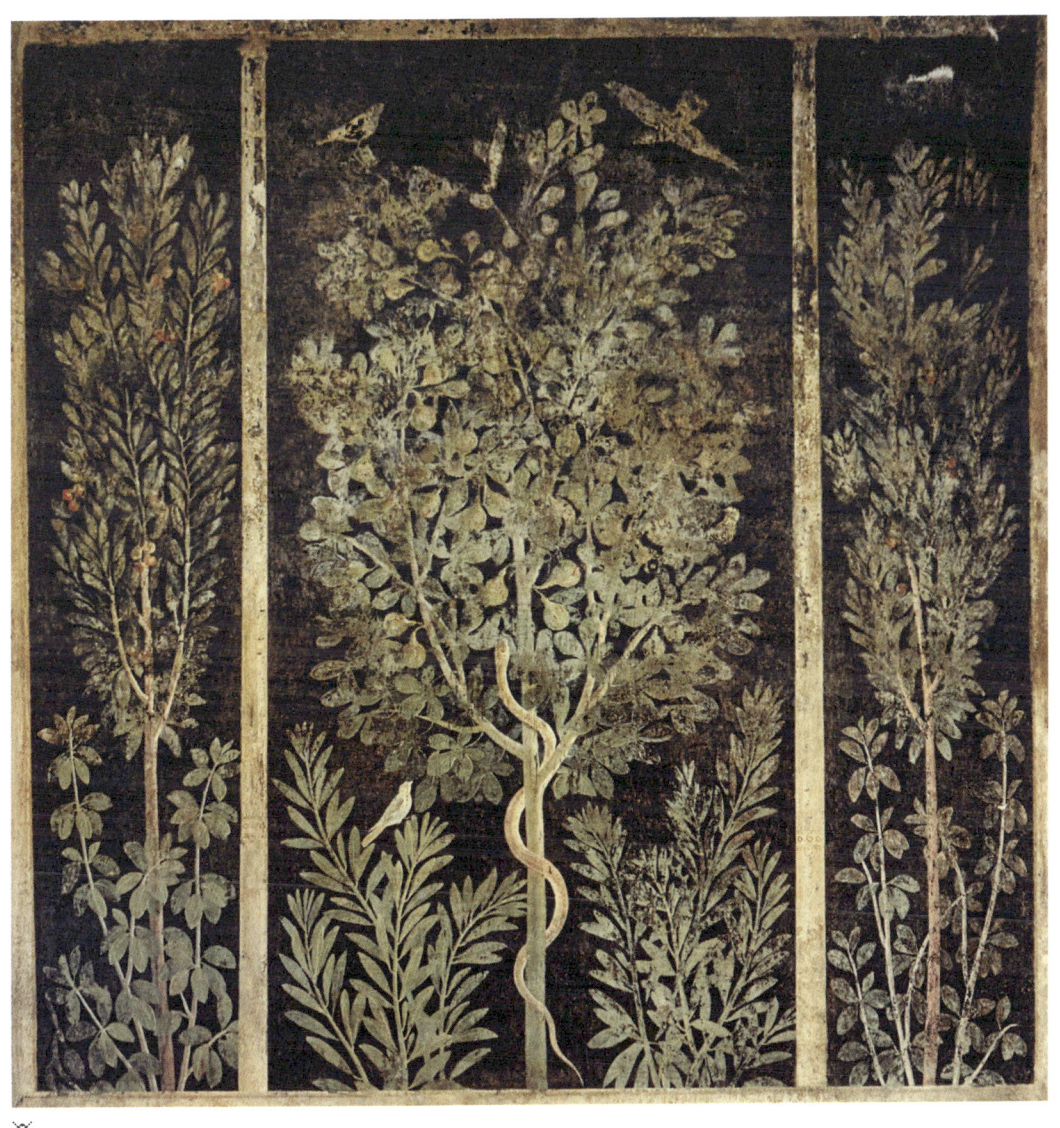

⊠ Roman fresco from House
of the Orchard or of the
Floral Cubicles (detail), first
century CE. Pompeii, Italy.

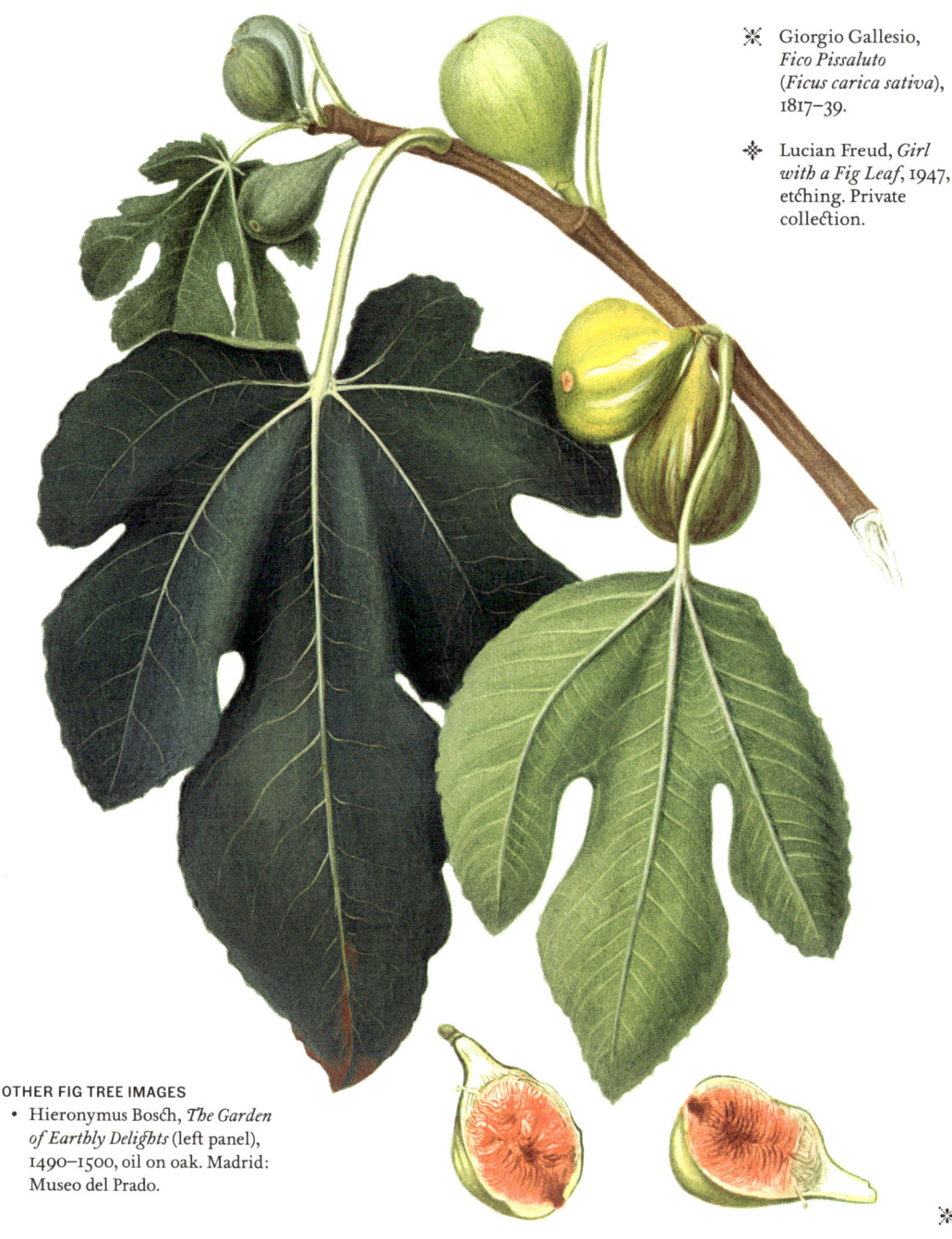

✳ Giorgio Gallesio,
Fico Pissaluto
(*Ficus carica sativa*),
1817–39.

❖ Lucian Freud, *Girl
with a Fig Leaf*, 1947,
etching. Private
collection.

OTHER FIG TREE IMAGES
• Hieronymus Bosch, *The Garden
of Earthly Delights* (left panel),
1490–1500, oil on oak. Madrid:
Museo del Prado.

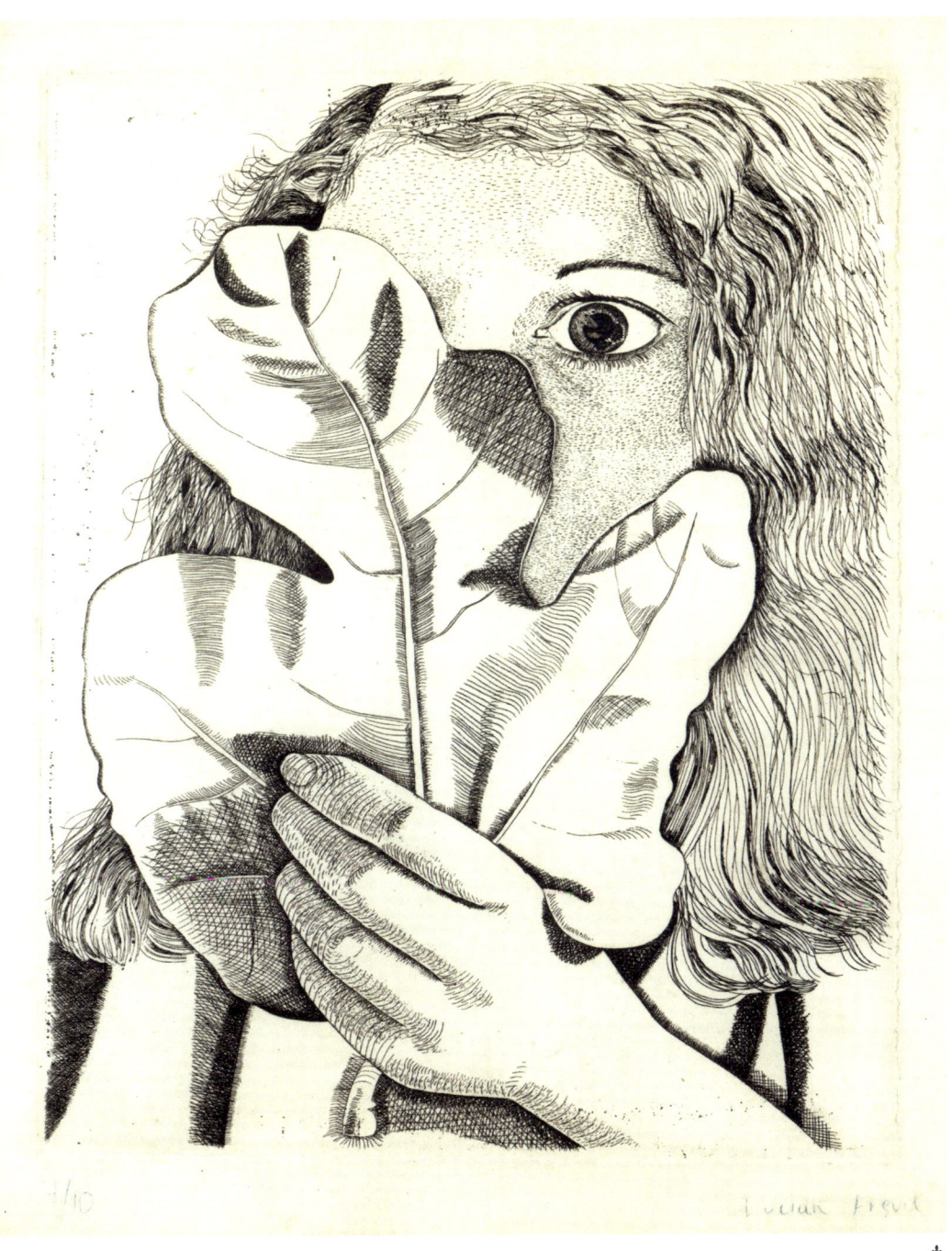

1/10

Lucian Freud

FAMILY Oleaceae

The ash is a candidate for the World Tree (p. 24), the tree that grows at the centre of the universe, houses all life and connects all realms. According to Norse myth, the Great Mother/Goddess was born from the elm, and her consort from the ash.

During the troubled late 1970s, the sculptor David Nash planted a circle of twenty-two ash trees near his home in Wales. Of the circle, which is still growing today, he says:

To make a gesture by planting something for the twenty-first century, which was what Ash Dome is about, was a long-term commitment, an act of faith. I did not know what I was letting myself in for.

The dense wood of the European ash was used to make tools. It was also important in folklore and medicine; belief in its healing powers gave rise to the ritual of passing sick children through clefts in the trunk, and its leaves, bark and sap were used to treat various ailments.

A fungal pathogen from East Asia, first identified in Britain in 2012, may result in the death of eighty per cent of English ash trees in a matter of decades. One can only hope that Nash's circle survives. A similar threat currently affects the ash in the United States and Canada, but the cause is a beetle, the emerald ash borer. Introduced from Asia in 2002, it kills all species of North American ash. So far it has wiped out tens of millions of ash trees in twenty-five states, and it is advancing westwards. Although treatments are available for individual trees, the scope of the problem makes prevention close to impossible.

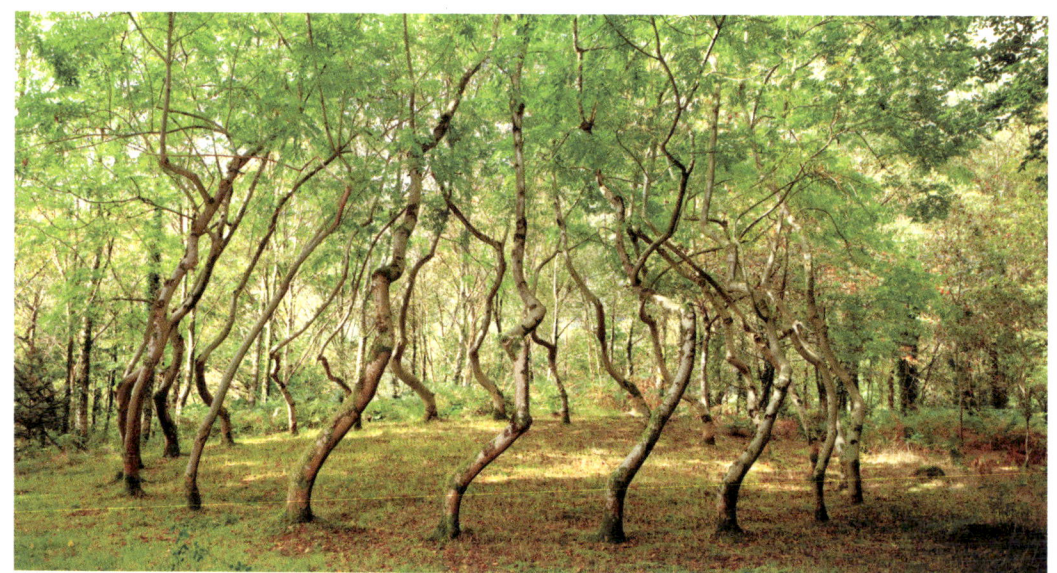

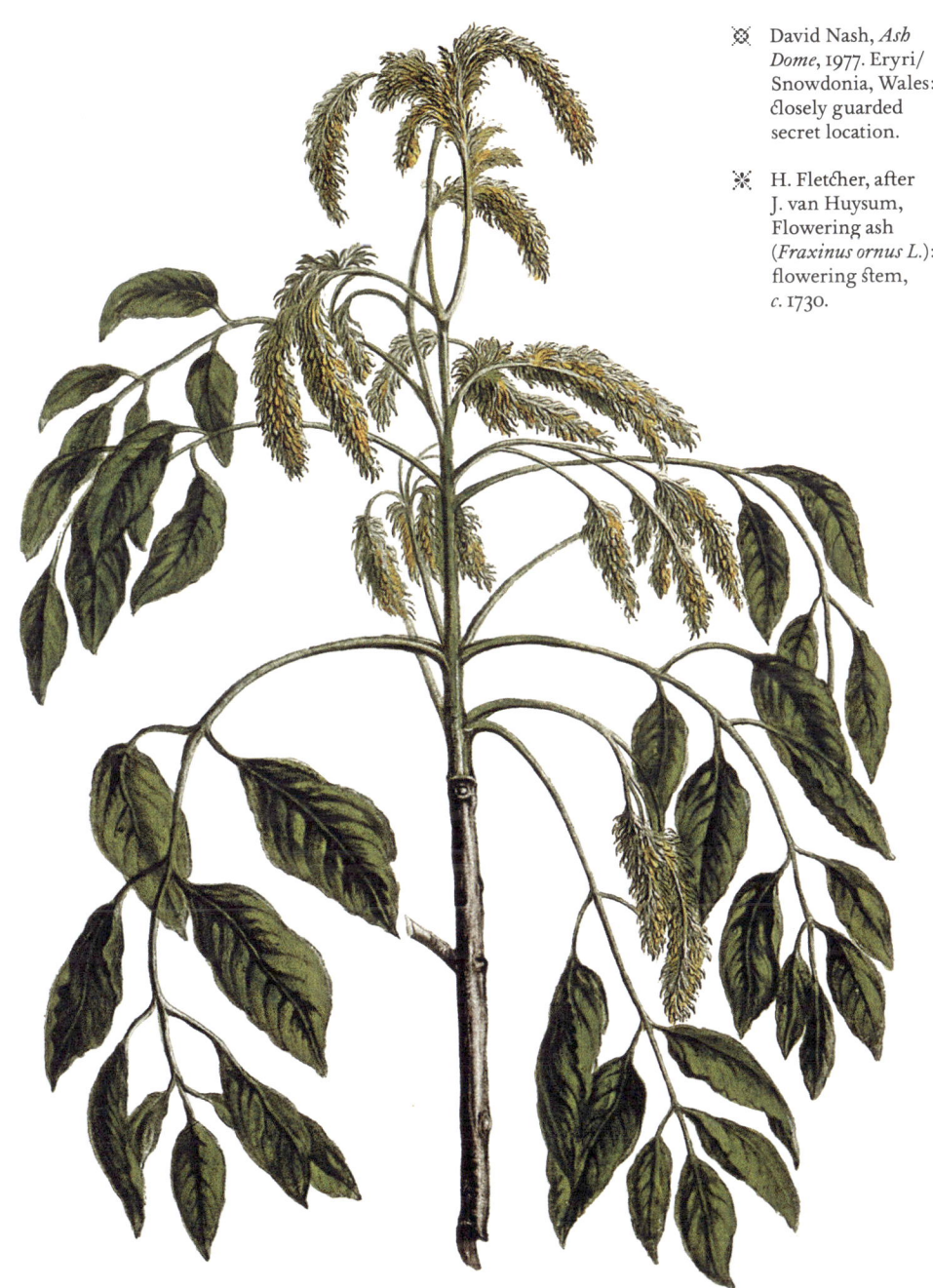

※ David Nash, *Ash Dome*, 1977. Eryri/ Snowdonia, Wales: closely guarded secret location.

※ H. Fletcher, after J. van Huysum, Flowering ash (*Fraxinus ornus L.*): flowering stem, *c.* 1730.

※

FAMILY Aquifoliaceae

These evergreen flowering plants – trees, shrubs and climbers – are found in the tropics and temperate zones worldwide.

Holly was sacred to Saturn, the Roman god of agriculture, and featured in Saturnalia, which was celebrated in mid-December. In medieval European survivals of Saturnalia, three kings – oak, ivy and holly – symbolized wildness and the eternal and enduring forces of nature. When paired with ivy (pp. 212–13), holly has been said to symbolize the male principle in nature and the return of light and life. The being associated with holly, also known as the Green Knight or Wildman, appears in the thirteenth-century long poem *Sir Gawain and the Green Knight*. A huge, mysterious green being appears at an Arthurian New Year's Eve feast riding a mammoth green horse, holding a holly branch in one hand and an axe in the other. There are many translations of the poem, and various interpretations have been offered. It has been understood as involving the opposition of nature and culture, an interpretation relevant to the environmental challenges that are currently facing the world.

In Germany, holly berries symbolized the life-giving blood of the Teutonic Underworld goddess Holle, and its evergreen leaves signified immortality. As a Mother Goddess, Holle was a patron of newborns and named them, an equivalent to giving them their souls.

Holly leaves symbolized Christ's Crown of Thorns, and its berries stood for his blood. It has also been linked with St Jerome and John the Baptist, both of whom were connected with Christ's Passion. The ubiquitous appearance of holly in Christmas decorations, like that of mistletoe, combines its Christian and pre-Christian symbolism.

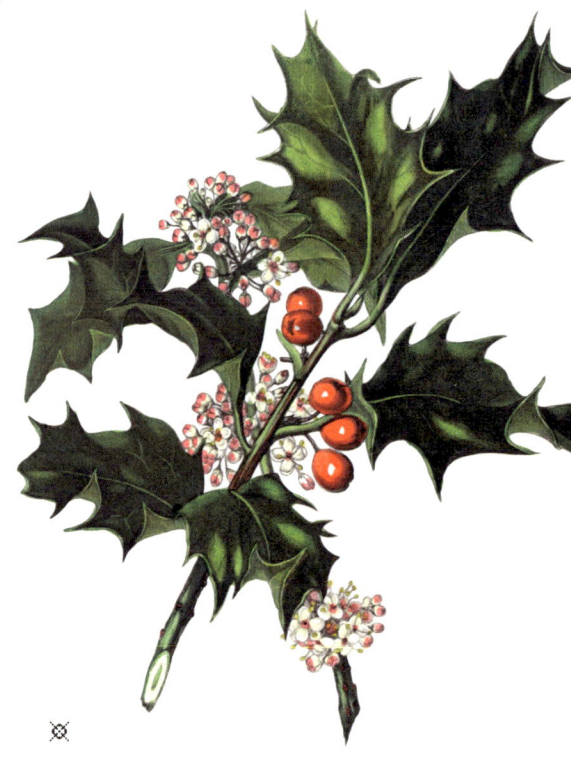

🞝 Rebecca Hey, Holly, 1837.

🞬 Carlton Alfred Smith, *Christmas Eve* (detail), 1901, oil on canvas. Private collection.

🞷 *The Unicorn Surrenders to a Maiden* (detail), Unicorn Tapestries, 1495–1505, wool and silk threads. New York: The Cloisters.

🞝

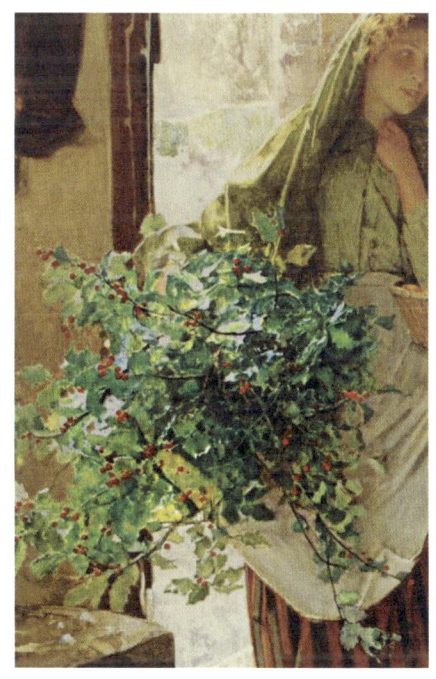

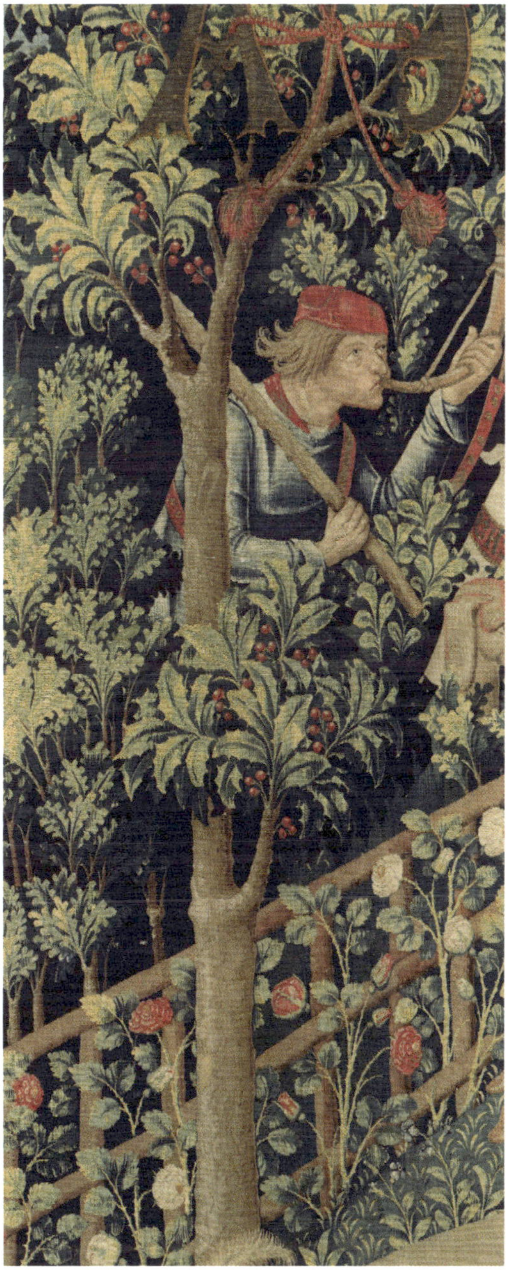

※

❋

FAMILY Cupressaceae

These coniferous trees in the cypress family are widely distributed throughout the northern hemisphere and grow at some of the highest altitudes of any tree.

Some junipers are given the common name cedar and widely used as timber. Juniper berries are used as a spice, as an essential oil, in herbal remedies and for flavouring alcoholic drinks like gin and jenever. Its oldest recorded use – 1500 BCE – was in ancient Egypt, where

its berries were used to treat tapeworm. The Romans used juniper berries for purification and stomach ailments.

The juniper has long been associated with chastity, because its berries are protected by thorny leaves, much as the chestnut is protected by its husk. Pliny wrote of the tree's incorruptibility, giving as an example a Spanish temple in perfect condition, sacred to Artemis, that had been built of juniper beams some 200 years before the Trojan War. This symbolism continued in Christian art, where it sometimes appears in Nativity scenes, while the tree's thorny leaves recall Christ's Passion and the Crown of Thorns. In portraiture its presence sometimes relates to the sitter's name, as in

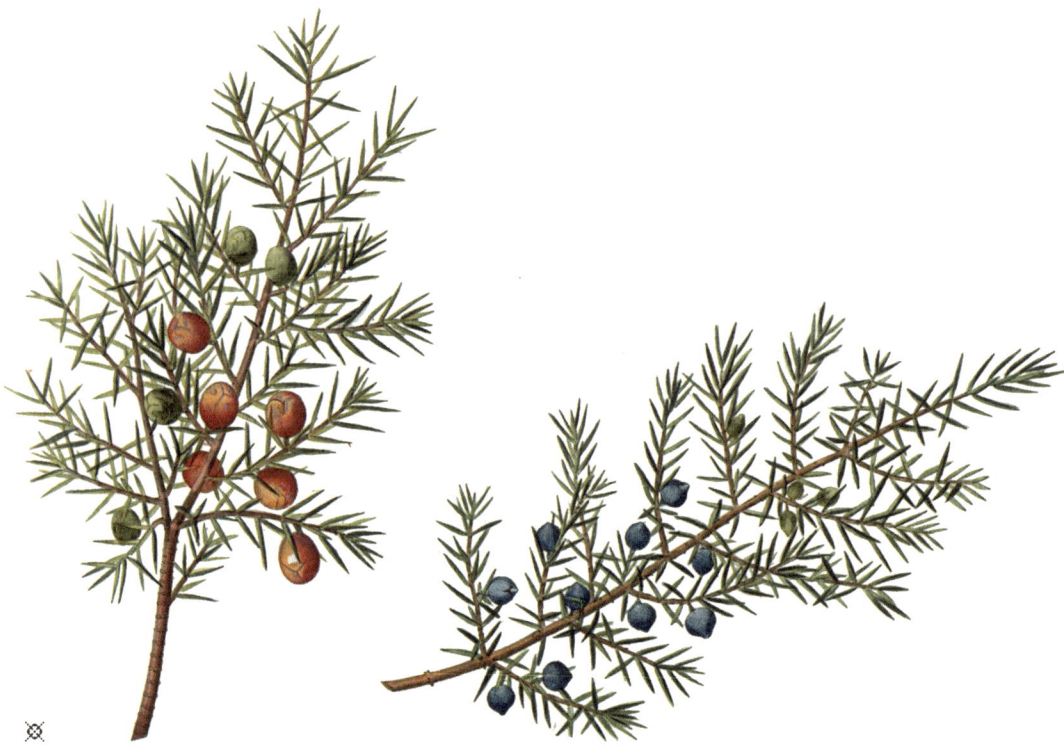

Leonardo's *Portrait of Ginevra de' Benci* (1474–75), which features a juniper on the reverse.

The Brothers Grimm are believed to have adapted the fairytale entitled 'The Juniper Tree' from the German Romantic artist Philipp Otto Runge. It is indeed a grim tale involving an evil stepmother, murder and unwitting cannibalism. The tree itself serves as a burial place. Illustrated volumes include images of the tree; the English artist Walter Crane contributed one showing a bird arising from the tree, implying the survival of the soul (1882).

The Canadian artist and writer Emily Carr painted trees over and over again. Junipers as well as other trees signify the spiritual connection and boundless energy she found in nature – as is clear from a passage in her journal:

Go into the woods alone and look at the earth crowded with growth, new and old bursting from their strong roots hidden in the silent, live ground, each seed according to its own kind expanding, bursting, pushing its way upward toward the light and air, each one knowing what to do, each one demanding its own rights on the earth.

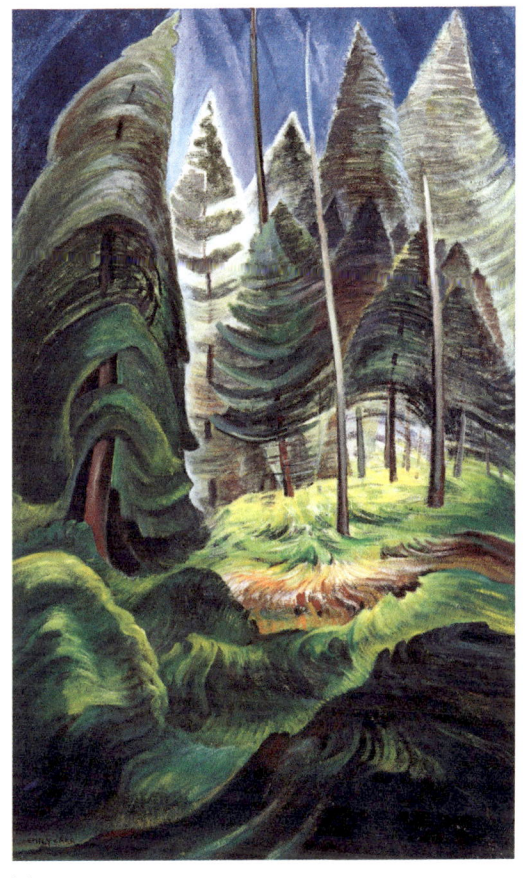

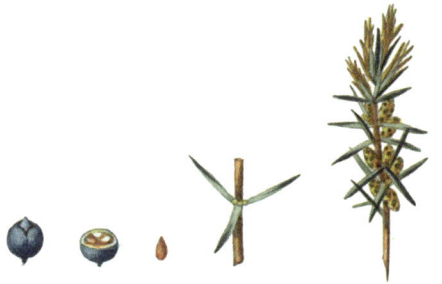

  Pierre-Joseph Redouté, *Juniperus communis* (Common juniper), *Juniperus oxycedrus* (Prickly juniper), 1801–19.

  Emily Carr, *A Rushing Sea of Undergrowth*, 1935, oil on canvas. Vancouver, British Columbia: Vancouver Art Gallery, Emily Carr Trust.

FAMILY Lauraceae

The laurel – also known as bay laurel, sweet bay or true laurel – is an evergreen shrub or small tree. Native to the Mediterranean, it now grows worldwide.

It is commonly an ornamental plant, and its leaves are used for seasoning, as well as having medicinal purposes. The bay leaf is sometimes categorized as a herb.

In ancient Greece, the plant was called *daphne*, after the nymph of the same name. Apollo pursued her, and she pleaded with Gaia, Mother Earth, who transported her to Crete and left a laurel tree in her place. Ovid says that she was immediately transformed into a tree. Apollo took the laurel as a personal symbol, and so it came to symbolize inspiration and immortal fame. Laurel leaves and crowns adorn artists, athletes, rulers, soldiers and philosophers, and the modern title Laureate means 'laurel-crowned one'. Laurel is associated with several other Greco-Roman deities: Artemis, Dionysus, Hera and Zeus; the priestesses of the Delphic oracle chewed its leaves to promote prophecies.

One of the most memorable depictions of Ovid's story can be found in Piero del Pollaiuolo's *Apollo and Daphne* of about 1470–80 at the

National Gallery, London. Daphne is shown undergoing transformation, her arms sprouting into leafy branches. Apollo appears as an aristocratic youth, and the scene is set in the Florentine countryside. The painting is small and would probably have been kept in a velvet bag when not on display. The museum's

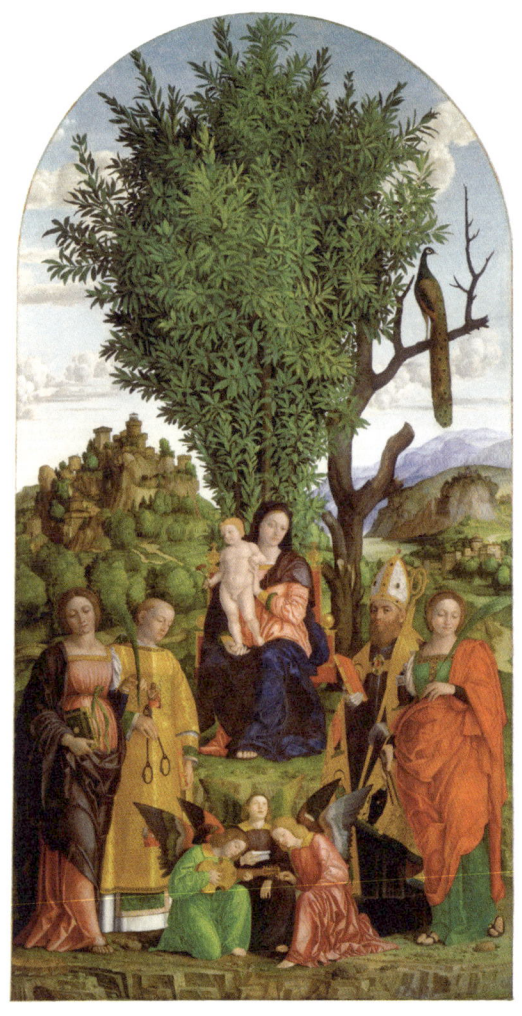

⊗ Girolamo dai Libri, *Madonna and Child with Saints*, *c.* 1520, tempera and oil on canvas. New York: Metropolitan Museum of Art.

⊗ William Clark, Bay laurel (*Laurus nobilis*), 1834.

⊗ Lorenzo Lotto, *Venus and Cupid* (detail), 1520, oil on canvas. New York: Metropolitan Museum of Art.   ⊗

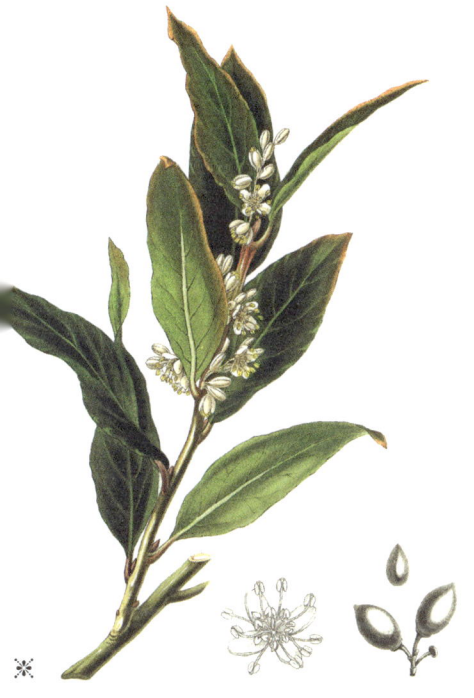

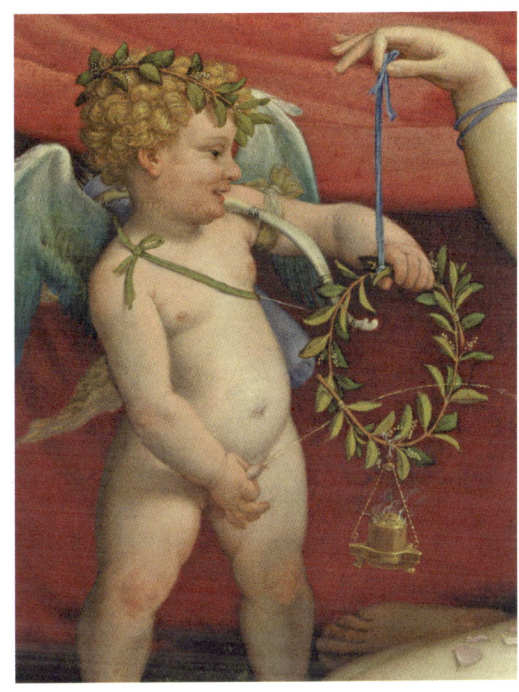

caption mentions the literary connection to Petrarch's fourteenth-century verses about the unattainable Laura, a platonic passion that became the ideal form of courtly love and the pursuit of beauty. The laurel tree and its leaves were sometimes also included in portraits of individuals who shared the plant's name: Laura or Lorenzo, for example.

The subject of Daphne and Apollo would be incomplete without mention of Gian Lorenzo Bernini's breathtaking sculpture (1622–25), now in the Galleria Borghese, Rome. Here, too, Daphne is caught mid-transformation, and marble mimics bark, slowly embracing her leg and her hair, while her fingertips sprout leaves.

The tree's symbolism of immortality also featured in Christian art. The Virgin Mary's intimate connection with the plant inspired Girolamo dai Libri to place her and the infant Jesus under the tree in his painting *Madonna and Child with Saints*. In Renaissance works such as Lorenzo Lotto's *Venus and Cupid*, Venus holds a laurel crown; in others, winged, allegorical figures of Victory convey laurel crowns.

See also 'Mullein', pp. 200–1, for a discussion of the laurel in Bellini's *St Francis in the Desert*.

FAMILY Oleaceae

Evergreen olive trees are cultivated in all countries in the Mediterranean basin, as well as in the Americas, Africa, China and Australia.

The fruit, also called the olive, is of major agricultural importance, olive oil being a core ingredient of Mediterranean cuisine. The tree may have originated some 20–40 million years ago.

The olive tree, together with its fruit and oil, is replete with symbolism: peace, fruitfulness, purification, strength, victory and reward. A small replica of an olive branch in gold was left on the moon by the astronauts of NASA's

Apollo 11 in 1969 to represent the wish for peace on earth.

According to Greek legend, Athena and Poseidon competed for the honour of giving a name to a newly created city. Poseidon threw his trident and a salty spring issued forth – or, according to some versions, a horse. Athena struck the ground with her spear and an olive tree sprang up. The gods declared Athena the winner, since her tree symbolized peace as well as being more useful, and the city was named Athens. Descendants of the original tree are said to flourish on the Acropolis today. Victors in Athena's Panathenaic games were crowned with wreaths of olive leaves. The sacred grove at Olympia was made up of olive trees, and

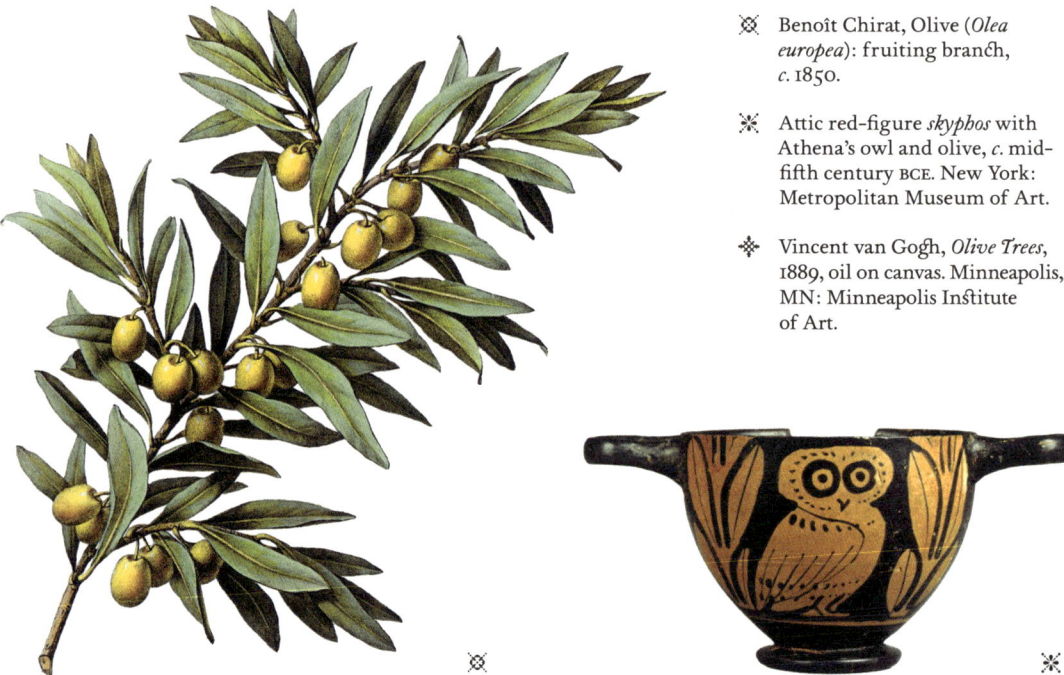

※ Benoît Chirat, Olive (*Olea europea*): fruiting branch, *c.* 1850.

※ Attic red-figure *skyphos* with Athena's owl and olive, *c.* mid-fifth century BCE. New York: Metropolitan Museum of Art.

❋ Vincent van Gogh, *Olive Trees*, 1889, oil on canvas. Minneapolis, MN: Minneapolis Institute of Art.

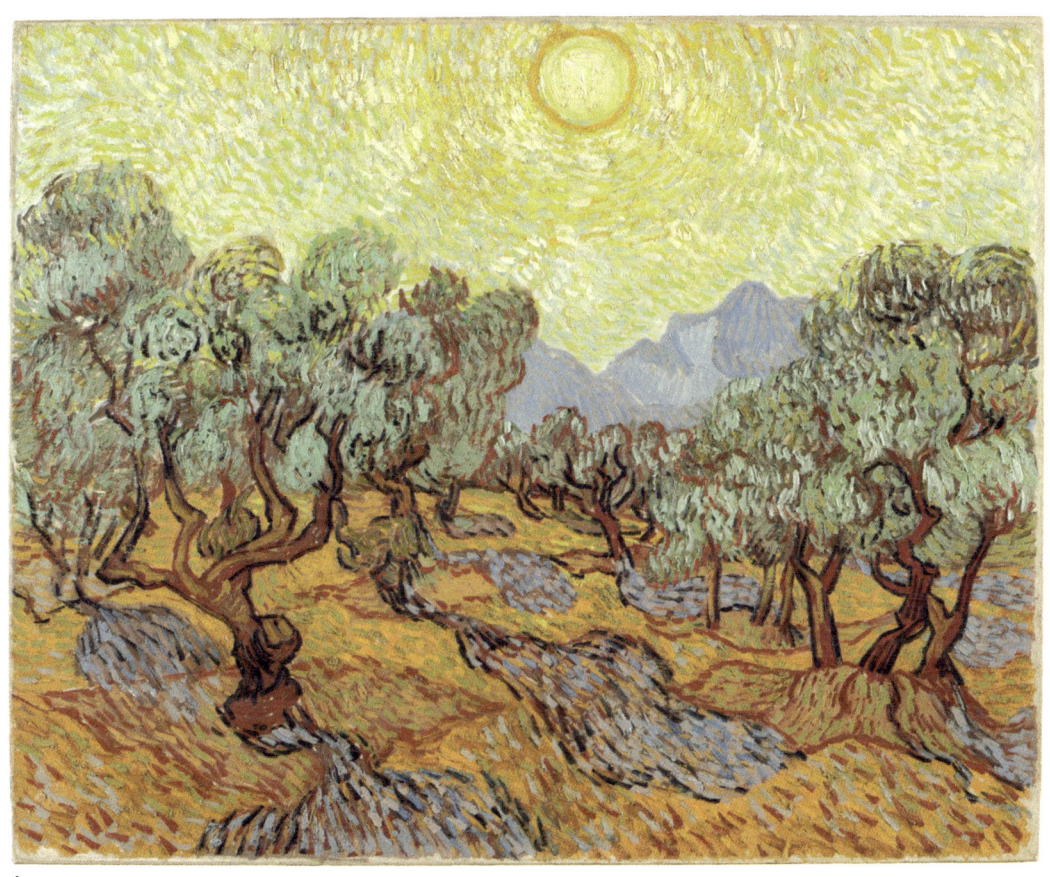

branches were presented to the winners of the games.

In the Torah the olive branch symbolizes safety, since when the dove returned with it, Noah knew the waters of the Great Flood had abated. Olive oil is poured on troubled waters; Jacob poured oil on the stone of Bethel after his dream of the ladder extending to heaven, and in Hebrew *messiah* means 'the anointed one'. Olive oil was used to treat wounds and, mixed with balsam and aromatic herbs, made the chrism

(consecrated oil) used for Christian baptism, confirmation, holy orders and the anointing of the sick.

OTHER OLIVE IMAGES
- Dove and olive branch, fourth century CE, fresco. Catacomb of San Lorenzo, Rome.
- El Greco, *Christ in the Olive Garden, c.* 1600, oil on canvas. Lille, France: Palais des Beaux-Arts.

FAMILY Arecaceae

There are many different species of palm, though this entry refers primarily to the genus *Phoenix*, the date palm.

Important as a food source in the ancient Mediterranean, the palm has long been a candidate for the Tree of Life, since it grows in arid lands and desert oases. Almost universally, palm branches symbolize triumph, victory and immortality.

The Egyptian date palm was a sacred tree, its branches symbolizing the god Heh, the personification of eternity. The god held a palm branch with several notches, each symbolizing a year, so that the branch signified never-ending life. This meaning also applies to Virgil's *Aeneid* and to the Eleusinian Mysteries of ancient Greece. In Greco-Roman culture the palm served as a symbol of military success – a meaning shared by many later societies – and Romans returning victorious from campaigns were met with palm bearers, as was Christ when he entered Jerusalem.

Images of martyred saints bear palms as a symbol of their triumph over death. A fourth-century Roman martyr born into a wealthy family, St Lucy was persecuted, tortured and killed for attempting to distribute her riches to the poor. Lucy's story was expanded in the thirteenth-century *Golden Legend*, a collection of lives of the saints. Her captors had gouged out her eyes, but while her body was being prepared for burial, they were miraculously restored. Lucy is thus the patron saint of the blind and of those suffering from eye ailments. In Francesco del Cossa's painting, Lucy holds the martyr's palm in one hand and, in the other, her eyes,

which look rather like strange little flowers on a single stem.

The Virgin Mary's association with the palm comes from the Song of Solomon (7:8): 'This stature of yours is like a palm tree, and your breasts like its clusters.' The Archangel Gabriel sometimes holds palm fronds in Annunciation scenes, and they appear again in the Virgin's death scenes. She apparently asked that they be carried in her funeral procession.

Images depicting the Holy Family's journey to Egypt usually include a palm bending so that Joseph could pick the fruit. The story of

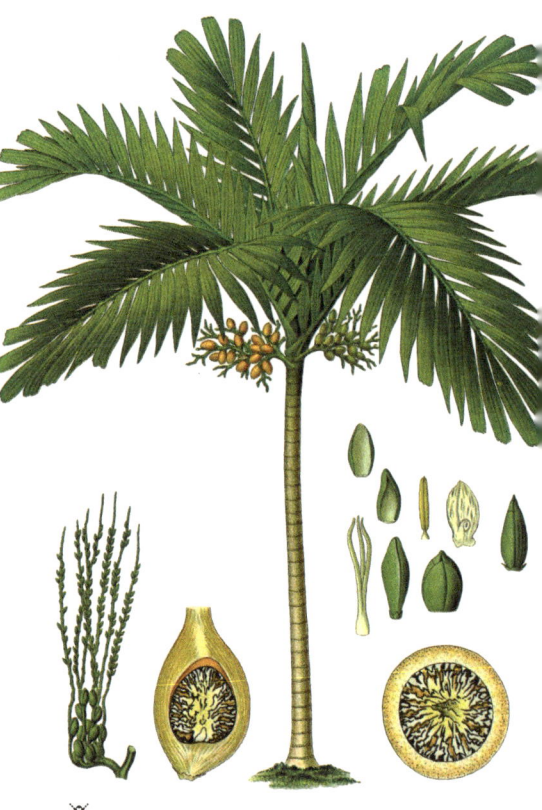

the flight is told briefly in Matthew 2:13–18, without mention of the palm tree. A more complete version appears in the apocryphal eighth–ninth-century Pseudo-Matthew, chapter 20. Images of the flight were popular with Renaissance and Baroque artists, such as Caravaggio, Gerard David, Albrecht Dürer, Lucas van Leyden, Hans Memling, Joachim Patinir and Martin Schongauer. Not all the elements of Pseudo-Matthew's text are included; other types of tree are sometimes substituted, since many European artists had never seen a palm. Indeed, most of the landscapes look decidedly un-Egyptian.

✖ Fr. Eugen Köhler, *Areca catechu* (Areca palm), 1890.

✖ Francesco del Cossa, *Saint Lucy*, c. 1473–74, tempera on panel. Washington, DC: National Gallery of Art.

OTHER PALM IMAGES
- Funeral ritual in a garden, facsimile by Charles K. Wilkinson of an image from the Tomb of Minnakht, Egypt, c. 1479–1425 BCE. New York: Metropolitan Museum of Art.
- Martin Schongauer, *The Flight into Egypt*, c. 1470–75, engraving. Washington, DC: National Gallery of Art.
- Andrea del Verrocchio and Leonardo da Vinci, *The Baptism of Christ*, c. 1470–75, tempera and oil on panel. Florence: Le Gallerie degli Uffizi.

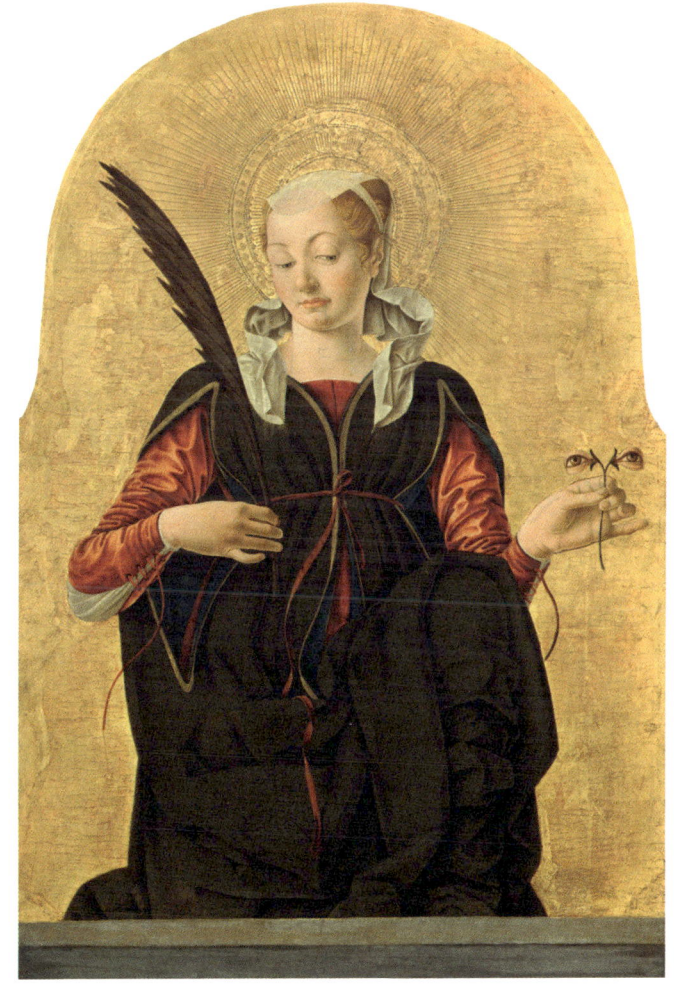

✖

FAMILY Pinaceae

Pines are evergreen, coniferous trees native to the northern hemisphere and may live for 1,000 years or more ('Methuselah', a bristlecone pine, is said to be about 4,600 years old).

They are thought to have evolved about 153 million years ago. Outside the wild, pines are grown largely for timber, harvested when the trees reach twenty-five years of age. Pines were used medicinally in China, and pine nuts are an important by-product. The word 'pine' can be traced to an Indo-European root word meaning 'resin'. Before the nineteenth century, pines were often referred to as fir trees.

In common with all evergreen trees, the pine and pine cones symbolize immortality. Many myths tell of the transformation of the dead into pine trees, and the rustling of their needles has been said to be the voices of gods. In Greece and Rome, the pine was sacred to Cybele, a fertility goddess. The Roman cult of Cybele conducted a multi-day spring ritual in which a pine was cut down and carried to the Palatine Temple, where it was bandaged like a corpse and wreathed with violets to represent the body of Cybele's lover Attis. On the final day, the rebirth of Attis was celebrated with great rejoicing.

Pine cones appear in art all over the world, usually with meanings of fertility and immortality. The ancient Egyptians depicted a pine cone encircled by twin cobras atop the staff of the god Osiris. Some scholars have claimed that pine cones also adorned the top of the ivy-entwined staff – the *thyrsus* – carried by Dionysus and his maenads, but more recently that shape has been linked with the artichoke (p. 166). The world's largest pine cone was created or commissioned by the Roman

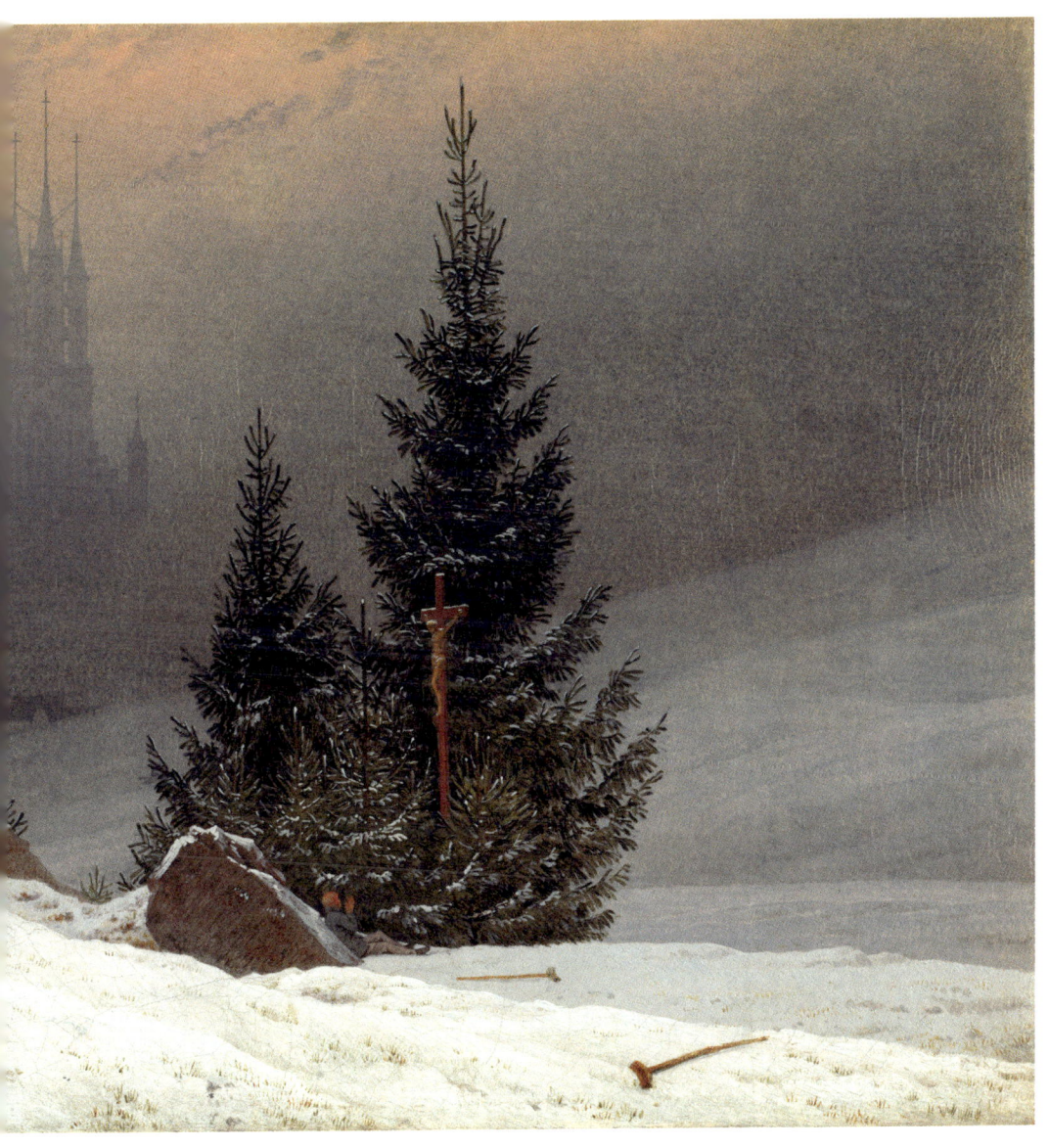

⌗ Caspar David Friedrich, *Winter Landscape*, probably 1811, oil on canvas. London: National Gallery.

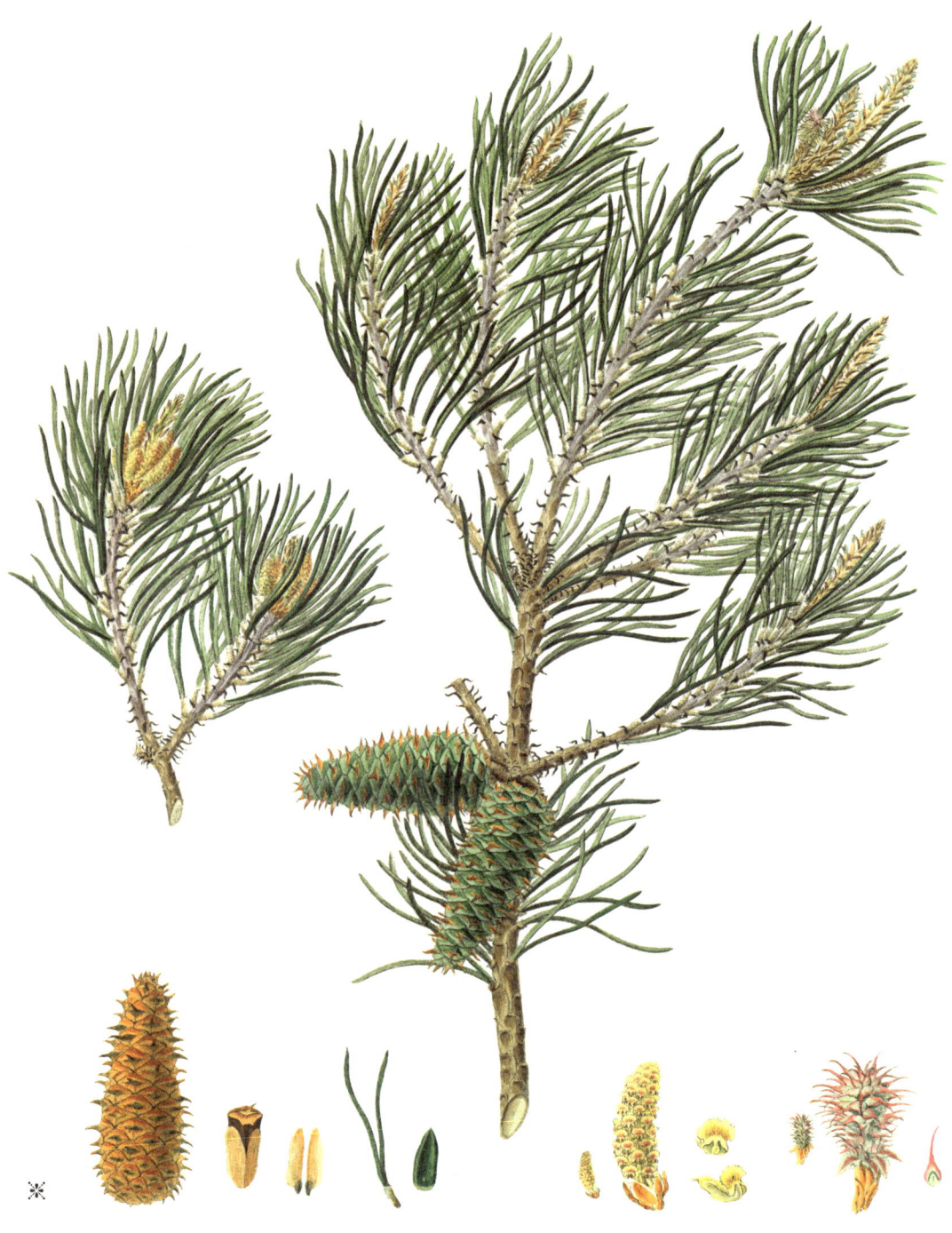

Publius Cincius Salvius, whose name appears on its base. The bronze cone was 3.4 m (11 ft) tall, and probably graced a fountain, water being another symbol of fertility. Unearthed near the Pantheon, the sculpture was moved in 1608 to the Vatican's Cortile della Pigna, where it now rests at the top of a double staircase designed by Michelangelo.

The pine tree was also important among the ancient Celts and possibly provided one of the letters in the ogham alphabet. There is a Germanic story about a church steeple bent by the wind and subsequently straightened by a shepherd, who attached it to a pine and uttered invocations. In 1492, the Virgin Mary is said to have appeared in a pine tree and spoken to the bishop of Gran Canaria. The basilica that was built as a result of this revelation contains an extraordinary statue of the Virgin (patron saint of the island) that is thought to have healing properties.

One of the miracles of St Francis of Assisi involved a pine. Taking refuge on the island of San Francesco del Deserto in the Venetian lagoon during a storm, Marilyn Aronberg Lavin, Jinyu Liu and Adam Gitner write that the saint is said to have taken a limb of pine to serve as a walking stick: 'Before leaving the island, Francis planted his staff in the ground where it miraculously germinated, becoming a pine tree that grew to an extraordinary height.' The island subsequently housed a Franciscan monastery, and the tree 'flourished in the monastery cloister until it had to be taken down. The remains now rest in a side chapel.' Lavin, Liu and Gitner suggest that the story serves as a metaphor for Francis's spreading of the holy word.

The symbolism of the pine continued to be evident in Romantic art, as in the work of the German artist Caspar David Friedrich.

In *Winter Landscape*, a group of conifers occupies the foreground, their shape repeated in the misty silhouette of a church in the background. Having cast his crutches aside, a man rests against a boulder and prays before a crucifix standing in the trees. Taken together, the dawn light, church, cross and trees symbolize hope and rebirth. The trees are identified as firs on the National Gallery website; however, because of their clustered needles, they are likely to be pines.

The pine cone has been associated with the third eye and the pineal gland, defined by Merriam-Webster's Dictionary as follows: 'a small, typically cone-shaped structure in the brain that arises from the third ventricle, is enclosed by the pia mater, and functions primarily as an endocrine gland secreting the sleep-influencing hormone melatonin'. Thought to be a vestigial eye, the pineal gland became associated with enlightenment, as did its pine-cone-like shape. Both the pine cone and the third eye figure in Masonic symbolism.

The pine cone also forms a perfect logarithmic (or equiangular) spiral. This pattern is found frequently in nature, such as in the growth of plants – in cacti, the seeds of the sunflower (pp. 114–17), and elsewhere – the chambered nautilus and spiral galaxies. The spiral's beauty, energy and endlessness probably explain the frequency with which pine cones appear in symbolic art.

✳ Jersey pine (*Pinus inops*), 1837.

FAMILY Rosaceae

Native to Iran and surrounding regions in West Asia and North Africa, almond trees are now cultivated elsewhere. The tree is one of the earliest domesticated, beginning around 3000 BCE.

A traditional symbol of sweetness and delicacy, almond trees are among the first to bloom in the spring and are therefore vulnerable to frost. The precise knowledge of the plant's life cycle acquired by its early farmers led to its symbolism: the tree's early bloom makes it a symbol of rebirth, survival and immortality.

In Jewish folklore, the almond fruit is regarded as female and the tree as male. The word *luz* means almond, and is also the name of a mysterious city, one of the 'Seats of the Immortals', which can be accessed at the foot of an almond tree. Thus, the tree is associated with immortality. In Exodus (25:31–40), God reveals the design of the golden menorah to Moses – it was to have cups shaped like almond flowers with buds and blossoms. The menorah from the Second Temple was carried off by the Romans in 70 CE, and it is depicted among the spoils of war on the Arch of Titus in Rome. Moses's elder brother Aaron's rod of almond wood, a symbol of authority, flowered, signifying divine favour, and in Jewish art, the almond is a symbol of Aaron. In the Christian New Testament, Joseph's rod also flowered, with the same symbolism; by extension, it signified the Virgin's purity.

The almond nut signifies awakening, revival, spring, hope, divine approval, virginity and fruitfulness. As Jean Chevalier puts it,

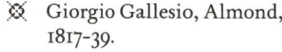

⊗ Giorgio Gallesio, Almond, 1817-39.

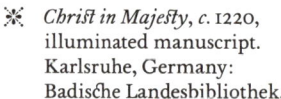

✴ *Christ in Majesty*, *c.* 1220, illuminated manuscript. Karlsruhe, Germany: Badische Landesbibliothek.

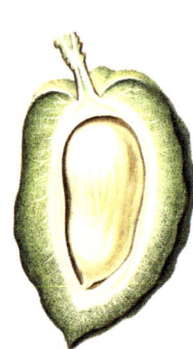

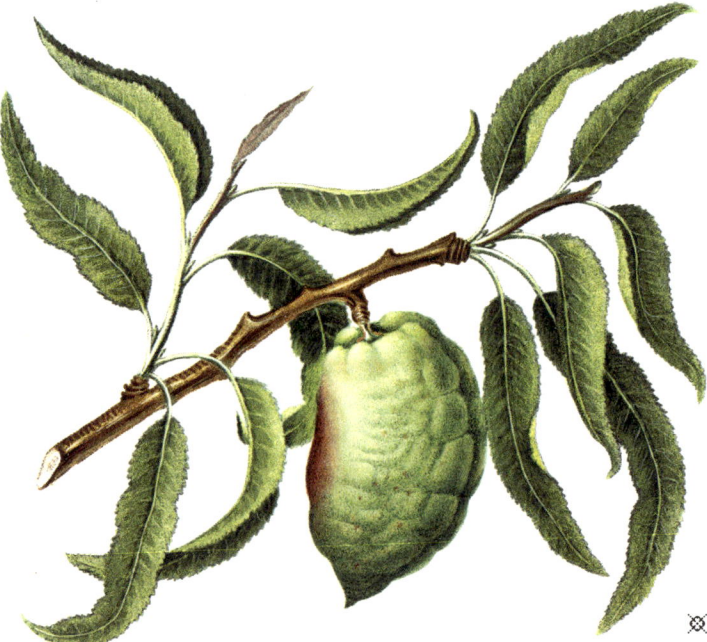

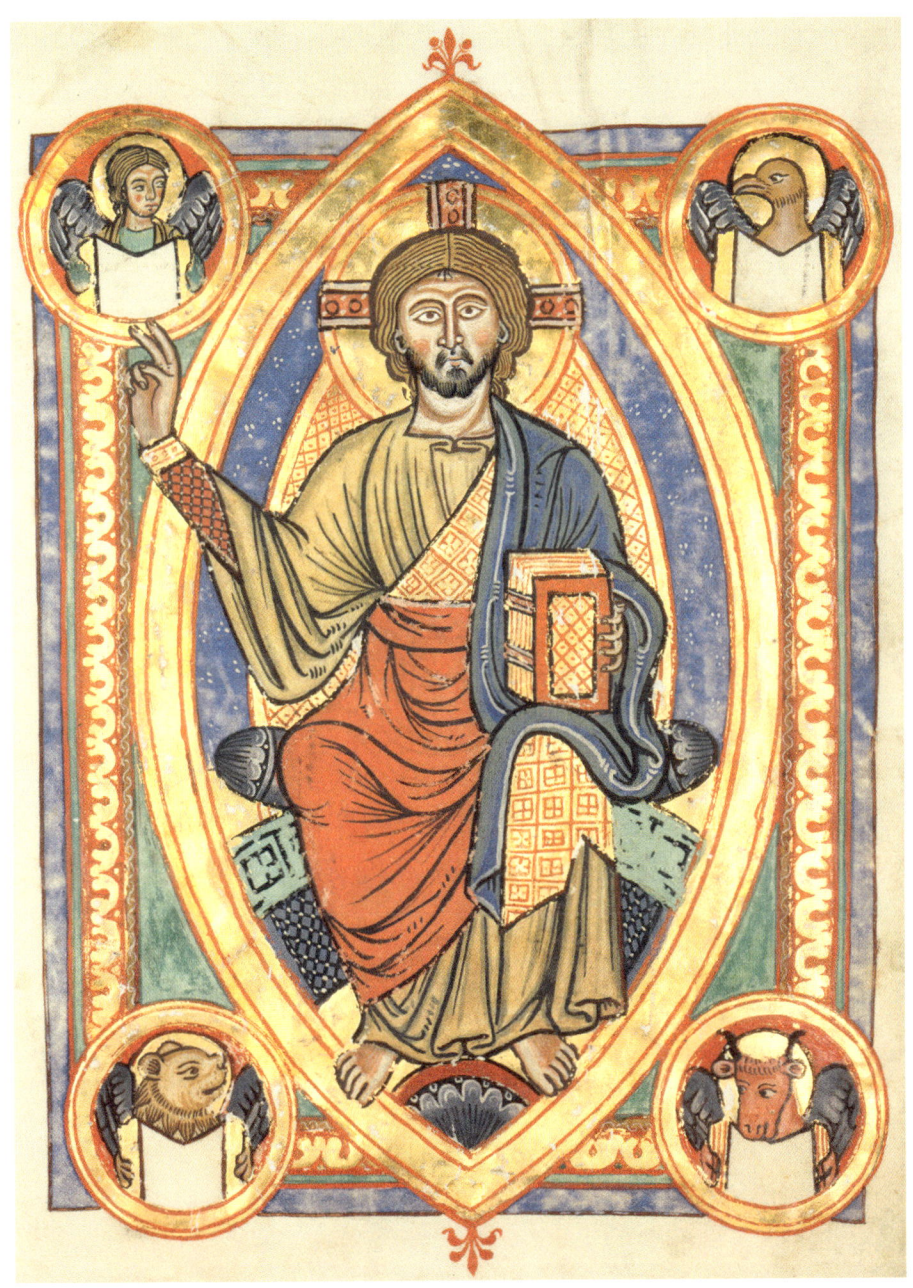

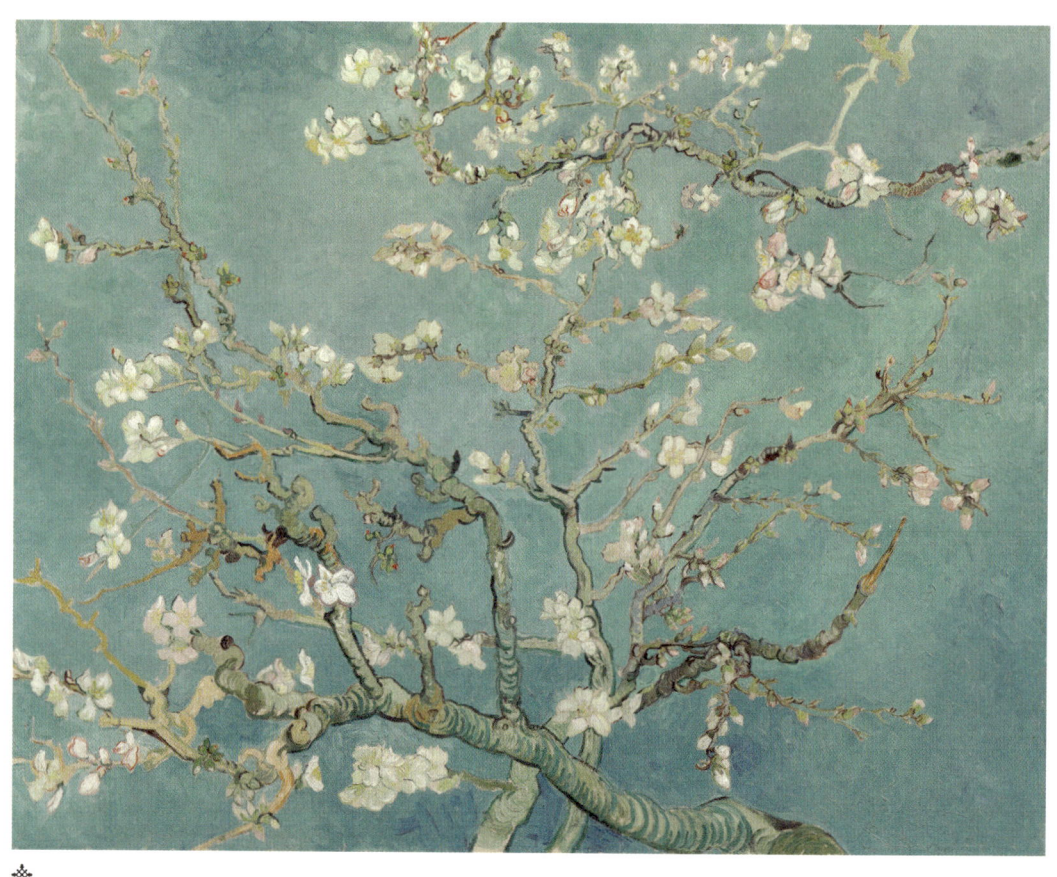

❖ Vincent van Gogh, *Almond Blossom*, 1890, oil on canvas. Amsterdam: Van Gogh Museum.

'in common parlance', to eat an almond means to have sexual intercourse. He also suggests that passing from its secular to sacred symbolism serves only to strengthen its connotation of the primordial womb, the beginning of time and creation.

Myth has it that the Greek and Phrygian god of vegetation, Attis, was conceived from an almond. The Greek traveller Pausanias recounts a complex story of abandonment, madness, self-castration, death and rebirth – all from an almond. Almond oil was also linked with Zeus, regarded as his seed.

Mandorla, the Italian word for almond, describes the almond-shaped halo of light surrounding the body of Christ and other holy beings. The mandorla first appeared in the fifth-century mosaics of the Church of Santa Maria Maggiore in Rome. From the sixth until the early fifteenth century, it became common in depictions of the Transfiguration and many other Christian subjects. It is often found in Eastern Orthodox art and in medieval architectural sculpture, where the frame may be adorned with decorative mouldings filled with inscriptions or symbols, such as Alpha and Omega (A and Ω), stars and/or flowers (such as the five-petalled almond blossom), but the device was abandoned by Renaissance artists as being unrealistic.

The mandorla can also take the form of a lens (the intersection of two circles) called the *vesica piscis* (Latin for 'bladder of a fish'). The *ichthys* (fish), the secret symbol of early Christians, consisted of similarly intersecting arcs, extending on one side to create the fish's tail. The Greek letters were additionally linked with Christ's name (I=Iesous/Jesus, C=Christos, Q=Theou/God's, U=Uios/Son, S=Soter/Saviour).

The almond within its skin symbolizes Christ – the divine nature hidden within the human form. More generally, the almond in its skin signifies substance hidden by external accident: spirituality masked by dogma and ritual, reality concealed by appearance, the yet-to-be-revealed truth.

Probably the most famous almond blossom in the history of art is the charming painting Van Gogh created for his newborn nephew and namesake, born in early 1890, drawing on the early-blooming tree's symbolism of spring and abundant yet vulnerable new life. The artist wrote to his own mother:

How glad I was when the news came...I should have greatly preferred him [Vincent's brother Theo] to call the boy after Father, of whom I have been thinking so much these days, instead of after me; but seeing it has now been done, I started right away to make a picture for him, to hang in their bedroom, big branches of white almond blossom against a blue sky.

Theo elected to hang the painting over the piano after Vincent sent it to Paris in April. The artist's viewpoint is unusual; the blossoms are shown close up, as if seen from below. One need not look far to see it as a new flowering of the Van Gogh family tree. The Van Gogh Museum website entry states: 'Unsurprisingly, it was this work that remained closest to the hearts of the Van Gogh family.'

FAMILY Fagaceae

Native to the northern hemisphere, oaks can be either deciduous or evergreen. North America has the most oak species, spread throughout the United States and Mexico. Oaks' fruit are called acorns, and both leaves and acorns are poisonous to livestock when consumed in large amounts.

Ancient cultures venerated the oak because it was widely believed to be the first tree, from which humans sprang. Its sacred status among the Hebrews stemmed from the meeting of Abraham and the angel beneath an oak. In Greco-Roman culture, the oak functioned as the World Tree. The presence of oaks at the oracle at Dodona linked the tree and its fruit, the acorn, to the king of the gods, Zeus or Jupiter, as well as to thunder, lightning and rain. It also stood for the Roman goddess Diana and the 'Kings of the Wood', her lovers.

Ancient Egyptian tomb paintings and mummy cases show crowns made of oak leaves and acorns, and some ancient rulers also wore oak crowns. Roman soldiers who saved civilians received a prestigious crown formed of oak leaves and acorns. The acorn was also important in Greco-Roman culture, since the oak was sacred to Zeus, representing strength and immortality. Many museum collections contain gold acorn jewelry, and some of the pendants may have originally adorned wreaths similar to the one illustrated overleaf, which may also reflect Egyptian models. Soldiers carried acorns into battle for protection, and women wore them to preserve their youthfulness.

In a Catholic context, the acorn symbolizes the power of the spirit and the virtue of truth, which probably explains the acorns on the cords of Catholic cardinals' hats, said to signify

⊗ Pierre-Joseph Redouté, *Quercus robur* (Pedunculate Oak, Truffle Oak, Common Oak, English Oak, Irish Dair), 1801–19.

※ Samuel Palmer, *Oak Tree and Beech, Lullingstone Park*, 1828, pen-and-ink drawing. New York: Morgan Library and Museum.

❋ Patricia Day, *Whispering Oak*, 2023, pastel on paper. Courtesy of the artist.

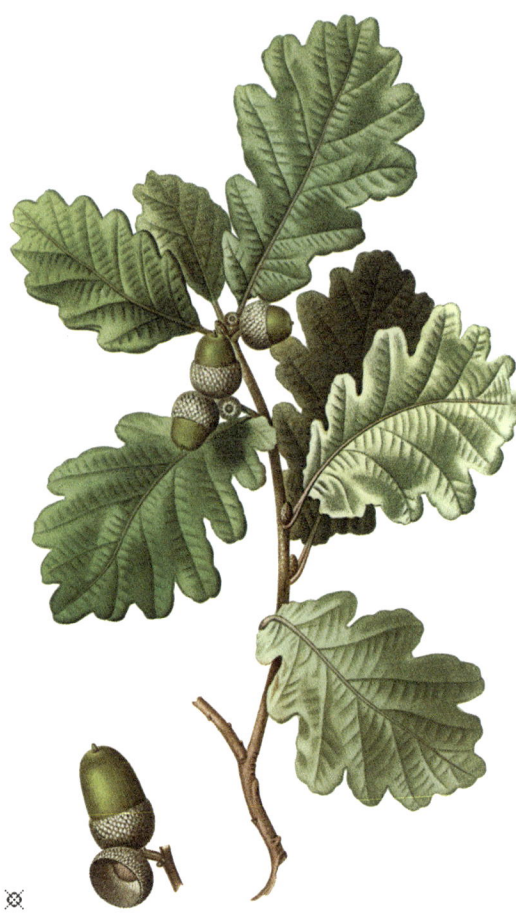

⊗

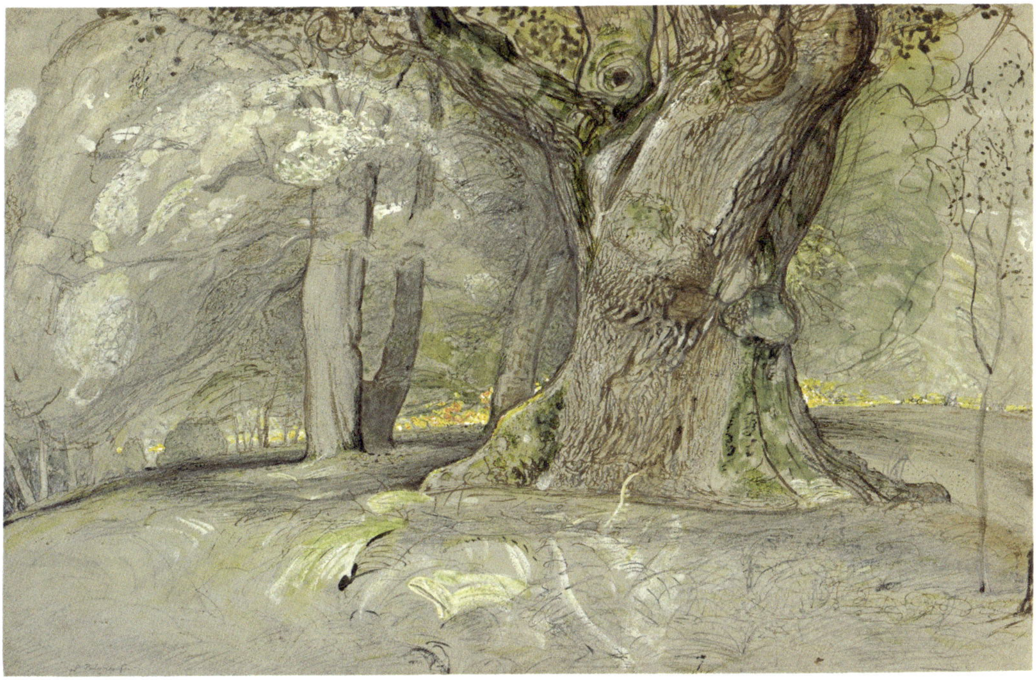

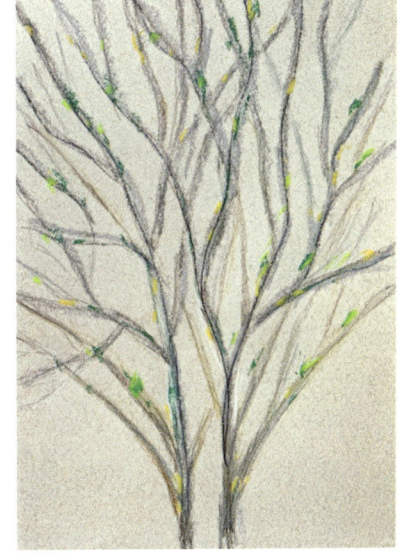

※

the spiritual growth that comes from a kernel of truth.

Sacred to Thor among the Teutons of northern Europe, the oak also served as the Tree of Life there. The oak's identification as the Tree of Life continued after the rise of Christianity, and, because its wood was held to be incorruptible, it came to symbolize immortality. Its attributes of strength, longevity and steadfastness made it an analogue of the Christian faith in the face of adversity.

Samuel Palmer's *Oak Tree and Beech, Lullingstone Park* was commissioned by his friend and mentor, the painter John Linnell. The artist's approach appears to be distinctly anthropomorphic. In a letter, he described the tree as having a 'muscular belly and shoulders; the twisted sinews'. After meeting William

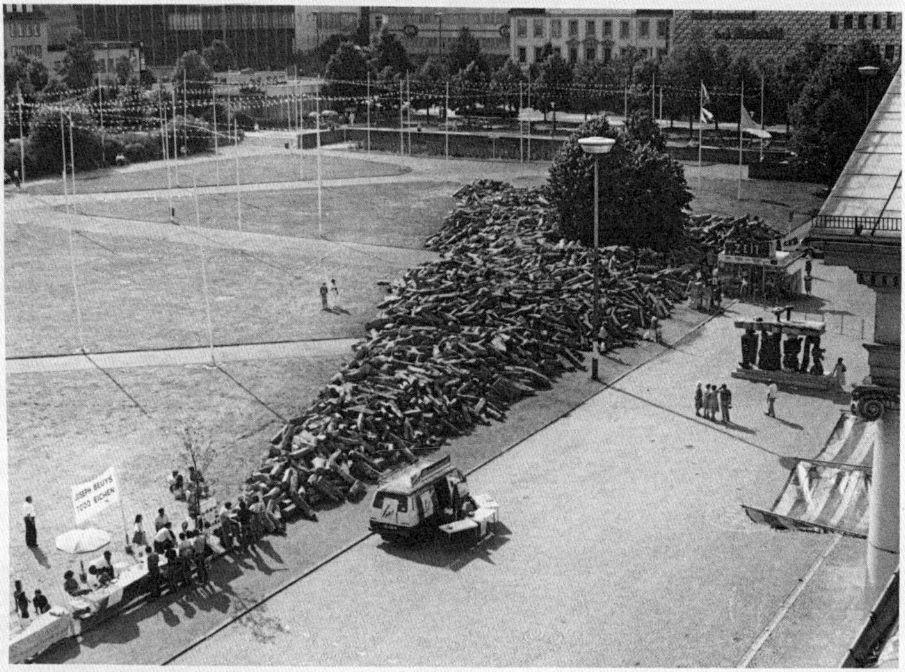

  Joseph Beuys, *7,000 Oak Trees*, 1982. Kassel, Germany: documenta arċhiv.

✳ Gold funerary wreath, imperial Rome, firſt or second century CE. New York: Metropolitan Museum of Art.

OTHER OAK IMAGES
- Caspar David Friedriċh, *Abtei im Eiċhwald* (*Abbey among Oak Trees*), 1809/10, oil on canvas. Berlin: Alte Nationalgalerie.
- Limbourg Brothers, 'November', from the *Belles Heures* of Jean de France, Duc de Berry, 1405–8/9, tempera, gold and ink on vellum. New York: The Cloiſters.
- Frida Kahlo, *Portrait of Luther Burbank*, 1931, oil on panel. Mexico City: Museo Dolores Olmedo.

Blake, Palmer combined naturalism with a visionary approach, resulting in memorable Romantic images. In this drawing, the close-up details powerfully suggest strength, endurance and longevity.

Joseph Beuys's *7,000 Oak Trees* project began with a mound of black basalt rocks piled in front of a museum in Kassel. From above, the rocks formed an arrow pointing at a single oak tree. Beuys said a rock could be moved from the pile, but only if a tree were planted next to it. In 1982, the artist, with the help of volunteers, started planting 7,000 trees; the work was completed on the anniversary of Beuys's death in 1987 by his son. Initially controversial, the project is now a valued part of Kassel's cityscape. In a conversation with the gallerist Richard Demarco, Beuys said of the project:

I think the tree is an element of regeneration which in itself is a concept of time. The oak is especially so because it is a slowly growing tree with a kind of really solid heartwood. It has always been a form of sculpture, a symbol of this planet. . .The tree planting enterprise provides a very simple but radical possibility...when we start with the seven thousand oaks.

The contemporary artist Patricia Day lives on the edge of a ravine populated by California live oaks. Her recent work focuses on trees, especially the oaks' entwined structure, strength and resilience despite urban pollution and the threat of fire.

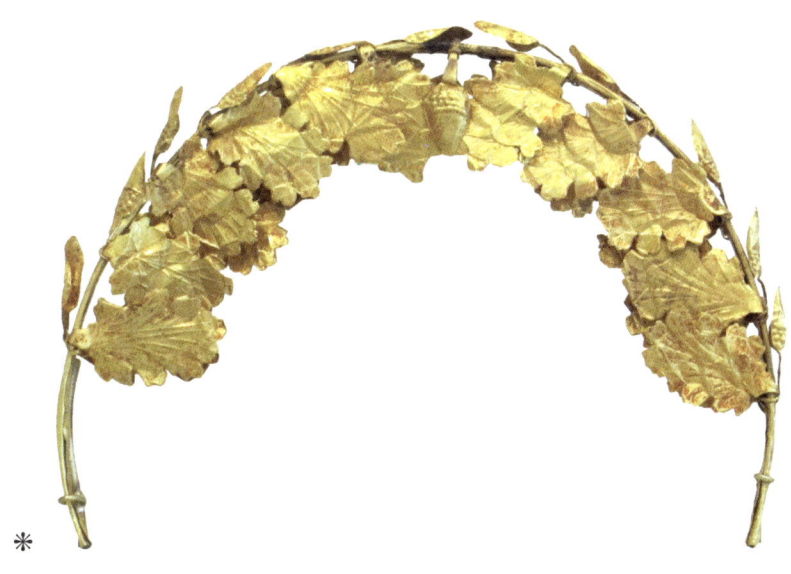

*

FAMILY Salicaceae

Willows, also called sallows (for those with broad leaves) and osiers (narrow leaves), are a group of deciduous trees and shrubs primarily found in moist soils in the northern hemisphere.

Willow bark has been known since 500 BCE as an analgesic because of its high concentration of salicylic acid, the ingredient in aspirin.

Willow symbolism, while not uniform, encompasses water, grief, healing and eternal life. The willow is also sometimes linked to the moon.

The ancient Egyptians saw the willow as sacred and protective, and linked it with miraculous births. Osiris was found in a willow clump, and Moses, abandoned at birth, was discovered floating safely on the Nile in a willow basket. In ancient Greece and Rome, both Homer and Pliny attached negative symbolism to the willow, holding it to be infertile, since it sheds fruit before it ripens. The goddess Hera was said to have been born on the island of Samos under a willow tree, which was long preserved in her temple there.

The willow is one of four trees associated with the Jewish Feast of Tabernacles (Leviticus 23:40). Participants circle the Torah table seven times, then strike the ground with willow branches; the branches symbolize repentance, and the action signifies the beating out of sin.

In Christian art, the tree was both positive (symbolizing faith and the faithful) and negative (sin and grief). The negative reading comes from Psalms, and the positive from Isaiah 44:4, in which God promises Jacob to bless his descendants: '[who] will spring up among the grass like willows by the watercourses'.

The weeping willow is associated with death in Western art. Favoured in the nineteenth century as an embroidery image, the weeping

⊗ Gravestone with weeping
willow, nineteenth century.
Rainham, Kent.

※ Babylon Willow
(*Salix Babylon*), n.d.

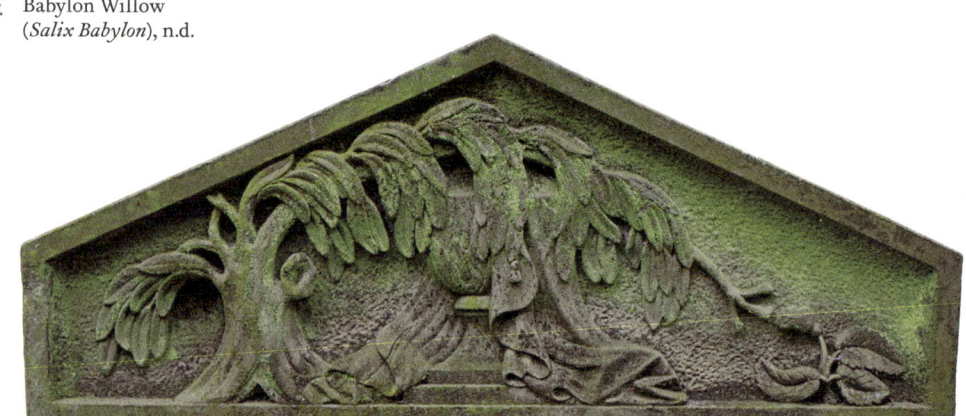

⊗

willow sometimes adorned *memento mori* samplers complete with the name and date of the deceased. It also appears frequently as a motif of grief and loss on Victorian gravestones.

The popular blue 'Willow Pattern' was obtained from Chinese sources by Minton, an English ceramics firm, in 1780. The design includes a story of forbidden love, elopement, pursuit by a parent and, finally, the transformation of the lovers into turtle doves.

Willow branches were used as divining rods to locate water, presumably because willows like to have their roots wet and grow prolifically near rivers and streams.

OTHER WILLOW IMAGES
- Albrecht Dürer, *St Jerome Seated Near a Pollard Willow Tree*, 1512, drypoint print. London: British Museum.
- Mary Bechler, mourning sampler, *c.* 1830. Private collection.
- Vincent van Gogh, *Garden with Weeping Willow*, 1888, oil on canvas. Private collection.
- Piet Mondrian, *Haystack with Willow Trees*, 1897/98, oil on canvas. Private collection.
- Claude Monet, *Weeping Willow* series, several variations by 1919 in various museums.
- Brothers Hildebrandt, 'Old Man Willow', illustration for a calendar after J. R. R. Tolkien's *The Lord of the Rings*, 1978.

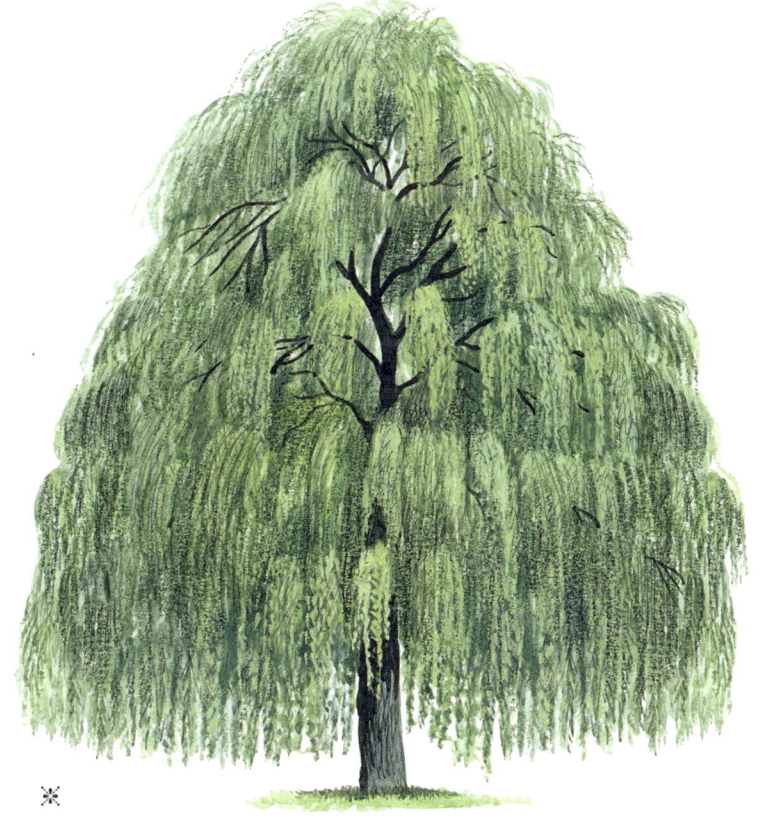

FAMILY Taxaceae

An evergreen conifer, the common yew is native to most of Europe as well as parts of Africa and Asia. Also called the English or European yew, it is grown primarily as an ornamental.

Fred Hageneder, an ethnobotanist and the author of *Yew: A History* (2007), believes that the yew is the original World Tree, the only tree that has existed throughout the entire territory of cultures with a World Tree tradition.

Sacred to the Greek goddess Hecate (witchcraft, death, necromancy), the tree was said to purify the dead as they entered Hades. In the British Isles, the yew was traditionally associated with war because the wood was so hard that shields, longbows and spears were commonly made from it. It was revered by pagans as the oldest tree of all, and is now often found in cemeteries; indeed, such trees are often older than the church next to which they grow.[8] New sprigs appear when old branches touch the ground, or from dead or dying stumps, and so perhaps unsurprisingly the yew has served as a symbol of immortality, rebirth and connection to ancestors. The tree was sacred to the Druids, for whom it carried a range of meanings – from death to resurrection.

In the UK, the Ancient Yew Group is dedicated to identifying and protecting veteran (400 to 900 years old) and ancient (over 900 years old) yews.

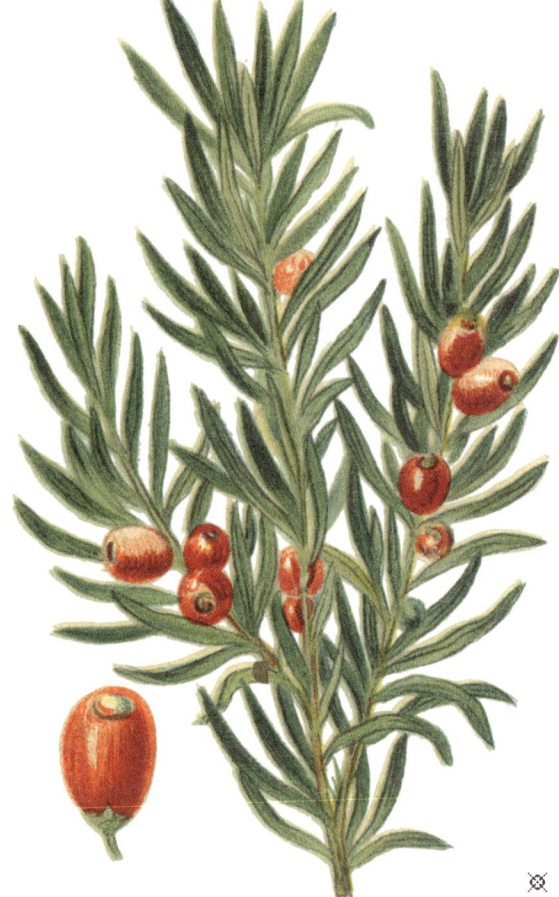

⊗ Yew (Ground Hemlock), 1862–69.

⊗ Old yew trees, north door of St Edward's Church, Stow-on-the-Wold, Gloucestershire, twelfth to fifteenth century. The door itself dates from the seventeenth or eighteenth century.

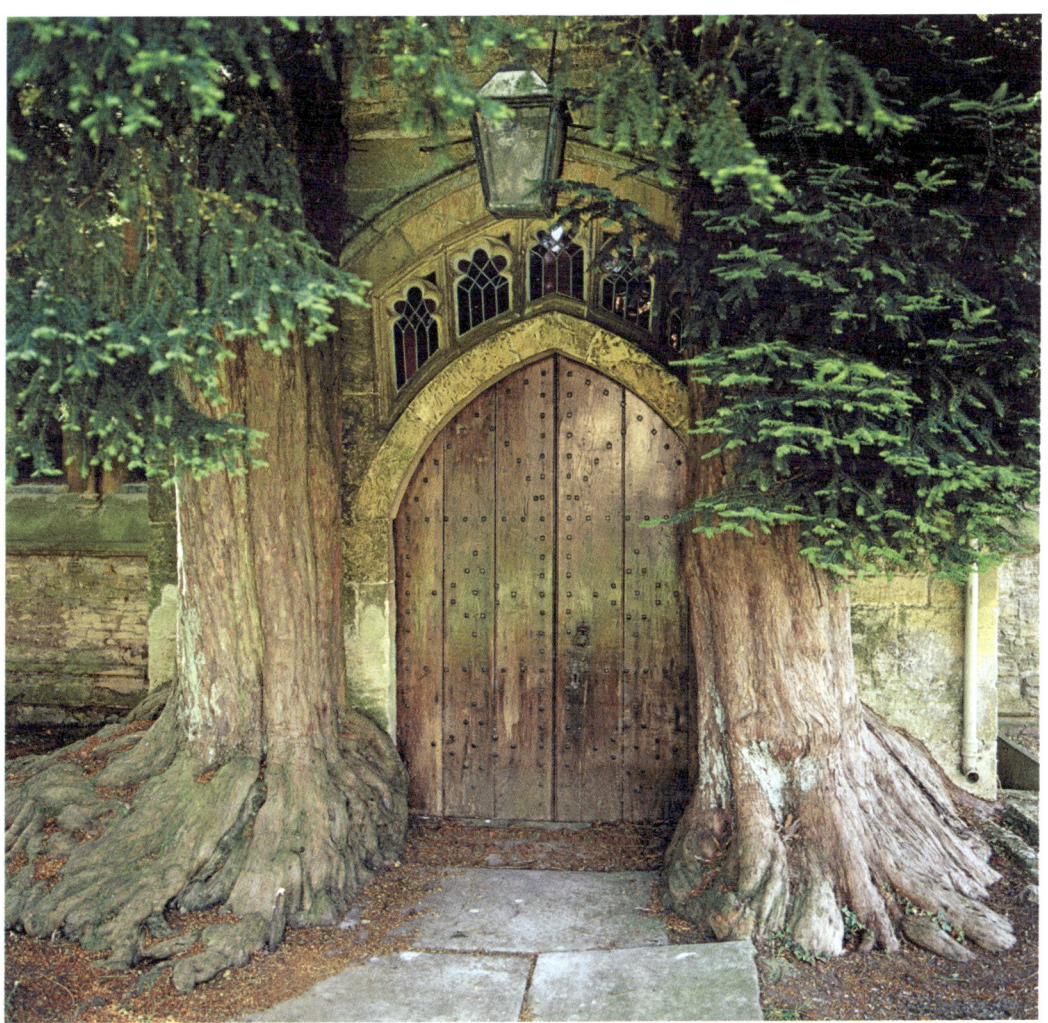

The seeds of the sticky red fruit and the needles are highly toxic; the flesh of the fruit is the only non-toxic part of the tree. The Pacific yew (*T. brevifolia*), on the other hand, is the source of paclitaxel, an anti-cancer drug.

Stripping the bark kills the tree, but it has since been discovered that the drug can also be produced from the leaves of the English yew.

FAMILY Ulmaceae

Elm trees first appeared about twenty million years ago, in Central Asia. They flourished and, before the appearance of Dutch elm disease in the twentieth century, spread over most of the northern hemisphere.

Caused by a microfungus dispersed by bark beetles, the disease killed most mature elms in Europe and North America, although the development of disease-resistant cultivars has now begun to restore the elm to forests and urban landscaping. The oldest elms in the world were planted in the 1860s by Frederick Law Olmsted in Central Park, New York. Most of the 1,200 elms – which make up half of the trees in the park – were saved from disease by aggressive management.

Elm wood is quite hard, and in ancient times it was used to make ploughs and chariots. The elm is sometimes associated with the Great Mother, and it has been suggested that Adam and Eve were born from the Goddess's Tree of Life, rather than created as is reported in Genesis. The Goddess was herself born from the elm, and her male consort was born from the ash. Elm symbolism is complex. On the one hand, it symbolizes birth, life and immortality, but the tree is also linked with death and the Underworld, and its wood was commonly used to make coffins. After Orpheus failed to rescue Eurydice from Hades, it is said that a grove of elm trees sprang up upon hearing his lyre played in mourning.

Constable's *Study of the Trunk of an Elm Tree* is almost photographic in its realism. It embodies the artist's humble attitude towards nature, and captures a sense of the impetus of life. Lucian Freud admired Constable deeply and attempted to copy the elm painting when he was a student, but gave up because it was so difficult. In 2002 Freud arranged an exhibition of Constable's work at the Grand Palais in Paris, and created an etching entitled *After Constable's Elm* for the catalogue.

Thomas S. Sinclair, Thomas's Elm (*Ulmus racemosa*), 1842–49.

John Constable, *Study of the Trunk of an Elm Tree*, c. 1821, oil on paper. London: Victoria and Albert Museum.

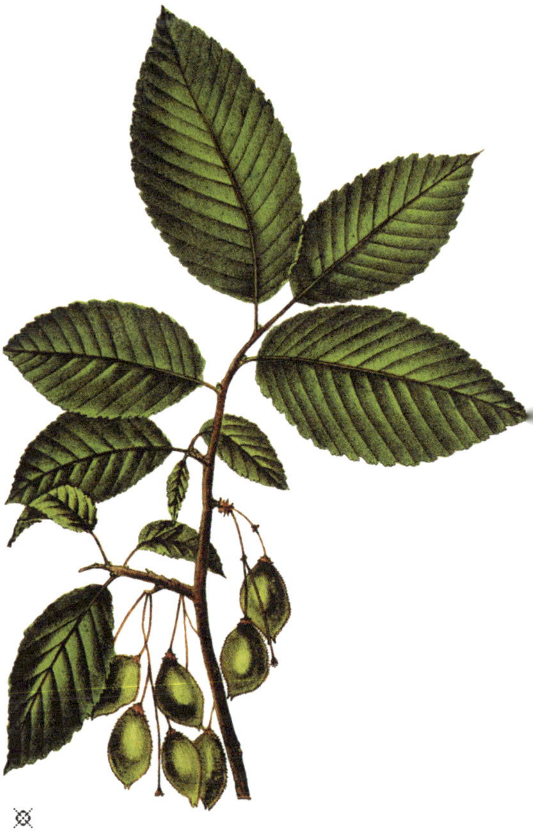

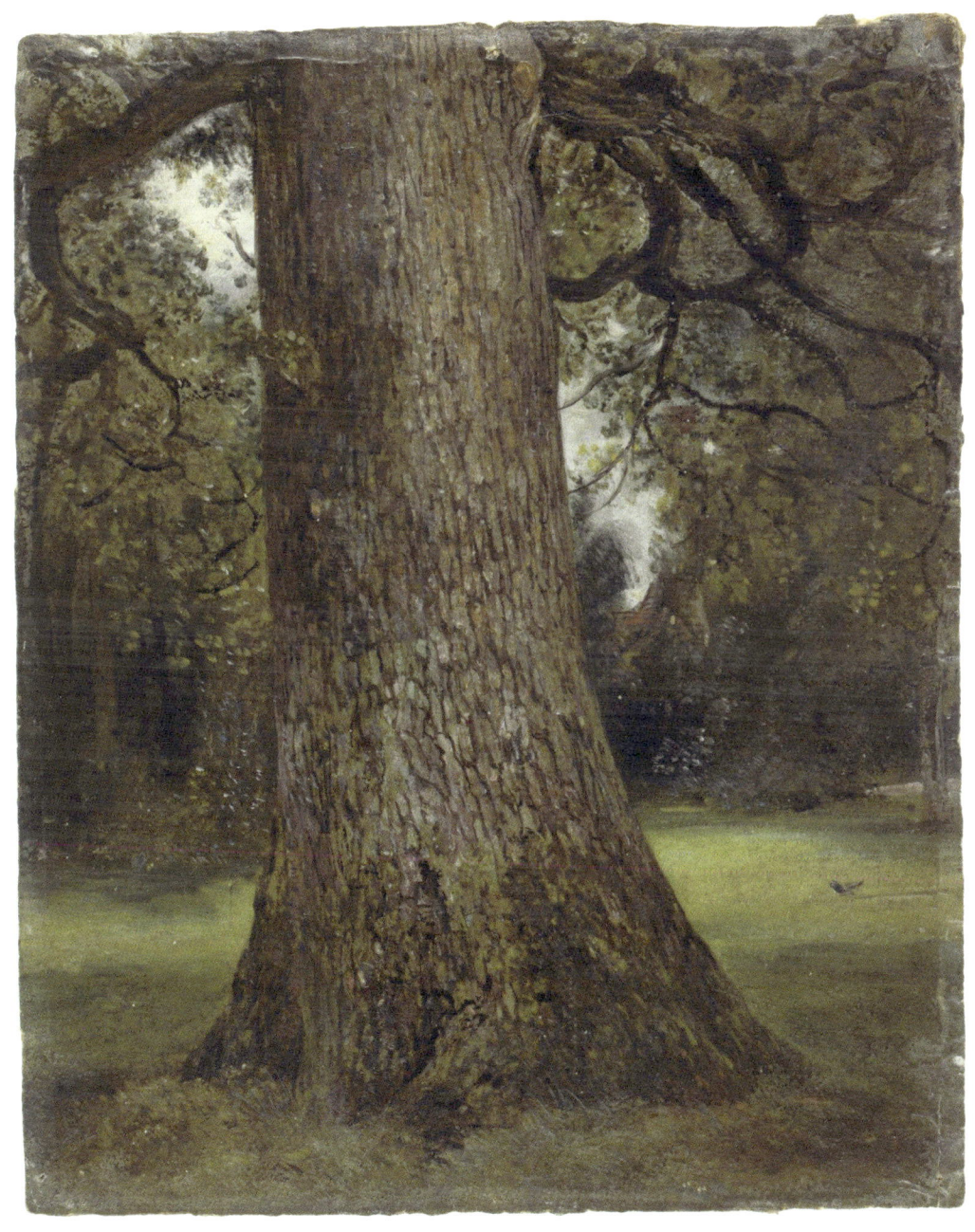

�֍

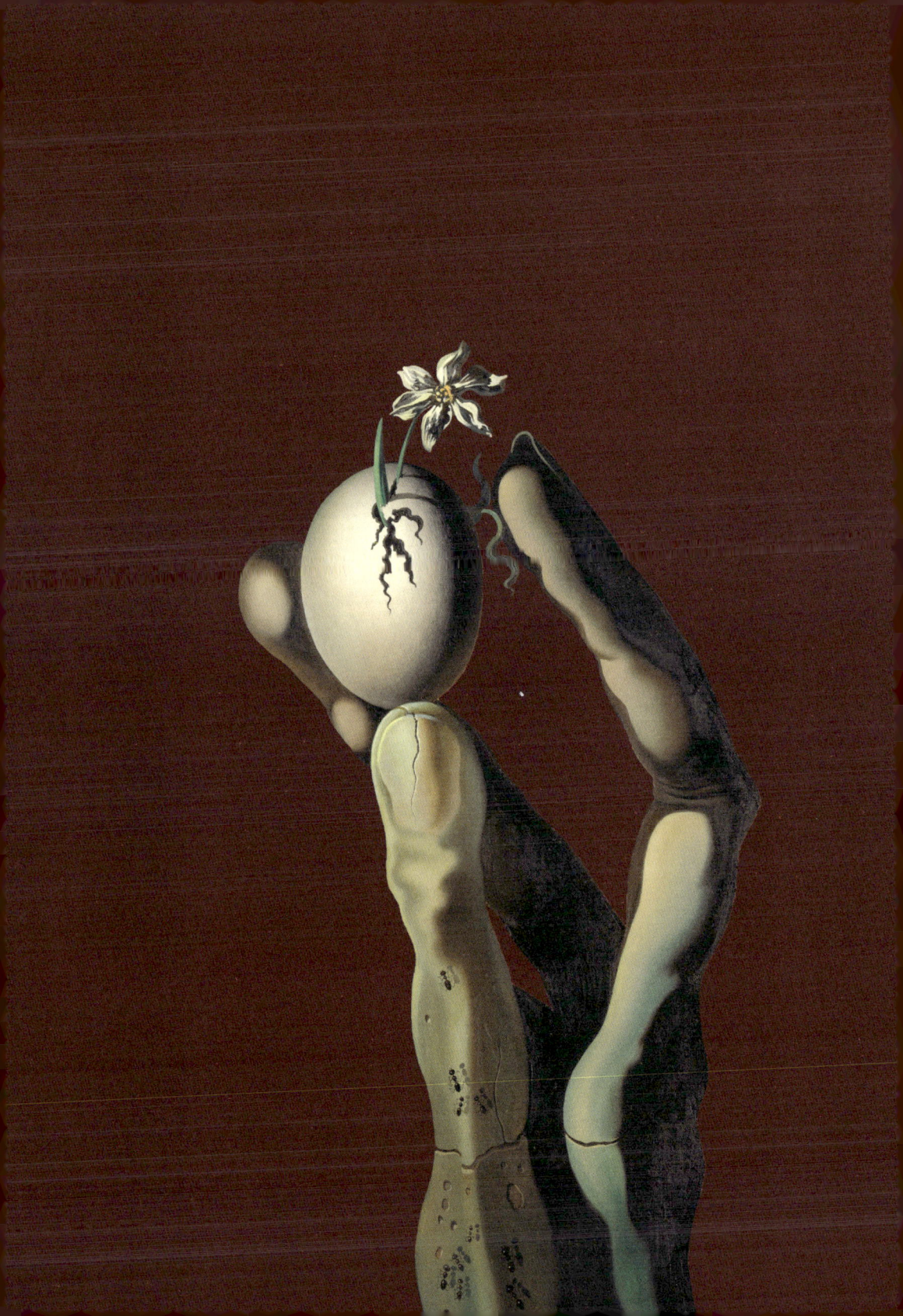

FLOWERS

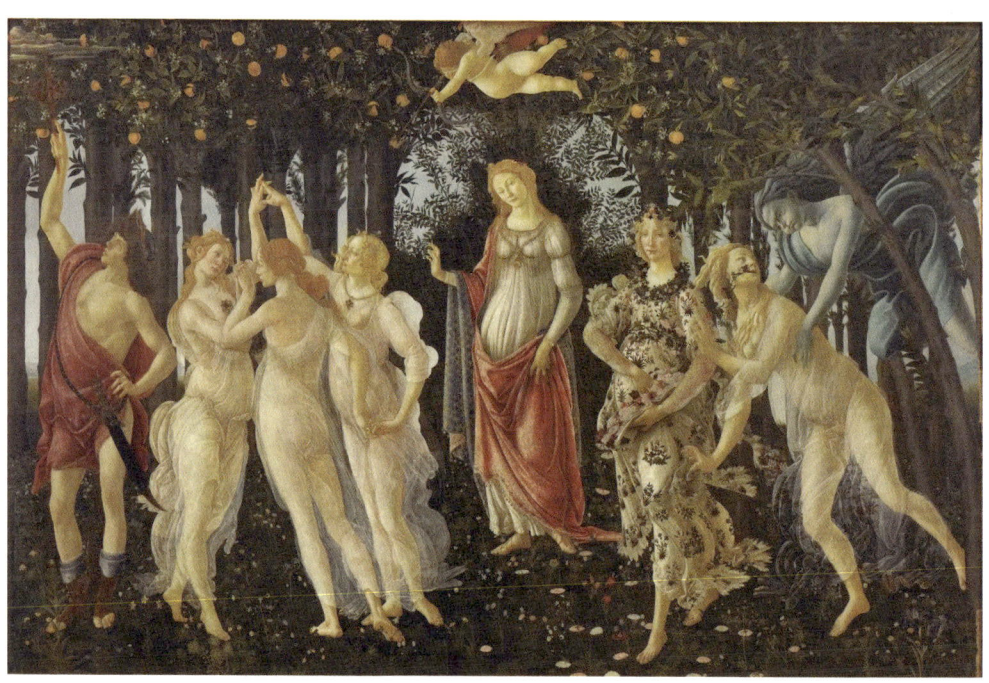

Sandro Botticelli, *Primavera*, c. 1480, tempera on wood. Florence: Le Gallerie degli Uffizi.

Jeff Koons, *Puppy*, 1992, stainless steel, soil and flowering plants. Bilbao: Guggenheim Museum.

Joseph Stella, *Flowers, Italy*, 1931, oil on canvas. Phoenix, AZ: Phoenix Art Museum.

It seems that flowers have always been loved and regarded as meaningful – although in ways that vary by era, fashion and geography.[9] Before the second half of the seventeenth century, flowers were categorized by smell, taste, colour and medicinal use; botanical classification occurred fairly late.

Both the flower and the blossom are universal symbols of young life and of beauty, and their transitory nature is sometimes used to evoke *joie de vivre* or the fragile quality of childhood. Colour has a great deal to do with symbolism: red stands for love, passion and blood; white for innocence and blamelessness, or sometimes death. Udo Becker adds that yellow signifies the sun; blue, dreams and mystery.

Flowers are connected to all aspects of love, from the fresh innocence of young love and spring to lust, passion and the realm of the erotic. They have been especially linked to the vulva and used as a symbol of purity or virginity.

Scattered flowers often mean joy, especially in the context of wedding flower-bearers.

Individual flowers carry specific meanings, many of which begin in the ancient world. The popular and widespread *Language of Flowers*, originating in Persia, was introduced to Europe in the early eighteenth century. Flowers have also functioned as personal, national or state symbols and appear in calendars of the months and seasons.

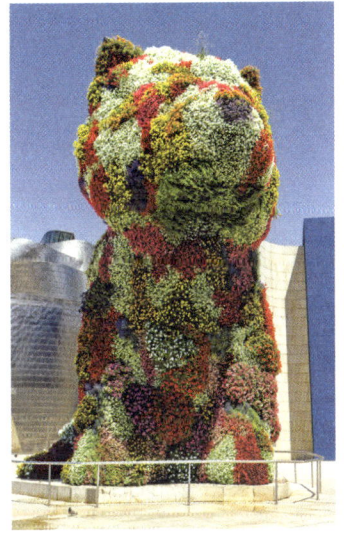

Some artists depict individual blooms to convey specific meanings. Combinations of flowers appear in still-life images and in landscapes. One of the most sumptuous of all is Botticelli's masterpiece *Primavera*. Tiny, identifiable flowers (the *millefleur* style is said to be anachronistic, recalling medieval tapestries) are sprinkled like stars throughout the landscape, and more spill from the mouth of Chloris. Several theories have been proposed to explain this enigmatic, complex painting. Most agree that it celebrates spring. Additional suggestions include the occasion of a Medici wedding or a celebration of the senses, smell in particular, as well as love and beauty – both human and natural. More than 500 species are depicted, among them approximately 190 flowers, of which 130 have been identified.

In the hippy culture of the 1960s, as consumerism began to be questioned and social consciousness grew, flowers became symbols of peace and love. Widespread sentiment against authority, shown by anti-war and student demonstrations, also led to overt reactions against the exploitation of nature. More recently, Jeff Koons's *Puppy* incorporates flowers into a 13-metre-high (43 ft) living sculpture of a West Highland terrier, reprised from an image of his own little white dog in 1993. It refers to both eighteenth-century elite topiary gardens and the excesses of modern pop culture (sentimentality and Hallmark-card-cute puppies set against the reality of puppy farms). Despite the negative implications of the sculpture, the public response has been overwhelmingly positive, inspiring optimism, love, joy and, as Koons himself intended, 'confidence and security'. The flowers are renewed in May (begonias, impatiens and petunias) and October (pansies), and fed and watered by a network of pipes inside the artwork.

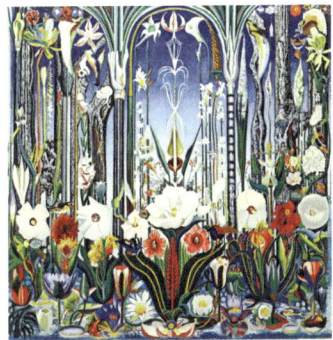

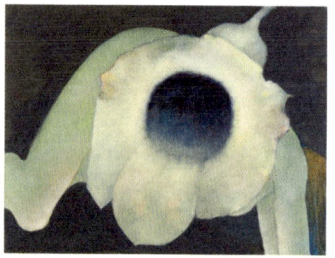

A Persian tradition, the *Language of Flowers* was introduced to Europe by the Swedish king Charles II on his return to Sweden from exile in Turkey in 1714. The tradition became widespread, nearly universal, in the eighteenth and nineteenth centuries.

Two others are credited with bringing the *Language* to Europe: the writer and medical pioneer Mary Wortley Montagu (England, 1717) and the traveller Aubry de La Mottraye (Sweden, 1727). Throughout the nineteenth century, the symbolism of the *Language of Flowers* could be found in the composition of wreaths, baskets, bouquets, Valentines and other greetings cards, *billets-doux* and visiting cards, as well as tussie-mussies and posies. Modern florists continue to find it of interest, as is evident in the many commercial websites that list flowers and their meanings as a sales pitch.

Books devoted to floriography were published all over Europe and in the United States. The historian and Orientalist Joseph Hammer-Purgstall's *Dictionnaire du langage des fleurs* (1809) may be the earliest, but among the most popular (and still in print) is Kate Greenaway's *Language of Flowers* (1884). In Vanessa Diffenbaugh's novel *The Language of Flowers* (2011), the main character gradually comes to realize that flowers have multiple meanings, sometimes contradictory. She devises her own 'Language' by studying plant characteristics and selecting suitable meanings.

Dorothea Tanning depicted a dozen newly created flowers in her collection *Another Language of Flowers* (1998). She did not wish to rival nature, but rather to pay homage. The flowers, accompanied by poetry, have fictional names that convey meaning. For instance, *Windwort* initially seems to be a rather indistinct flower, but a closer look reveals its hybrid nature, with female breasts on the right and a profile face on the left. A nude female body arches over the delicate petals. The circular hole in the centre recalls other forms – apples, melons, cabbage – associated with sexuality and fecundity. Tanning's last work, these paintings convey the mysteries of nature and the marvel that is the artist's imagination.

Dorothea Tanning, *Zephirium apochripholiae (Windwort)*, 1997–98, oil on canvas. From *Another Language of Flowers: Paintings* by Dorothea Tanning, James Ingram Merrill et al., Braziller, 1998.

John William Waterhouse, *The Awakening of Adonis* (detail), 1899, oil on canvas. Private collection.

J. M. Seligmann, *Anemone plant, c.* 1768.

FAMILY Ranunculaceae

The anemone, native to temperate zones, is nearly always bluish violet, white, pink or red; one species is yellow.

The word *anemone* means 'daughter of the wind' in Greek, and the flower is said to herald spring breezes. It can stand alone, letting the wind ruffle its petals, but a strong gust may pluck it – thus the flower embodies both the profusion of life and its transience.

In Book 10 of the *Metamorphoses*, Ovid tells how Venus loved a mortal hunter named Adonis so much that she neglected heaven. Adonis ignored her warnings of the danger of hunting and was gored by a wild boar. The goddess heard his dying groans and declared that his blood would become a flower. A bloom sprang up, but 'the joy it gives to man is short-lived, for the winds which give the flower its name, Anemone, shake it right down'. The flower thus became a symbol of death and sorrow. In John William Waterhouse's painting Venus awakens Adonis with a kiss; her garden is in full flower, anemones included, signifying the renewal of nature.

The anemone may be the flower referred to in the Bible as the 'lily of the fields', since there are no white lilies in Palestine, but anemones are widely distributed. Anemones are also said to have sprouted from Christ's blood and thus to have grown at the foot of the Cross. The flower may also signify the blood of saints.

Anemones appear in many still-lifes, especially Dutch *vanitas* paintings, and in decorative ceramics.

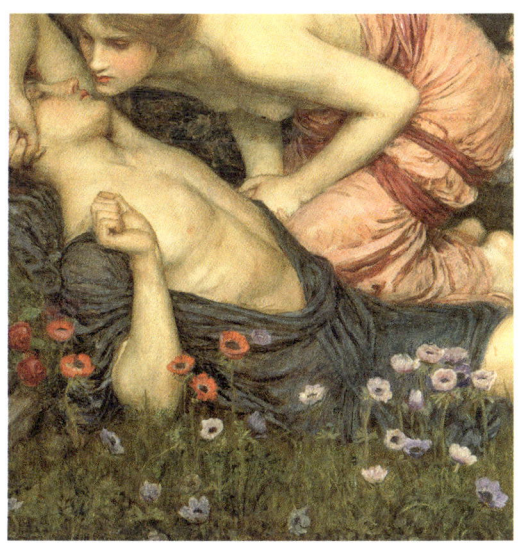

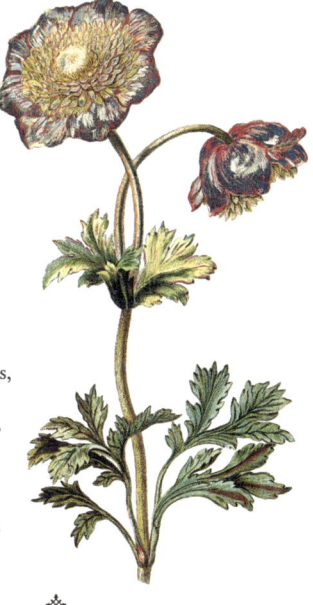

OTHER ANEMONE IMAGES
- Nicolas-Bernard Lépicié, *Adonis Transformed by Venus into an Anemone*, 1782, oil on canvas. Versailles, France: Petit Trianon.
- Pierre-Joseph Redouté, 'Anemone Simple', from *Choix des Plus Belles Fleurs*, 1827.
- Raoul Dufy, *Anemones*, 1937, lithograph after a watercolour.

FAMILY Ranunculaceae

Perennial columbine plants are found in meadows and woodlands.

The Latin name of the genus comes from the word for eagle (*aquila*), because the petals are said to resemble an eagle's claw. By contrast, the common name comes from the Latin word for dove (*columba*), because the inverted flowers look like five doves clustered together. The flower is closely related to those of *Actaea* (baneberry) and *Aconitum* (monkshood), and is, like them, poisonous.

The columbine is associated with many goddesses. In Norse mythology it was sacred to Freya, and among the ancient Greeks it was the symbol of Aphrodite.

In Christian art, the flower symbolizes the dove of the Holy Spirit. Six doves signify the gifts of the Holy Spirit – identified by the prophet Isaiah as wisdom and understanding, counsel and might, knowledge and fear of the Lord (11:2) – and the flower often bears six blooms on a stem. The leaves have three lobes and thus can also symbolize the Trinity. The flower appears in paintings depicting the Virgin Mary, specifically symbolizing

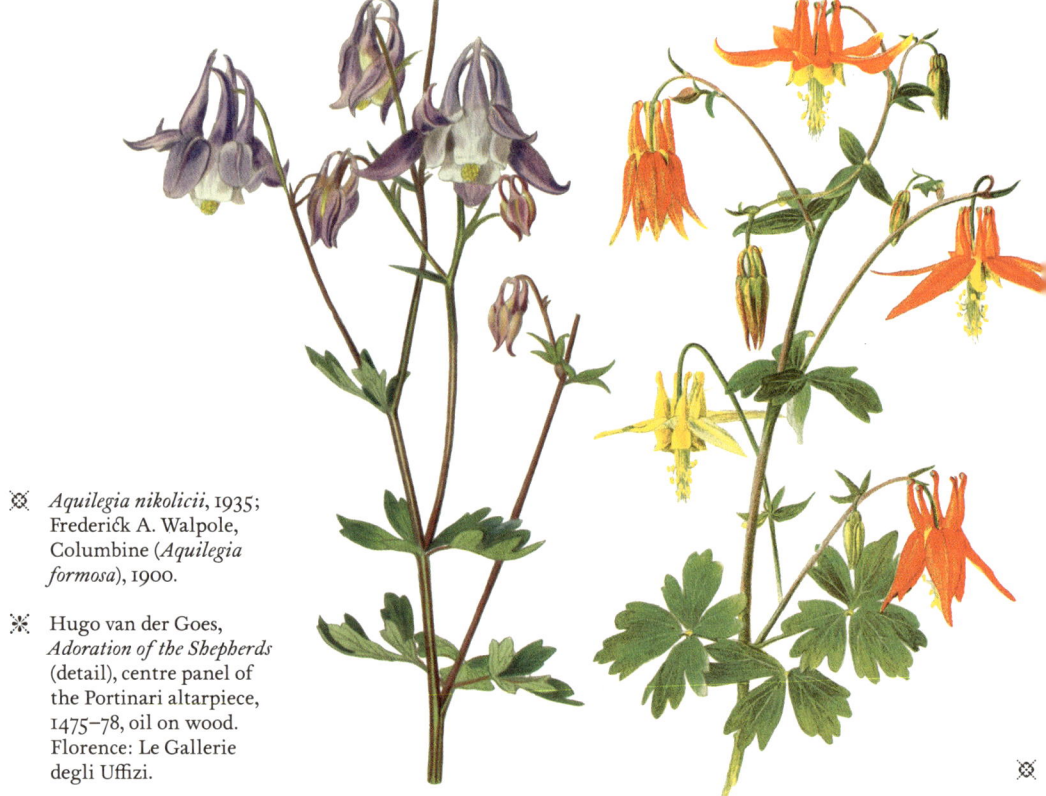

⊗ *Aquilegia nikolicii*, 1935; Frederick A. Walpole, Columbine (*Aquilegia formosa*), 1900.

✳ Hugo van der Goes, *Adoration of the Shepherds* (detail), centre panel of the Portinari altarpiece, 1475–78, oil on wood. Florence: Le Gallerie degli Uffizi.

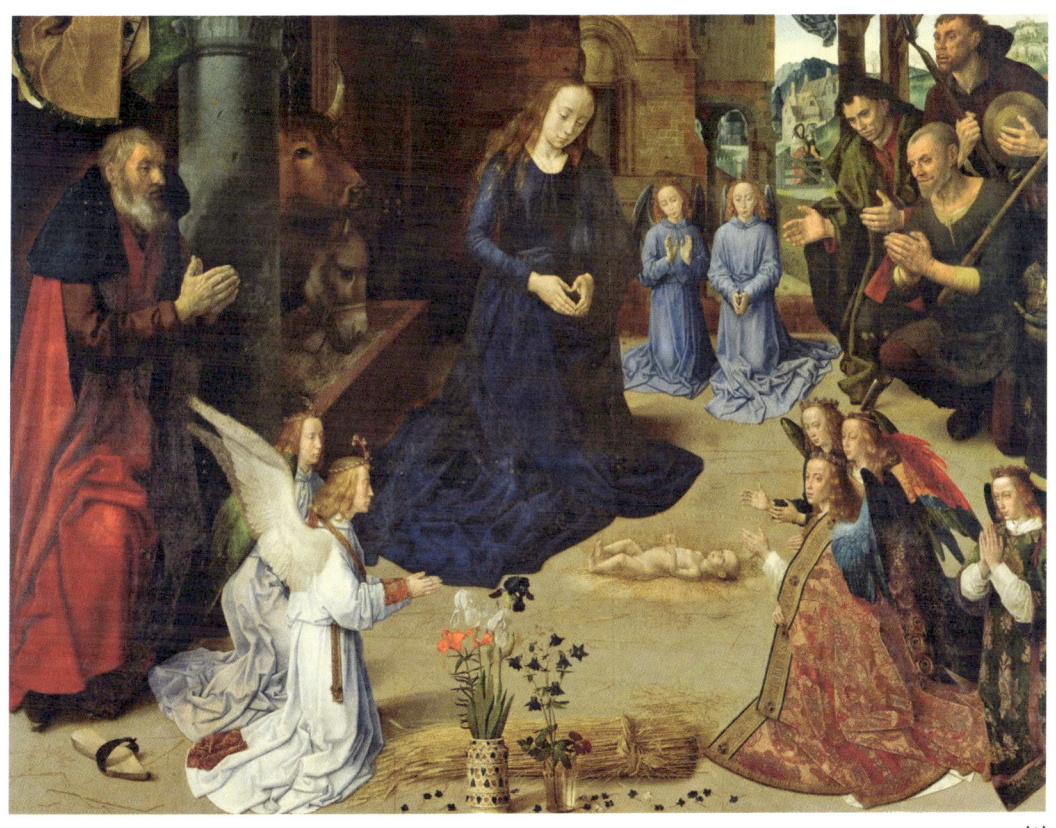

her sorrows. This led, in turn, to the Renaissance association of this flower with the Passion of Christ and the death of the Virgin.

Hugo van der Goes seems to have loved painting flowers. The columbine appears in a lovely still life sited below the kneeling Virgin in the centre panel of the Portinari altarpiece, foreshadowing the Virgin's grief over the suffering and death of Christ. The painting also includes carnations, red, blue and white irises, scattered violets and stalks of wheat.

OTHER COLUMBINE IMAGES

- Hans Multscher, Wurzach altarpiece, 1437, tempera on panel. Berlin: Gemäldegalerie.
- Hugo van der Goes, Monforte altarpiece, c. 1470, oil on panel. Berlin: Gemäldegalerie.
- Anon., *Spinola Hours*, c. 1510–20, illuminated manuscript. Los Angeles, CA: J. Paul Getty Museum.

FAMILY Araceae

Various species of arum are widespread throughout Europe, North Africa and West Asia.

The plant goes by several common names, such as Adam and Eve, Jack-in-the-pulpit, lords-and-ladies and naked girls/boys. Many have sexual implications because the shape of the plant is reminiscent of male and female genitalia, suggesting copulation. Because of its sexual connotations, the plant was often touted as an aphrodisiac. The growth stages involve a cone-shaped flower with an erect central male spathe; in the autumn the lower ring of flowers transforms into vertical clusters of bright red berries. Despite its links with sex, the plant is extremely poisonous. The flower resembles, but is unrelated to, the calla lily.

The arum isn't depicted often in art, although it symbolizes the Virgin Mary in medieval paintings. This may have come about because of the phonetic similarity between arum and Aaron, Mary and her cousin Elizabeth being descended from the house of Aaron.

Van Gogh drew arum lilies in the garden of the asylum at Saint-Rémy, and included them in a painting of a moth that he mistakenly identified as a death's-head hawkmoth (it is actually a giant peacock moth). Not wishing to kill the moth for his studies, he made quick drawings that he later referred to when creating the painting. The painting also includes the later berry stage of the arum in the upper centre. The regenerative symbolism of the arum may counteract the deathly associations of the death's-head hawkmoth, which gets its name from the skull-like pattern on its thorax.

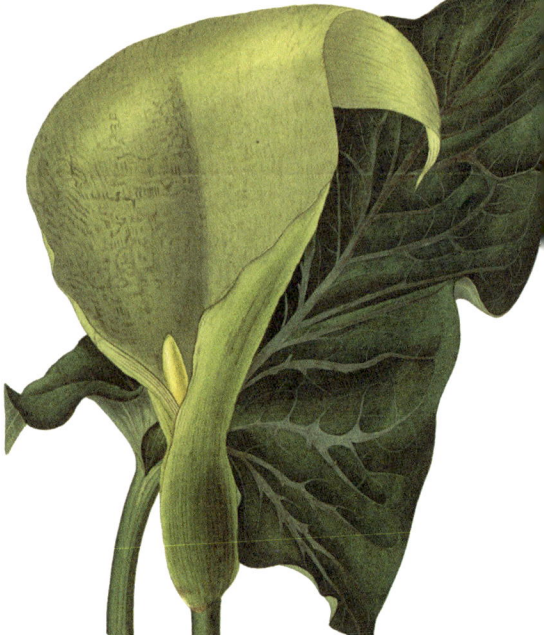

※ John Curtis, *Arum italicum*, 1823.

❋ Vincent van Gogh, *Giant Peacock Moth*, 1889, oil on canvas. Amsterdam: Van Gogh Museum.

※

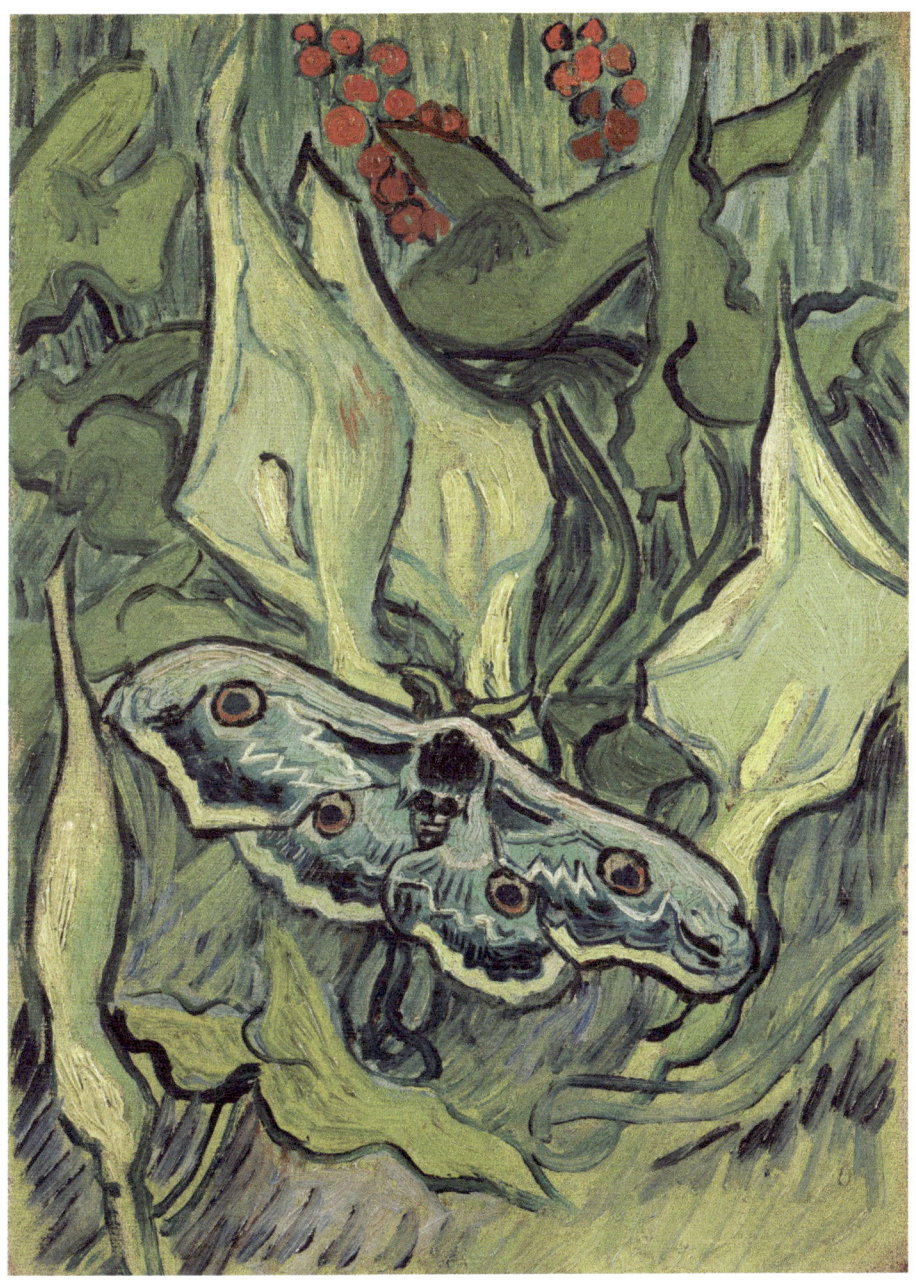

FAMILY Asteraceae

The daisy is one of the less showy members of the
family Asteraceae, in which are also classified
the chrysanthemum (pp. 104–5) and the sunflower
(pp. 114–17). The common name comes from the
Saxon *daes eage*, 'day's eye', describing its bright
yellow centre. Uses include food and herbal medicine.

The name of the genus stems from Roman
legend. Vertumnus, the god of vegetation and
the seasons, fell in love with a nymph or dryad
named Belides. He pursued her, and to avoid
his unwanted attention she transformed herself
into a daisy.

Towards the end of the fifteenth century
– possibly for the first time in paintings by
Botticelli – daisies appear in Annunciation
scenes, symbolizing the Christ Child's
innocence and purity; they were thought to
be more fitting than the austere lily, which
represents the same attributes in his mother.
Botticelli painted daisies not only in images
of the Virgin and Child but also in *The Birth
of Venus*, in which they are embroidered on
the robe held out by the Hora (a minor Greek
goddess) of Spring. The Neoplatonic concepts
of the time may have suggested a link between
Aphrodite/Venus and the Virgin Mary, in terms
of human and divine love.

Daisies are among the blooms scattered
throughout the landscape of Botticelli's
Primavera (see p. 90). The flower also appears
in Giovanni Bellini's *St Francis in the Desert*
(see 'Mullein', pp. 200–1), where it may indicate
the saint's guileless simplicity and virtue. In his
Annunciation of 1482, Domenico Ghirlandaio
adorned the Virgin's writing desk with a vase
of roses, daisies and jasmine, symbolizing love,
innocence and divine hope.

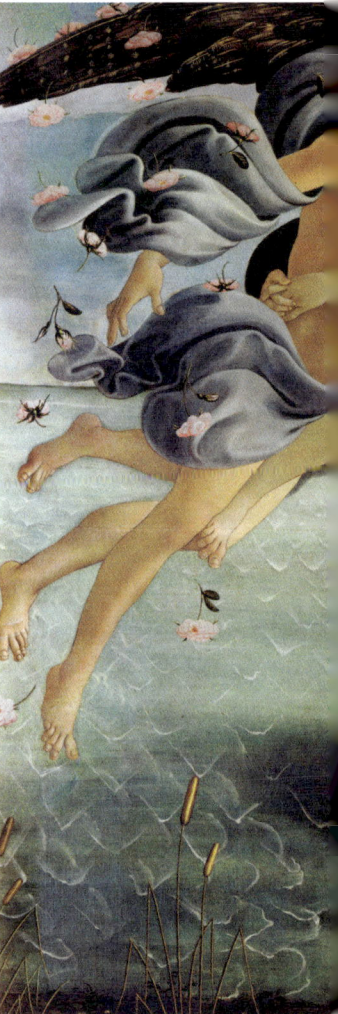

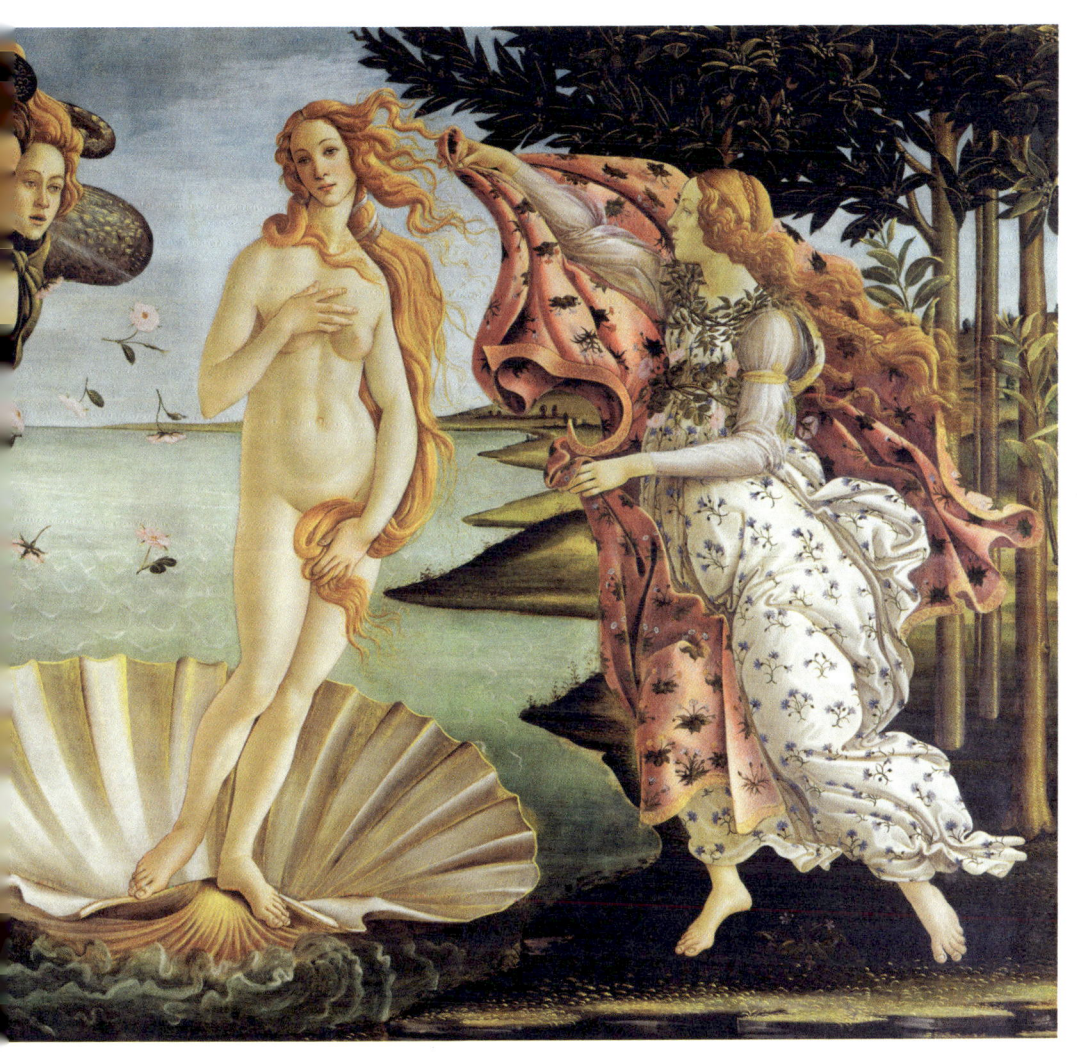

Sandro Botticelli, *The Birth of Venus*, c. 1485, tempera on canvas. Florence: Le Gallerie degli Uffizi.

✣ Jane Elizabeth Giraud,
Daisies, 1846.

✳ Richard Dadd, *The Fairy
Feller's Master-Stroke*,
1855–64, oil on canvas.
London: Tate.

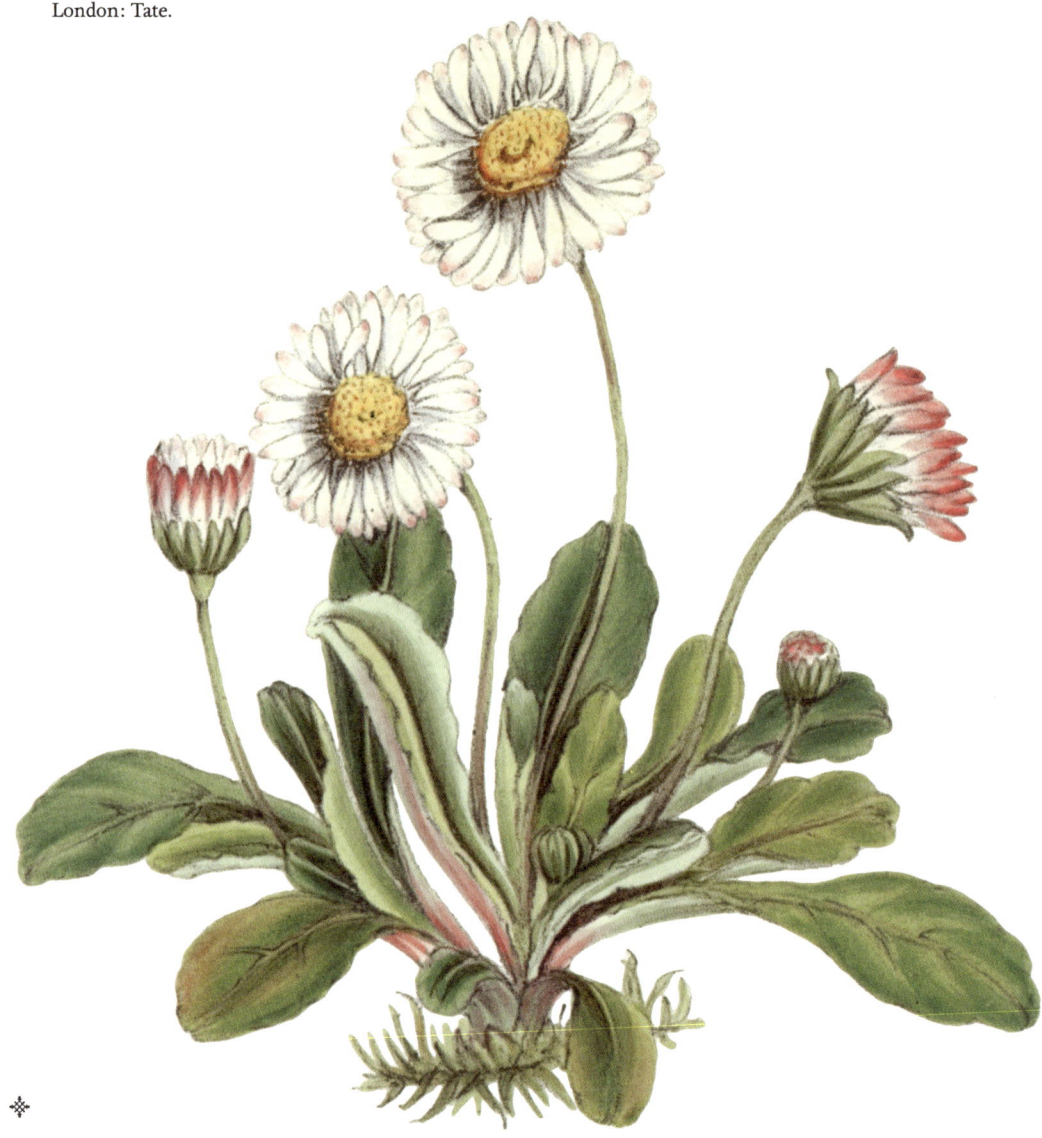

✣

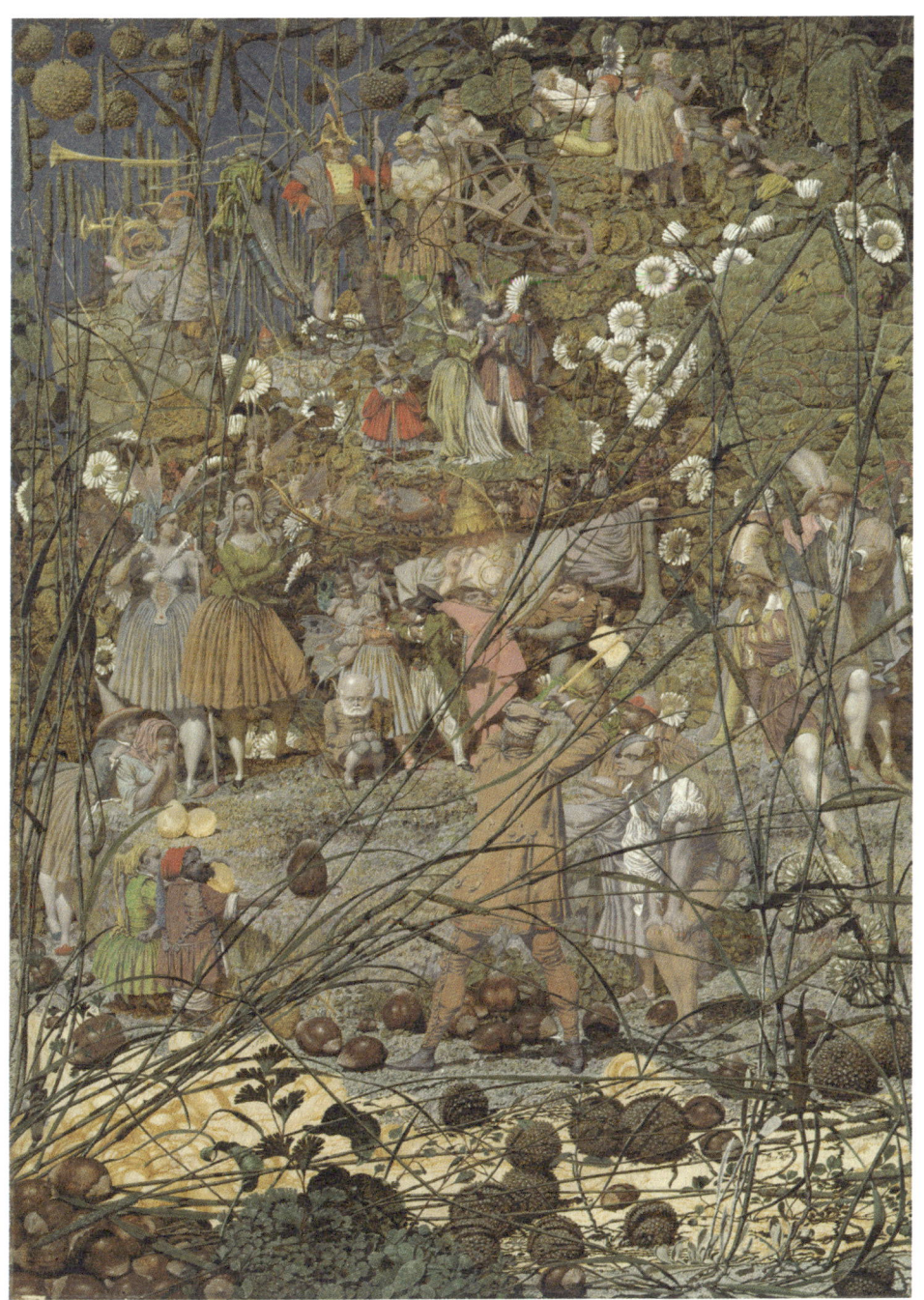

*

FAMILY Asteraceae

Thistle is the common name for a group of prickly flowering plants. Medicinally, thistles may provide remedies for headaches, mouth ulcers, vertigo and jaundice.

The thistle has been the national emblem of Scotland since the thirteenth century; it appears in Scots heraldry and in coinage, badges and tattoos. Many thistle images can be found in botanical illustrations, and the flower was popular in Art Nouveau and Arts and Crafts jewelry, textiles and ceramics.

Some thistles are troublesome and/or poisonous weeds (such as the yellow star-thistle, *Centaurea solstitialis*), but others are important sources of nectar for butterflies and honeybees.

In ancient times thistles were believed to guard against evil and demonic powers, and possibly to have aphrodisiac potential. Medieval medicinal uses of the plant included the treatment of internal disorders.

The thistle, along with the thorn (Genesis 3:17–18), functioned as a Christian symbol of sorrow and sin; thistles often appear at the foot of the Cross in paintings by northern European artists and have symbolized Christ's suffering. Martyred saints are sometimes depicted grasping thistles.

At the age of twenty-two, having just completed his apprenticeship, Albrecht Dürer

painted a self-portrait holding a thistle to symbolize conjugal fidelity. He married (not altogether happily, it would turn out) the year it was painted, and judging from the symbol, intended to be faithful to his wife. He may also have been aware of medieval herbalists' belief that the thistle could combat depression. Indeed, the portrait may reflect the artist's melancholic temperament, religious intentions and philosophic doubts. He added an inscription next to the date; translated, it reads: 'My affairs follow the course allotted to them on high. Marriage has in part determined his destiny – the Bridegroom puts his future life in the hands of God'.

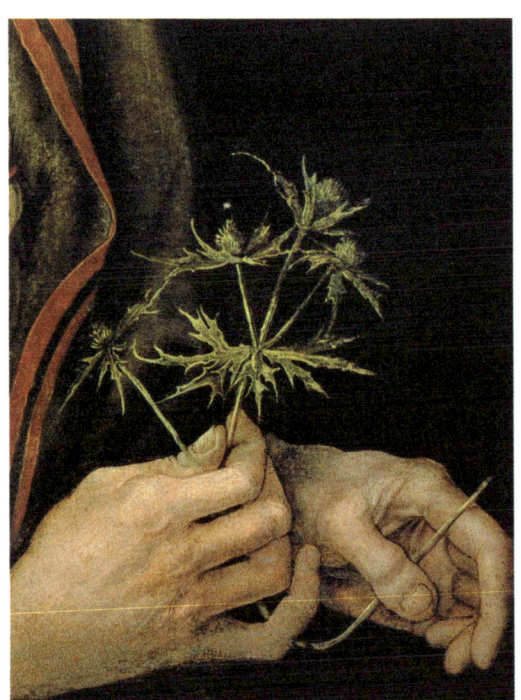

OTHER THISTLE IMAGES
- Hans Hoffmann, *A Hare in the Forest*, *c.* 1585, oil on panel. Los Angeles, CA: J. Paul Getty Museum.
- J. J. Grandville, *Les Fleurs animées*, 1847.

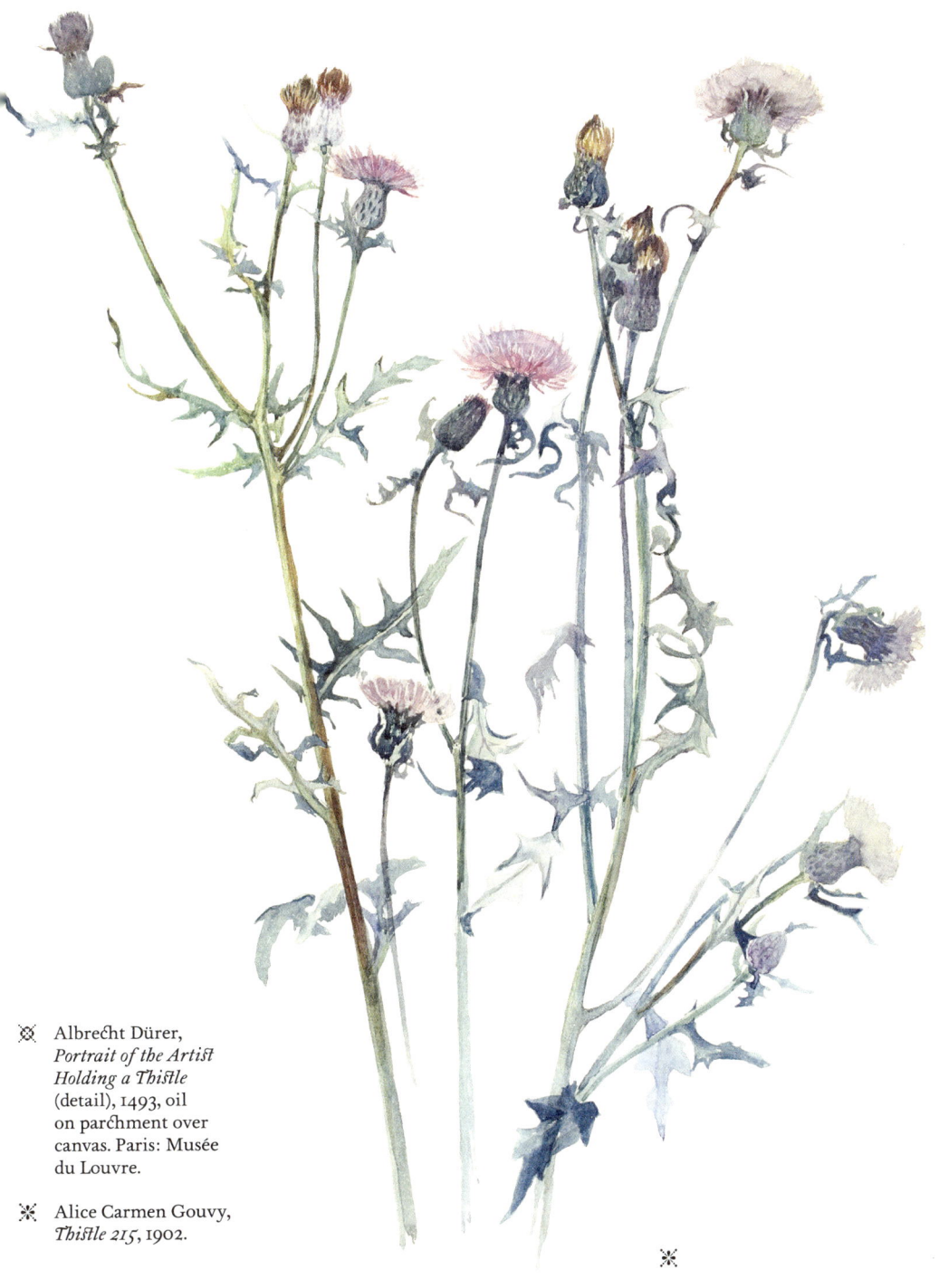

※ Albrecht Dürer,
*Portrait of the Artist
Holding a Thistle*
(detail), 1493, oil
on parchment over
canvas. Paris: Musée
du Louvre.

※ Alice Carmen Gouvy,
Thistle 215, 1902.

※

FAMILY Asteraceae

Chrysanthemums are native to East Asia and northern Europe, and are popular as a cut flower. They have traditionally symbolized cheerfulness in adversity and a love of truth, but also slighted love.

Beginning in 1897, Piet Mondrian drew and painted hundreds of images of flowers, which vary from naturalistic to semi-abstract. Often just single blossoms, the flowers stand centred and isolated against neutral grounds. This enabled the artist to devote his full attention to rendering subtle geometry and minute detail. 'Mums' bloom late in the year, providing brilliant colour when other flowers are absent. Mondrian must have appreciated this, and apparently wished to show the cycle of life, since some of his chrysanthemums exude energy and life force, while others begin to droop and decay.

This early *Chrysanthemum* is said to reflect Mondrian's interest in the work of Van Gogh and in theosophy. From 1875, members of the British Theosophical Society had sought to grasp the hidden essence of reality through transcendent spiritual states. According to the activist and president of the society Annie Besant, flowers emit auras that link with higher spheres of existence; the chrysanthemum is said to evoke the moon, while the sunflower (pp. 114–17) recalls the sun. The energetic symmetry of this bloom seems to disclose what the artist identified as 'the deeper beauty' hidden within. He apparently saw the chrysanthemum as an ideal embodiment of this beauty, and may have depicted as many as 150 of these flowers.

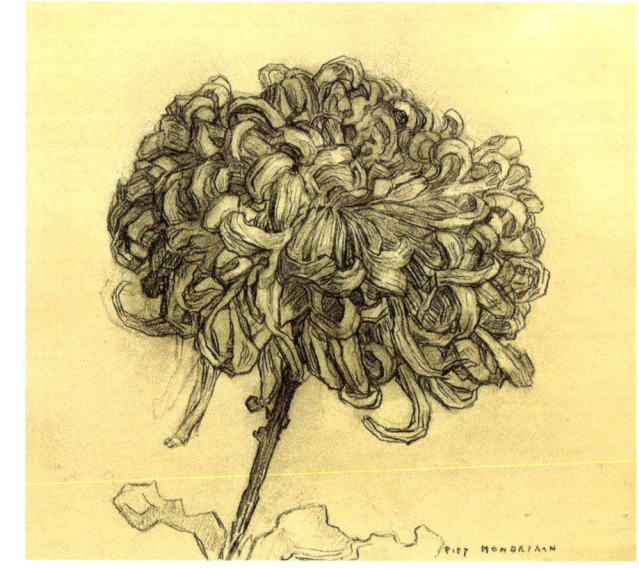

⊗   Piet Mondrian,
Chrysanthemum, *c.* 1908–9,
crayon on paperboard.
New York: Guggenheim
Museum.

※   Pieter de Pannemaeker
after Jean Linden,
Autumn chrysanthemum
hybrids, 1888.   ⊗

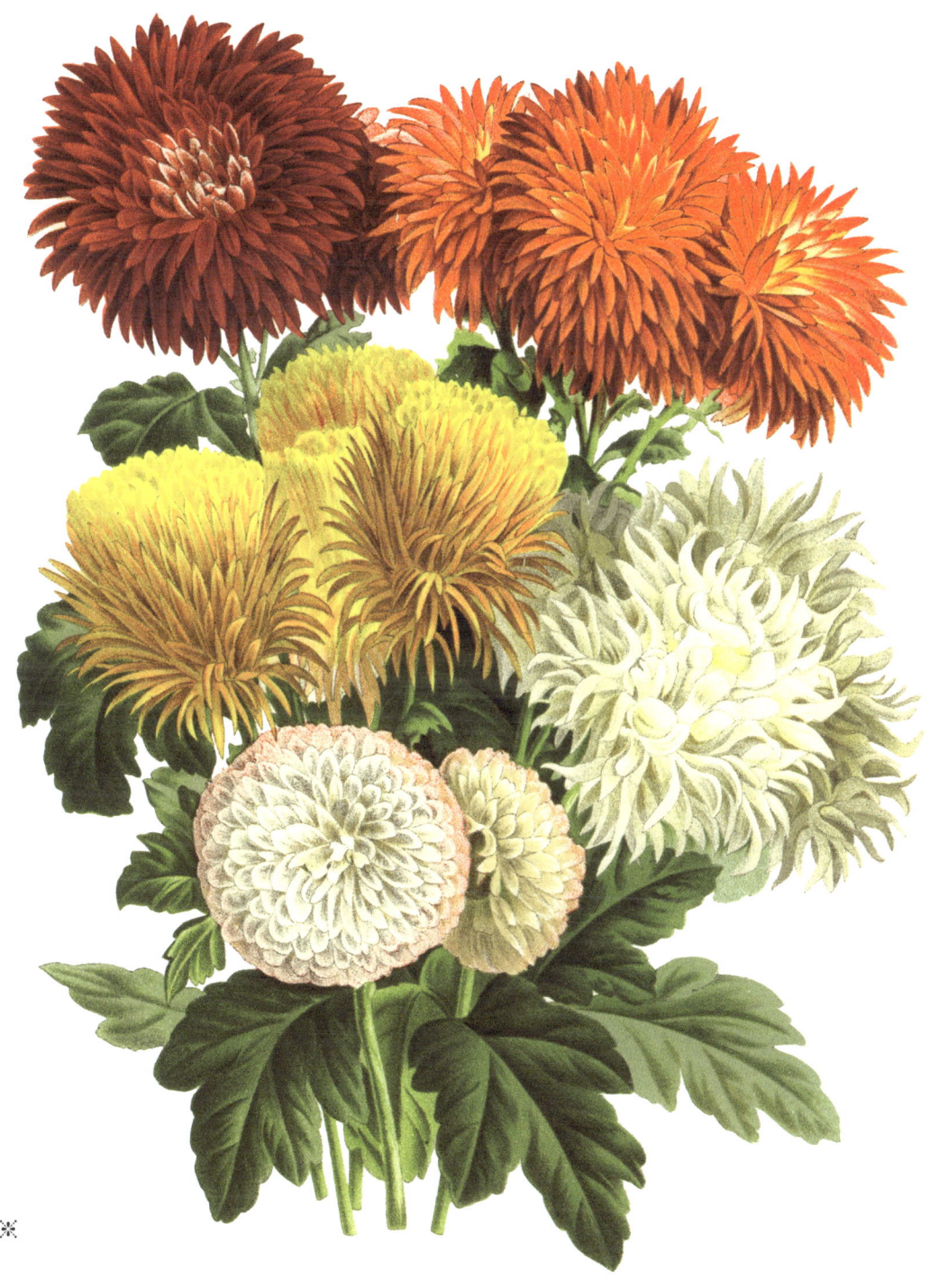

FAMILY Iridaceae

A genus of flowering plants in the iris family, the crocus is native to woodland and meadows nearly worldwide. The spice saffron comes from the stigmas of *Crocus sativus*, which is common in the Mediterranean, notably on the islands of Crete and Santorini.

The ancient Minoans of Bronze Age Crete depicted the natural world around them with enthusiasm and accuracy. The crocus was the source of saffron, an important commodity, used in medicine, dye and perfume, and traded throughout the Mediterranean. According to the archaeologist Rachel Dewan, it also played a role in Minoan worship of the Mother Goddess and served as a symbol of Minoan female identity. It may have been at this time that saffron came to be considered an aphrodisiac.

According to Greek legend, the flower is named after a youth who unrequitedly loved a shepherdess named Smilax. When he pined away and died, the gods changed him into the crocus flower. Because of this association with love, the flower became linked with weddings. The Romans grew it and sprinkled its blooms to perfume banquet halls, gardens and courtyards.

The crocus continues to be a significant source of saffron, and is still mostly grown in Greece. Brilliant yellow clothing dyed with saffron symbolized light and majesty, and often adorns gods and kings.

The colour of Buddhist robes varies according to culture. The Buddha himself wore robes made from discarded cloth that was dyed by being boiled with vegetable matter and spices such as turmeric or saffron, which gives cloth a yellow–orange colour. The colour of the robes indicated that the monks were fulfilling their vows of poverty.

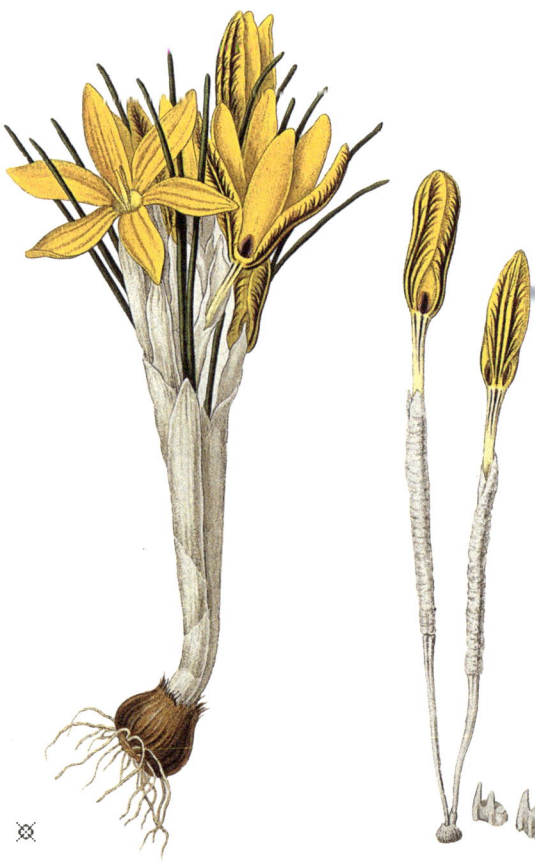

OTHER CROCUS IMAGES
- *The Saffron Walden Charter*, 1514. Saffron Walden, Essex: Saffron Walden Museum.
- Raymond C. Booth, *Crocus*, 1962, oil on canvas. Warrington, Cheshire: Warrington Museum & Art Gallery. A bird's skull rests beneath the crocus flowers.

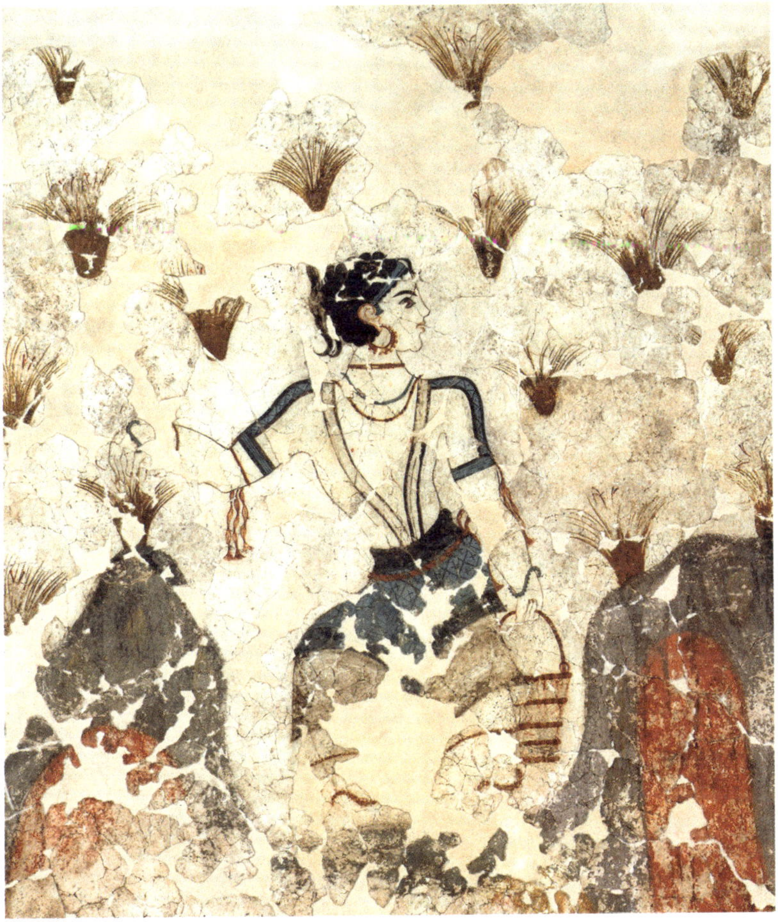

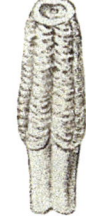

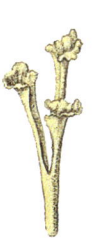

Crocus (*Crocus stellaris*): entire flowering plant and its anatomical segments, *c.* 1812.

'Saffron Gatherers', detail of fresco, *c.* 1500 BCE. Xeste 3, Akrotiri, Santorini.

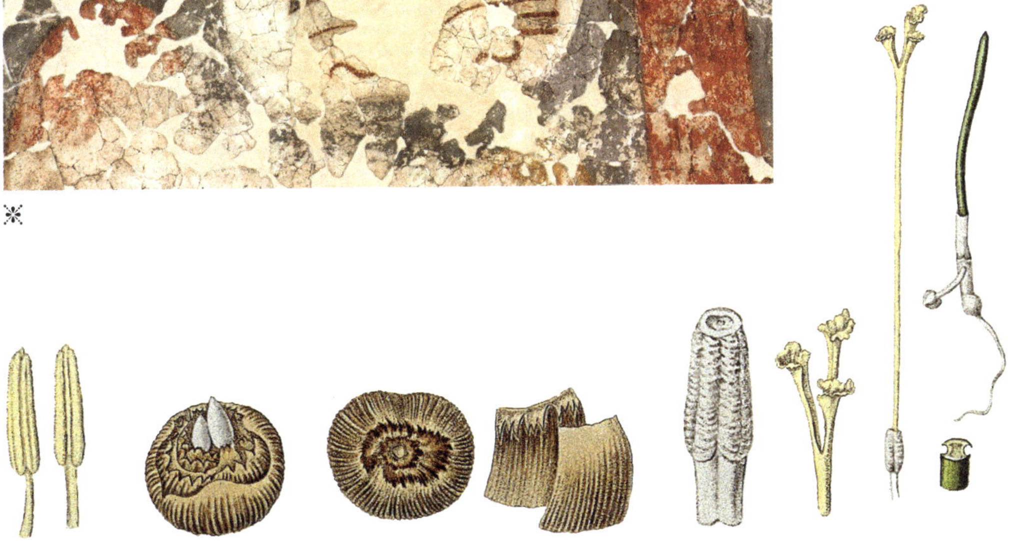

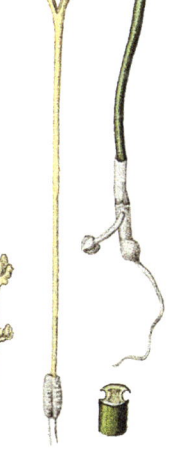

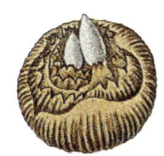

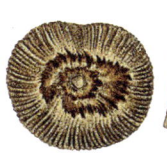

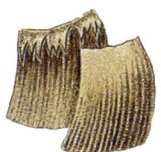

FAMILY Primulaceae

A genus of twenty-three species of flowering plant native to Europe and the Mediterranean, cyclamen are grown today for decorative use both indoors and outside.

Theophrastus claimed that the cyclamen was an aphrodisiac that promoted conception. Sacred to Hecate, who presided over all magical spells, it was believed to purify the ground on which it grew. In Christian art, it became sacred to the Virgin Mary. The little red spots sometimes found on the inside of the flower symbolized her sorrow over Christ's death.

Moshe Gershuni's work is autobiographical, recalling his childhood in Israel. His series *Hai Cyclamen* (*18 Cyclamens*) relates to war, regeneration and atonement. The number eighteen, *Chai* in the Kabbalah, means world or life, and donations to synagogues are made in multiples of this figure. Persian cyclamen (*Cyclamen persicum*) grows wild across the Levant and North Africa. After the 1948 Arab–Israeli War, the cyclamen became a national symbol of Israel. Hebrew inscriptions around the edges of the painting (opposite) refer to Psalms, expressing forgiveness and reconciliation.

In Japanese culture, the cyclamen is a sacred flower to lovers and is often given as a gift on Valentine's Day.

⊗ James Sowerby, Cyclamen (*Cyclamen coum*), 1787.

※ Moshe Gershuni, *Hai Cyclamen*, 1984, mixed media on paper. Private collection.

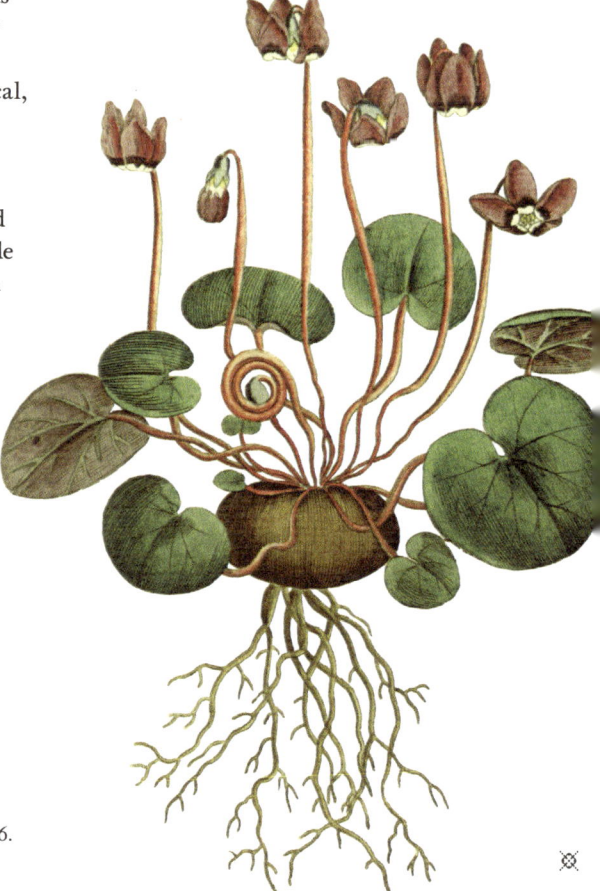

OTHER CYCLAMEN IMAGES
- Ernst Ludwig Kirchner, *Cyclamen*, 1918–19, oil on canvas. New York: Metropolitan Museum of Art.
- Ellsworth Kelly, several cyclamen lithographs, 1966. New York: Museum of Modern Art.

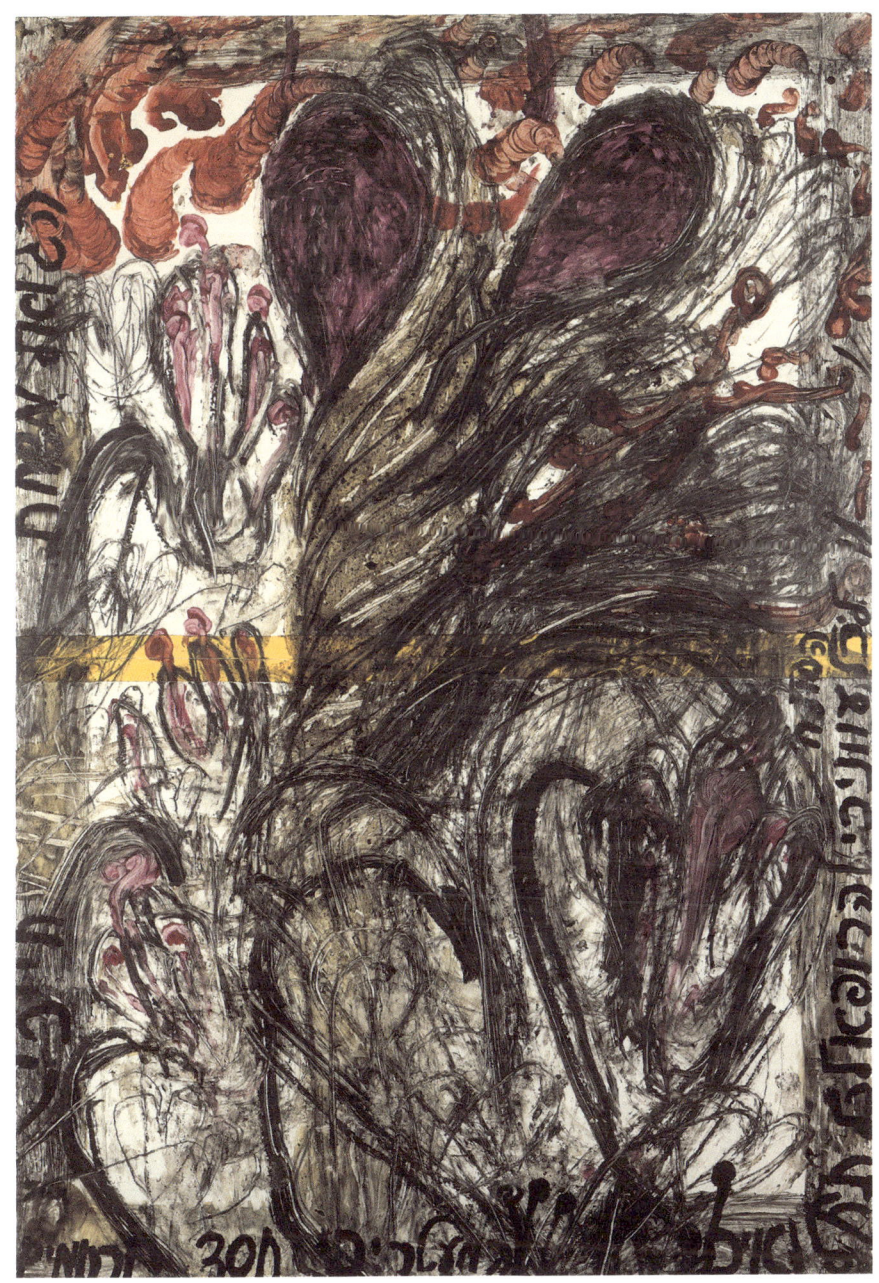

※

CYCLAMEN CYCLAMEN

FAMILY Caryophyllaceae

Imported from Tunisia in the thirteenth century, the carnation has been cultivated for about 2,000 years.

Its Greek name, *dianthus*, mentioned by Theophrastus and taken up by the naturalist Carolus Linnaeus in the eighteenth century as its botanical name, comes from the words for divine (*dios*) and flower (*anthos*). According to legend, the goddess Artemis, having been rejected by a shepherd boy, took revenge by tearing out his eyes. When the eyes fell to the ground, they sprouted, becoming carnations. The flower was used in Greco-Roman ceremonial crowns.

In Christian imagery, carnations sometimes appear in the Virgin's or Christ's hand, or in the Garden of Eden. Medieval legend attributes the flower's origin to the tears shed by the Virgin Mary at the Crucifixion.

In northern Europe, the flower was commonly worn by brides and became associated with marriage. Indicating a promise of marriage or a pledge of love, carnations sometimes appear in Flemish portraits. They also appear in still lifes, most notably in Dutch Baroque *vanitas* works, where they and the other objects recall the brevity of life and pleasure, and serve as a reminder of the dangers of overindulgence.

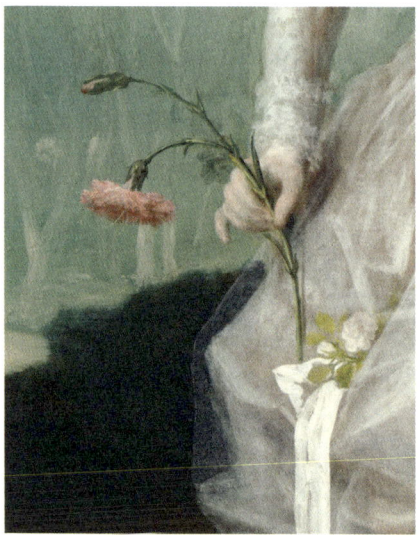

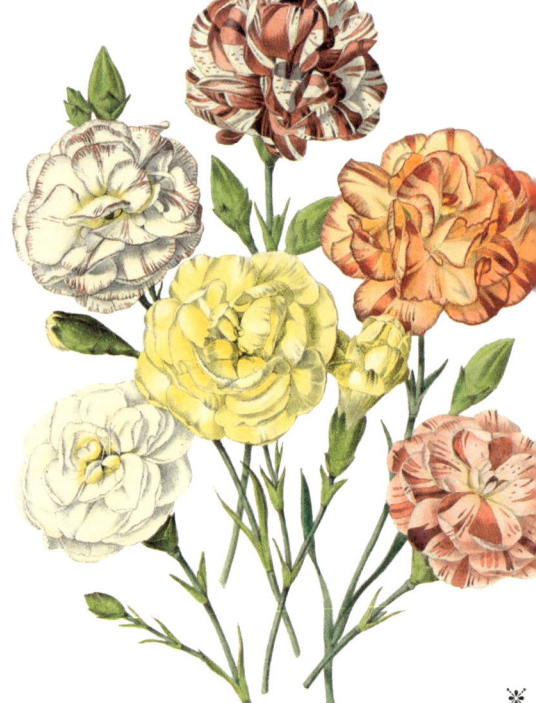

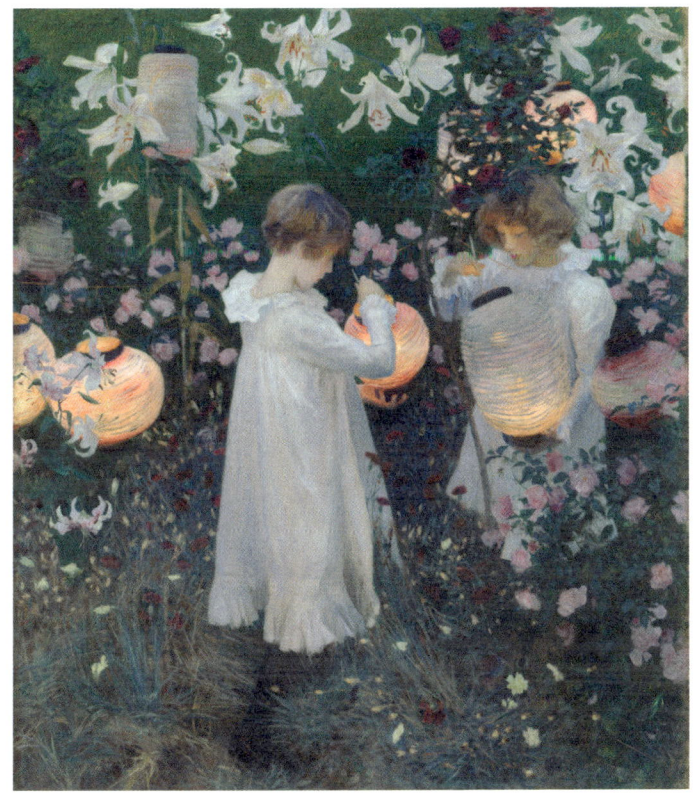

⊗   Francisco Goya,
*The Marquesa de
Pontejos* (detail),
c. 1786, oil on canvas.
Washington, DC:
National Gallery
of Art.

❋   Augusta Withers,
Tree carnation, 1857.

❖   John Singer Sargent,
*Carnation, Lily, Lily,
Rose*, 1885–86, oil on
canvas. London: Tate.

❖

Carnations, lilies and roses appear in John Singer Sargent's *Carnation, Lily, Lily, Rose*. The title comes from 'Ye Shepherds Tell Me', a song by the British composer Joseph Mazzinghi popular in the 1880s. The refrain asks, 'Have you seen my Flora pass this way?' '[B]eauty's queen' – and goddess of flowers – in the song, Flora wears a wreath of lilies, carnations and roses, symbolic of love, purity and spring rebirth. Although it is unclear whether Sargent meant this painting to be symbolic, it certainly celebrates the beauty of nature and flowers, as well as the innocence of childhood.

The carnation has been the emblem of Mother's Day in the United States since 1907, and red and pink carnations are the symbol of Parents Day in Korea.

OTHER CARNATION IMAGES
- Leonardo da Vinci, *The Madonna of the Carnation*, 1478–80, oil on panel. Munich: Alte Pinakothek.
- Nicolaes van Verendael, *Flowers in a Glass Vase on a Stone Ledge*, between 1657 and 1691, oil on canvas. Aachen: Suermondt Ludwig Museum.

FAMILY Plantaginaceae

Native to and widespread throughout temperate Europe, this plant is popular in gardens worldwide. It is the source of digoxin, a heart medicine.

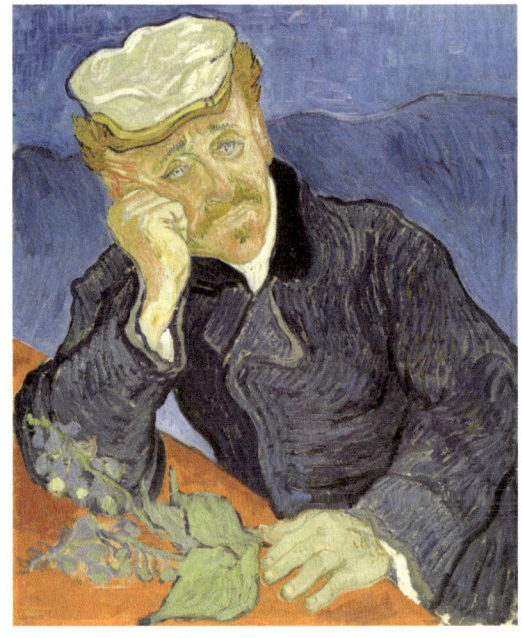

The colour of the blossoms varies; typically purple in their wild form, when cultivated the plants may bear pink, yellow or white blooms. The flowering stem can measure between 0.9 and 1.8 m (3–6 ft) tall, and the plant is poisonous to varying degrees.

Probably the most famous foxglove in art appears in Van Gogh's *Portrait of Dr Gachet*. There are two versions: the earliest is now in an unknown private collection, and the second, originally owned by Gachet himself, is in the Musée d'Orsay in Paris. The doctor, a homeopath and amateur artist, cared for Van Gogh after his release from the asylum at Saint-Rémy. Van Gogh, who felt a kinship with Gachet, wrote that he had attempted to create a modern portrait to capture 'the deeply sad [often translated as heartbroken] expression of our times'. The foxglove in both versions of the painting reflects the doctor's role as both healer and fellow sufferer.

The contemporary Irish artist Dorothy Cross spent twenty years studying the foxglove, creating sculptures of individual specimens in bronze and thereby, according to Giovanni Aloi, elevating the plant to mythological status. The artist's interest in the plant stemmed from her childhood, when she was warned of its dangers. One wonders whether Cross was aware of suggestions that Van Gogh suffered from digitalis intoxication, since other aspects of her work deal with altered states of mind induced by psychotropic substances, poison and sex.

OTHER FOXGLOVE IMAGES
- Paul Ranson, *Digitalis*, 1899, tempera on canvas. Tokyo: National Museum of Western Art.

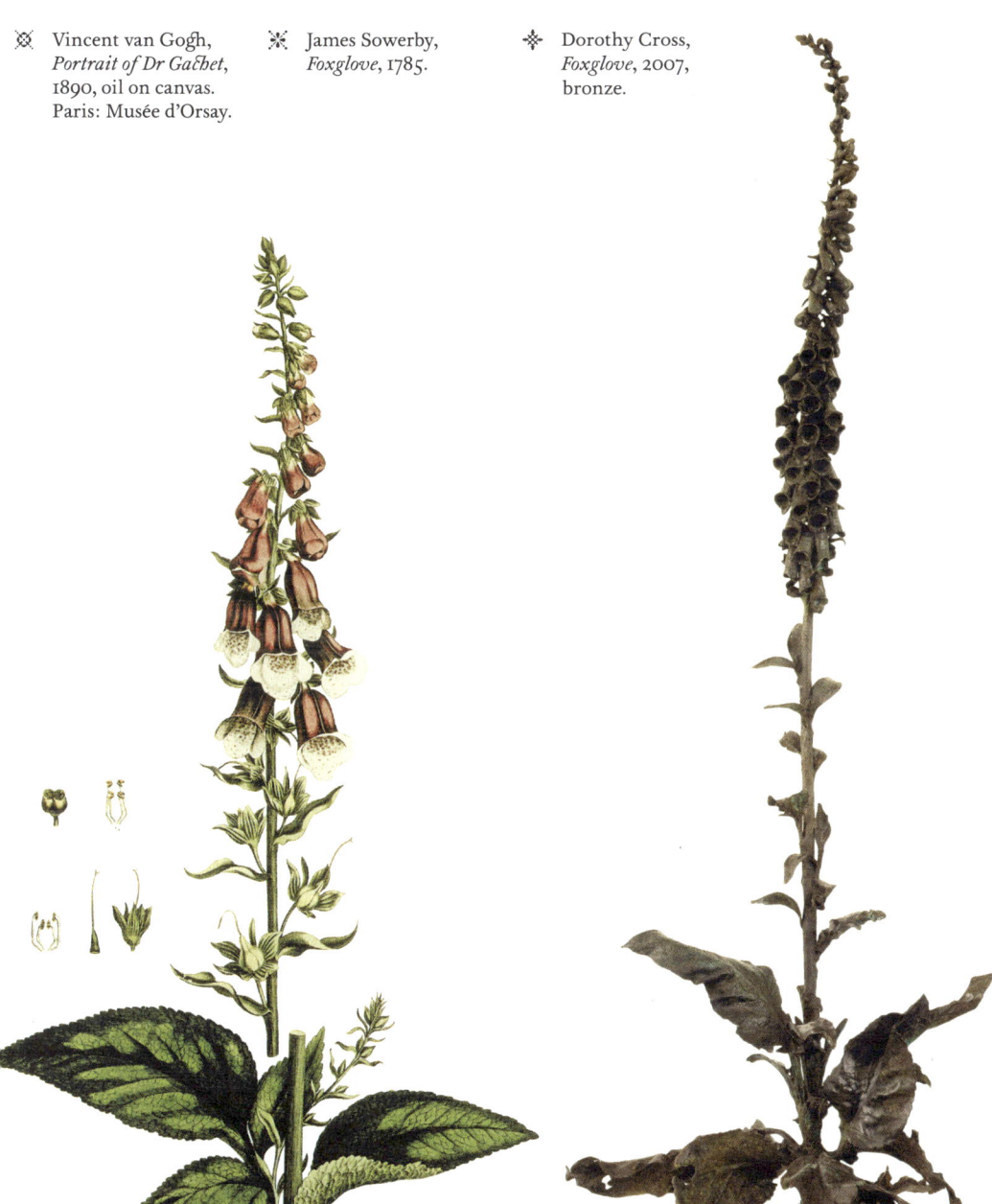

※ Vincent van Gogh,
Portrait of Dr Gachet,
1890, oil on canvas.
Paris: Musée d'Orsay.

※ James Sowerby,
Foxglove, 1785.

✤ Dorothy Cross,
Foxglove, 2007,
bronze.

FAMILY   Asteraceae

All species except one are native to North and Central America, domesticated in Mexico around 2100 BCE. The common or giant sunflower was brought back to Europe by Spanish explorers. Sunflowers provide edible seeds and oil and are used as fertilizer. The sunflower's face is said to follow the sun across the sky, and its petals spread out like the sun's rays – hence the genus name, from the Greek *hēlios*, 'sun'.

Baroque artists – such as Anthony van Dyck, who painted a self-portrait holding a sunflower – played on its meaning of unconditional devotion, related to the way its flowers turn to face the sun. In Van Dyck's case, it signified his allegiance to Charles I of England, for whom he served as court painter.

   The flower was beloved by the Pre-Raphaelites, and a little later in the nineteenth century sunflowers were also popular as decorative motifs in the Arts and Crafts Movement. The sunflower became Oscar Wilde's iconic symbol after a caricature of him appeared in *Punch* in 1881; Wilde adopted the sunflower, praising its 'gaudy leonine beauty'. Thereafter, the flower became associated with the Aesthetic Movement.

   Dorothea Tanning's *Eine Kleine Nachtmusik* dates from the artist's time in Arizona, where she lived with Max Ernst. A huge sunflower head rests at the top of a stairway on a red carpet. Two girls occupy the hallway, one of them apparently especially threatened by the

flower, to the extent that her hair is literally standing on end. Tanning, who connected the flower with the intense Arizona sun, wrote of the painting:

It's about confrontation. Everyone believes he/she is his/her drama. While they don't always have giant sunflowers (most aggressive of flowers) to contend with, there are always stairways, hallways,

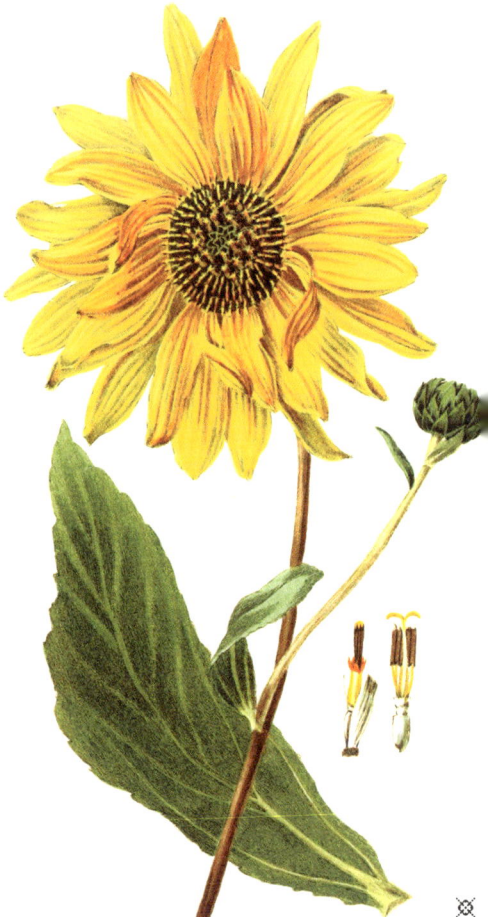

  ⊠   William Clark, *Sunflower*,
        1826.

  ✳   Dorothea Tanning, *Eine Kleine*
        Nachtmusik, 1943, oil on canvas.
        London: Tate.

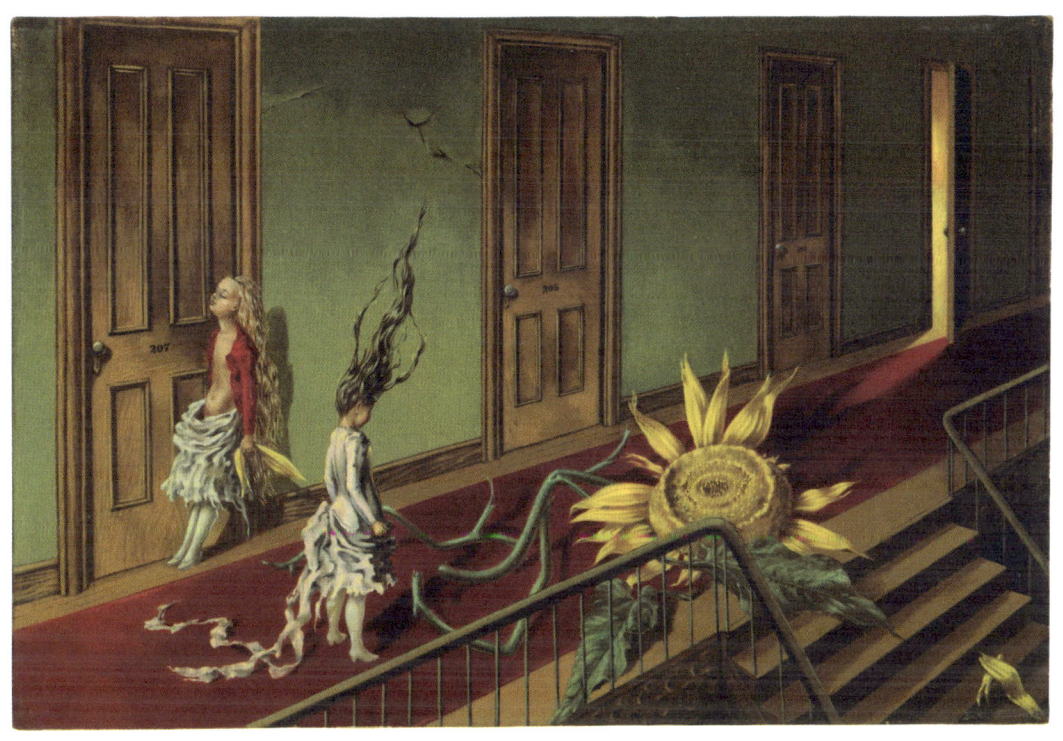

❋

even very private theatres where the suffocations
and the finalities are being played out.

Vincent van Gogh painted sunflowers before
he left Paris and created many more to adorn
Paul Gauguin's room in Arles, where the
artists shared a house – known as the Yellow
House – for several weeks in late 1888. He hoped
Gauguin would be a mentor and looked forward
to discussing art and literature with the older
painter, so the flowers doubtless embody his
admiration. Unfortunately, the feeling wasn't
reciprocated, and Gauguin's visit famously
ended in a violent quarrel.[10]

Van Gogh's celebrated sunflowers continue
to inspire contemporary art, for instance Faith
Ringgold's story quilt *The Sunflower Quilting
Bee at Arles* (part of her *French Collection*), of
which several versions exist. The quilts depict
influential African American women and
feature Van Gogh himself holding a sunflower
still life. The works celebrate community,
creativity and the challenges these women
overcame. One of the quilts includes the Yellow
House. The quilts highlight the contribution of
Black women as well as honouring Van Gogh.

Anselm Kiefer, among the twenty-first
century's most complex and important artists,

works in diverse media. Plants play a significant role in his art. For instance, huge sunflowers appear in *The Orders of the Night*,[11] hovering over the supine body of a man, a self-portrait.[12] The sunflowers symbolize adoration; but these appear to be dying, their seeds falling to earth to grow again. His works are unstable; surfaces crack, bloom and grow. Building on Van Gogh's visions, Kiefer evokes the vast, eternal cycles of nature, divine mystery and human strength and frailty.

❧ Anselm Kiefer, *Die Orden der Nacht* (*The Orders of the Night*), 1996, acrylic, emulsion and shellac on canvas. Seattle, WA: Seattle Art Museum.

✳ Faith Ringgold, *The Sunflower Quilting Bee at Arles*, 1991, acrylic on canvas with pieced fabric border. Private collection.

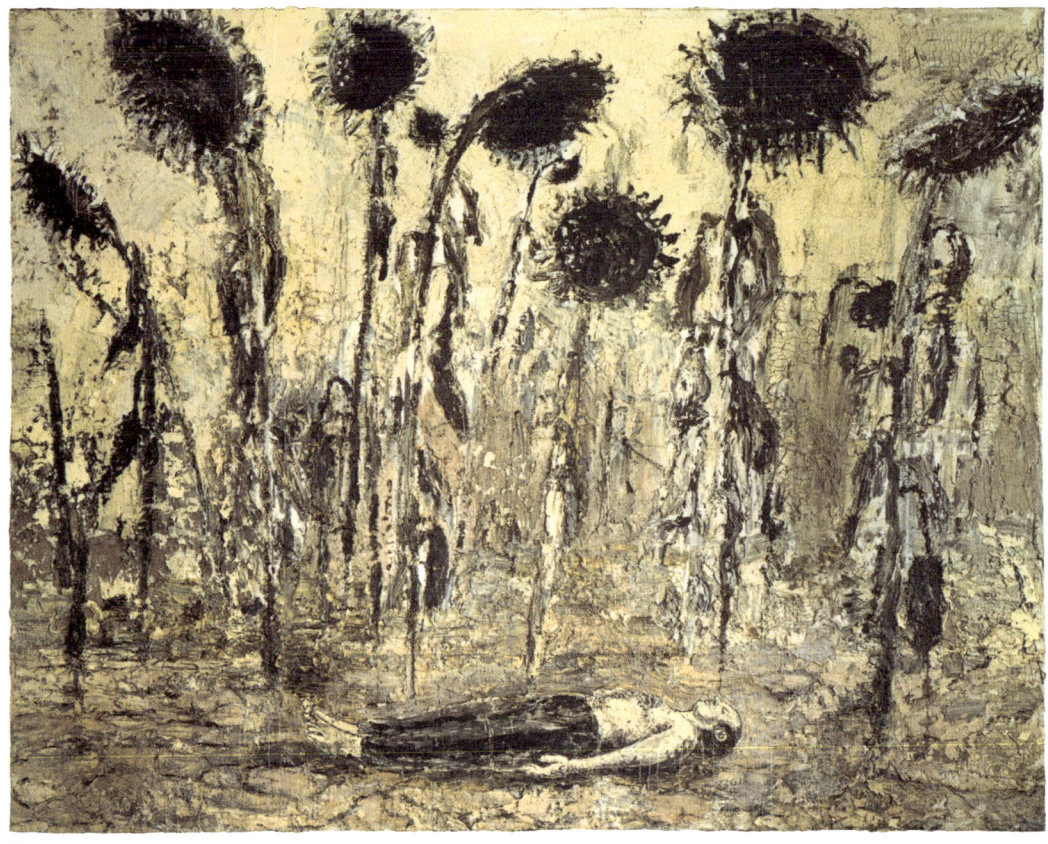

❧

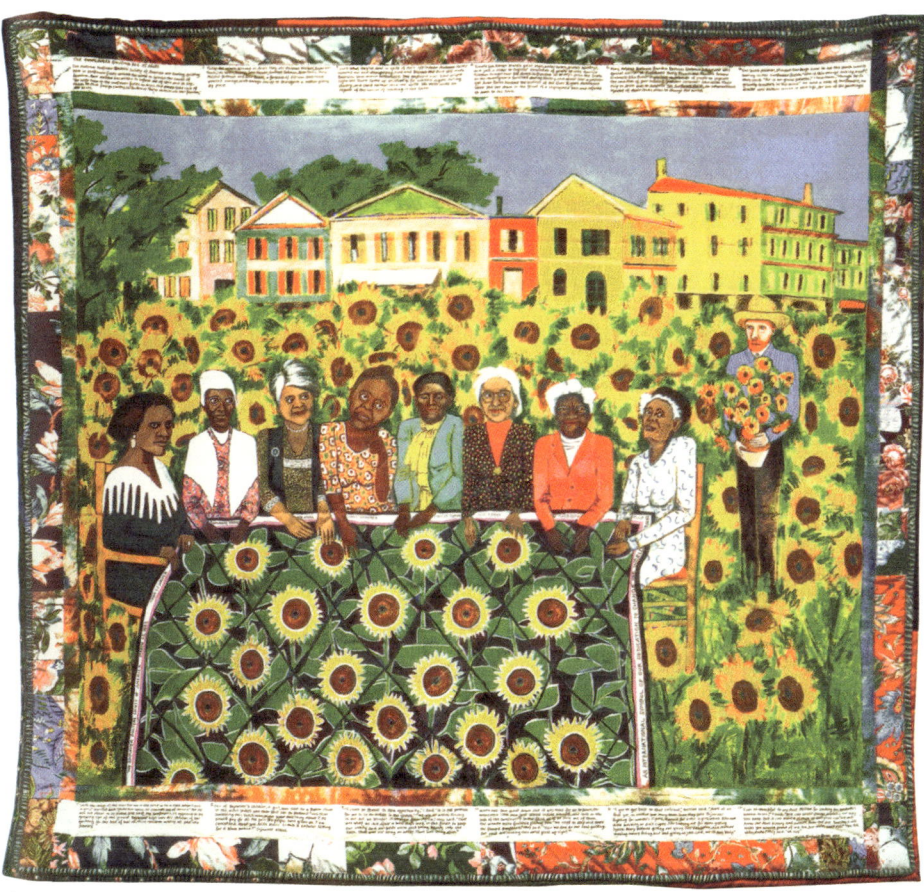

*

FAMILY Asparagaceae

This small genus of perennial flowering plants is native to the eastern Mediterranean and known by the common name hyacinth. The bulbs are poisonous.

The hyacinth's name comes from the Greek poet Homer, or possibly from Ovid. There are several variants of the story: in some, the youth Hyacinth was killed by Apollo and in others by the wind god Zephyrus. A number of sources suggest that the relationship between Apollo and Hyacinth was sexual. In all versions, Apollo changes Hyacinth's blood into the hyacinth flower. It has also been suggested that Hyacinth was a pre-Hellenic vegetation deity whose importance was eclipsed by the Olympian gods.

The hyacinth appears in the garden of Flora in Renaissance art, growing at the lower edge of Botticelli's *Primavera* (p. 90), and it also graces still lifes. In Christian art, it is a symbol of prudence, depicted only rarely. It sometimes appears in Nativity scenes.

While living in Paris in 1949, Ellsworth Kelly bought a potted hyacinth to cheer up his room. Kelly drew throughout his life, often returning to accurate line drawings of plants, perhaps as a foil to the increasing abstraction of his paintings. While his plant drawings may not have had any deeper meaning, they clearly convey his appreciation for the simple beauty of the world around him.

Hyacinths often appear in botanical illustrations and are favourites with contemporary floral artists. William Morris combined the hyacinth with other flowers in a stunning wallpaper design; it also appears in pattern #480, manufactured in 1917 after his death.

⊗ Pierre-Joseph Redouté, *Hyacinthus orientalis*, 1827.

⊗ Ellsworth Kelly, *Hyacinth*, 1949, ink on paper. Private collection.

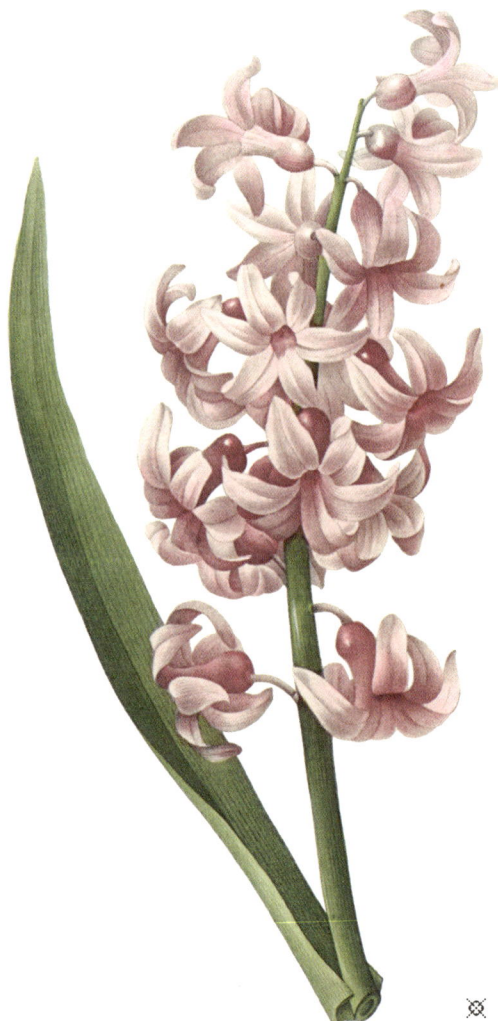

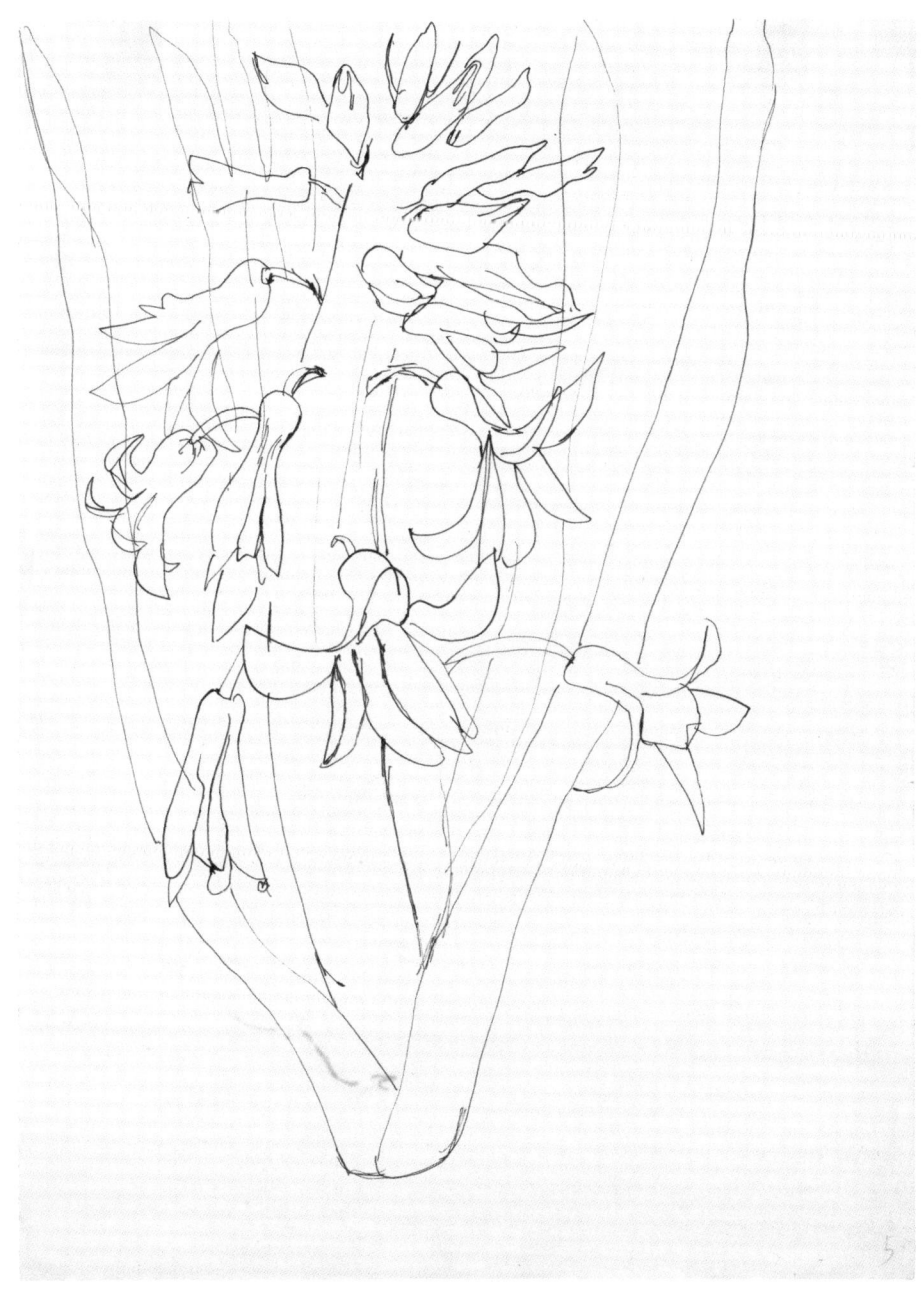

FAMILY Iridaceae

The Iris's name comes from the Greek goddess of the rainbow, possibly referring to its many colours. Irises grow in nearly all temperate zones of the northern hemisphere, and are widely cultivated as an ornamental. Their uses include aromatherapy, the flavouring and colouring of alcoholic drinks, and perfume. They have also been used in plantings for water purification, but can become invasive.

The ancient Egyptians placed the iris on the brow of the Sphinx, symbolizing power. The Greek goddess Iris also acted as the female messenger of the gods, paired with Hermes. Iris led the souls of dead women to the Elysian Fields, and irises were planted on women's graves.

In Christianity, the iris is one of the flowers linked with the Virgin. It sometimes takes the place of the lily in Annunciation scenes, probably because of another of its common names: sword lily. The sharp leaves may also signify the Virgin's sorrow over the death of Christ, as stated in the Gospel of Luke: 'a sword will pierce through your own soul also' (2:35). According to a medieval French legend, the petals of all irises were golden until Christ's death, when they turned purple as a sign of mourning.

The flower served as a symbol of French royalty as early as the first century CE. The first twelve Louis signed their names with an iris or perhaps a lily (pp. 124–27), giving rise to the *fleur-de lys* emblem that is still associated with France today. The three large petals signified

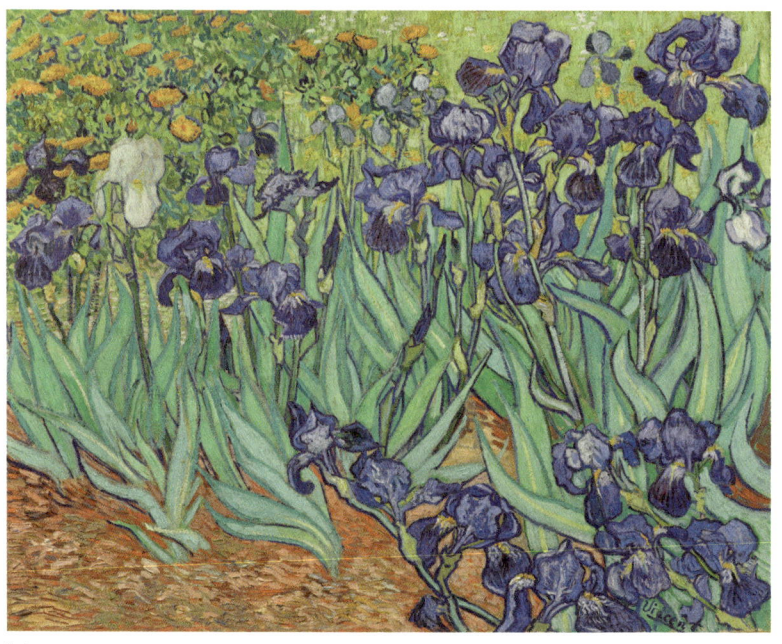

※ Vincent van Gogh, *Irises*, 1889, oil on canvas. Los Angeles, CA: J. Paul Getty Museum.

※ Kazumasa Ogawa, *Iris Kæmpferi* , 1896, coloured collotype. Los Angeles, CA: J. Paul Getty Museum.

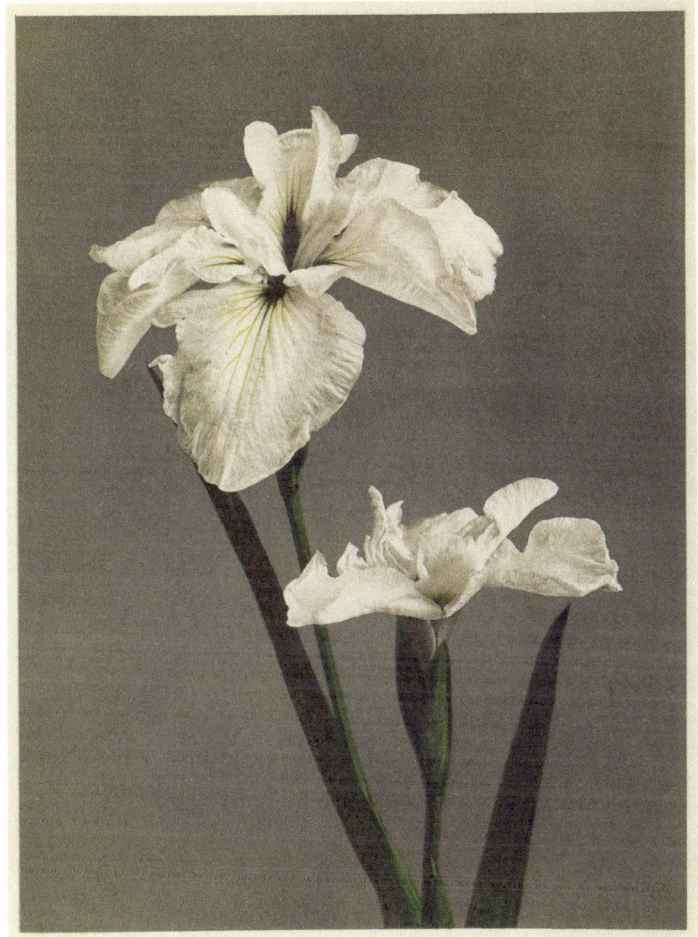

OTHER IRIS IMAGES

- Hugo van der Goes, *Adoration of the Shepherds*, centre panel of Portinari altarpiece, 1475–78, oil on wood. Florence: Le Gallerie degli Uffizi.
- James Atkinson Grimshaw, *Iris, Spirit of the Rainbow*, 1876, oil on canvas. Leeds: Leeds Museums and Galleries.
- Fernand Khnopff, *Portrait of Yvonne Suys*, 1890, oil on panel. Private collection.
- Louis Comfort Tiffany, *Magnolias and Irises*, c. 1908, stained-glass window. New York: Metropolitan Museum of Art.

※

faith, wisdom and valour, and the purple colour stood for royalty and nobility.

Among the most famous of all iris images is Van Gogh's *Irises*. The artist voluntarily admitted himself to the asylum at Saint-Paul de Mausole in May 1889. As soon as he was able to go out into the hospital garden, he began this painting. Most of the flowers are purple, but there is a single white iris, as well as marigolds. The individuality of the flowers is evidence of Van Gogh's very close observation, while the single white flower among the deep purples is sometimes said to represent his loneliness.

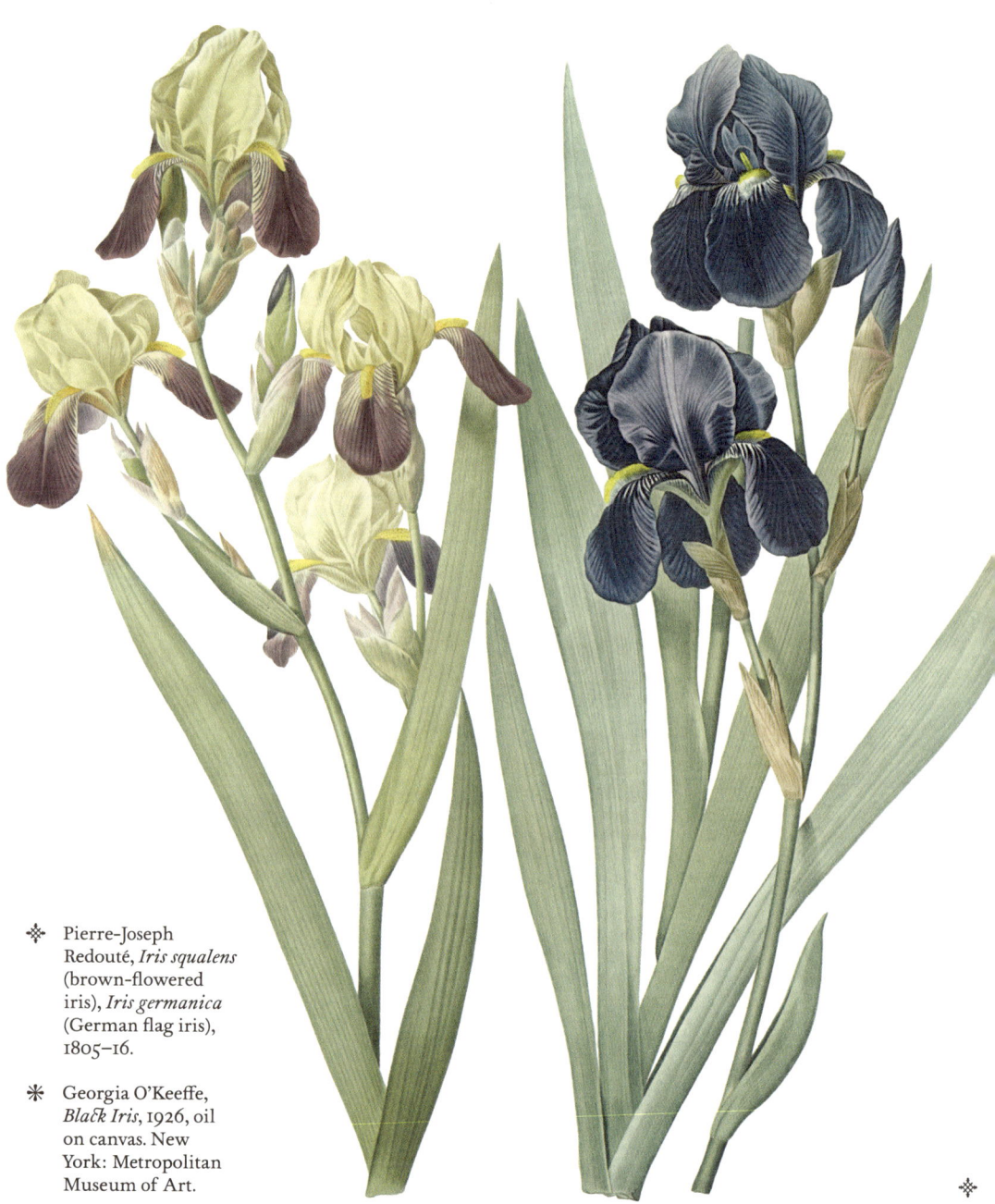

✳ Pierre-Joseph
   Redouté, *Iris squalens*
   (brown-flowered
   iris), *Iris germanica*
   (German flag iris),
   1805–16.

✳ Georgia O'Keeffe,
   Black Iris, 1926, oil
   on canvas. New
   York: Metropolitan
   Museum of Art.

✳

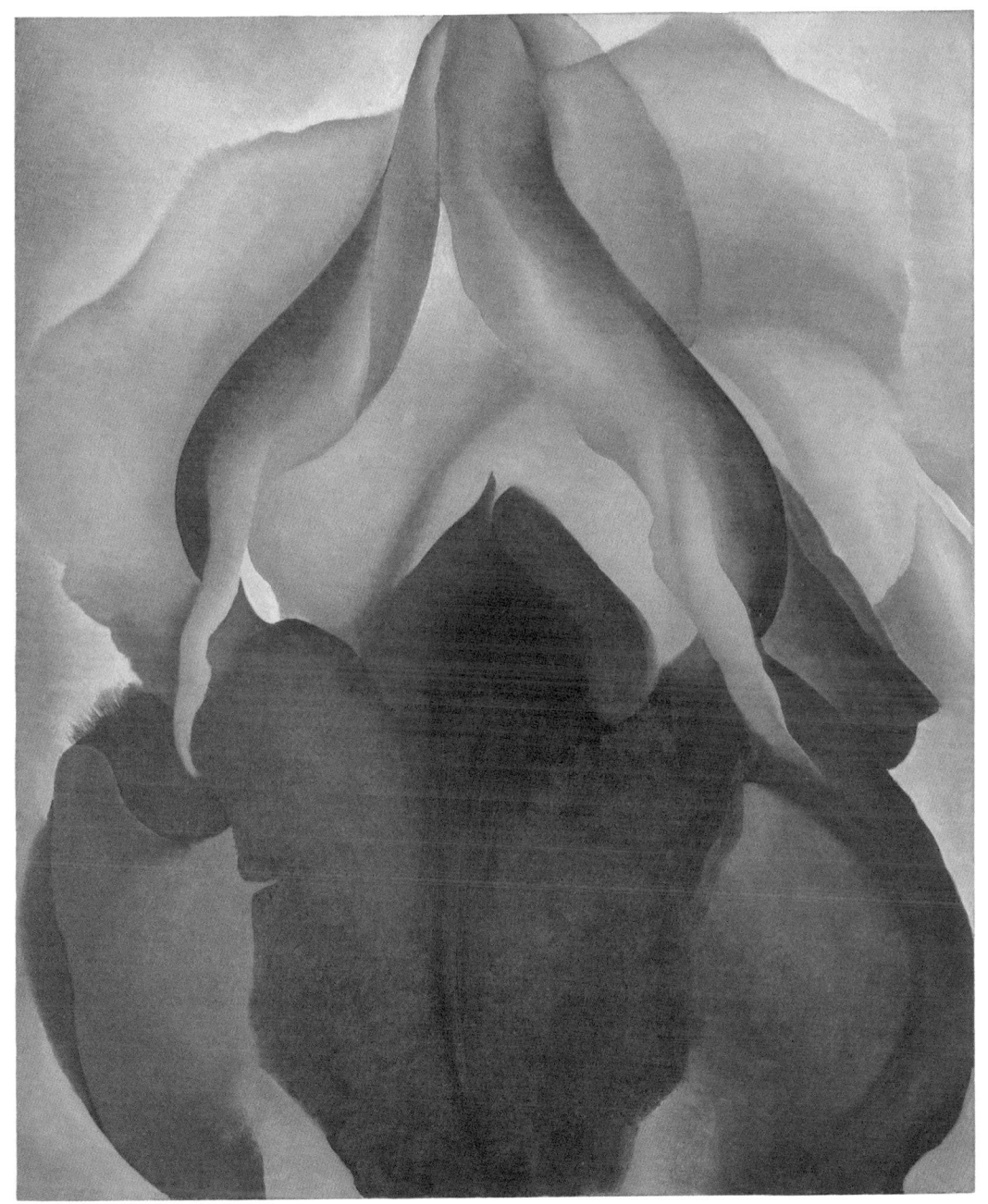

*

FAMILY Liliaceae

Lilies belong to a genus of flowering plants that grow from bulbs, most of them native to the temperate northern hemisphere.

Generally symbolizing femininity, the lily is the sacred flower of motherhood and fruitfulness in Mediterranean and Egyptian mythology. In ancient Greece and Rome, it was sacred to Hera/Juno. The lily is said to have sprung from Hera's milk, some drops of which fell to earth when the Milky Way was created.

According to Semitic legend, the flower sprang from Eve's tears after leaving the Garden of Eden and finding that she was pregnant. In Christianity the lily represents purity, innocence and chastity, and is the favoured symbol of the Virgin Mary. The flower appears in Annunciation scenes from the medieval period, and since the Renaissance, three lilies have been favoured, signifying the Trinity – Father, Holy Spirit and yet-to-be-born Christ. Examples can be found in Leonardo and Botticelli, and later in Rossetti.

Simone Martini's *Annunciation with St Margaret and St Ansanus* was painted for the altar of St Ansanus in the transept of Siena Cathedral. The archangel Gabriel, bearing the olive branch of peace, appears to a startled Virgin Mary. A vase of lilies occupies the centre

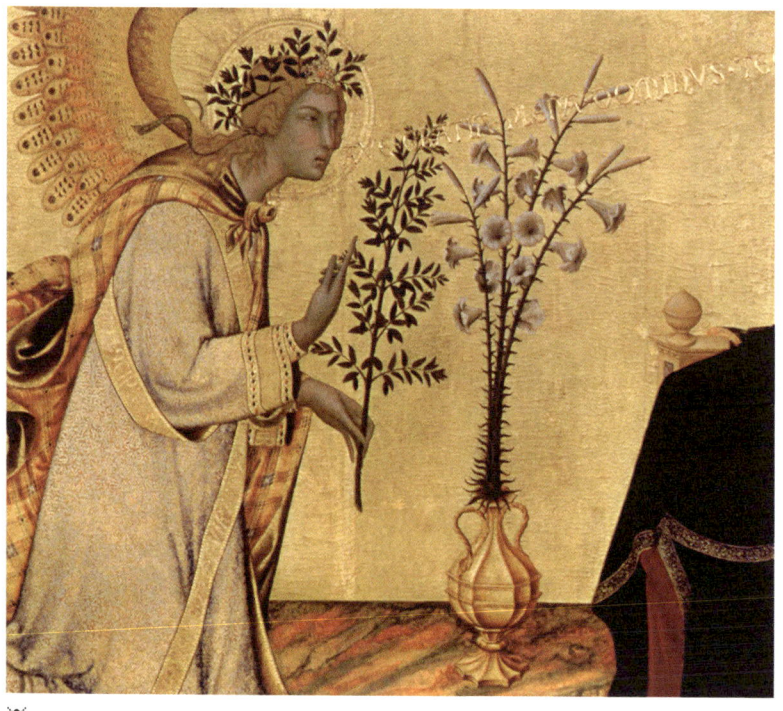

✼ Simone Martini, *Annunciation with St Margaret and St Ansanus* (detail), 1333, tempera on wood with gold background. Florence: Le Gallerie degli Uffizi.

✼ Charlotte Sowerby, *Lilium speciosum*, 1857.

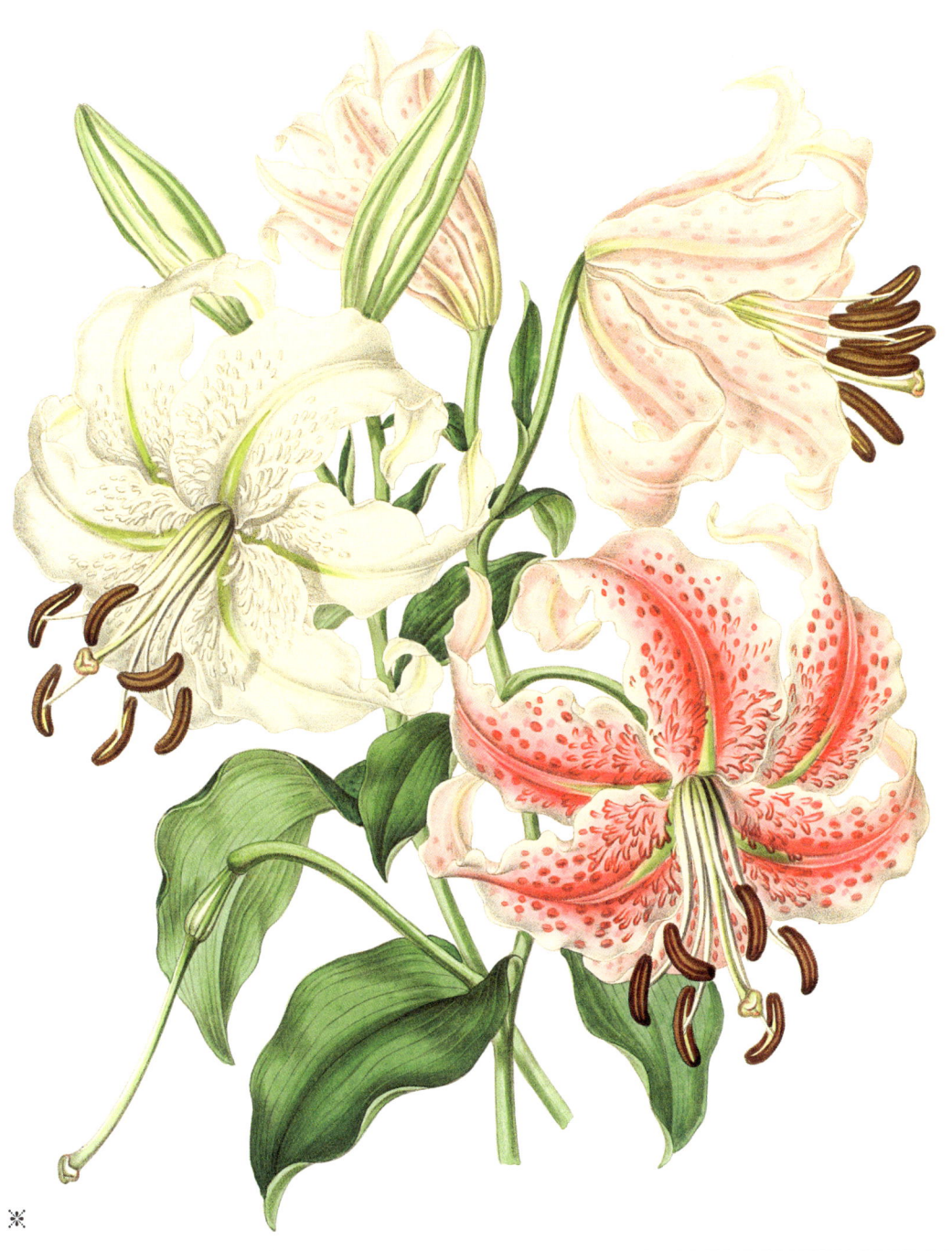

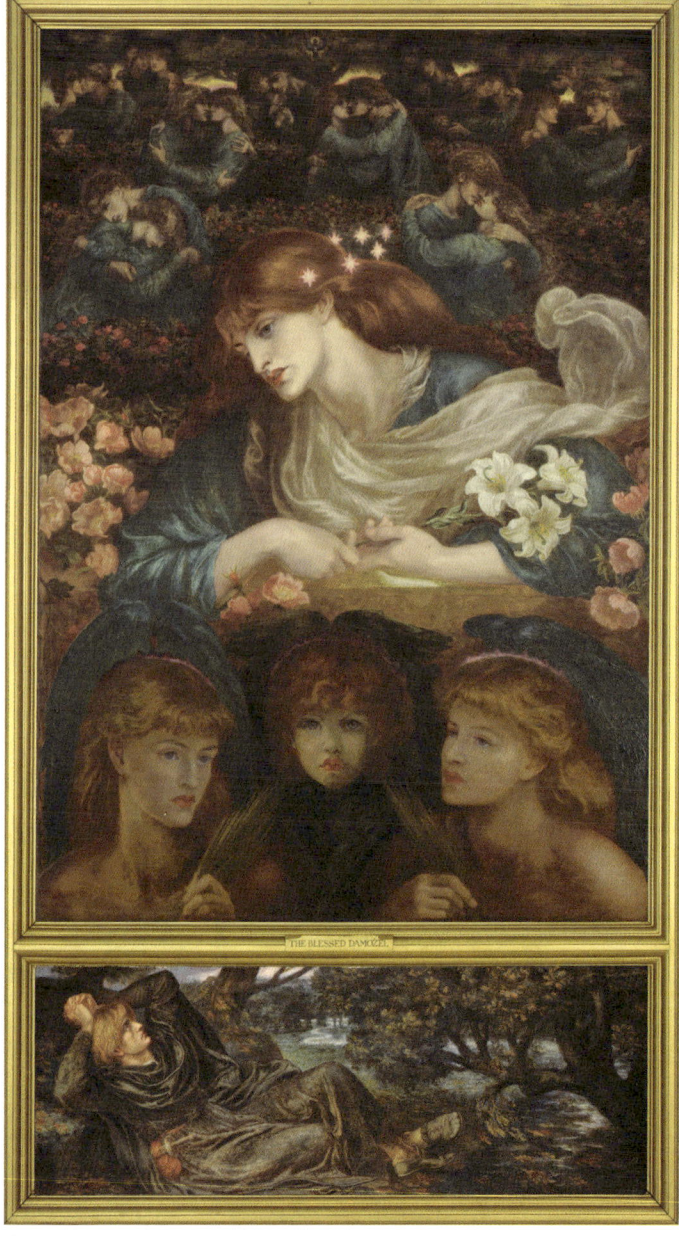

❧ Dante Gabriel Rossetti, *The Blessed Damozel*, 1871–78, oil on canvas. Cambridge, MA: Fogg Museum/Harvard Art Museums.

✳ David Hoćkney, *Mr and Mrs Clark and Percy*, 1970–71, acrylic on canvas. London: Tate.

OTHER LILY IMAGES
- Francisco de Zurbarán, *Christ and the Virgin in the House at Nazareth*, *c.* 1640, oil on canvas. Cleveland, OH: Cleveland Museum of Art.
- Paul Gauguin, *Contes barbares*, 1902, oil on canvas. Essen: Museum Folkwang.
- Stanley Spencer, *The Resurrection, Cookham*, 1924–27, oil on canvas. London: Tate.

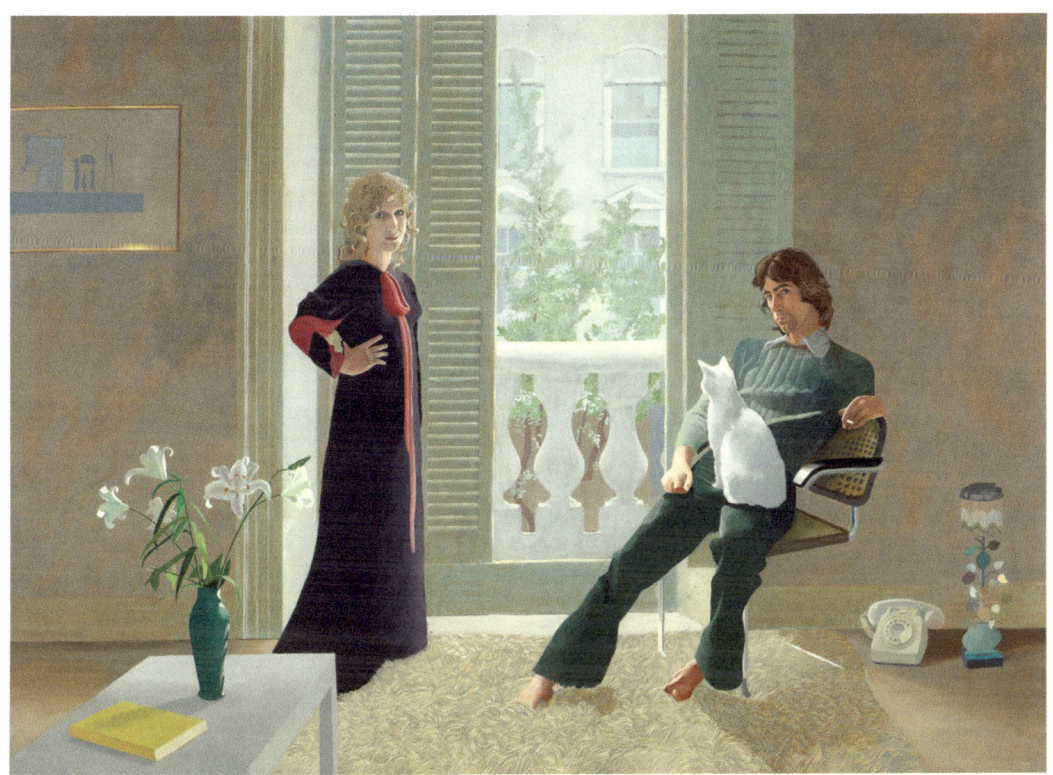

*

of the composition, symbolizing the Virgin's chastity, innocence and purity.

Lilies also appear in images of the Assumption of the Virgin and, focusing on the flower's attributes of purity and innocence, in depictions of the Christ Child. The lily is associated with saints including Catherine of Siena, Clare, Philomena, Joseph, Anthony of Padua and Francis of Assisi. A lily and a sword in images of the Last Judgment symbolize the separation of the innocent and the sinful.

The lily became a favoured heraldic symbol, primarily of the city of Florence and the kings of France. There is some disagreement as to whether the lily or the iris is the basis for the *fleur-de-lys* (see 'Iris', pp. 120–23).

The Blessed Damozel was inspired by a poem Rossetti wrote when he was eighteen, taking the theme of separated lovers who will be rejoined in heaven from Dante's *La Vita Nuova* (1294). The Damozel holds three lilies, which are said to symbolize purity (or possibly the Trinity). Her lover appears in the 'earthly sphere' below, an arrangement reminiscent of Italian Renaissance altarpieces.

FAMILY Caprifoliaceae

Honeysuckle symbolizes pure happiness. Because of its tenacious, clinging habit, it also signifies affection, love and everlasting bonds, while its fragrance links it to sweet pervasiveness.

Honeysuckle has also been believed to repel evil and protect the home. Medicinally, the flowers are natural antibiotics, and can be used to treat staphylococcus infections and upper respiratory problems.

In Greek mythology, the lovers Daphnis and Chloe could remain together only while the honeysuckle bloomed. Daphnis asks Eros, the god of love, to make the plant flower for longer, and it is said to be for this reason that some honeysuckle species bloom for an extended time.

The Druids gave the honeysuckle a place in the ogham alphabet, the twenty-third letter of which is usually ascribed to this flower. Later, Scottish farmers hung honeysuckle wreaths over barn doors or around the necks of cattle as a form of protection.

In 1609, Peter Paul Rubens painted an image of himself and his first wife, Isabella Brant, just before their marriage. The couple is seated on a honeysuckle branch, the foliage of which surrounds and embraces them. The artist thus established a symbolic setting for wedded bliss. Tragically, Isabella died at the age of thirty-four from bubonic plague.

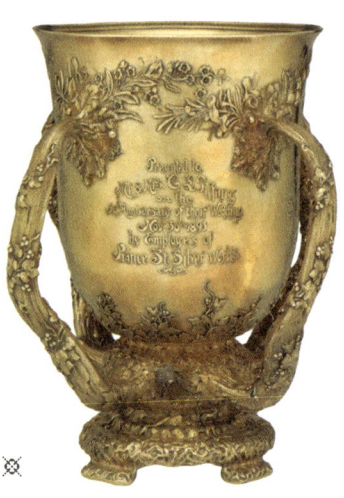

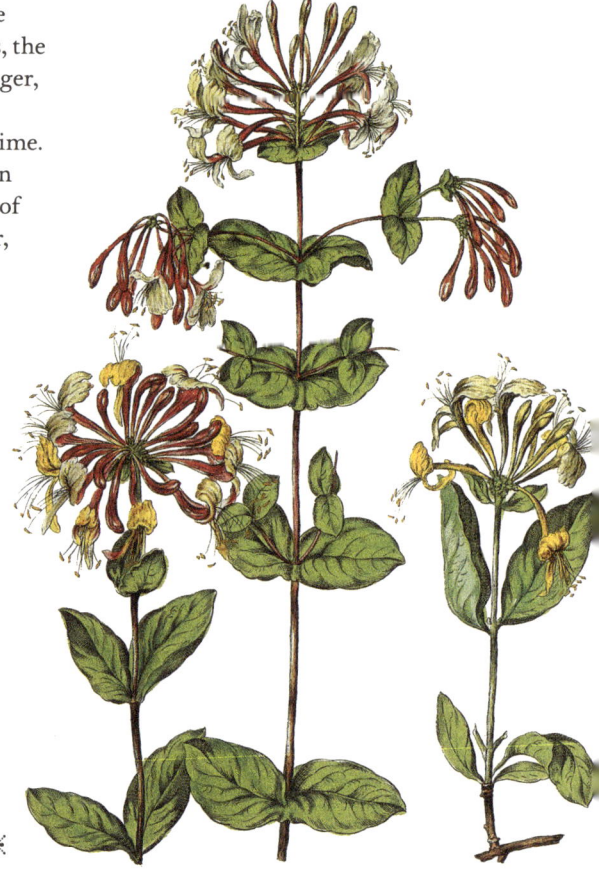

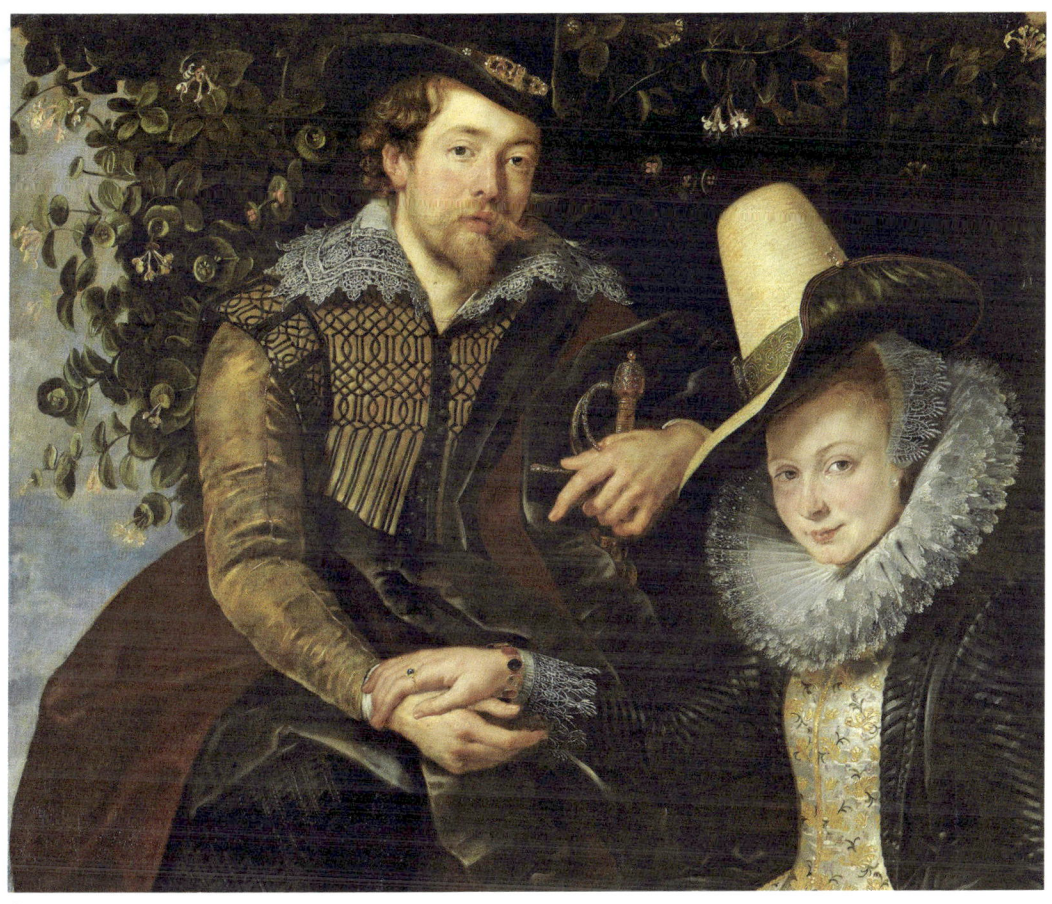

FAMILY Amaryllidaceae

A genus of spring-flowering perennial plants, narcissi were well known in ancient cultures both medicinally and botanically, and became increasingly popular in Europe after the sixteenth century. The plant may be poisonous if accidentally ingested.

An ancient Greco-Roman myth tells of a semi-divine youth, Narcissus, who was so pampered by his mother and the other nymphs that he became extremely conceited. The nymph Echo fell in love with him, but he was too self-obsessed to notice, and she wasted away until only her voice remained. Incensed by his behaviour, Nemesis, the goddess of vengeance, caused him to fall in love with his own reflection in a pool of water. Narcissus, unable to reach his beloved, died and became a flower. Thus we are to understand that narcissism – excessive egotism – will eventually be punished. The flower was also connected with sleep, apparently because its bulb dies back but blooms again each spring. It was often planted on graves, linking death with sleep.

In Christian art, the narcissus appears in representations of Eden and in Annunciations as a symbol of the triumph of divine love over death, egotism and sin. Negative meanings include an allegory of self-love and stupidity.

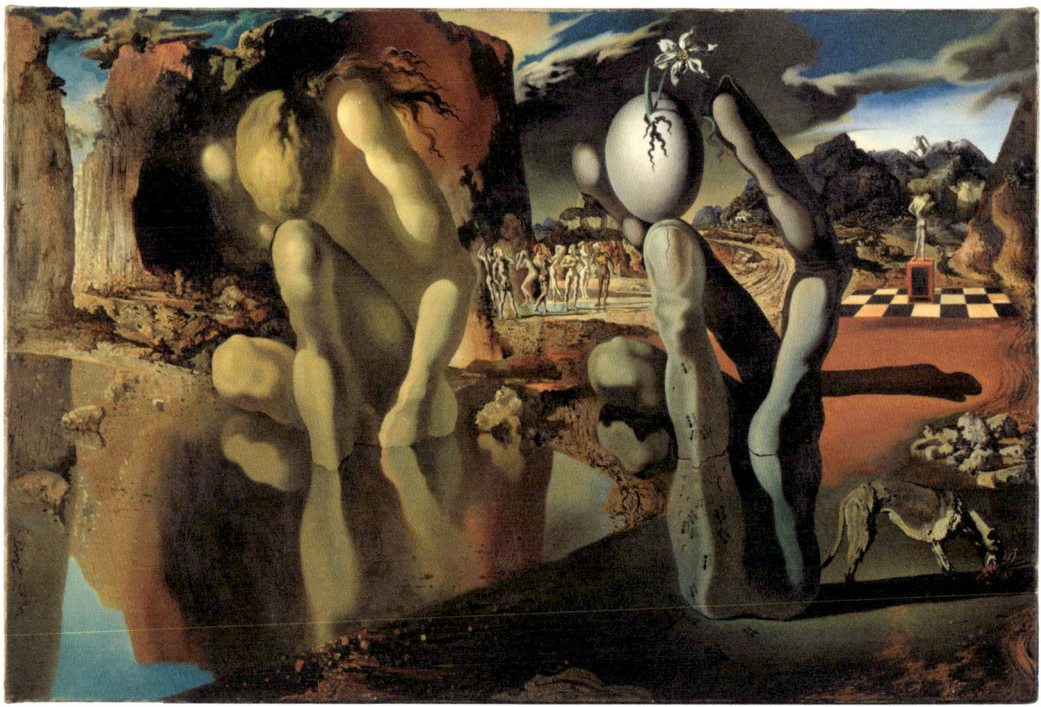

Salvador Dalí depicted the myth of Narcissus in his memorable *Metamorphosis of Narcissus*. Narcissus appears on the left-hand side of the painting, while on the right, a stone hand clutches a cracked stone egg from which the flower emerges. In a small book about the painting in 1937, Dalí wrote: 'If one looks for some time, from a slight distance and with a certain "distant fixedness", at the hypnotically immobile figure of Narcissus, it gradually disappears until at last it is completely invisible'. Dalí met Sigmund Freud the year after painting *Metamorphosis of Narcissus*. He took the painting to their meeting in order to discuss his theory of narcissism, which he had developed based on Freud's concept of paranoia.

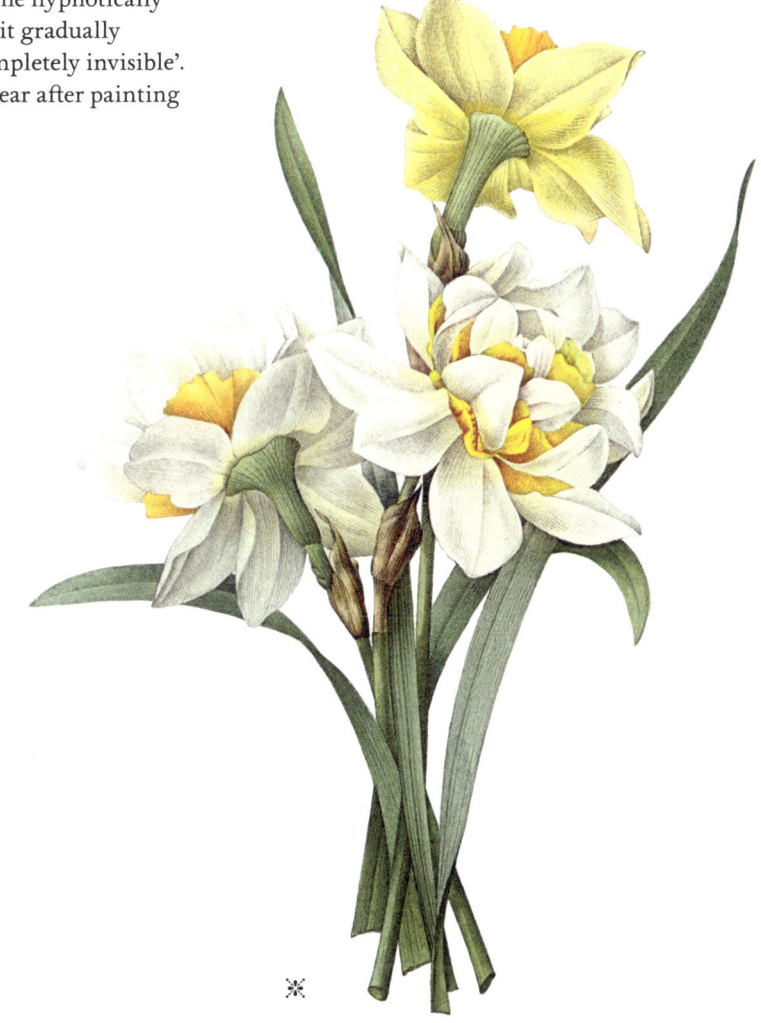

✳ Salvador Dalí, *Metamorphosis of Narcissus*, 1937, oil on canvas. London: Tate.

✳ Pierre-Joseph Redouté, *Narcissus gouani* (Double daffodil), 1827.

OTHER NARCISSUS IMAGES
• Lucian Freud, *Narcissus*, 1948, ink on paper. London: Tate.

FAMILY Nymphaeaceae

The water-lily family consists of aquatic herbs with large round leaves, and includes the plant known in ancient Egypt as the lotus. Rooted in the quiet riverbed, the flower rests on the surface of the water. It thus symbolizes life force and the eternal cycle of life.

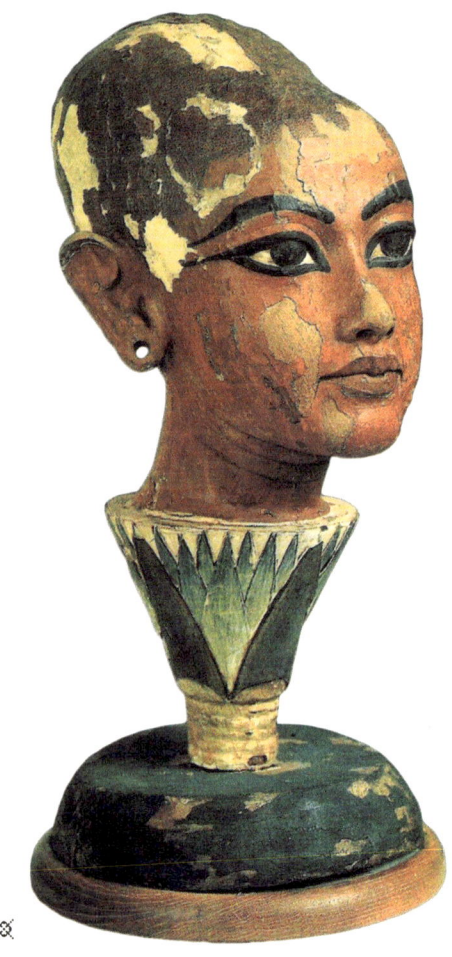

With flowers that open in the morning and close at night, the lotus symbolized the sun, creation and rebirth. It was sacred to Horus, the Egyptian hawk-headed god associated with the sun and the moon. He was the son of Osiris and Isis, and after his father's murder Isis hid him in the marshes of the Nile, where the lotus proliferates. When he grew up, Horus was strong enough to fight Seti, his father's killer, and assume the throne of Egypt; he is thus also linked with power and the pharaohs, who believed they were his descendants. Images of Egyptian water lilies – blue (*Nymphaea caerulea*) and white (*N. lotus*) – as symbols of power often appear in depictions of rulers and in tomb paintings, and inspire many column designs.

The Egyptian deity Nefertem emerged as a lotus from the primordial waters, signifying both sunlight and the delightful aroma of the lotus. A beautiful New Kingdom wooden head found in Tutankhamun's tomb is known as the 'Head of Nefertum' and is said to depict Tutankhamun as a child, emerging at the moment of lotus-birth. Wilson notes that the image links earthly political power with the divine regenerative powers of the gods.

The ancient Egyptian priesthood apparently used the lotus as a narcotic, and the elite classes soaked the petals in wine – with results both aphrodisiac and soporific.

The lotus is a sacred flower in Buddhism and Hinduism, representing enlightenment and resurrection. The lotus flower features prominently in much Asian art. In Hinduism the lotus is often featured alongside the divinities Lakshmi and Vishnu. In Buddhist art, the Buddha is usually shown on a lotus throne.

Among the most admired water-lily paintings are those created by the French Impressionist artist Claude Monet. When

⊗ Head of Nefertem, 18th
Dynasty, 1332–1323 BCE.
Cairo: Egyptian Museum.

※ Louis van Houtte, *Nymphaea
stellata*, 1845.

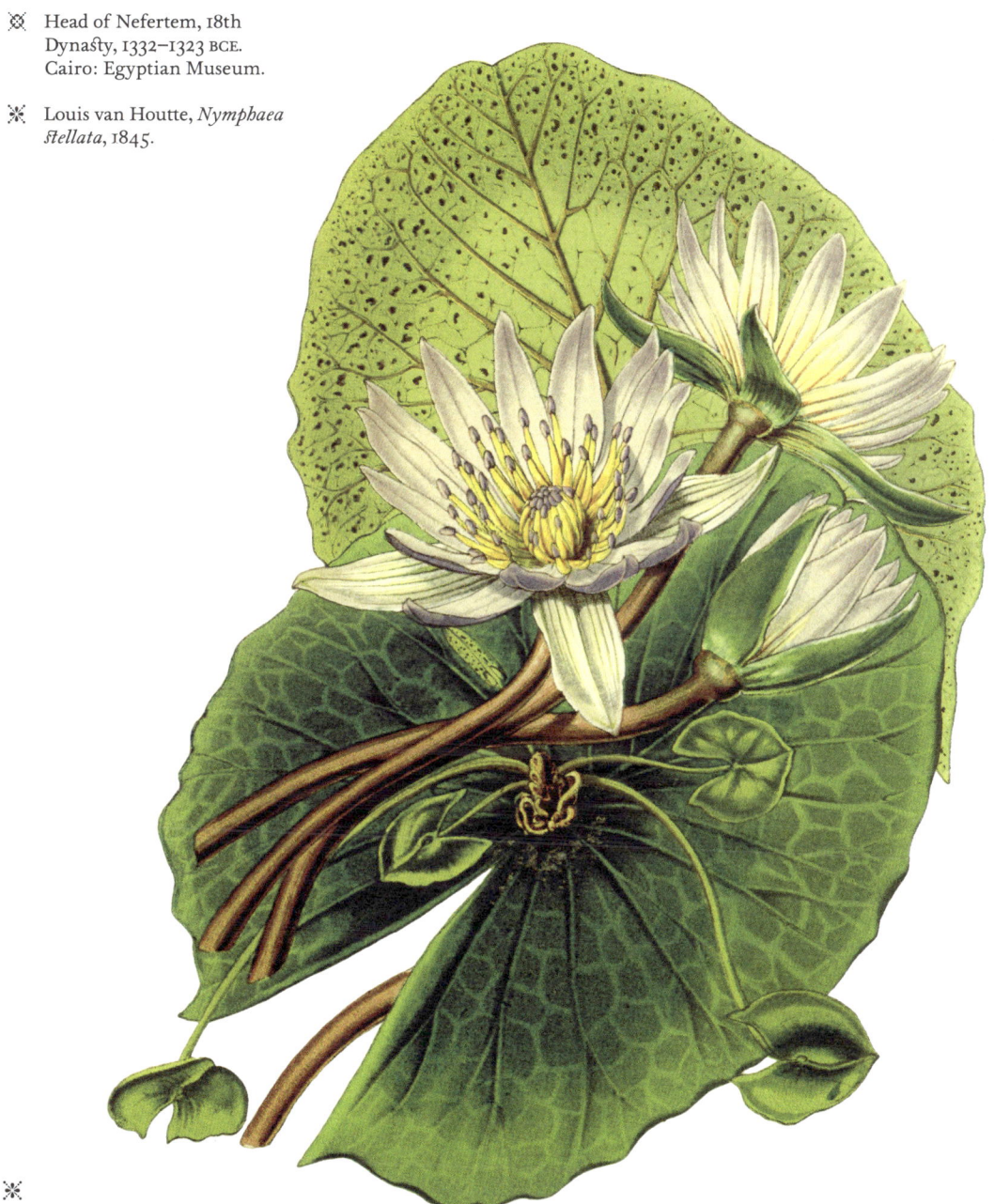

※

he purchased the house he had previously rented in Giverny, northern France, he began lavishing his attention on the garden, particularly the water-lily pond. To establish this, he diverted a local stream – causing problems with his neighbours, who also objected when he introduced water lilies imported from foreign sources. He spent the last three decades of his life painting approximately 250 images of them, ranging from small to mural-sized works.[13]

Giovanni Aloi looks at Monet's water lilies without 'disciplinary-specific filters'. He notes that Monet's love affair with water lilies began with the exhibition of hybrids raised by the botanist Joseph Bory Latour-Marliac at the 1889 World's Fair in Paris:

Open form and lack of detail free the represented body from many economic, social, and cultural implications – if there is a symbolic register to be found in these extremely open paintings, it is that the water lilies are interconnected with everything else around them: the sky, the water, the grass, the trees hanging over them, and the human perceiving them. There's an eco-continuity and interconnectedness at play in these paintings that is unprecedented in the history of representation.

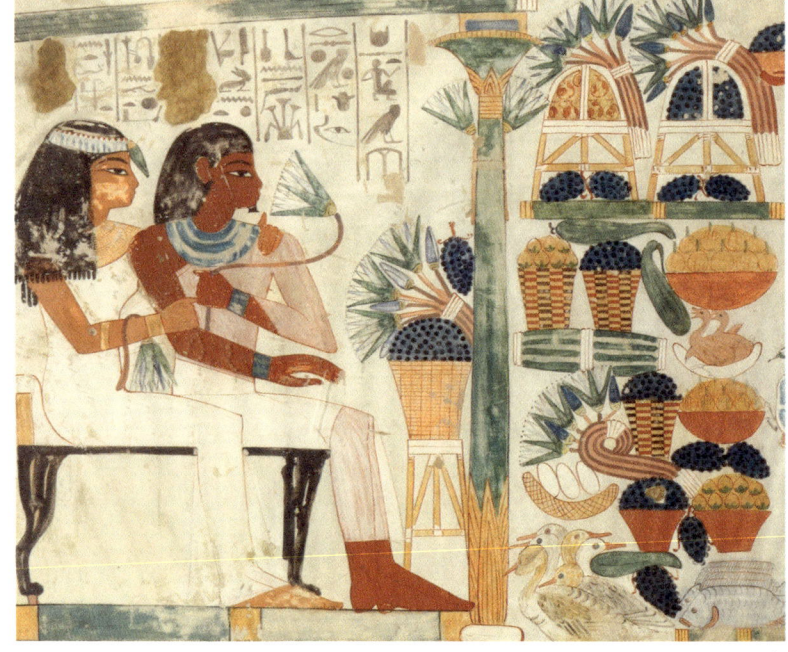

❖ Nakht and family fishing and fowling (detail), *c.* 1400–1370 BCE, tempera facsimile by Norman de Garis Davies and Lancelot Crane of image from the Tomb of Nakht, east wall, south side of offering chapel, 1908–10. New York: Metropolitan Museum of Art.

✳ Claude Monet, *Nympheas*, 1897–98, oil on canvas. Los Angeles, CA: Los Angeles County Museum of Art.

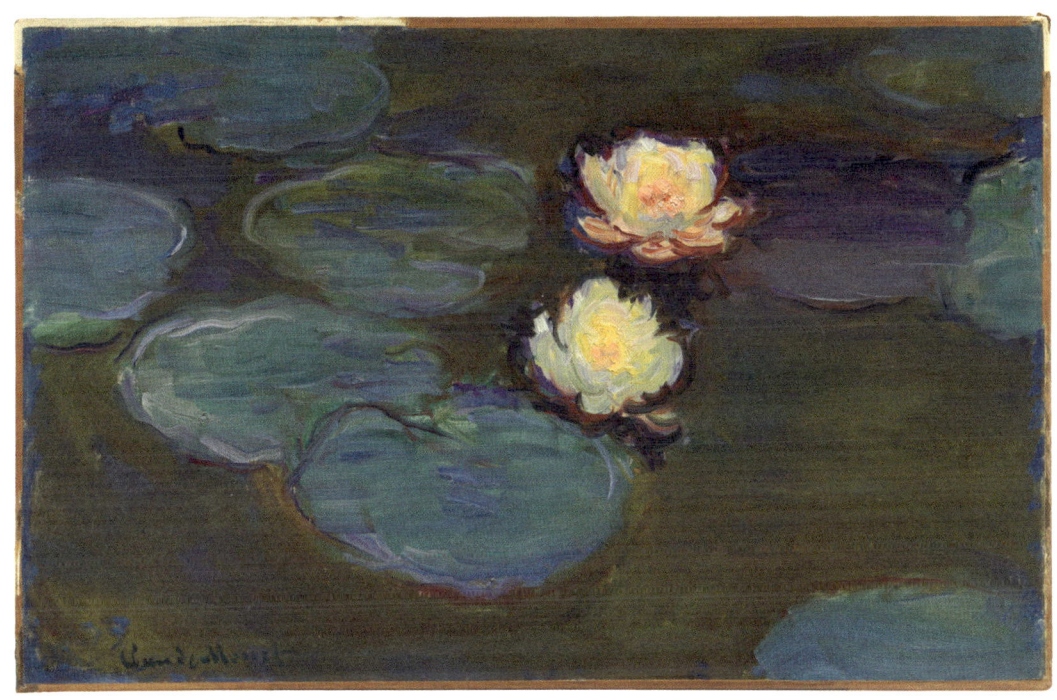

＊

Indeed, these paintings incorporate and go beyond the aims of Impressionism by capturing not only the fall of light and colour, but also the interconnectedness, eternal restlessness and movement of nature. Additionally, as embodiments of tranquillity and peace, they stand outside a modern world racked with troubles. Aloi also points out that Monet's water lilies resulted from selective breeding and hybridization, a fact that gives his paintings of them a 'more modern edge'.

OTHER EGYPTIAN LOTUS AND WATER-LILY IMAGES

- The hawk-headed god Horus holding a bouquet of lotus blossoms, *c.* 237 BCE. Edfu, Egypt: Temple of Horus.
- 'William' the hippo, 12th Dynasty, 1961–1878 BCE, faience. New York: Metropolitan Museum of Art.
- Banksy, *Forgive Us Our Trespassing*, 2011, acrylic, spray-paint and marker pens on wooden panels. Commissioned by the Museum of Contemporary Art, Los Angeles.

FAMILY Orchidaceae

Orchids comprise one of the two most numerous flowering plant families in the world, the other being the daisy family (Asteraceae). They evolved some 78–84 million years ago; a bee trapped in amber bearing orchid pollen has been dated to 15–20 million years ago. Orchids appear in almost every environment, even glaciers.

In the ancient world, the name orchid comes from the Greek word for testicle because of the shape of the flower's bulbs. The Romans claimed that orchids sprang forth from the semen of copulating satyrs, or from the scattered body parts of the ritually sacrificed Orchis, son of

a satyr. The orchids that appear on the Ara Pacis Augustae altar in Rome are the oldest orchid images in Western art.

Not surprisingly, given the flower's sexual associations, it was connected with potency and was a common ingredient in love potions. In the *Language of Flowers* it conveyed seduction.

In the second half of the nineteenth century 'Orchid Mania' took over, and orchids were valued above all other flowers. The demand led to ecological disaster, wiping out many orchids in the wild. Strangely, by the twentieth century it had become valued as a floral gift for dates and school proms, possibly because of their expense.

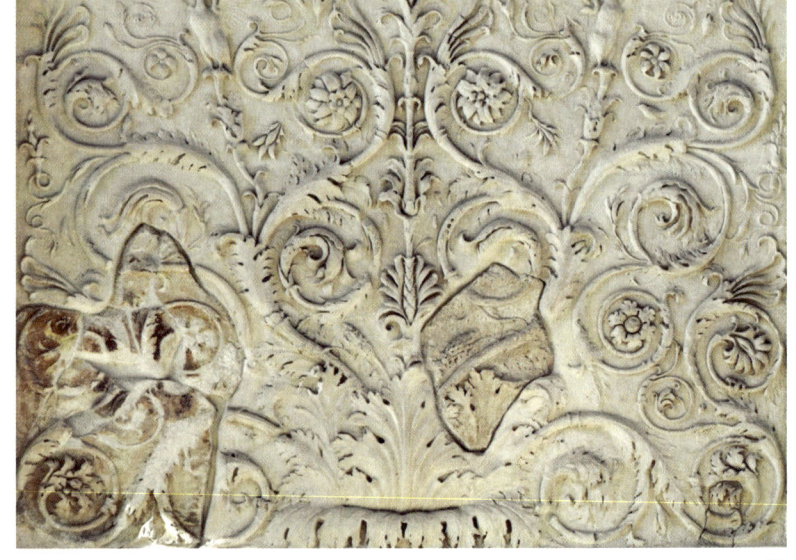

⊗ Orchids in low relief,
     9 BCE. Rome: Ara
     Pacis Augustae.

⊛ John Nugent Fitch,
     Cattleya velutina,
     1882–97.

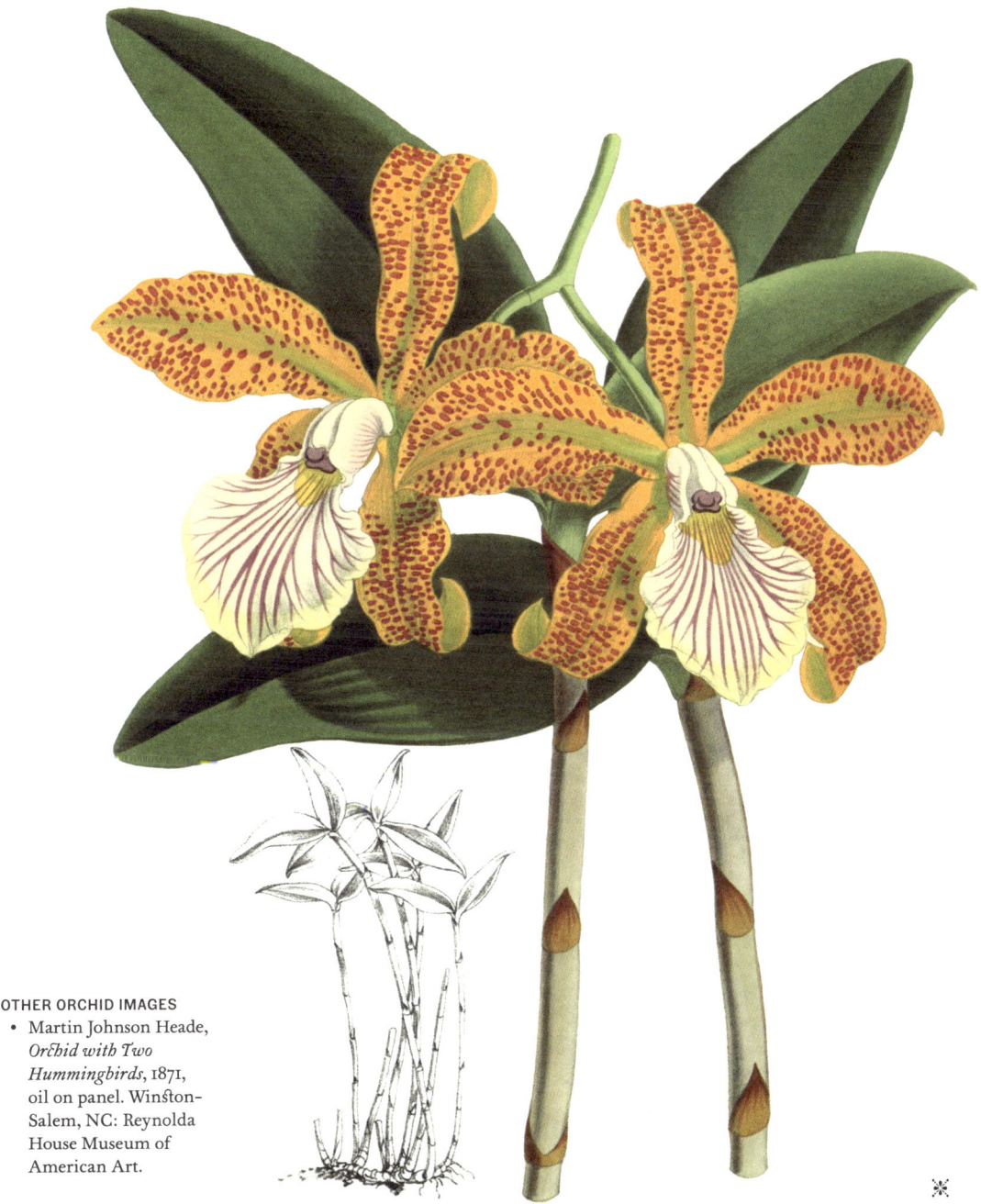

OTHER ORCHID IMAGES
* Martin Johnson Heade,
  *Orchid with Two
  Hummingbirds*, 1871,
  oil on panel. Winston-
  Salem, NC: Reynolda
  House Museum of
  American Art.

FAMILY Papaveraceae

Poppies are herbaceous annuals, biennials or short-lived perennials. They come in many colours and bloom in the spring and early summer in temperate zones.

Opium is produced from the seeds of the opium poppy (*Papaver somniferum*), but despite the drug's popularity, little is known of its ancient history. It originated in the Neolithic period, and the locations suggested vary across West Asia and Europe. Egyptian doctors used poppy seeds to relieve pain, and poppy images occur in both Greek and Assyrian art of the fifth millennium BCE. It is possible that the poppy symbolized sleep and death in ancient Egypt, since poppies were included in the floral collars from Tutankhamun's embalming cache.

The ancient Greek god of sleep, Hypnos, is usually depicted wearing a crown of poppies. Ovid describes the realm of sleep as a hidden cavern, with at one end a lush field of poppies and at the other herbs of drowsiness that night

gathers to sprinkle over the lands. The poppy was also linked with Morpheus, the god of dreams, and over time it became associated with death and eternal sleep. Poppies also figure in Virgil's *Georgics*, which tells how the Shades were placated by a gift of poppies. This later facilitated the fictional Dante's entry into Hades in search of Beatrice in the *Divine Comedy*.

Because of the flower's bright red colour, Christian doctrine took it as a symbol of Christ's Passion and blood, and it appears in some Crucifixion scenes. Wild poppies grow in wheatfields, thus conveying a Eucharistic connection.

The poppy in Rossetti's *Beata Beatrix* symbolizes death and grief, both Dante Alighieri's for his beloved Beatrice and Rossetti's

⊗   Roman sarcophagus with the myth of Selene and Endymion, early third century, marble. New York: Metropolitan Museum of Art.

⚘   *Papaver somniferum*, 1887.

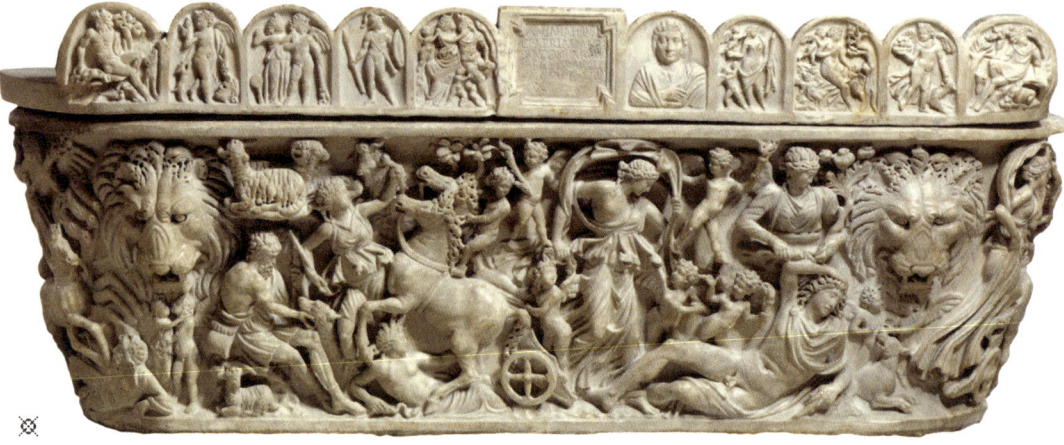

⊗

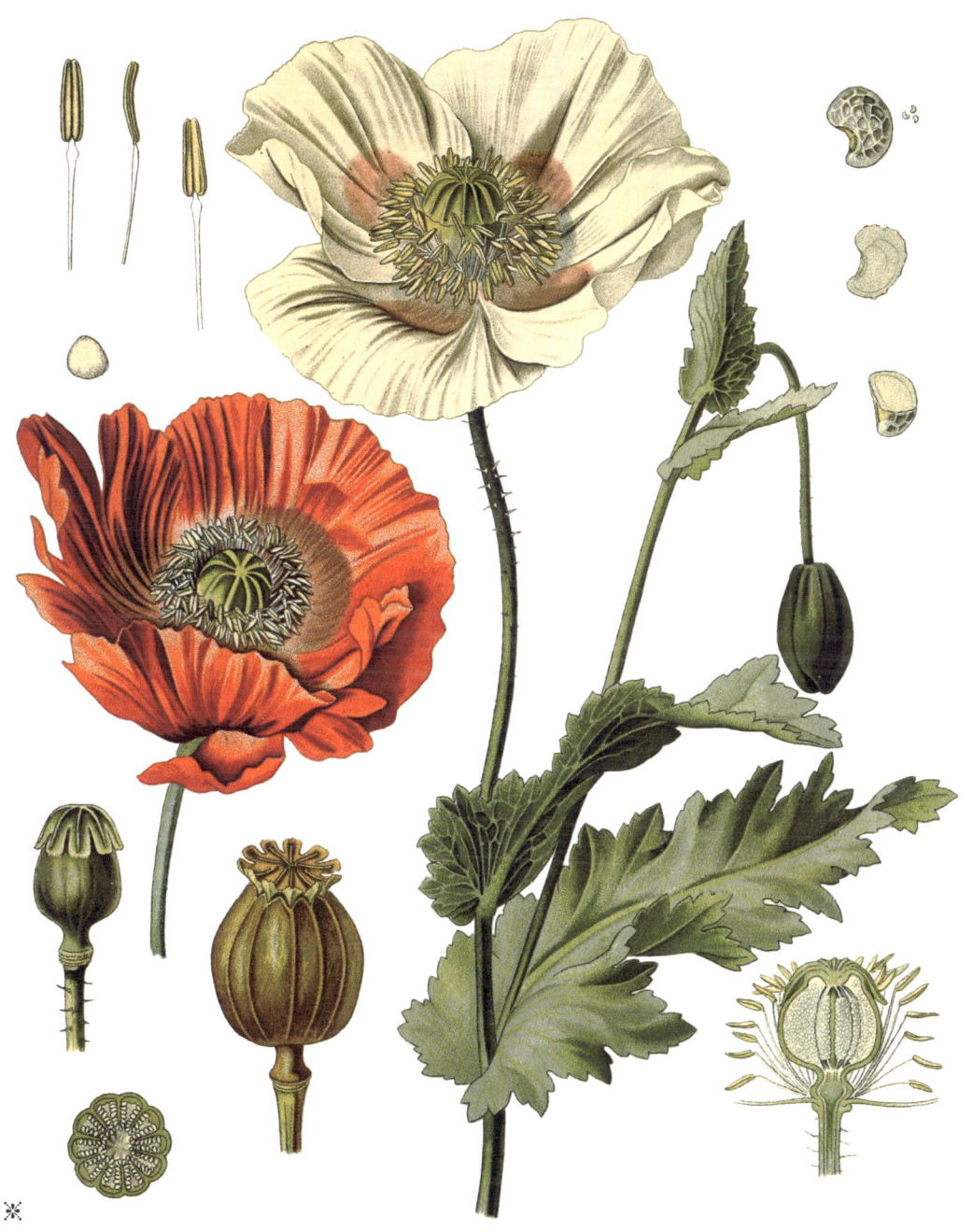

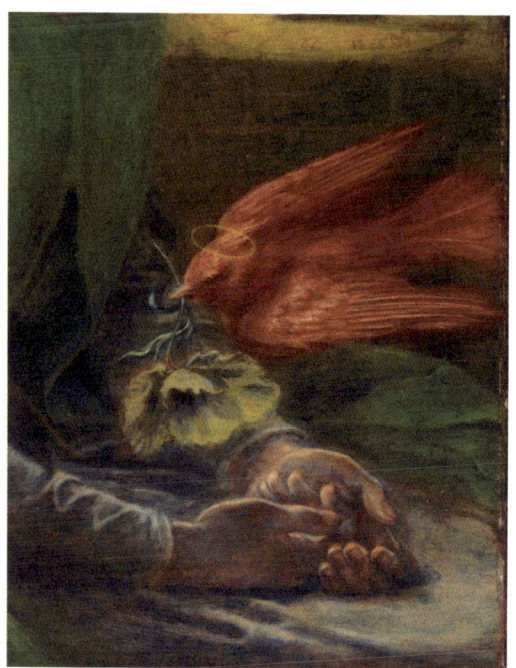

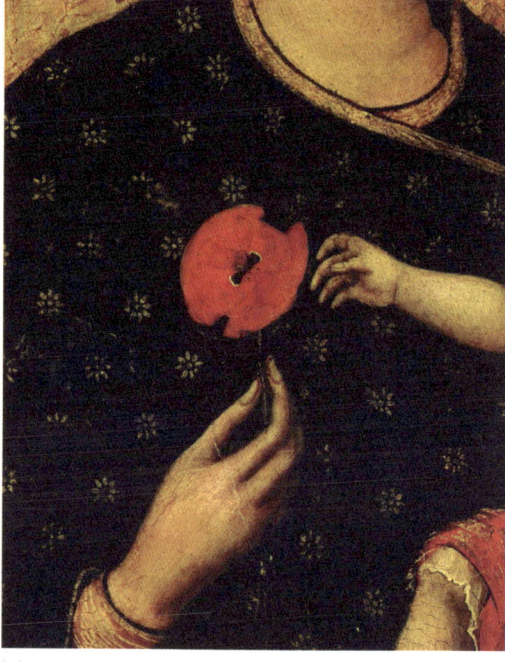

for the death of his wife, Elizabeth Siddal, the model for the image. Siddal died of an accidental overdose of laudanum, an opium tincture. A dove brings Beatrice a white poppy. The dove symbolizes the Holy Spirit, and the poppy signifies death; Rossetti additionally envisioned the bird as a messenger of love, and depicts Beatrice as if in a dream-like ecstasy, transformed, he writes in a letter in 1873, by 'sudden spiritual transfiguration'. The sundial shows the moment of her death, nine o'clock on 9 June 1290.

A Canadian doctor, John McCrae, noticing poppies growing amid the graves of First World War dead in the graveyard of Ypres, wrote a poem entitled 'In Flanders Fields' (1915). The poem led, in part, to the establishment of

Remembrance Sunday, on which the fallen of various conflicts are honoured by wearing red poppies.

In 2014, the contemporary artist Paul Cummins, with the set designer Tom Piper and volunteers, created 888,246 ceramic poppies, one for each British and colonial soldier who died during the First World War. It took several thousand volunteers to install the poppies in the moat of the Tower of London. The first poppy was planted on 28 July 2014 and the last on 11 November 2014, and the flowers were subsequently sold to recoup expenses and for charity.

⊗ Dante Gabriel Rossetti, *Beata Beatrix*
   (detail), *c.* 1864–70, oil on canvas.
   London: Tate.

※ Paolo Veneziano, *Madonna of the Poppy*
   (detail), *c.* 1325, oil on panel. Venice:
   San Pantalon.

❖ Paul Cummins and Tom Piper,
   Blood Swept Lands and Seas of Red,
   2014, ceramic poppies. Installation
   at the Tower of London.

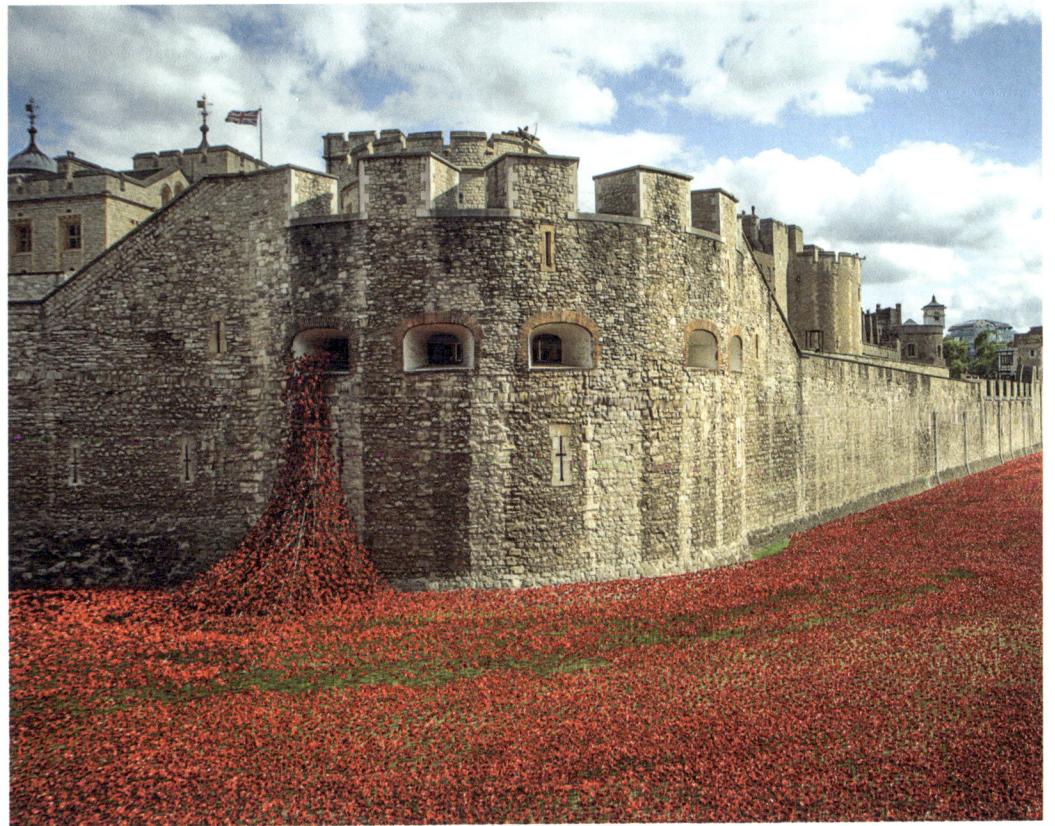

❖

FAMILY Passifloraceae

A fast-growing perennial climbing plant, the passionflower has large, intricate flowers and grows wild as well as in cultivated environments.

The passionflower is native to South and Central America and the southern United States. It was used traditionally as an anti-inflammatory and a calming herb, as well as being cultivated for food and drink.

Jesuit settlers in South America understood the flower as symbolic of the Passion of Christ, hence their name for it. Its radial filaments represent the Crown of Thorns; the three-pronged stigma indicates the three nails; the petals refer to the ten faithful Apostles; the five anthers represent Christ's five sacred wounds; and the central vertical element is the pillar to which he was tied before being beaten.

Charles Allston Collins depicted many flowers in his painting *Convent Thoughts*.

A nun stands in a *hortus conclusus* holding what appears to be an illuminated book of hours; she studies a passionflower (representing Christ's Passion and Crucifixion), and there are forget-me-nots (remembrance), lilies (the Madonna's purity) and honeysuckle (constancy). Water lilies (purity of heart) float in the pond at her feet. Collins was not a member of the Pre-Raphaelite Brotherhood, although the painting clearly reflects the style of that group of painters, and the frame, ornamented with lilies, was created by John Everett Millais, who was a member. Debra Mancoff suggests that the painting shows

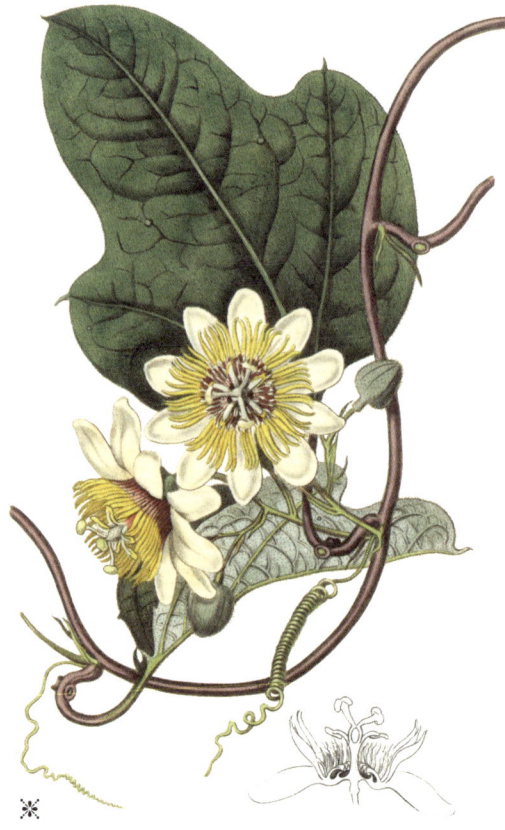

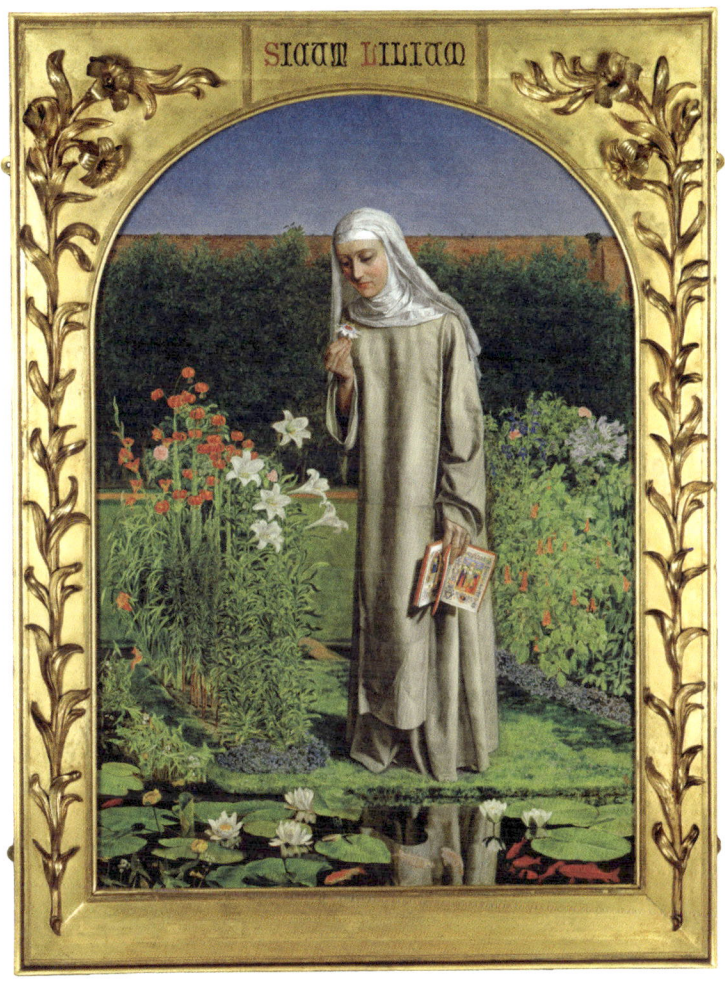

* John Everett Millais, *Isabella* (detail), 1849, oil on canvas. Liverpool: Walker Art Gallery.

* *Passiflora holosericea*, 1815.

* Charles Allston Collins, *Convent Thoughts*, 1851, oil on canvas. Oxford: Ashmolean Museum.

the novice learning lessons of piety from nature and symbolic flowers, and 'confirm[ing] her commitment to her calling'.

Passionflowers are found carved into gravestones as well as in church decor. In the US, several cemeteries feature gravestones by Louis Comfort Tiffany, many of them adorned with flowers; in Green-Wood Cemetery, Brooklyn,

passionflowers emerge from the granite of the so-called Child's cross (1913). Tiffany, who died in 1933, is buried nearby.

OTHER PASSIONFLOWER IMAGES
* Tiffany Studios, Child's cross, *c.* 1913. Brooklyn, New York: Green-Wood Cemetery (National Historic Landmark).

FAMILY Rosaceae

The rose is a perennial flowering plant; the term is also used to refer to the flower itself. Most species are native to Asia, with smaller numbers being native to Europe, North America and northwestern Africa.

Roses are among the most valued and favoured plants in human history and, along with the lotus, the most symbolically significant. Symbolism varies by colour and by the number of petals. The blue rose, for instance, symbolizes impossibility.

Based on fossil evidence, the rose is around 35 million years old and has been cultivated for some 5,000 years in China. Consisting of a large number of species, it is one of the most widespread, cultivated and hybridized plants in history. It is not surprising, then, that the rose is one of the most frequently represented flowers in art, nor that it is associated with some of the most important figures in world culture. In most world cultures, roses were linked with goddesses – Aphrodite, Cybele, Psyche, the Three Graces, Flora and Eve – the Virgin Mary, who was believed to have been conceived while her mother, Anne, was smelling a rose, and female saints. Roses symbolize love, beauty, youth, war and politics.

In ancient Greece, the rose was sacred to Athena and Aphrodite. An origin story tells of Chloris, the goddess of flowers, who, when walking in the woods, found the dead body of a beautiful nymph. Wishing to give the nymph new life by transforming her into a flower, she called upon the other gods to help, and each contributed something to the creation of the rose. According to another myth, the rose was white until Aphrodite's lover Adonis was mortally wounded. The goddess, running to

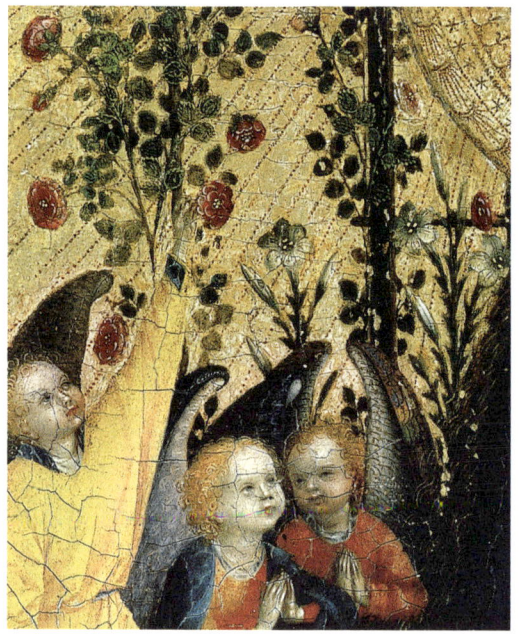

him, pricked herself on a thorn, and her blood coloured the rose red.

The term *sub rosa* originated from the practice of attaching a rose to the ceiling of council chambers to swear all present to secrecy. In Rome, the rose was associated with death, and Rosalia, a celebration of roses, was linked with the cult of the dead.

In Christian art, the white rose signifies the Virgin's purity. She is called 'the rose without thorns', since she was untouched by Original Sin (it is said that roses grew thorns only after the Fall). The red rose symbolizes Christ's blood and his Passion, and the Christ Child sometimes holds a rose as he is depicted sitting in his mother's lap. The enthroned Virgin and Child often appear in a rose arbour or a *hortus conclusus* filled with roses. The German artist

Stefan Lochner loved plants and includes many in the work pictured here; not just red and white roses, but also lilies, strawberries and possibly a tiny apple.

Roses are a favourite flower in heraldic emblems and coats of arms, signifying nobility, sacrifice, triumph, war (the Romans believed the war god Mars was born from a rose), generosity and discretion. Another connection of the rose with war stems from the English Wars of the Roses (1455–85), fought between the houses of Lancaster (the red rose) and York (the white rose). The conflict ended with the establishment of the Tudor monarchy, the emblem of which includes both a white and a red rose, symbolizing peace.

The use of strings of beads as a mnemonic for prayer originated in antiquity and is found in several Asian religions. The Catholic version, the rosary, served as a meditation on the mysteries of the Virgin Mary. Rosaries have long been made of compressed rose petals. The word itself comes from the Latin *rosarium*, meaning a garden or garland of roses and, by association, a garden or bouquet of prayers.

OTHER ROSE IMAGES
- Pieter Vanderlyn, attrib., *Young Lady with a Rose*, 1732, oil on canvas. New York: Metropolitan Museum of Art.
- Dante Gabriel Rossetti, *The Beloved* ('*The Bride*'), 1865–66, oil on canvas. London: Tate.
- Herman de Vries, *Rosa Damascena*, 1984, dried flowers. Installation at 56th Venice Biennale.

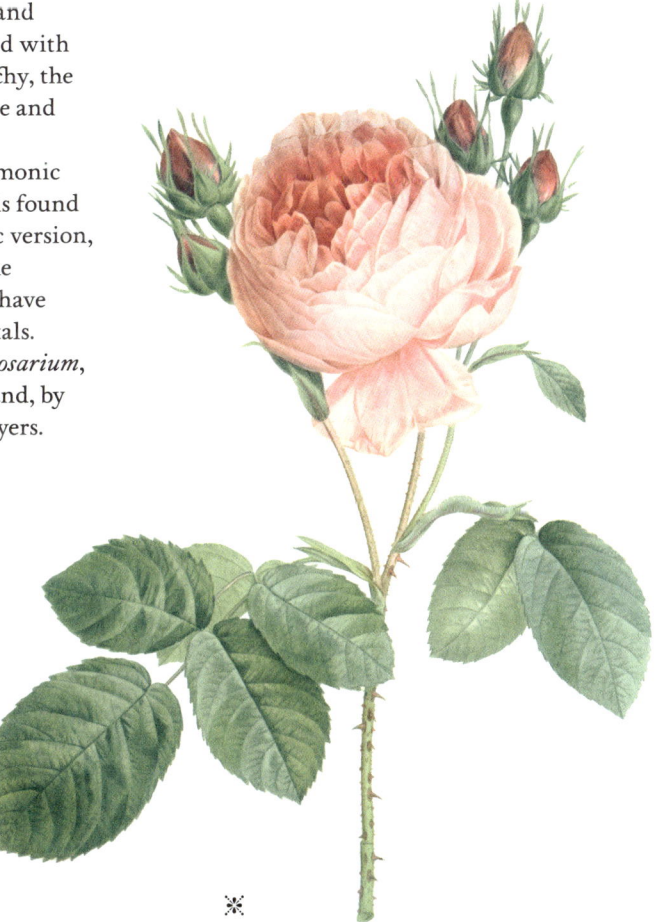

※ Stefan Lochner, *Madonna of the Rose Bower* (detail), *c.* 1440–42, oil on panel. Cologne: Wallraf-Richartz Museum.

※ Pierre-Joseph Redouté, *Rosa centifolia*, 1817–24.

FAMILY Liliaceae

Tulips grew wild in West Asia and the Mediterranean, and were being cultivated in Istanbul by the mid-eleventh century. They are perennials that grow from bulbs and flourish in temperate climates.

In Persia, the flower – believed to have sprung from the tears of a disappointed lover – stood for perfect love. The petals are edible, but there is some question as to the toxicity of the bulbs.

The herbalist Conrad Gesner first described and illustrated the tulip for Europeans in 1561. It was brought to Vienna by an Austrian politician in the second half of the sixteenth century and soon spread throughout Europe. It reached the height of popularity in Holland, bringing about 'tulipomania', which resulted in great fortunes for some and financial ruin for others, until the entire market collapsed in 1657.

Dutch still lifes often included tulips alongside many other plants. Since many of these paintings depicted flowers that bloomed at different times, they have been called 'fantasy bouquets'. The Denver Art Museum website points out that such paintings were a 'cheap' alternative to buying real flowers;

they lasted longer and could still be enjoyed in the winter. The flower also appears in *vanitas* paintings, where tulips in various stages of life, from fresh to wilted, signify the fragility and brevity of existence.

The presence of so many plant and flower species in Van Oosterwyck's sumptuous painting, opposite, relate to the fragility and brevity of life. The striped tulip on the left – a beautiful symbol of worldly greed and ephemeral wealth – seems to confront the sunflower (pp. 114–17), the ultimate symbol of the sun and the divine.

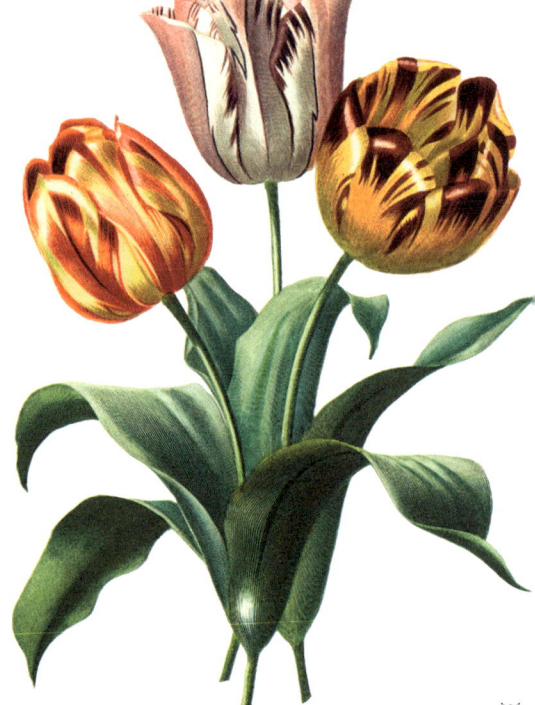

⊗ Charles Dessalines D'Orbigny, *Tulipa gesneriana*, 1849.

❋ Maria van Oosterwyck, *Bouquet of Flowers in a Vase*, c. 1670s, oil on canvas. Denver, CO: Denver Art Museum.

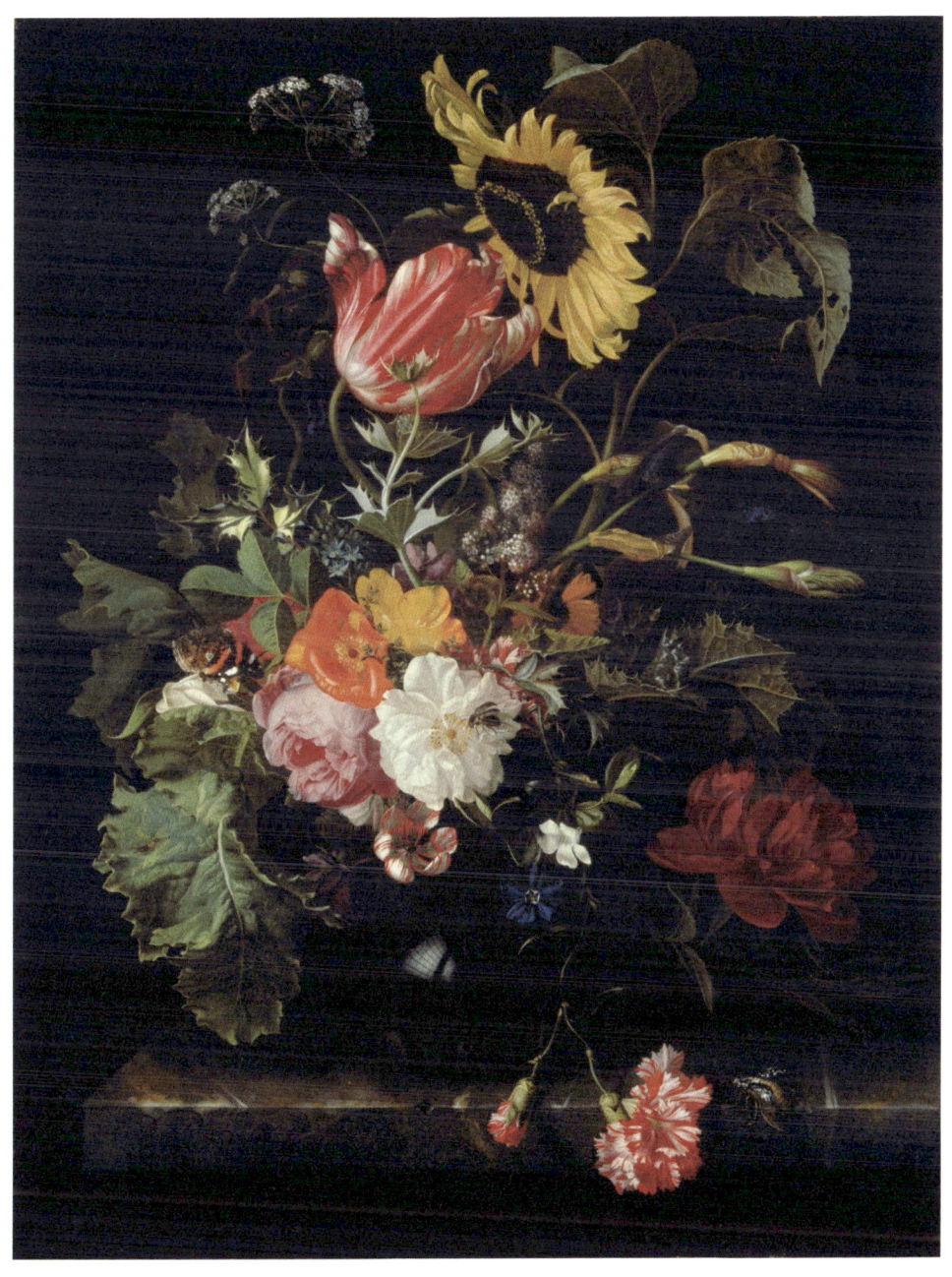

FAMILY Violaceae

The names 'violet' and 'viola' usually refer to small-flowered annuals or perennials, including wild species. Most are found in the temperate northern hemisphere.

Violets serve as garden plants, for decorative culinary use and for medicinal purposes (as antioxidants, and for insomnia and skin conditions). *Viola odorata* is also used as a source of scent in the perfume industry.

The violet symbolizes modesty and humility. It also stands for the balance between heaven and earth, sense and spirit, passion and reason, and love and wisdom. Clarity of mind and deliberate action are qualities associated with this flower.

In mythology, the violet is said to have grown from the blood of the Phrygian god of vegetation, Attis, who incited the jealousy of Cybele; she, driven mad by him, struck him so that he self-mutilated and died. Cybele, regaining her sanity, begged Zeus to keep Attis's corpse from decaying, resulting in the bloom. Another story involving jealousy is told of Zeus, who loved Io and, to avoid Hera's wrath, turned the mortal into a white heifer. When the heifer shed tears on the grass, Zeus transformed her tears into violets, more suited to her delicate

OTHER VIOLET IMAGES
• Pauline Powell Burns, *Violets*, *c.* 1890, oil on cardboard. Washington, DC: Smithsonian National Museum of African American History and Culture.

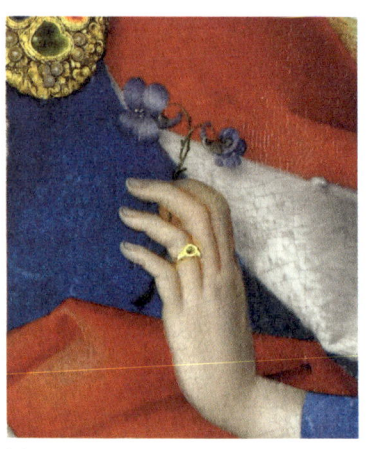

✳

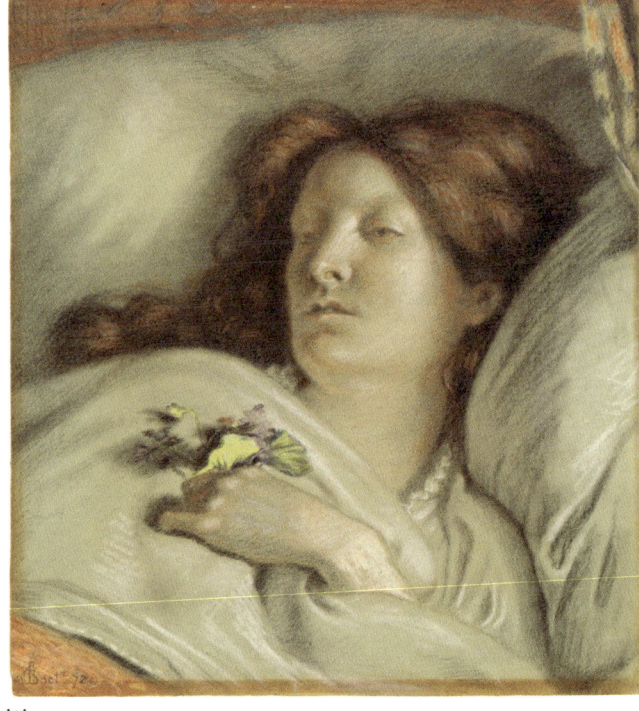

✳

taste. Because of violets' association with incorruptibility, the Romans decorated graves with the flower on *dies violaris*, violet day.

The flower's core symbolism led to its association with the Virgin Mary, as well as Christ in his humble human form. The flower appears in paintings of the Madonna and Child, in Adoration scenes and, although rarely, at the foot of the Cross. In medieval art Christ sometimes wears a purple robe, the colour of the violet, symbolizing both his humble humanity and the acceptance of divinity.

※ Stefan Lochner, *Virgin with the Violet* (detail), *c.* 1450, oil and tempera on wood. Cologne: Kolumba Museum.

※ Ford Madox Brown, *The Convalescent (A Portrait of the Artist's Wife)*, 1872, pastel on paper. New York: Metropolitan Museum of Art.

✤ Jacques Le Moyne de Morgues, Violets, *c.* 1575.

FAMILY Violaceae

The pansy is derived from the hybridization of *Viola tricolor* and other wild violets, and the words pansy, violet and viola are sometimes used interchangeably.

Pansies have two petals pointing up and three to the sides and downwards, although *V. melanium* has four upward-pointing petals. The flower's name comes from the French *pensée*, the feminine form of the verb *penser*, to think or ponder something. The French word was derived from the Latin *pensare* or *pendare*: to consider, to take everything into

consideration; by extension, to remember. Early herbals, referring to the 'heartsease pansy', touted the plant's curative powers, especially for painful disorders of the heart. Wild varieties of the plant are still often called heartsease.

The flower, which can also symbolize humility and love, has been a favourite of writers and poets, including Shakespeare, Ben Jonson, Edmund Spenser, Wordsworth, Nathaniel Hawthorne and D. H. Lawrence. In *A Midsummer Night's Dream*, the fairy king Oberon tells how the once white pansy turned 'purple with love's wound' when shot by Cupid's arrow. Older names for the flower linked it with wanton affection.

Pansies were a popular subject in nineteenth-century art. In Van Gogh's painting, opposite, a basket of pansies rests on a small stool shaped like a tambourine. Such stools and tables graced the Café du Tambourin in Paris, which Van Gogh frequented and where he exhibited his own art and a selection from his collection of Japanese prints. He had a brief relationship with the proprietor, Agostina Segatori, so the flowers may signify his affection and indicate that she was in his thoughts.

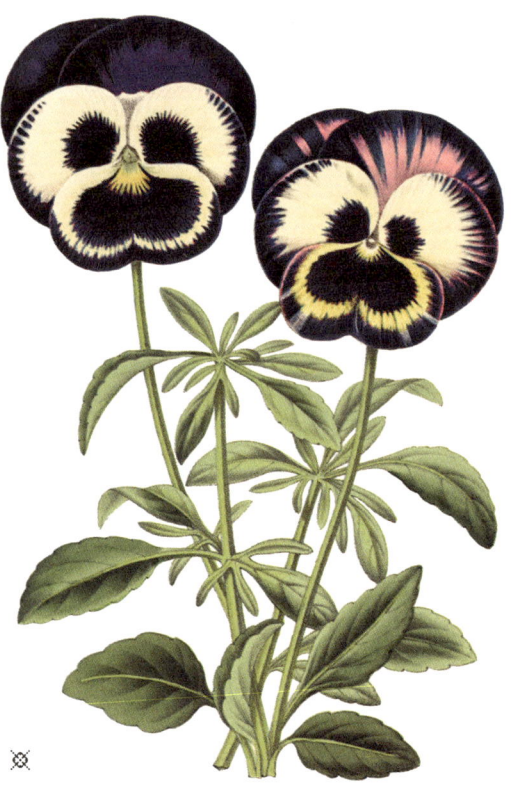

OTHER PANSY IMAGES
- Henri Fantin-Latour, *Still Life with Pansies*, 1874, oil on canvas. New York: Metropolitan Museum of Art.
- Georgia O'Keeffe, *Black Pansy and Forget-Me-Nots*, 1926, oil on canvas. Brooklyn, NY: Brooklyn Museum.
- Joe Brainard, *Three Pansies*, 1967, watercolour on paper. New York: Metropolitan Museum of Art.

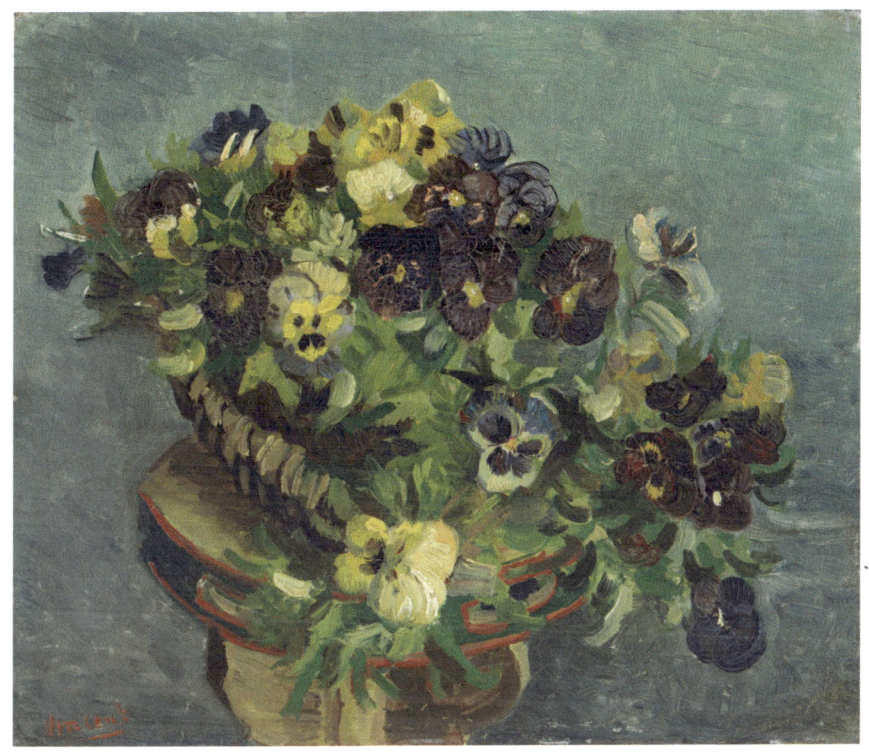

⊗ J. Vandamme, *Viola tricolor*
(1. *Gloire de Bellevue*; 2. *Reine
des Panachées*), 1854.

※ Vincent van Gogh, *Basket
of Pansies*, 1887, oil on canvas.
Amsterdam: Van Gogh
Museum.

❖ British Queen Elizabeth I's
embroidered bookbinding,
created at the age of eleven for
her stepmother Katherine Parr,
1544. Oxford: Bodleian Library.

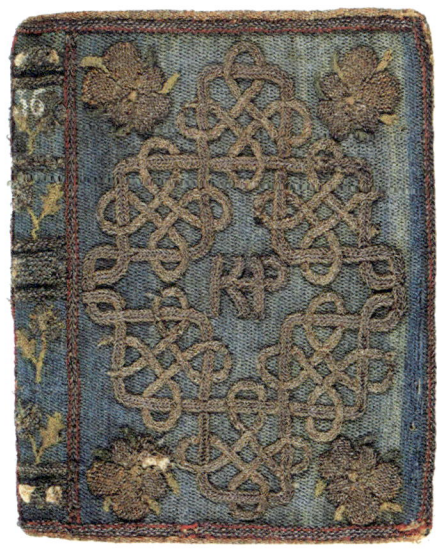

❖

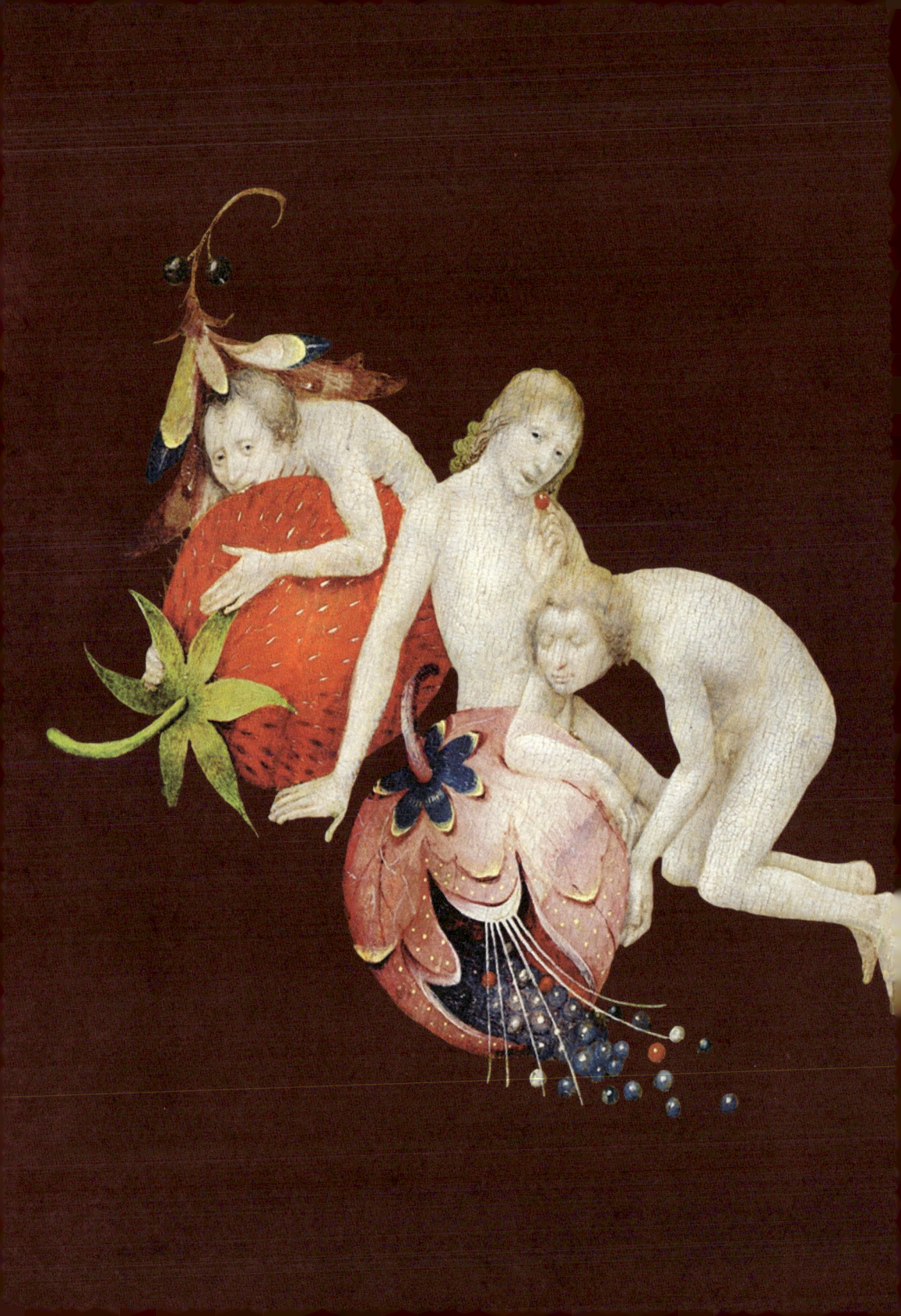

FRUIT,
VEGETABLES
& SEASONINGS

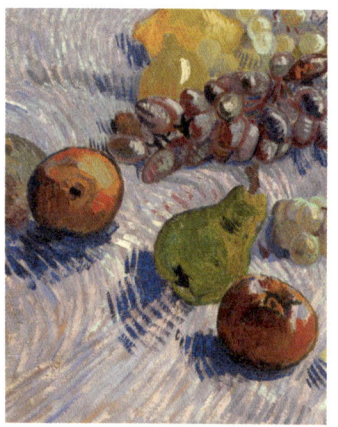

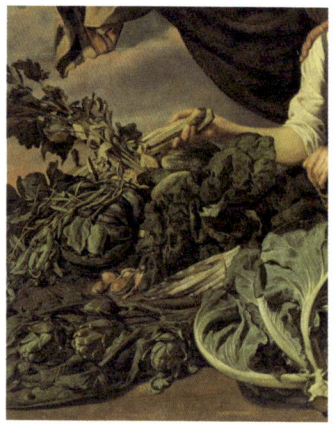

Like flowers, fruit and vegetables often appear in art because of their beauty and sensuous appeal. This aspect of their symbolism is most evident in still lifes.

The earliest depictions of fruit are found in ancient Egypt, where paintings of food appear on tomb walls. The Egyptians believed the images became tangible in the afterlife and thus provided sustenance for the dead.

Mosaic *emblemata* representing fruit and other food adorned the walls of wealthy Romans, signifying the hospitality that would be extended to guests. The images also presented a visual celebration of the seasons.

Later depictions of fresh fruit convey fertility, vitality, youth and abundance. In a state of decay, they signify transience and mortality. This can be seen in Cézanne's *Still Life with Skull*, in which a prominent piece of decaying fruit has dark cavities that mimic the skull's eye and nasal holes.

Vegetables are classified in various ways. The most useful system divides them by the part of the plant that is consumed: bulbs (such as onion), flowers (broccoli), leaves (lettuce), stalks (celery), tubers (potato) and roots (carrot).

When it comes to seasonings, the words 'spice' and 'herb' are often used interchangeably, but they are actually two different things, made from different parts of plants and processed in different ways. Spices are generally more highly flavoured because they come from parts of the plant that contain essential oils. Even so, the distinction between herb and spice is not always clear, and some plants provide both herbs and spices. Coriander (*Coriandrum sativum*) produces a seed that is ground to serve as a spice. The leaves that provide the herb are also known as coriander (cilantro in the United States). Dillweed, mustard and myrrh's seeds also all provide spices, while their leaves are used as herbs.

⊗ Vincent van Gogh, *Grapes, Lemons, Pears, and Apples* (detail), 1887, oil on canvas. Chicago, IL: Art Institute of Chicago.

✳ Adriaen van Utrecht and Theodoor Rombouts, *An amorous couple with lettuce, artichokes, peas and other vegetables, with a squirrel* (detail), *c.* 1630, oil on canvas. Private collection.

❖ Paul Cézanne, *Nature morte au crâne* (*Still Life with Skull*), 1890–93, oil on canvas. Philadelphia, PA: Barnes Foundation.

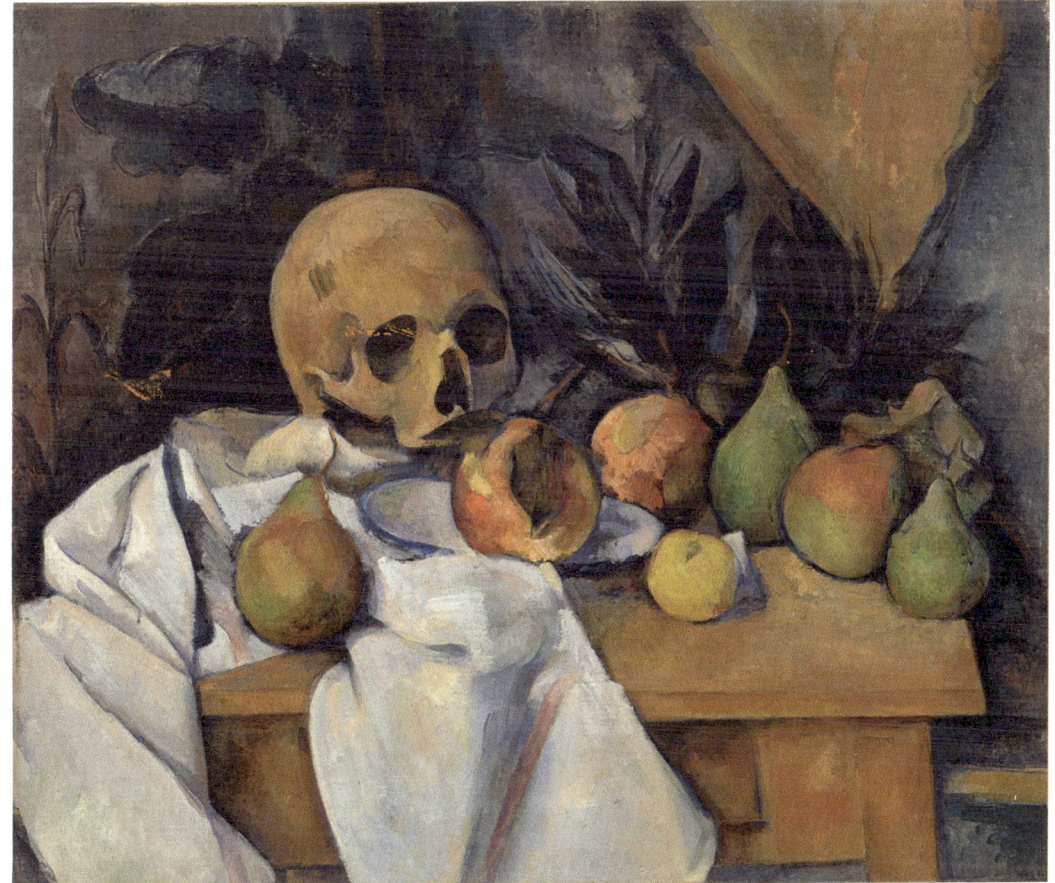

❖

FAMILY Amaryllidaceae

The onion, like garlic, spring onions, shallots, chives and leeks, is a member of the amaryllis family, and is categorized as a vegetable. It has been cultivated for 7,000 years.

Onions were known to the ancient Egyptians, and Homer mentioned them in his writings. The Romans substituted onions and fish for human heads in sacrificial ceremonies to Jupiter. Onions figure in folk medicine and have been viewed as an aphrodisiac. In Europe, they have also carried the reputation of being food for poor people, due in part to the fact that they are cheap to buy or grow.

Giuseppe Arcimboldo arranged fruit and vegetables to form human heads. Aside from their immediate whimsicality, the artist's works show his keen appreciation and knowledge of plants; *Spring* (1573) contains some eighty identifiable plants. *The Vegetable Gardener* features an onion cheek. The bountiful vegetables have sexual connotations, like the fleshy mushrooms that make up the lips; the onion has been compared to a woman's breast, the tangle of roots positioned where a nipple would be. Inverted, the image becomes a bowl

with vegetables in it. Arcimboldo's work has been interpreted as criticizing the wealthy elite's behaviour and their frivolous approach to nature. Aloi suggests that the images served as an 'attention-seeking device' that expressed anthropocentric concerns.

Broadly speaking, onions, because they cause eye irritation, are regarded as useful but superficially unpleasant – suggestive of life's woes. With its many concentric rings, the onion sometimes also serves as a metaphor for mystery and life.

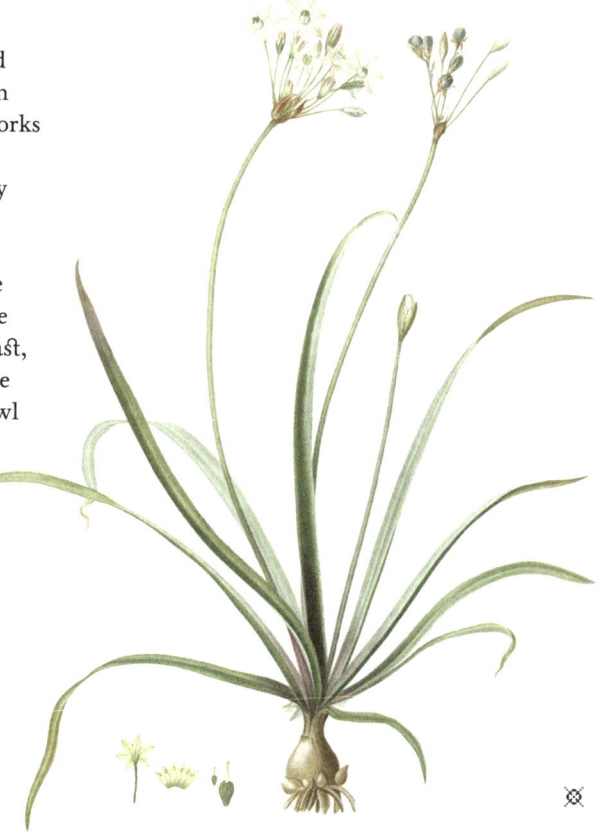

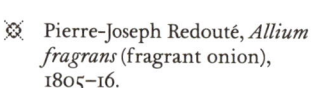 Pierre-Joseph Redouté, *Allium fragrans* (fragrant onion), 1805–16.

✳ Giuseppe Arcimboldo, *L'Ortolano* (*The Vegetable Gardener*), 1587–90, oil on panel. Cremona, Italy: Museo Civico Ala Ponzone.

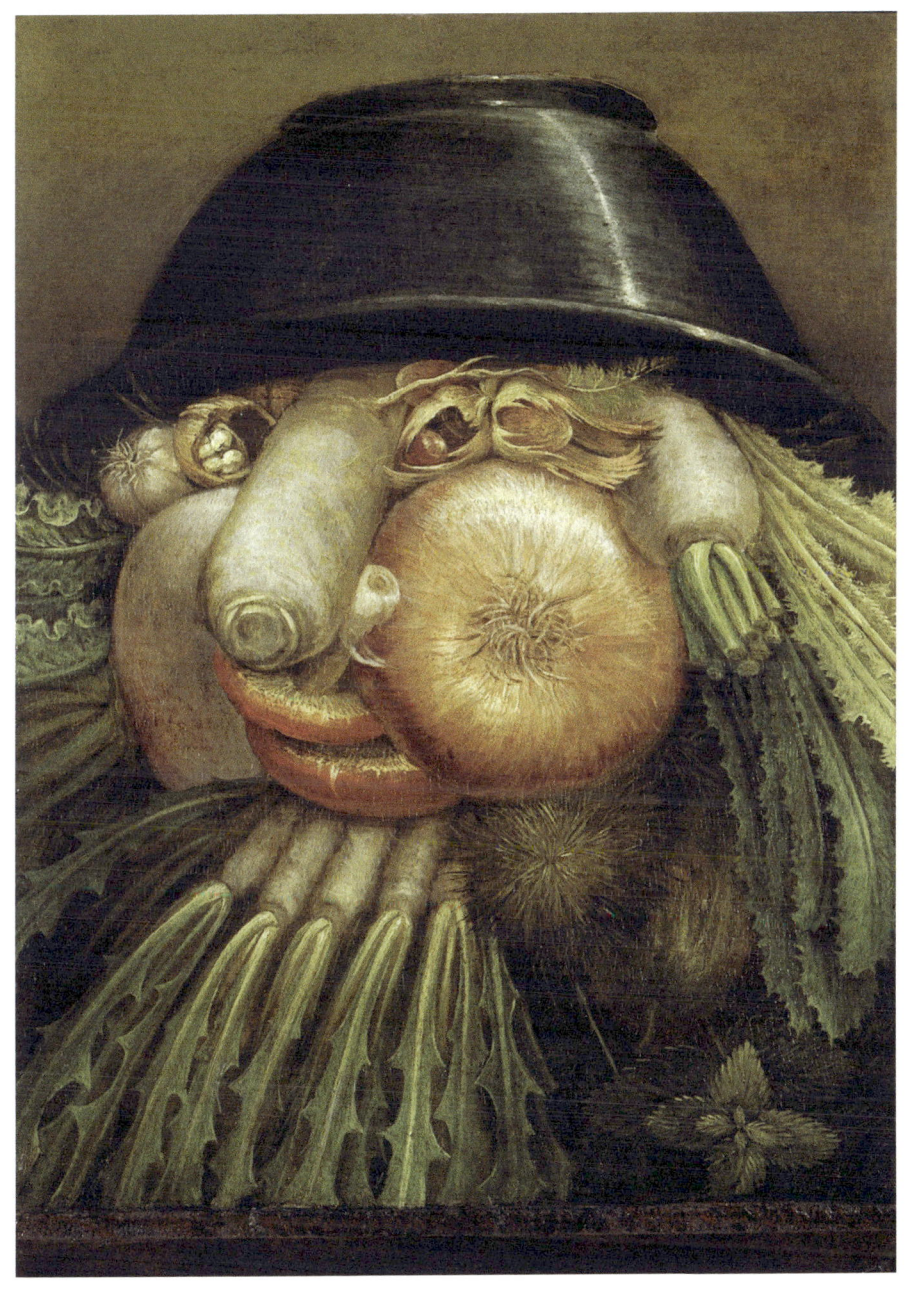

※

FAMILY Bromeliaceae

A tropical plant with edible fruit, the pineapple originated in South America, where it was an important source of food and medicine to the Tupinambá people in the Amazon region. It is thought to have symbolized hospitality and fertility.

First cultivated in Europe in the seventeenth century, it became a symbol of wealth and luxury. Though they are not native to the islands, Hawai'i is now the most active producer of pineapples.

As a symbol of hospitality, sculpted and painted pineapples ornament architecture and interiors. In colonial Virginia, sailors placed a pineapple on the gatepost to announce their safe return home. The 'Dunmore Pineapple' summerhouse in Scotland, built for the 4th Earl of Dunmore, last Governor of Virginia, announced his return home somewhat more dramatically. Acquired by the Scottish National Trust in the 1970s, it is now a holiday guest house.

⊗ Sir William Chambers, 'The Dunmore Pineapple', after 1777. Dunmore, Scotland.

✳ Georg Ehret, *Ananas aculeatus* (pineapple), *c.* 1742.

✳ Terracotta *pinax* (votive tablet) showing Persephone and Hades enthroned, 500–450 BCE. Reggio Calabria, Italy: Museo Nazionale

✳ Cesare Ubertini, Wild celery (*Apium graveolens L.*), 1772–93.

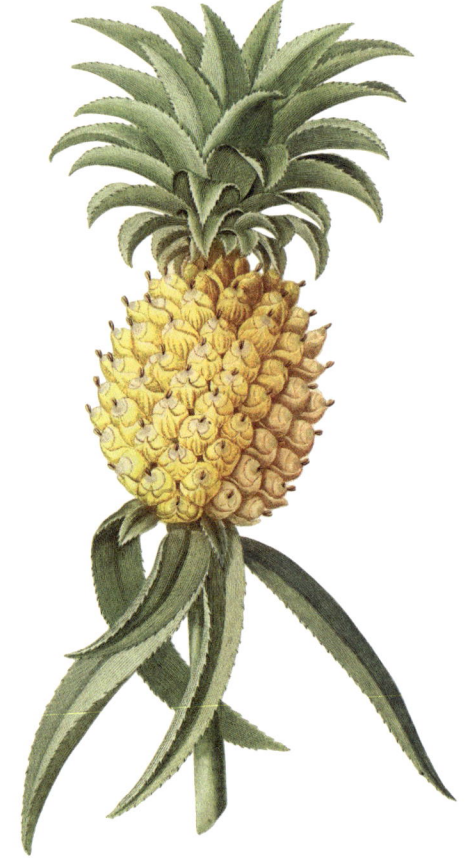

⊗

✳

FAMILY Apiaceae

Celery was first cultivated in the ancient Mediterranean. It is a diuretic and has been known as an aphrodisiac, an effect that some researchers attribute to androsterone, a steroid that acts as a pheromone.

Celery leaves were found in garlands in the tomb of Tutankhamun, and the Cairo Agricultural Museum owns a wreath with celery leaves from the grave of a Theban nobleman. The Greeks and Romans also garlanded their dead with celery, and victorious athletes were crowned with the plant, possibly reflecting its links with bravery and victory.

Celery had conflicting meanings in classical Greece. It plays an aphrodisiac role in Homer's *Odyssey*, growing on the isle of the nymph Calypso and possibly inflaming her lust for Odysseus. It was linked to the lusty god Silenus, but was also believed to have sprouted from

the blood of an Underworld deity, and thus associated with death. In this votive tablet from the Sanctuary of Persephone at Locri in southern Italy, Hades, god of the Underworld, holds a plant that has been identified as celery.

In the eighteenth century, Mme de Pompadour served King Louis XV celery soup for its aphrodisiac properties; it was also reputedly consumed by the adventurer Giacomo Casanova. Celery became an irresistible luxury in nineteenth-century Europe and North America, and in 1912 it was served in first class on the Titanic.

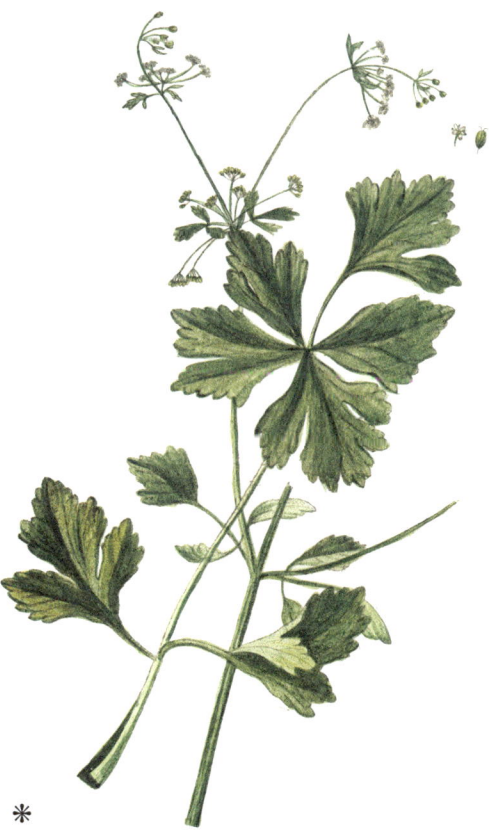

FAMILY Brassicaceae

The cabbage is generally regarded as a humble vegetable and a symbol of the everyday and ordinary. Formerly a member of the mustard family, it now has its own family. Brassicaceae contains many plants that have been domesticated and altered, including broccoli, Brussels sprouts, cauliflower and kale, as well as ornamentals like candytuft and honesty.

Stanley Spencer's *The Dustman* shows a family retrieving items from the rubbish. An overripe cabbage occupies the centre of the canvas. Spencer celebrates ordinariness, writing: 'All the signs and tokens of home life, such as cabbage leaves and teapot, which I have so much loved that I have had them resurrected from the dustbin because they are reminders of home life and peace'.

The Romans apparently used cabbage to alleviate hangovers. They placed its leaves on wounds and mixed it with honey to salve the eyes. In the sixteenth and seventeenth centuries the cabbage symbolized female sexuality and hidden beauty.

Leonora Carrington created a portrait of a red cabbage, of which she wrote: 'it...screams when dragged out of the earth and plunged into boiling water or grease – forgive us, cabbage...the cabbage is still the alchemical rose'. For Carrington, the 'ordinary' cabbage was extraordinary, sentient and mystical. Her cabbage is a Chinese cabbage (*Brassica rapa*), with a tightly packed head inside the graceful leaves.

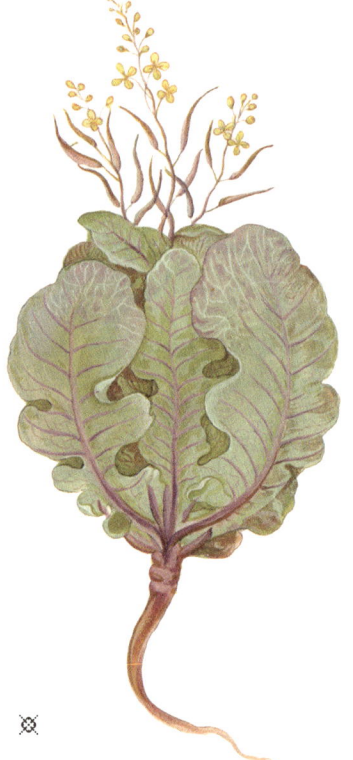

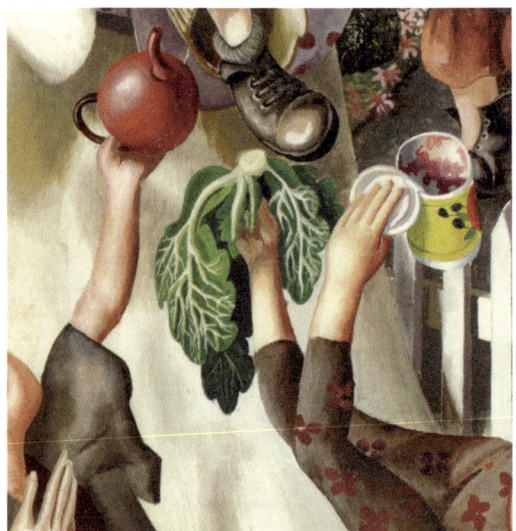

⊗ Anselmus Boëtius de Boodt, Cabbage (*Brassica oleracea*), 1596–1610.

✻ Stanley Spencer, *The Dustman* or *The Lovers* (detail), 1934, oil on canvas. Newcastle upon Tyne: Laing Art Gallery.

❖ Leonora Carrington, *Cabbage*, 1987, acrylic on canvas. Private collection.

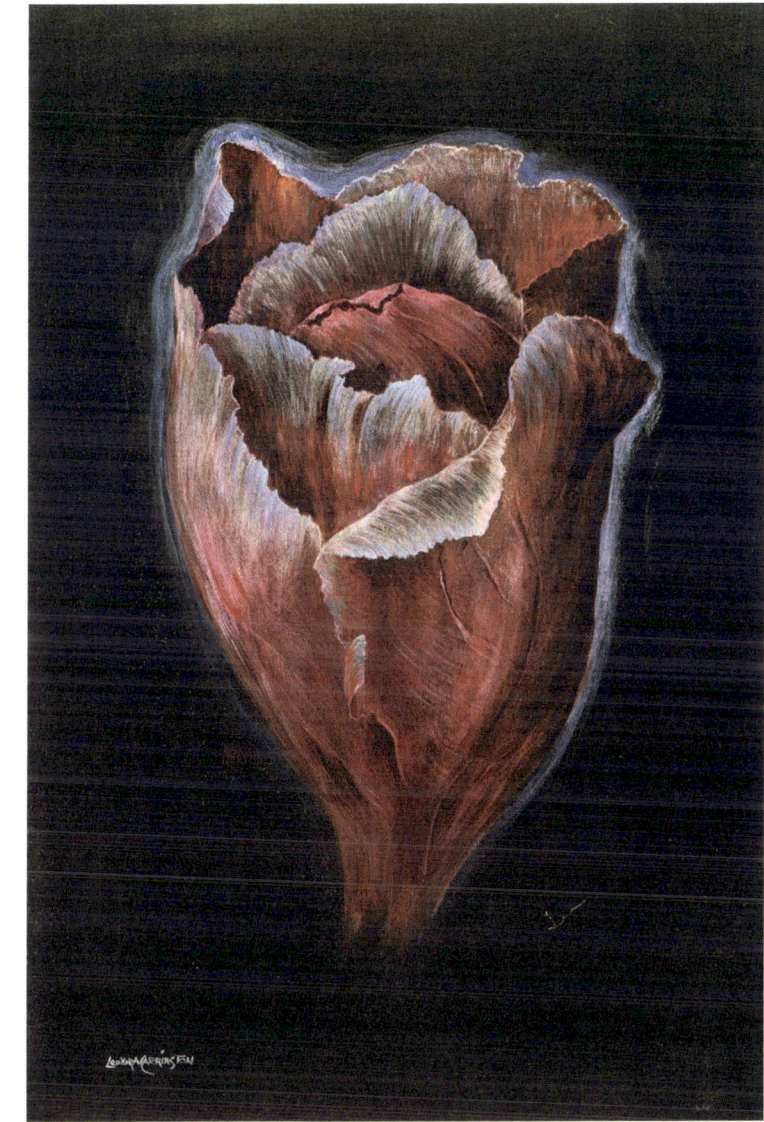

OTHER CABBAGE IMAGES
- Pieter Aertsen, *Market Scene*, 1569, oil on wood. Stockholm: Hallwylska Museet.
- Nathaniel Bacon, *Cookmaid with Still Life of Vegetables and Fruit*, 1620–26, oil on canvas. London: Tate.

❖

FAMILY Cucurbitaceae

Gourds include the fruit of flowering plants such as pumpkins, cucumbers, squash, courgettes and various melons.

In the context of art, the hollow shells of bottle gourds (also known as calabash, *Lagenaria siceraria*, and found on archaeological sites dating from as early as 13,000 BCE) served not only as musical instruments but also as decorated containers.

In some translations of 1 Kings 6 and 7, sacred gourds adorned the interior of the Temple of Solomon and the basin that held water for ritual use. They represent fertility, new life and the sunrise. The solar symbolism stems from the gourd's mature shape, which swells like God's emblem, the sun, as it rises in the morning.

Albrecht Dürer's *St Jerome in His Study* depicts the contemplative ideal of the Christian scholar. One odd feature is the huge gourd hanging from the ceiling. St Jerome mistranslated the Latin word *cucurbita* in the story of the prophet Jonah as a type of ivy, and debate ensued in letters he exchanged with St Augustine in 403–4 CE. By placing the gourd in the saint's study, Dürer refers to this erudite discussion.

The gourd symbolizes both transience and salvation, since God provided Jonah with a gourd as a shelter from the elements, and then sent a worm to destroy it. In Dürer's image, the hanging gourd relates to the skull on the windowsill, serving as a *memento mori*, a reminder of the brevity of life and, one could assume, philological discussions.

The many seeds of the gourd link it to fertility, but because it grows and withers quickly, it also symbolizes the brevity and fragility of life. In modern times, all over the world, gourds are carved, painted and inlaid for decorative purposes.

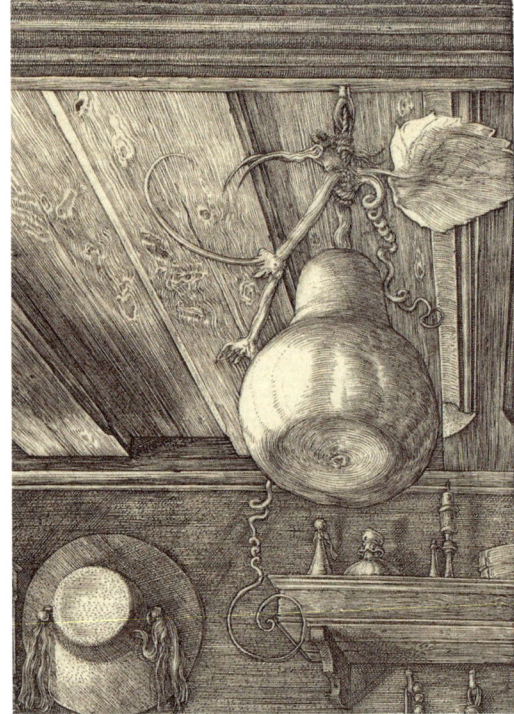

⊗ Albrecht Dürer, *St Jerome in His Study* (detail), 1514, engraving.

✳ Elizabeth Twining, *Cucurbitaceae*, The Gourd Tribe, 1849–55.

⊗

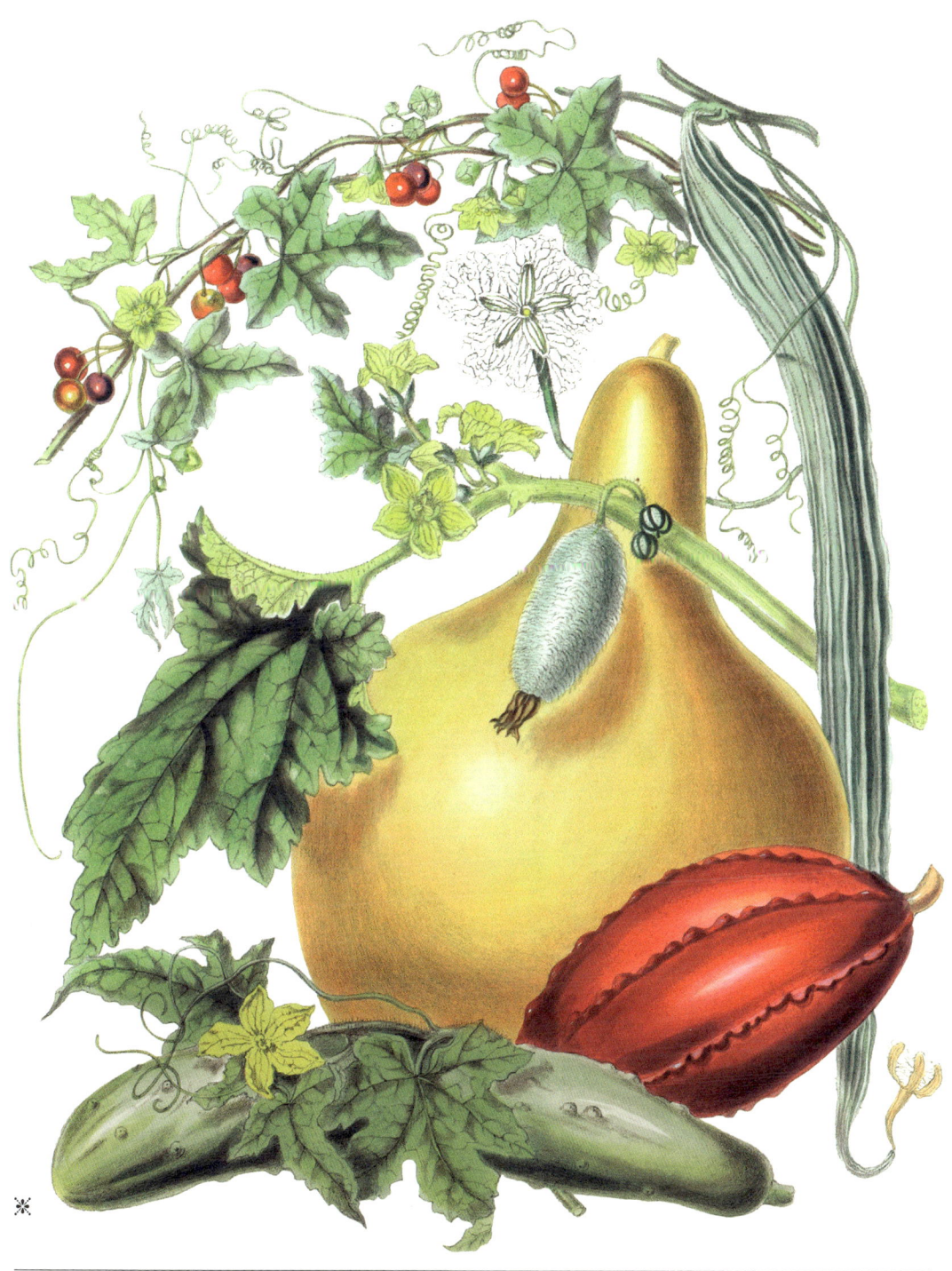

FAMILY Cucurbitaceae

The pumpkin often symbolizes prosperity, growth and abundance. It is native to the Americas and had reached Europe by the sixteenth century, first appearing in the Villa Farnesina, Rome, in festoons painted between 1515 and 1518.

Raphael supervised work in the Villa Farnesina's Loggia of Psyche; the fruit and vegetables there allude to love and sexuality. Giovanni Martini da Udine painted the bountiful festoons with more than 170 species, identified by Caneva and Janick as including a huge variety of cucurbits. Agostino Chigi, a banker and the original owner of the villa, was also pivotal in cultivating plants from the Americas in Europe.

The pumpkin is now linked most closely with Halloween, as jack-o'-lanterns that illuminate porches and shine from windows, traditionally a form of protection. The journalist Blane Bachelor writes in *National Geographic* that

⊗ Giovanni Martini da Udine, fruits, flowers and vegetables (detail), including *Cucurbita maxima* (pumpkin), 1515–81, fresco. Rome: Villa Farnesina, Loggia of Cupid and Psyche.

⁜ Cesare Ubertini, *Cucurbita aspera Pyriformis* (Pumpkin), 1772–93.

❋ Yayoi Kusama, *Pumpkin*, 1994. Naoshima: Benesse Art Site.

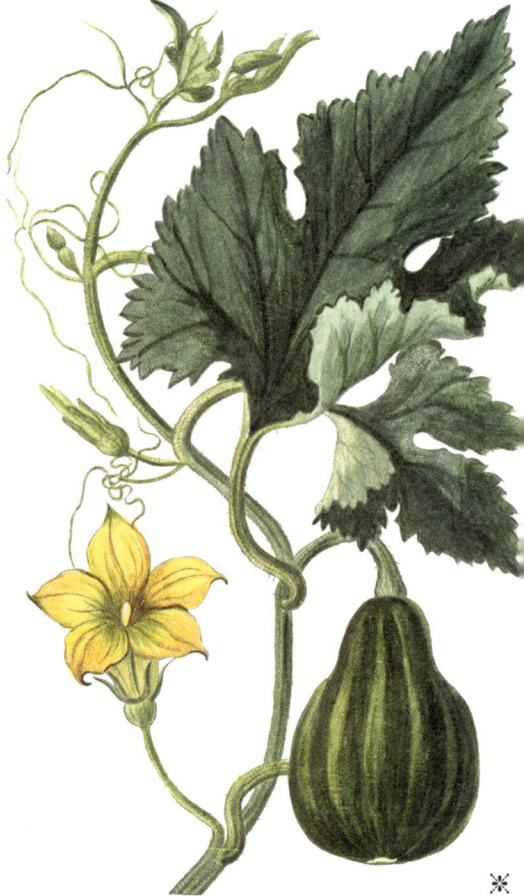

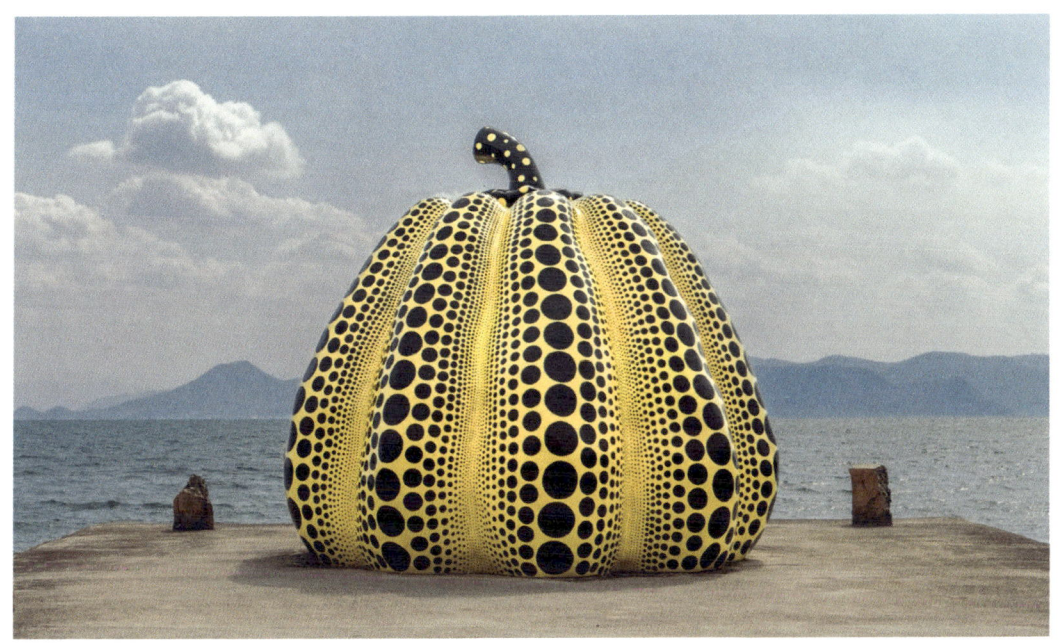

representations of the human head relate to the Celtic festival of Samhain, originally celebrated on 1 November. To ward off wandering spirits, the Celts carved scary faces into root vegetables such as beetroot, turnips and potatoes. The jack-o'-lantern is said to have been introduced to the United States by Irish immigrants, who quickly replaced the root vegetables of their homeland with pumpkins. A carved pumpkin appeared on the cover of *Harper's Weekly* in 1867, but perhaps the most memorable comes from Washington Irving's short story 'The Legend of Sleepy Hollow' (1820). And, of course, Cinderella's coach was a pumpkin. The demand for pumpkins today explains why in the US in 2022, more than a billion pounds were harvested. Professional pumpkin carvers work all year round. Some duplicate masterpieces of art, while others, such as Ray Villafane, depict squashed and manipulated heads.

Yayoi Kusama claims that, the first time she ever saw one as a child, the pumpkins on her family's seed farm spoke to her. The rotund forms she first created while in her teens brought her poetic peace, and symbolized her childhood, life and fertility. She says, 'I love pumpkins because of their humorous form, warm feeling and human-like quality and form. My desire to create works of pumpkins... continues. I have enthusiasm as if I were still a child'. Her pumpkins still speak to her, and have made her one of Japan's most important contemporary artists.

OTHER PUMPKIN IMAGES
- Disney Enterprises, *Cinderella*, 1950.
- Arthur Rackham, 'The Headless Horseman', from Washington Irving's 'The Legend of Sleepy Hollow', 1928.

FAMILY Asteraceae

The globe artichoke (also known as the French artichoke or green artichoke) is a variety of thistle that is cultivated as food.

The edible part of the vegetable consists of the leaves and central 'choke' before the flowers bloom. Artichokes can also be made into a herbal tea and the Italian liqueur Cynar, and artichoke leaf powder is being investigated for medicinal use to reduce cholesterol.

The ancient Greeks and Romans consumed artichokes, even though Pliny referred to them as monstrosities of nature. The thyrsus, a staff held by Dionysus and his maenads, was formerly said to be topped with a pine cone – but lately it has been re-identified as an artichoke.

After visiting Strawberry Hill, the former home of Horace Walpole, in west London in 2017, Caroline Murray wrote:

The artichoke (Cynara cardunculus var. scolymus) has to be one of the vegetables least likely to have been discovered to be edible – what desperate early inhabitant of the Mediterranean area first took the trouble to wrestle one into submission and find that this particular giant thistle was concealing something rather delicious under all the sharp points and choking bits?

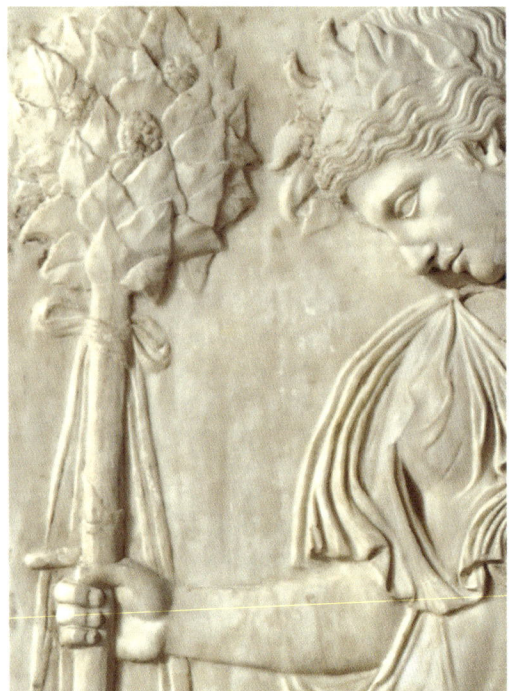

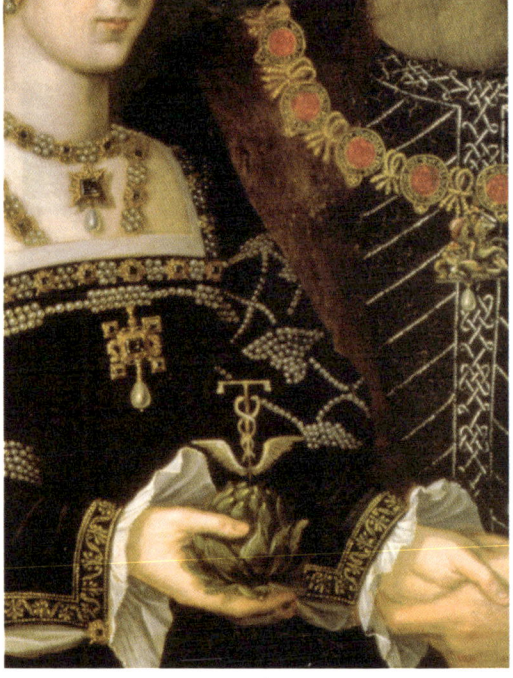

Murray also writes about the plant's contradictory meanings: sadness, hope for a prosperous future, disappointment, and – since it has a heart – love and devotion. This latter symbolism may be at work in the so-called *Bedford Double Portrait*, of which four versions exist. Mary Tudor and Charles Brandon, Duke of Suffolk, appear hand in hand. Mary's brother Henry VIII wished to cement political alliances by marrying her to the much older Louis XII of France, first by proxy and later in reality, but Louis died abruptly eighty-two days after the wedding, possibly thanks to his enthusiastic reception of the beautiful Mary. After a great deal of intrigue, Mary and Brandon returned to England and were married. The artichoke in Mary's hand has been compared to a royal orb and may relate to her brief stint as queen of France, but it is more likely to signify the love she felt for Brandon.

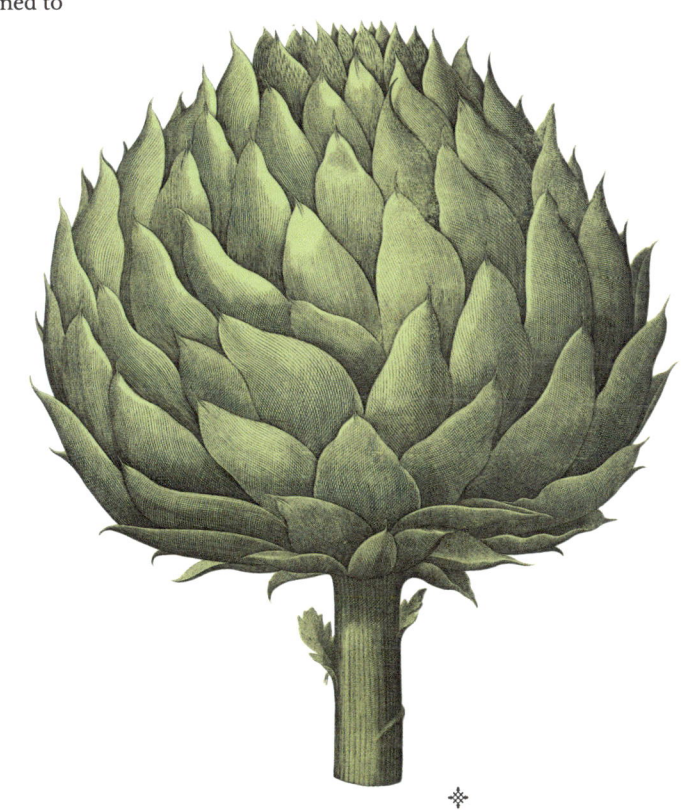

⊗ Dancing maenad holding a thyrsus (detail), Roman copy after fifth-century BCE Greek original, attributed to Callimachus. Madrid: Museo del Prado.

✳ British School, *Mary Tudor and Charles Brandon, 1st Duke of Suffolk* (detail), after 1515, oil on canvas. Cambridge, UK: Anglesey Abbey.

✣ Basilius Besler, *Fructus artischochi* (artichoke), 1613.

FAMILY Apiaceae

Carrots are associated with health, abundance and fertility, in part because, like other elongated, cylindrical fruit and vegetables, they are vaguely phallic.

The wild carrot probably originated in Persia, and evidence of its presence in Europe dates from as early as 3000 BCE. Heirloom carrots come in many colours; the characteristic orange developed from selective breeding in the seventeenth century. The bright orange colour comes from the concentration of beta-carotenes (sadly, despite all tales to the contrary, it doesn't improve vision). Carrots are also a good source of vitamins K and B6.

Along with myriad fruit and other vegetables, carrots appear in many images from the sixteenth century onwards, among them Dutch market and kitchen paintings. One of the more entertaining European images is by an unknown French artist and depicts a fantastic women's headpiece. This whimsical arrangement possibly stemmed from the earlier practice of lacing headdresses with carrot foliage as a substitute for feathers. Outrageously tall headdresses, apparently a craze begun by Queen Marie Antoinette of France in the late eighteenth century, incorporated faux materials of all sorts; caricatures of the period show servants following women with tools to keep their headdresses from tipping backwards. In addition to the carrots large and small in the illustrated headdress, lettuce and possibly *haricots verts* (green beans) appear.

The Surrealist René Magritte often played with plants in his art, creating hybrid images, mysterious forests and realistic bottles. The

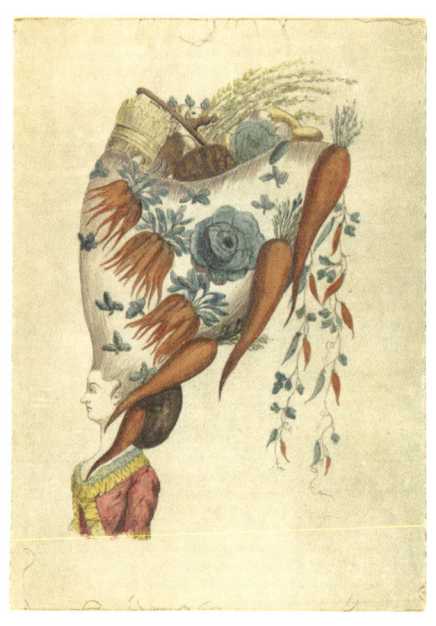

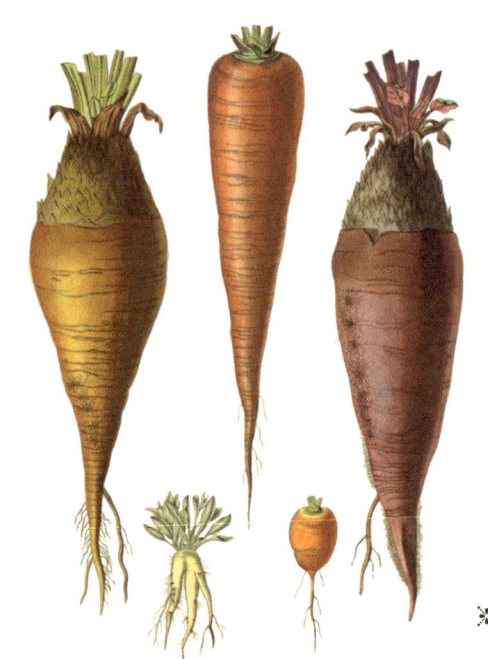

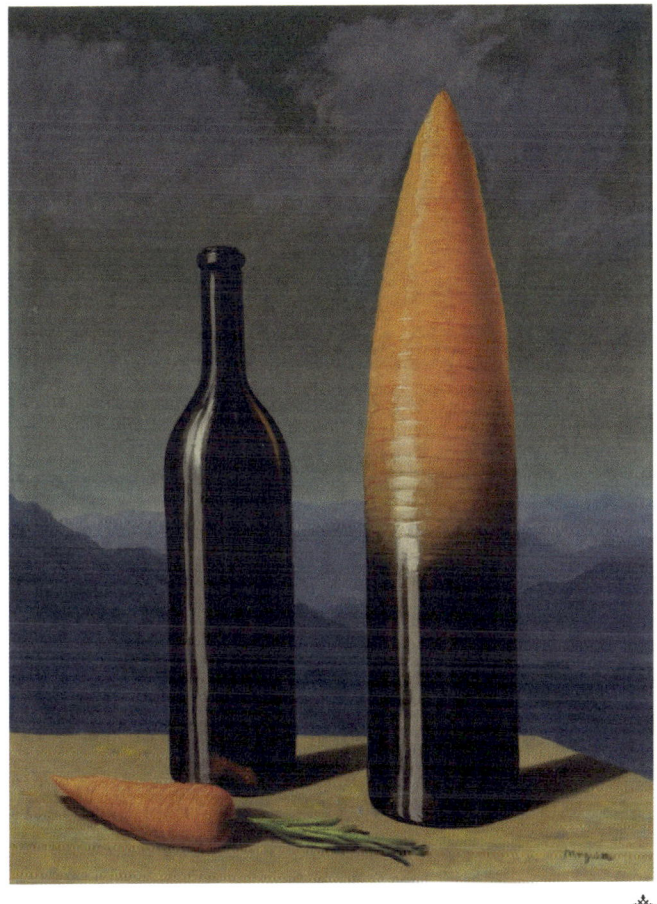

⊗ Unknown artist (French), 'Fantastic Hairdress with Fruit and Vegetable Motif', eighteenth century, watercolour on canvas over board. New York: Metropolitan Museum of Art.

✳ Maubert, Edible roots, 1864–69.

✣ René Magritte, *L'Explication* (*The Explanation*), 1952, oil on canvas. Private collection.

✣

first bottle, painted in 1940, probably reflects wartime material shortages, and he is said to have done it to amuse his friends. Magritte returned to the bottle form in sculpture and painting into the 1960s, and more than thirty survive. One of the most puzzling paintings is *The Explanation*. A bottle is depicted on the left next to another bottle that seems to be transforming into a carrot, its form a pointed cylinder. A rather anaemic-looking carrot lies in the foreground. The scholarly literature on Magritte lacks an explanation. The empty bottle may convey inebriation, and in combination with the the carrot's association with male genitalia and the bullet- or bomb-shaped cylinder, could be read as a suggestion, even explanation, of where things have gone wrong.

FAMILY Apiaceae

A flowering plant in the carrot family, fennel is indigenous to the Mediterranean basin and now widely naturalized elsewhere. It is classified as a herb, used to flavour absinthe, and various parts of the plant are also used in cooking.

It produces aromatic seeds that are sometimes confused with those of anise, which are similar in taste and appearance, although smaller.

According to Pliny, fennel cleared vision and provided spiritual rejuvenation. The herb was sacred to fire-making gods such as Prometheus, who was said to have brought fire down from the heavens as a gift to human beings. Greek islanders traditionally carried fire from place to place in the stalks of giant fennel, since the pith is fire-resistant. And in present-day Italy, ceremonial battles are fought with fennel stalks in a traditional attempt to avert agricultural disasters. The plant, when eaten by snakes, was believed to cause shedding, so it has also symbolized periodic renewal and rejuvenation.

In *The Blind Leading the Blind*, painted the year before the artist's death, Pieter Bruegel the Elder depicted a Flemish proverb, probably based on Matthew 15:14, in which Christ, referring to the Pharisees, says, 'They are blind leaders of the blind. And if the blind leads the blind, both will fall into a ditch.' The powerful painting not only illustrates several forms of blindness, but also contains symbolic plants. Guy de Chauliac, a contemporary doctor, wrote that blindness was caused by 'corrupt fumes, mounting from the stomach to the brain'.

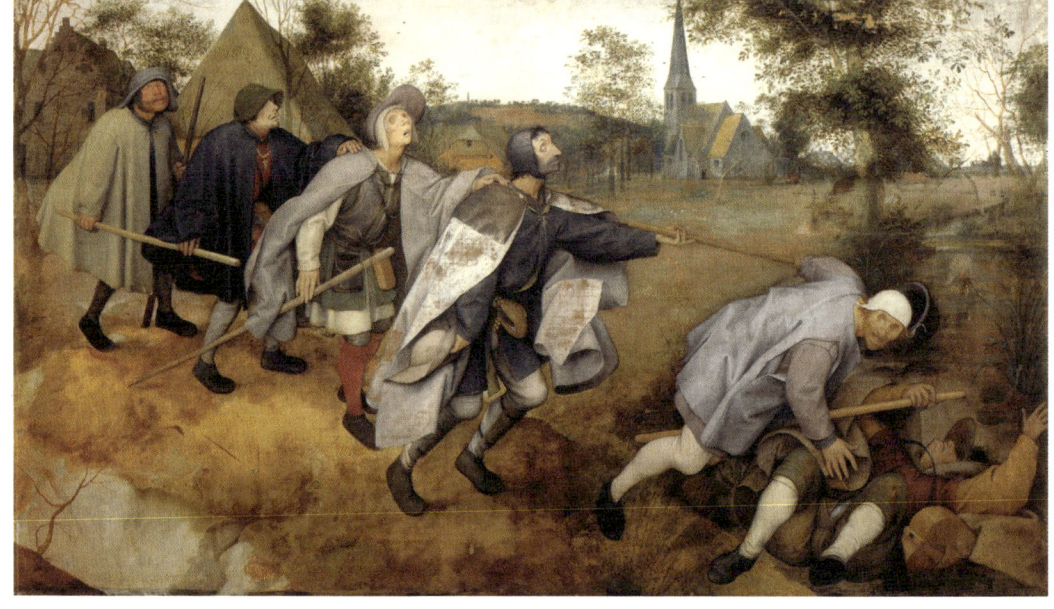

Sufferers could chew on cloves, cinnamon, fennel, anise, coriander and nuts of maquette, resulting in gentle, curative breath. The surface of the painting was abraded at some point, but plants that can be identified include fennel (immediately behind the figure in blue, second from the right) and an iris (above the fallen man on the far right).

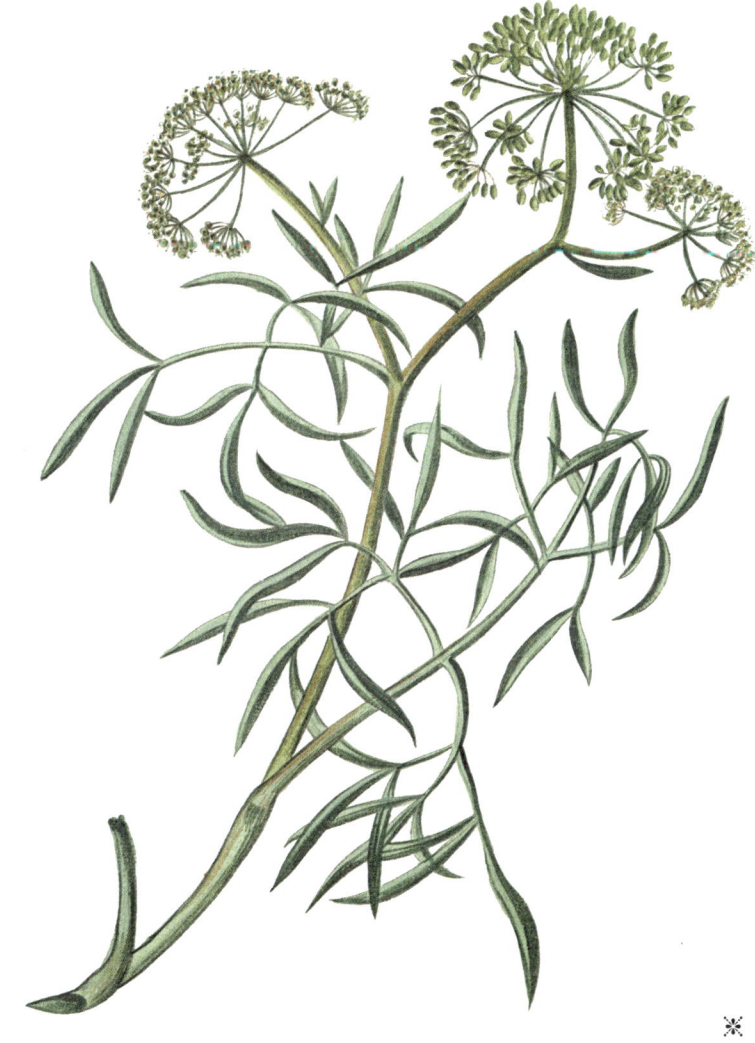

⊗ Pieter Bruegel the Elder, *The Blind Leading the Blind*, 1568, distemper on canvas. Naples, Italy: Museo e Real Bosco di Capodimonte.

※ Cesare Ubertini, *Crithmum maritimum* (Sea fennel), 1772–93.

※

FAMILY Rosaceae

Strawberries are cultivated worldwide for their fruit, which is appreciated for its sweetness, aroma and bright red colour.

Technically, the fruit is not a berry, because its flesh does not come from the ovary of the flower. The first garden strawberries were transplanted from the wild in the Middle Ages.

The strawberry is a symbol of harmony and spiritual nourishment. Although no mention of the fruit occurs in the Bible, it has often been considered part of the earthly paradise. The strawberry also appears in scenes of the Nativity and the Adoration, as well as in depictions of the Holy Family. The three-lobed leaves relate to the Trinity, the little white flower suggests innocence and humility, and, above all, the red fruit evokes blood and the Passion of Christ. For this

reason, it also appears in some Crucifixion and Deposition scenes.

In the medieval period, strawberries were carved on altarpieces and atop columns. They often appeared in illuminated manuscripts, partly for their decorative appeal but also as symbols of innocence and fruitfulness, the latter because of their many seeds. Probably for this reason, the strawberry is also associated with the Virgin Mary. Strawberry plants with fruit often adorn the Virgin's gardens, especially the *hortus conclusus*. This inclusion of strawberries in garden settings continued during the Renaissance.

Luscious-looking strawberries appear in the centre panel of *The Garden of Earthly Delights* by Hieronymus Bosch. The panel, representing humanity after Adam and Eve's expulsion from Eden, depicts a multitude of naked figures cavorting about. Set in a lush, intricate landscape, they indulge in delicious-looking

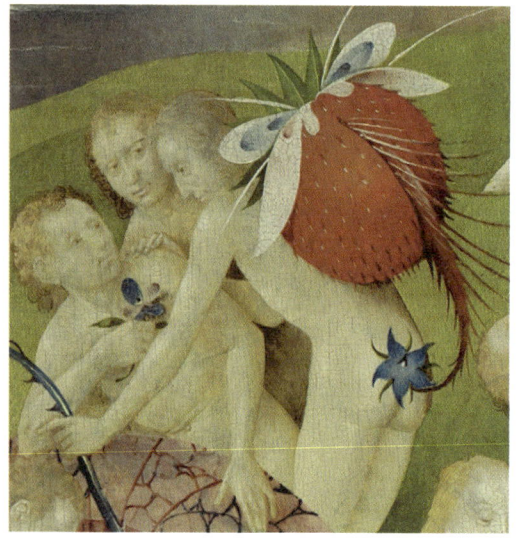

✠

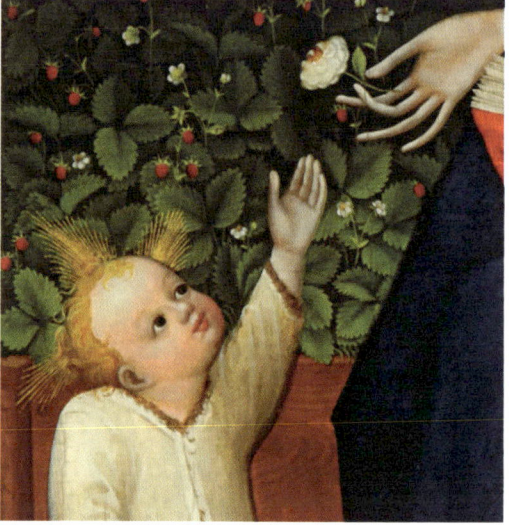

✳

edibles, amorous activities and other earthly pleasures. Bosch lived in a strict religious community, and some critics have suggested that the painting warns against most of the seven deadly sins, especially lust. Strawberries supposedly had aphrodisiac properties, but they may also signify the dangers of another deadly sin, gluttony. One detail shows a man embracing and biting a large berry; elsewhere, a ring of naked figures huddle beneath a giant strawberry that they seem almost to be worshipping. Generally, the centre panel sets out all sorts of sins, tempting but ephemeral. The huge strawberry pins the figures down, in much

the same way sin ensnares and weighs down the soul. The consequences of sin are made evident in the gloomy, menacing right-hand panel.

Fray José de Sigüenza, an early seventeenth-century monk and librarian at El Escorial, Spain, suggested that the strawberries in this painting symbolized the ephemeral, transient nature of earthly pleasures.

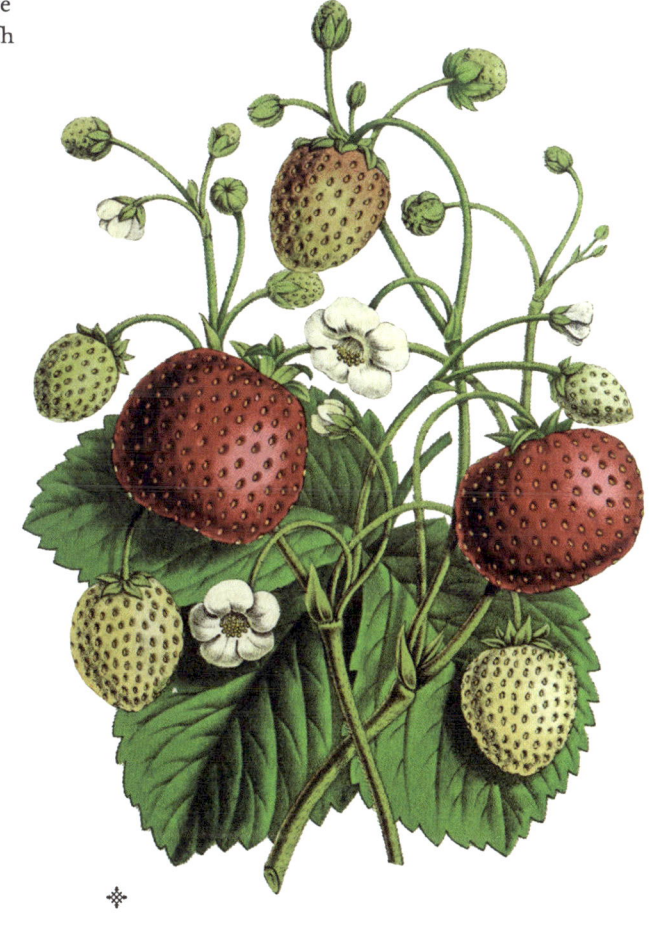

⊗ Hieronymus Bosch, *The Garden of Earthly Delights* (detail of centre panel), 1490–1500, oil on oak. Madrid: Museo del Prado.

⁂ Upper Rhenish Master, *Madonna in den Erdbeeren* (*Madonna of the Strawberries*) (detail), *c.* 1425, mixed media on spruce wood. Solothurn, Switzerland: Kunstmuseum Solothurn.

❖ G. Severeyns, Strawberries, 1851.

OTHER STRAWBERRY IMAGES
• Anon. (possibly Polish), *The Madonna with Wild Strawberry, c.* 1465–77, oil on panel. Kraków, Poland: Stanisław Wyspiański Museum.

FAMILY Rosaceae

Having originated in Central Asia, apples are now cultivated worldwide. A large number of species exist that vary in tree size and fruit yield.

In secular art, the apple can symbolize the cosmos or totality thanks to its perfectly spherical shape. In portraits, emperors and kings often hold an 'imperial apple' (orb) along with a sceptre. Apples were also linked with many goddesses and came to be regarded as magical fruit that granted immortality. The apple tree served as the World Tree in many cultures.

The fruit that tempted Eve in Eden is not named in Genesis, and many possibilities have been suggested. Having eaten the fruit, Adam and Eve obtained forbidden knowledge (Genesis 3:5), contrary to the Creator's will, and were banished from Eden. One reason for identifying the apple as the forbidden fruit is that the Latin word *malum* (from which the genus name comes) means both apple and evil.

The ancient Greeks believed that Dionysus, the god of wine and intoxication, created the apple, which he gave to Aphrodite, the goddess of love. Apples were also associated with beauty and sexuality. When Eris, the goddess of discord, called for 'the judgment of Paris', she threw down a golden apple and demanded that he choose the most beautiful goddess. Paris chose Aphrodite, who rewarded him with Helen of Troy. Helen's abduction led to the Trojan War.

The most famous apples in antiquity were the golden ones in Hera's garden at the ends of the earth, guarded by nymphs called the Hesperides and a 100-headed dragon. The apples, which granted immortality, were Gaia's wedding gift to Hera when she married Zeus. Obtaining the apples formed the eleventh labour of Hercules. The hero needed Atlas's help and agreed to hold the heavens aloft while the giant fetched the apples. When Atlas returned, he thought he would leave Hercules holding the heavens, but was, inevitably, tricked into taking the weight back.

In Christian art, Christ often reaches out for or holds an apple, signifying his role as a

⊗ Orchard Painter (attrib.),
    Women Gathering Apples,
    obverse of a red-figure column
    krater, *c.* 460 BCE. New York:
    Metropolitan Museum of Art.

✳ Giorgio Gallesio, *Malus
    appenninensis* (Pupina apple),
    1817–39.

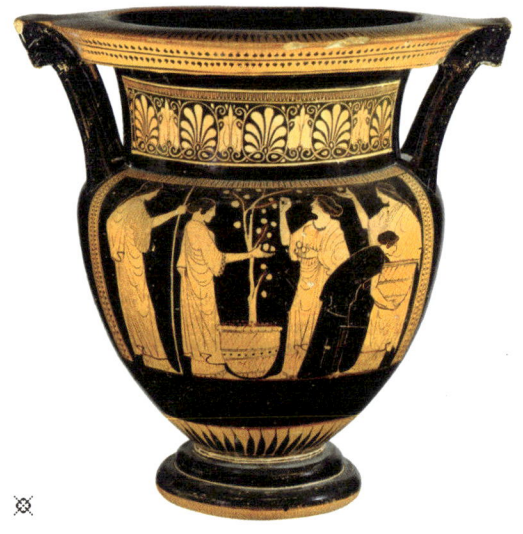

⊗

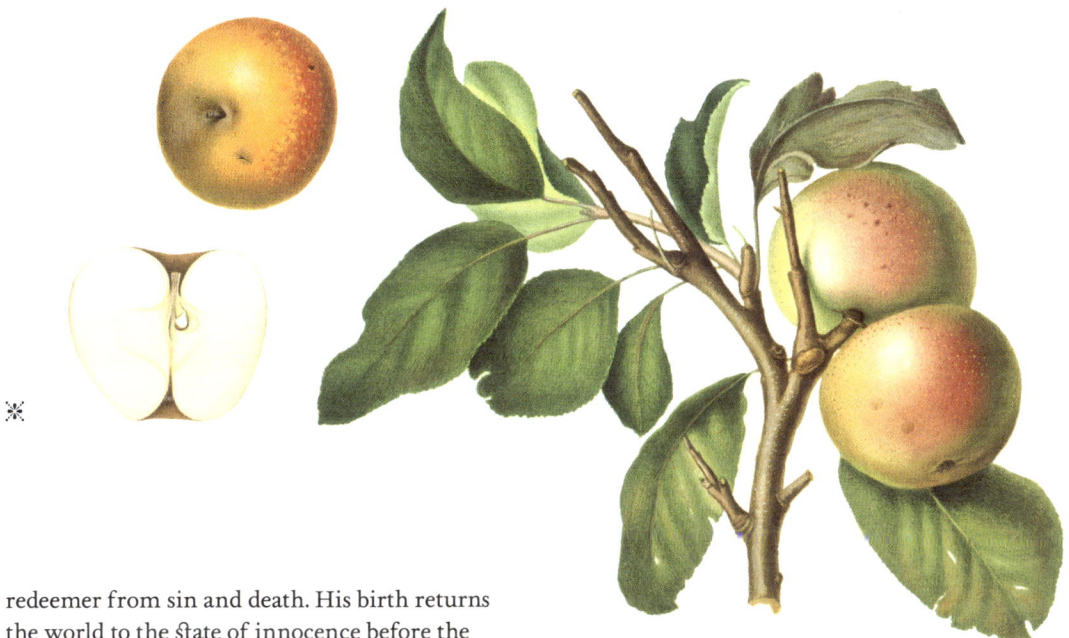

redeemer from sin and death. His birth returns the world to the state of innocence before the Temptation and Fall. In the Venetian painter Carlo Crivelli's *Madonna and Child*, a swag of apples and a cucumber-like gourd hang above the Virgin's head, signifying salvation.

One of the most famous twentieth-century apples appears in Magritte's *Son of Man* (1963). It started out as a self-portrait in response to a commission by Harry Torczyner, the artist's friend, advisor and patron. The face-obscuring apple and the title could refer to Original Sin and expulsion from Eden. The apple, the enigmatic setting and the bowler-hatted, well-dressed but rigid figure all recur in Magritte's work, evoking mystery and ambiguity. For Magritte, the painting involved the tension between the visible and the hidden. The whites of the eyes – just visible on either side of the apple – the flattened coat and the left arm, which seems to bend back at the elbow, add to the enigma of sight, the conflict between seen and unseen.

OTHER IMAGES OF APPLES

- Mary Cassatt, *Baby Reaching for an Apple*, 1893, oil on canvas. Private collection.
- Carlo Crivelli, *Madonna and Child*, c. 1480, tempera and gold on panel. New York: Metropolitan Museum of Art.
- René Magritte, *La Chambre d'écoute* (*The Listening Room*), 1952, oil on canvas. Houston: Menil Collection.
- Gabriël Metsu, *La Peleuse de pommes* (*The Apple Peeler*), 1662, oil on wood. Paris: Musée du Louvre.

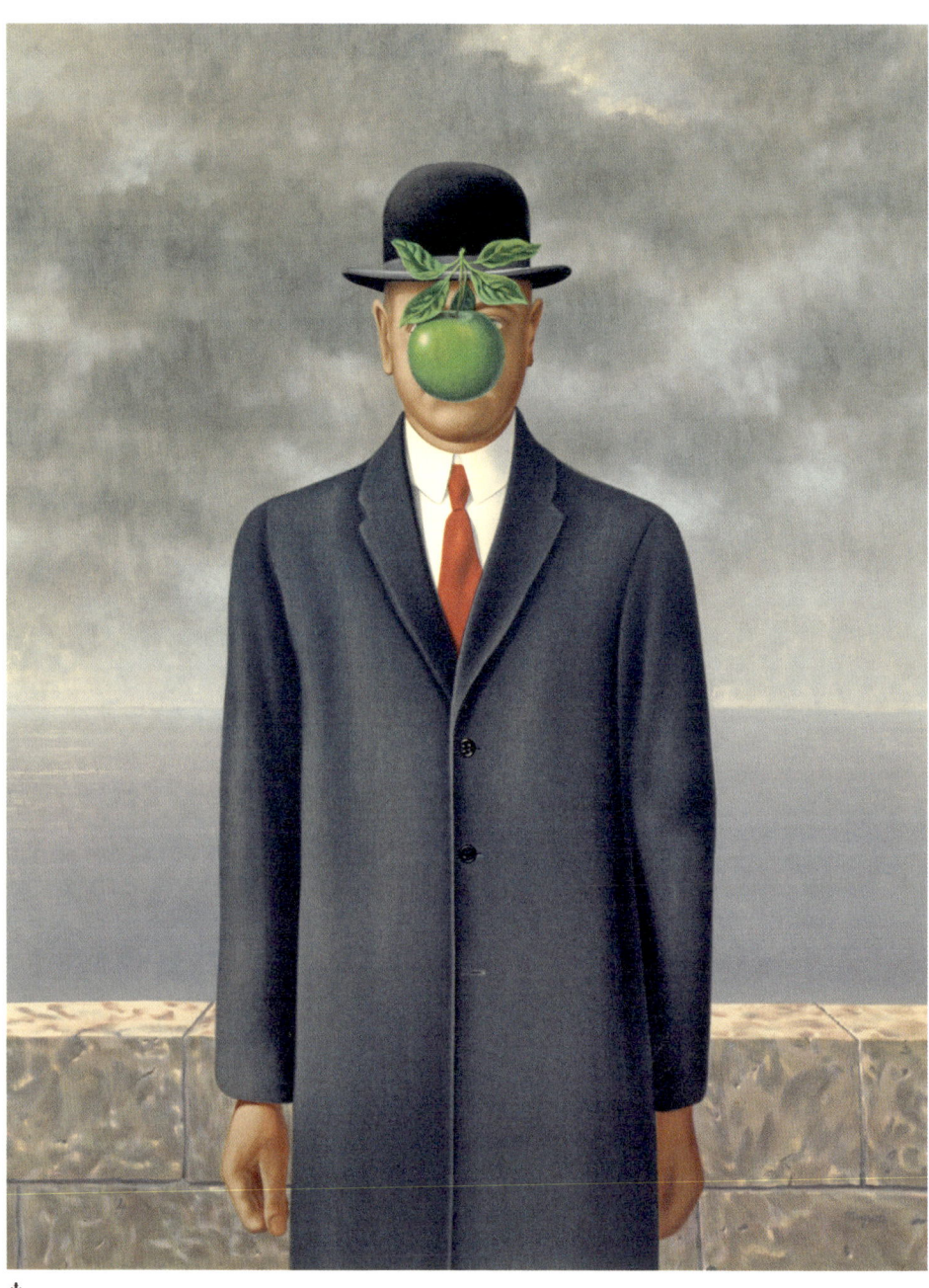

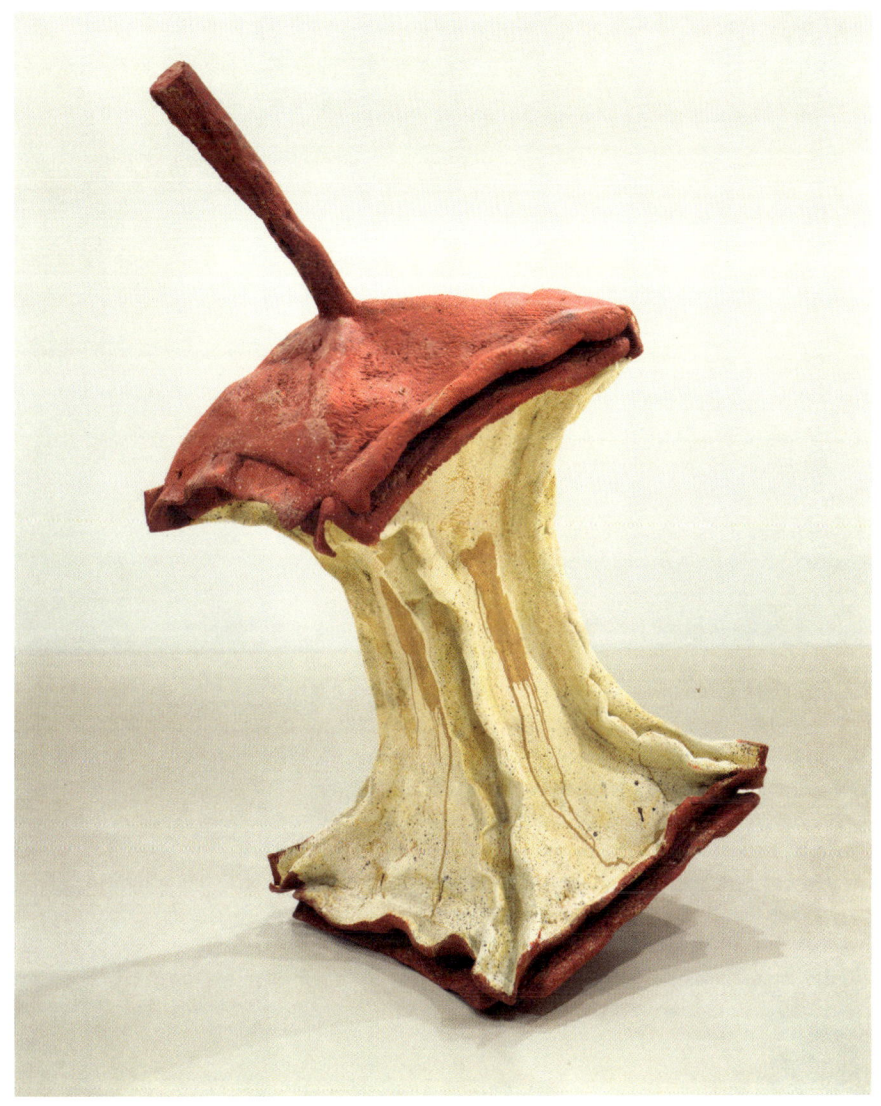

❖ René Magritte, *The Son of Man*, 1964, oil on canvas. Private collection.

✳ Claes Oldenburg and Coosje van Bruggen, *Geometric Apple Core*, 1991, latex paint, polyurethane and steel. San Francisco, CA: Museum of Modern Art.

FAMILY Musaceae

The banana is an elongated fruit (technically a berry) of several large flowering herbaceous plants. The words 'banana' and 'plantain' are sometimes used interchangeably. Generally, botanists do not consider the plant to be a tree since its 'trunk' consists entirely of entwined leaves.

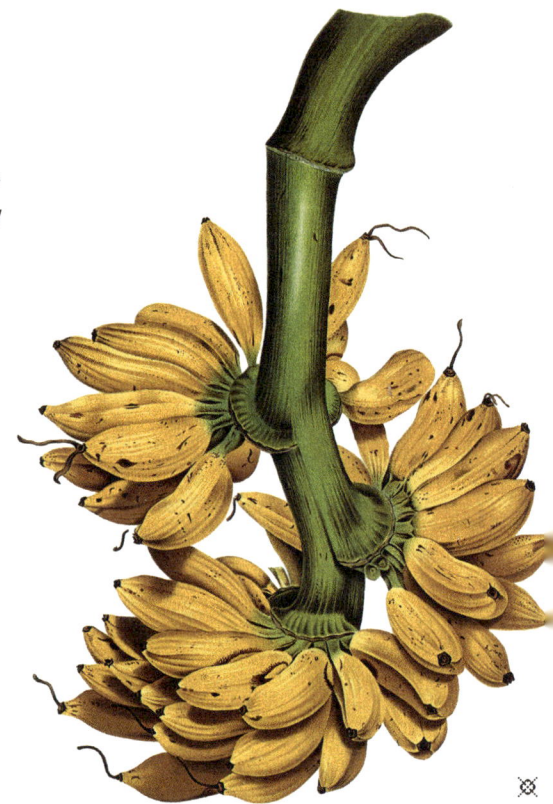

First domesticated in Polynesia, bananas now grow in 135 countries around the world. The fruit develops all year round in large clusters of approximately twenty, in between three and twenty tiers. Touted as a good source of potassium, bananas in fact deliver less of that nutrient than raw spinach, skinless cooked potatoes and soybeans, but according to Alex Abella's *The Total Banana* (1979) they do still have substantial benefits, including providing important vitamins, assisting with weight reduction and maintaining healthy digestion.

As they became more widespread in Europe and North America, bananas came to represent ideas of the 'exotic'. In 1924, Josephine Baker danced semi-naked at the Folies Bergère in Paris with only a string of artificial bananas around her waist, drawing on and challenging such imagery. Bananas have since featured in other costumes: in the 1930s, Carmen Miranda's costume included a fruit-bowl hat full of bananas and other tropical fruit; excessive numbers of oversized (not to mention suggestive) bananas appeared in Busby Berkeley's film *The Gang's All Here* (1943), which starred Miranda. Her popularity may have induced United Fruit to invent the brand name Chiquita Banana.

When bananas appear in art, it is often as a symbol of the erotic. De Chirico's *The Uncertainty of the Poet* depicts a rather twisted

antique sculpture that is said to represent Aphrodite, side by side with a cluster of twenty-three bananas that appear to have been ripped from a tree. One of the artist's most important paintings, it contains elements typical of de Chirico, among them a train belching smoke, long shadows and a sharply tilted arcade. The conjunction of bananas and the classical torso evokes both exoticism and a sort of mysterious, constrained eroticism.

In the twenty-first century, various banana-related works have raised questions about consumption and gender. Maurizio

Cattelan's *Comedian* consisted of a banana duct-taped to the wall at Art Basel, Miami, in 2019. The 'edition' of three bananas sold for between $120,000 and $150,000 each, with purchasers buying the concept and a certificate of authenticity. The Dadaist conceptual work attracted such crowds that the banana had to be removed. *Consumer Art*, a video work from the 1970s by the Polish artist Natalia LL showing herself eating bananas suggestively, was removed from view in Warsaw's National Museum in 2019. Almost 1,000 people gathered outside and ate bananas in protest, prompting the museum to put the video back on display.

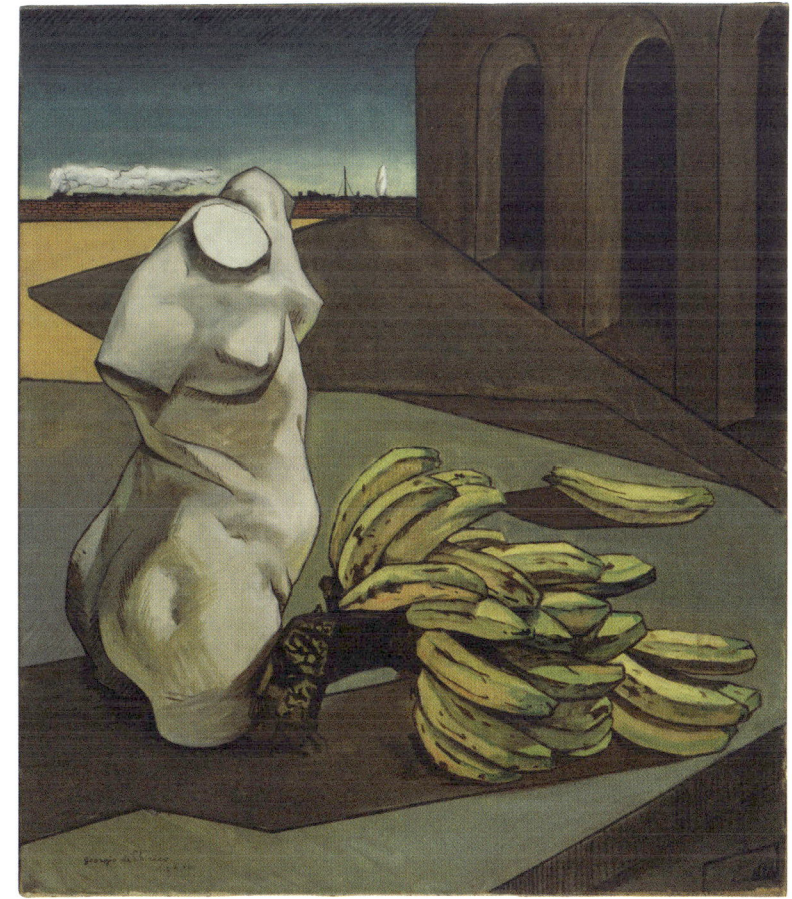

⊗ Berthe Hoola van Nooten, *Musa paradisiaca L.* (plantain banana), *c.* 1885.

✳ Giorgio de Chirico, *The Uncertainty of the Poet*, 1913, oil on canvas. London: Tate.

✳

FAMILY Myristicaceae

A seed or ground spice, nutmeg originated in Indonesia. Its health benefits are unclear, and in large amounts it can be hallucinogenic and even toxic.

The Indonesian Banda Islands remained its only source until the nineteenth century. In the seventeenth century, the Dutch East India Company killed, starved, exiled and enslaved the Bandanese in order to control the nutmeg market.

Today, nutmeg is an important crop in Grenada, having been introduced by English merchants in 1843. The spice mace, which features prominently in Caribbean food, comes from nutmeg's bright red seed cover.

The Norwegian sculptor Lene Kilde received a scholarship from Arts Council Norway that enabled her to travel to Grenada in 2014. Grenada's Underwater Sculpture Park, one of twenty-five gardens created by Jason deCaires Taylor, contains ecologically friendly sculptures that encourage marine growth and keep tourists away from nearby fragile coral reefs. Kilde's sculpture *The Nutmeg Princess*, inspired by a book of the same name by a Grenadian author, Richardo Keens-Douglas, stands 3.4 m (11 ft) tall. In the book, the Nutmeg Princess, who knows when the nutmeg is ripe, can be seen only by the brave and pure of heart. She encourages the children to believe in themselves and follow their dreams. Kilde's figure, eyes closed and apparently arising from a giant nutmeg, reaches upwards, her hands full of nutmeg. Once installed, Kilde notes, the sculpture has changed 'day by day, providing hiding places for marine life, and surfaces for corals and sponges to attach and grow'. The figure's rapt expression and pose convey generosity, contemplation and joy.

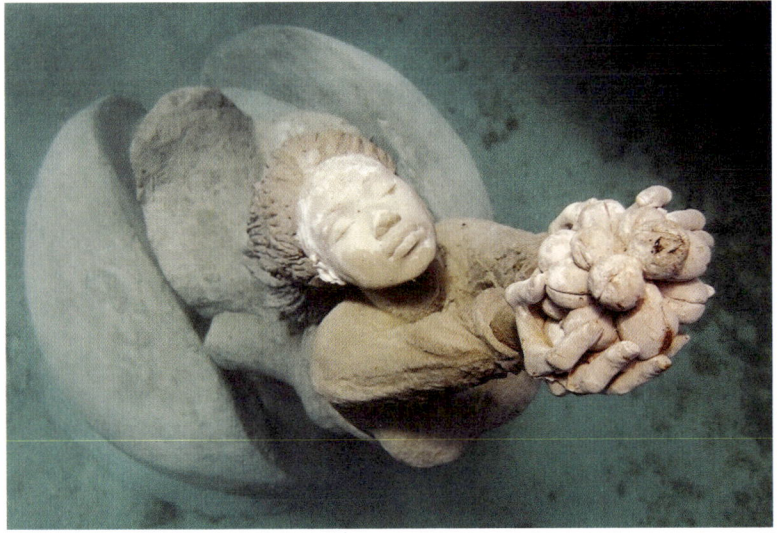

⊠ Lene Kilde, *The Nutmeg Princess*, 2014, concrete. Grenada: Underwater Sculpture Park at Molinere Bay.

⋇ *Myristica fragrans* Houtt., 1890.

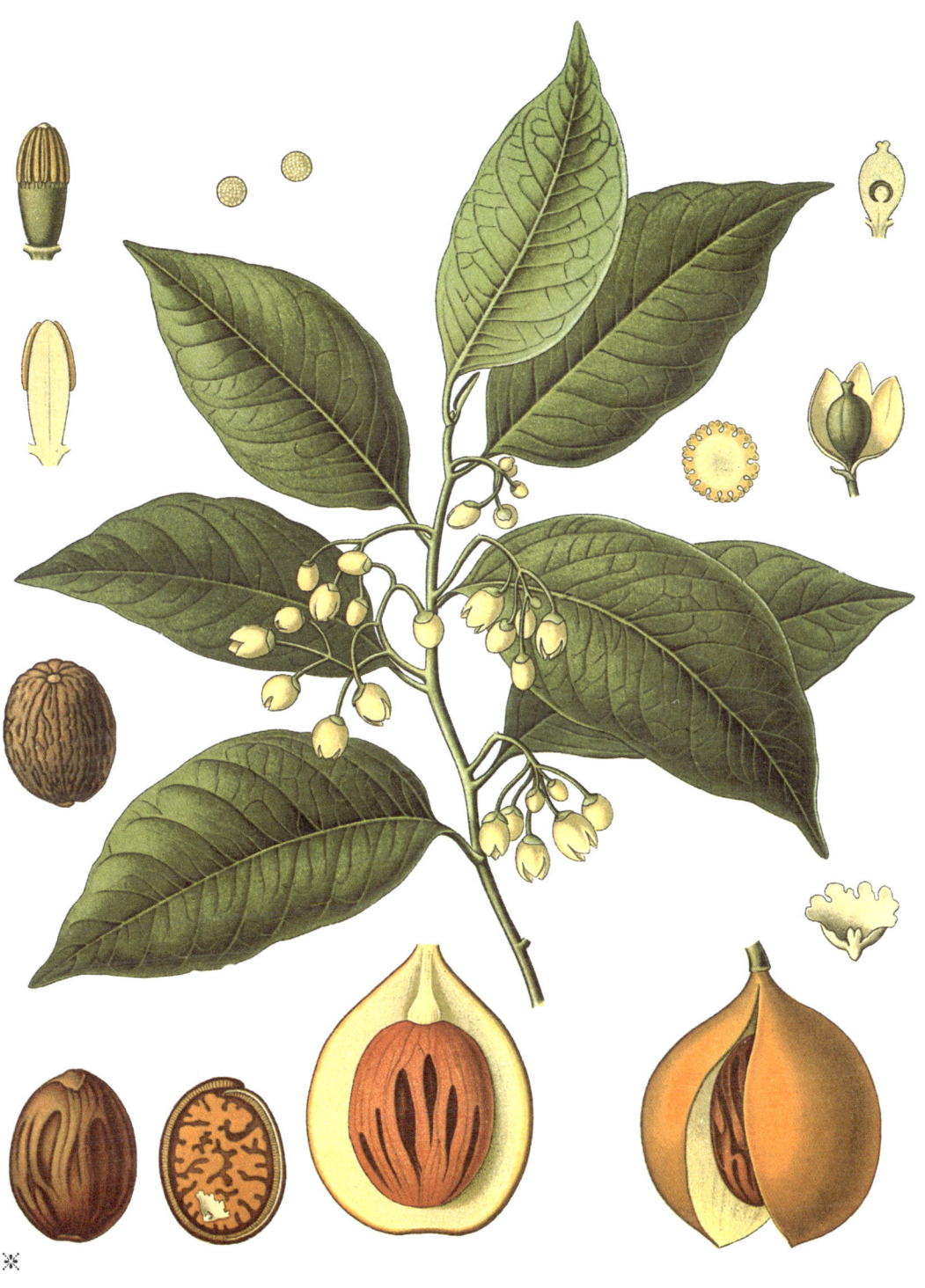

FAMILY Rosaceae

The cherry originated in the Mediterranean and is now grown worldwide. In Denmark and Lithuania, probably before the introduction of Christianity, demons were thought to live in cherry trees.

As a Christian symbol, the deep red cherry represents Christ's blood, which is why the fruit sometimes appears on the table in depictions of the Last Supper or his appearance at Emmaus. Cherries often appear in Renaissance images of the Madonna and Child, as sumptuous fruit and a harbinger of Christ's death and Resurrection. Sometimes Northern Renaissance painters substitute a cherry tree for the palm (pp. 68–69) in scenes of the 'Rest on the Flight to Egypt', possibly never having seen a palm.

Giovanna Garzoni is regarded as the finest Italian Baroque miniature painter. She served several aristocratic patrons, even becoming an official miniaturist in the Medici court. Few of her miniatures survive, however, and she is now better known for her painstaking still-life watercolours. Flowers, fruit and living creatures such as birds, bees, beetles and snails were rendered with great accuracy. Unusually for an Italian painter, her work often resembles Dutch Baroque *vanitas* images in style.

The art historian Mary Garrard notes the vitality and sensuality of Garzoni's still lifes and suggests that, during the plague, looking at them might have been thought to promote health. Garrard also sees in them associations with the human body (such as melons being equated with plump breasts). The images may therefore have conveyed the magic of sexual and cyclical regeneration in nature.

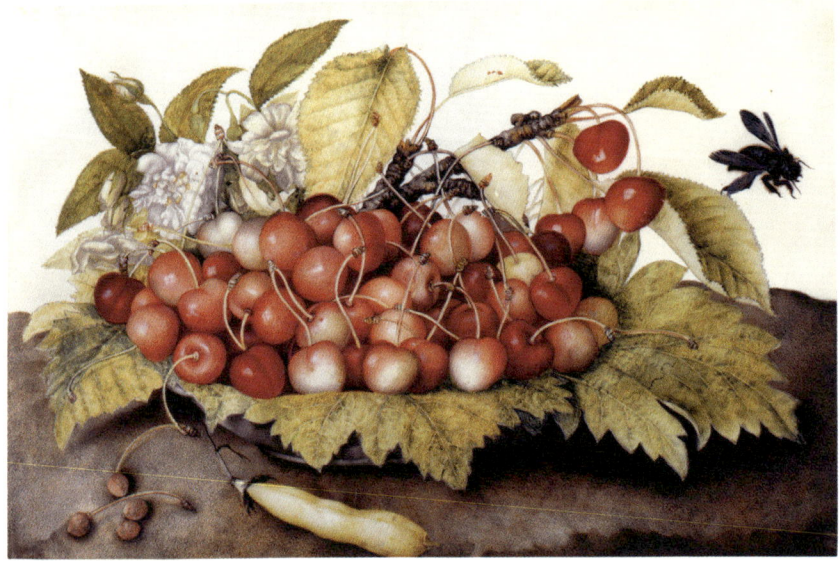

⊗

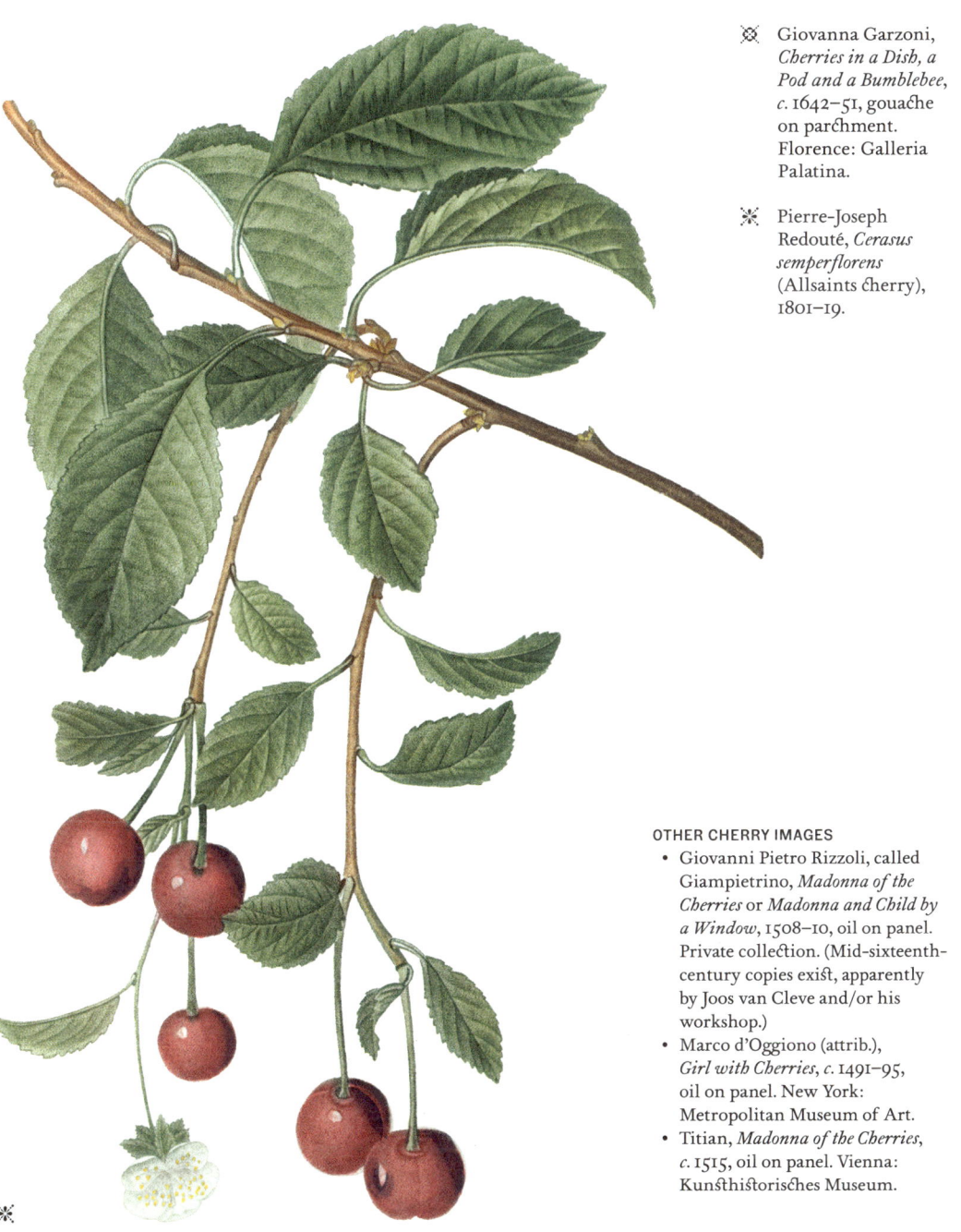

✗ Giovanna Garzoni, *Cherries in a Dish, a Pod and a Bumblebee*, *c.* 1642–51, gouache on parchment. Florence: Galleria Palatina.

✳ Pierre-Joseph Redouté, *Cerasus semperflorens* (Allsaints cherry), 1801–19.

OTHER CHERRY IMAGES
- Giovanni Pietro Rizzoli, called Giampietrino, *Madonna of the Cherries* or *Madonna and Child by a Window*, 1508–10, oil on panel. Private collection. (Mid-sixteenth-century copies exist, apparently by Joos van Cleve and/or his workshop.)
- Marco d'Oggiono (attrib.), *Girl with Cherries*, *c.* 1491–95, oil on panel. New York: Metropolitan Museum of Art.
- Titian, *Madonna of the Cherries*, *c.* 1515, oil on panel. Vienna: Kunsthistorisches Museum.

FAMILY Rosaceae

The deciduous peach tree originated between two and six million years ago in China, from where it migrated to Persia, then Europe.

The *Prunus* genus includes several other fruit trees; the nectarine, although distinguished commercially, is identical to the peach, but without the fuzzy skin. The tree and the fruit are particularly important in Asian cultures.

Tradition has it that the peach was brought to Greece by Alexander the Great following his conquests in Persia. Its presence in the Roman Empire is evident from a beautiful fresco in the ruined city of Herculaneum, where the peaches promote a sense of hospitality.

Peach trees bloom early and thus symbolize spring. The three parts of the fruit – flesh, stone and seed within the stone – link it to the Holy Trinity. The Christ Child sometimes holds a peach instead of an apple in depictions of the Madonna and Child, and in such images it has the same meaning as the fruit of salvation.

Renaissance artists revived an ancient tradition that the leaf and stem of the peach together symbolized the heart and tongue. It therefore signifies truth, in the sense of speaking the truth from the heart. The fruit also symbolized fertility. The four pieces of fruit on the left-hand side of Van Eyck's *The Arnolfini Portrait*, a painting widely discussed for its symbolism, have been identified as peaches and/or oranges. If they are oranges, they may signify wealth; if they are peaches, they may instead suggest the hope for a fruitful marriage.

Peaches adorned *vanitas* still-lifes throughout the Baroque period in the Netherlands, and

Giorgio Gallesio, *Persica Magdalena* (Peach), 1817–39.

Jan van Eyck, *The Arnolfini Portrait*, 1434, oil on oak. London: National Gallery.

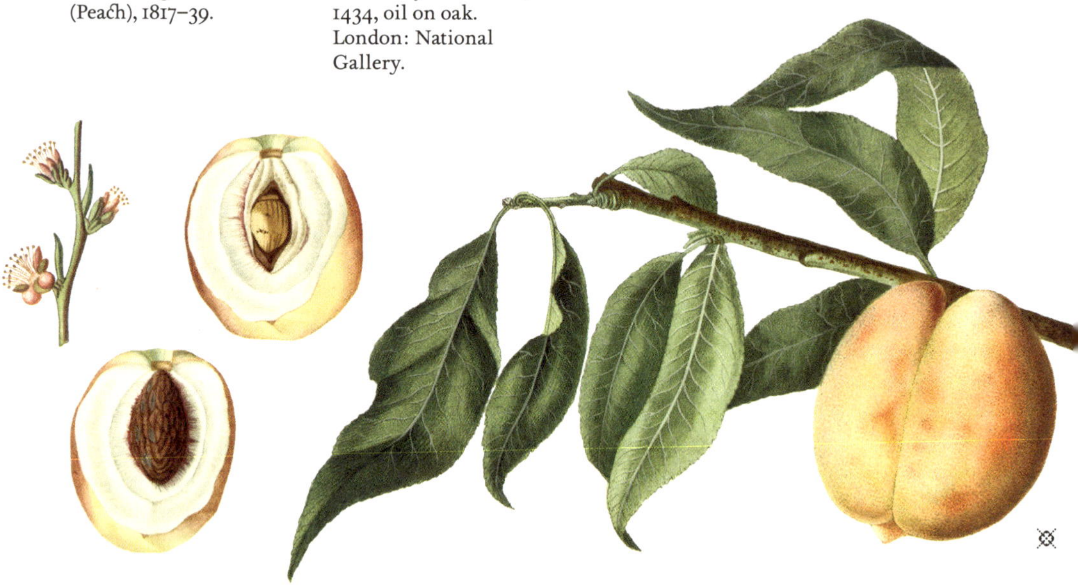

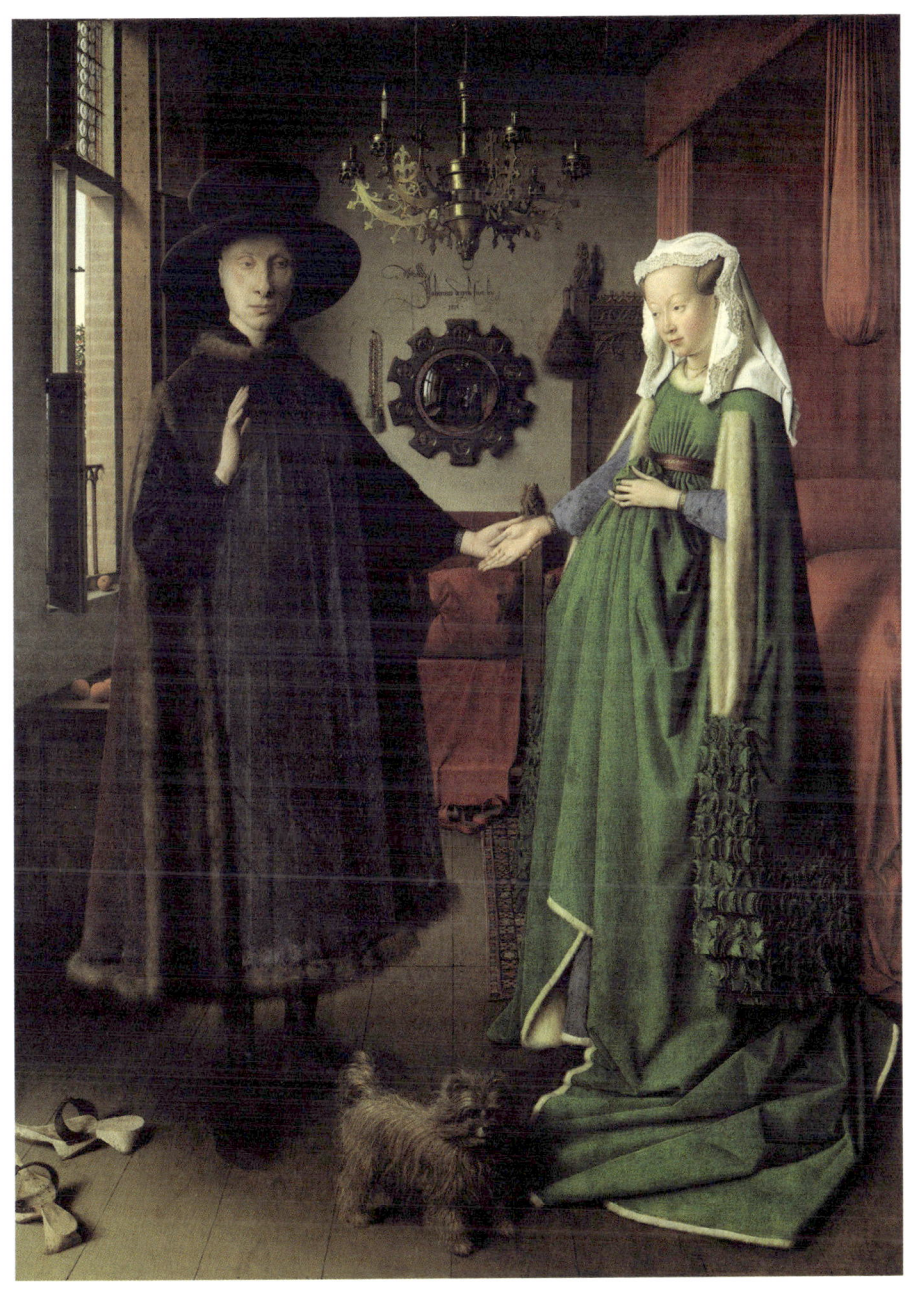

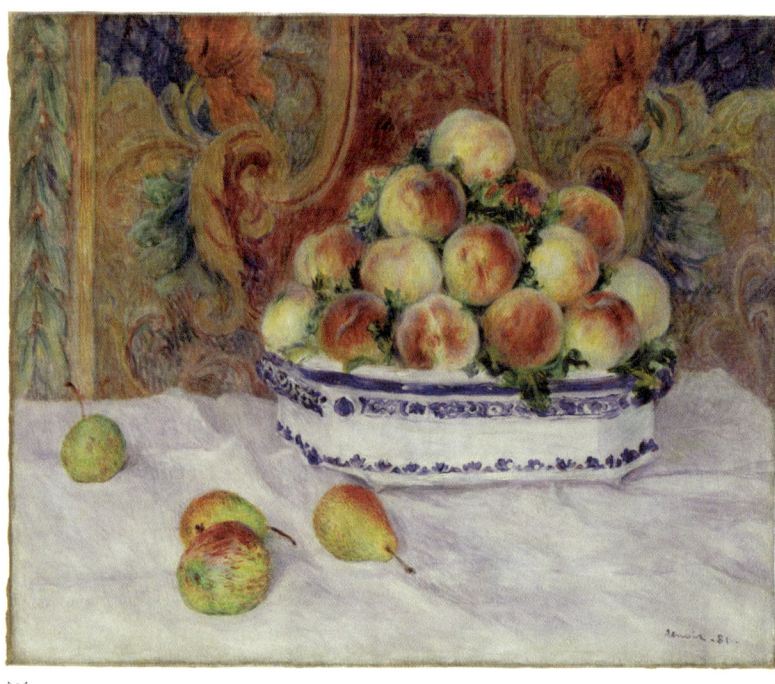

⊗

have continued to appear in European art long afterwards. Their fuzzy surface and variegated colours posed no challenge for Renoir, whose *Still Life with Peaches* depicts a pyramid of delicious-looking peaches, seen from different vantage points, in a faience jardinière. On the white cloth, complete with folds and violet shadows, rest two pears, an apple and a smaller green fruit. This arrangement is backed by a tapestry or wallpaper that adds to the energy and liveliness of the painting, contributing to the overall sense of *joie de vivre* and sensuous appeal.

Roald Dahl's children's story *James and the Giant Peach* (1961) has been reprinted with new illustrations several times. The story tells of an unhappy orphan boy who finds a tunnel into a giant peach, where he meets various giant-sized bugs that take him on magical adventures. The peach represents a nurturing, safe place where James can grow.

OTHER PEACH IMAGES
- Still life with peaches and a water jar, from Herculaneum, *c.* 62–69 CE. Naples, Italy: Museo Archeologico Nazionale.
- Carlo Crivelli, *Madonna col Bambino* (*Madonna and Child*), *c.* 1482, tempera on panel. Bergamo, Italy: Accademia Carrara.

FAMILY Lythraceae

The pomegranate originated in Afghanistan, Iran and northern India, and travelled westwards; it was introduced into the Americas in the sixteenth century.

Today, it is widely cultivated for juice and used in cooking, baking, garnishes and alcoholic drinks. The fruit is a rich source of dietary fibre and is high in several vitamins, although its precise health benefits are the subject of debate.

The pomegranate has a long history in art, beginning in the ancient Mediterranean. It is one of the candidates for the Tree of Knowledge in Eden, and is mentioned among the fruits of Paradise in the Qur'an. Pomegranates occur in several passages in the Old Testament; the fruit is one of the plants listed among the valued products of Israel.

The Greeks associated the pomegranate with female fertility; it was sacred to Aphrodite and Hera, as well as playing a role in the abduction of Persephone. The daughter of Demeter and Zeus, Persephone was picking flowers when Hades carried her off to the Underworld. Demeter, the goddess of agriculture, became so grief-stricken that famine ensued. Zeus interceded, ordering Hades to return the girl to her mother. But Persephone had eaten a pomegranate seed (in some tellings, several) while in the Underworld, so she could spend only certain months with Demeter each year; the months she spent in the Underworld correspond to the barren fields after harvest. Pomegranates are common in Greek art as early as the Geometric period, and the object illustrated below is one of many terracotta pomegranates. Probably because of its association with Persephone's release from the Underworld, the fruit often appears on ancient gravestones. Figures of young women holding pomegranates may have been devotees of Hera.

The dining-room frescoes from the Villa of Livia at Prima Porta (30–20 BCE; now in the

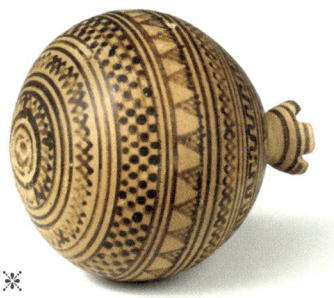

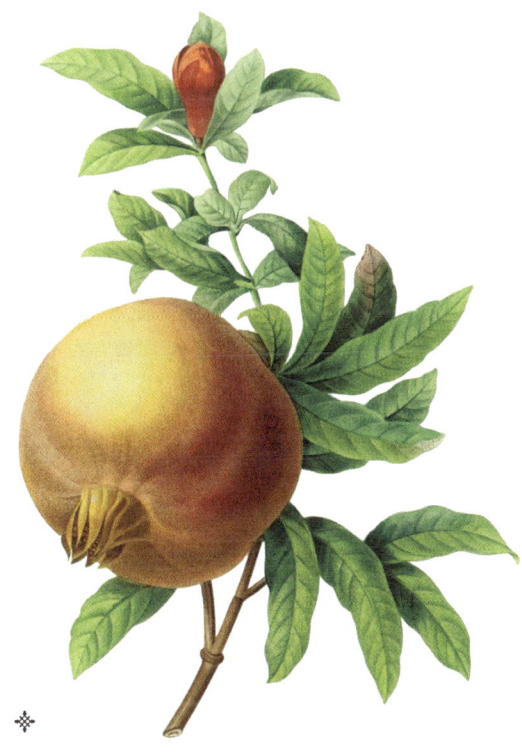

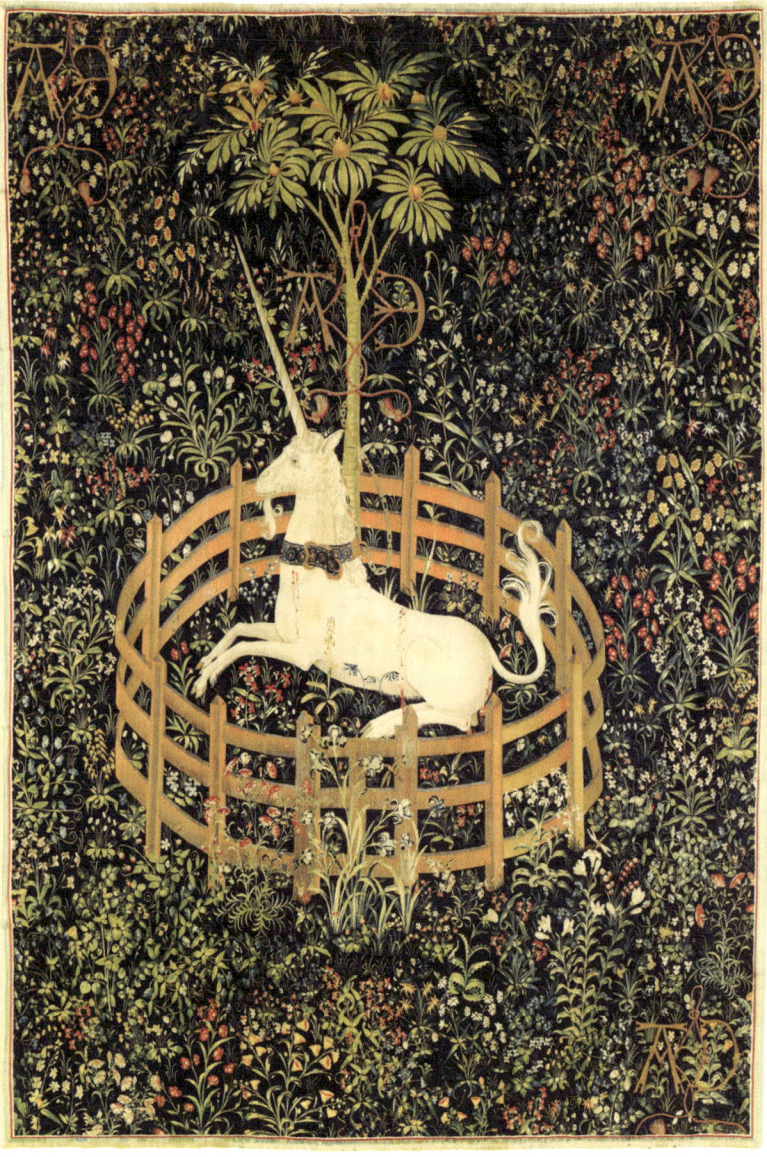

⊗ *The Unicorn Rests in a Garden*, Unicorn Tapestries, *c.* 1495–1505, wool and silk threads. New York: The Cloisters.

✳ Sandro Botticelli, *Virgin and Child with Angels* ('Madonna of the Pomegranate', also known as 'Madonna of the Magnificat') (detail), *c.* 1487, tempera on wood. Florence: Le Gallerie degli Uffizi..

✤ Dante Gabriel Rossetti, *Proserpine* (detail), 1874, oil on canvas. London: Tate.

FRUIT, VEGETABLES & SEASONINGS

Palazzo Massimo in Rome) feature many species of bird and plant, including pomegranate trees bursting with fruit. Here they would seem to indicate sheer energy and the bounty of life. This symbolism of bounty, fertility and rebirth continued into the medieval period and seems to have reached its height in the Italian Renaissance.

In *The Unicorn Rests in a Garden* (sometimes called *The Unicorn in Captivity*) from the Cloisters' Unicorn Tapestries, the unicorn – often said to symbolize Christ – reclines in a fenced circle beneath a pomegranate tree, its fruit having apparently dripped onto its white coat. The pomegranate symbolizes fertility, but the red spots on the unicorn resemble blood – signifying the immortality made possible by Christ's sacrifice. It has been suggested that the tapestries were created to celebrate a wedding; thus, the image may also indicate the desire for a fruitful marriage.

Italian painters included pomegranates in many images of the Virgin and Child, probably because the fruit's red juice, like wine, foreshadowed the Last Supper and Christ's death and Resurrection. In Botticelli's *Virgin and Child with Angels* the skin has burst, and some of the fruit's many seeds are visible. Just as seeds produce new plants, so Christ's sacrifice signifies rebirth. Pomegranates also appear in the works of Fra Angelico, Gentile da Fabriano, Filippino Lippi, Lorenzo di Credi and Raphael, among others.

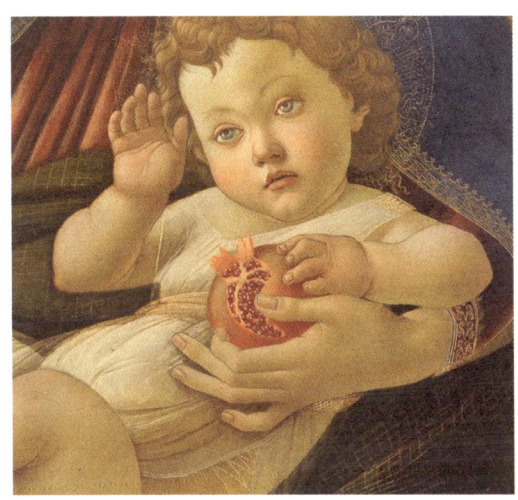

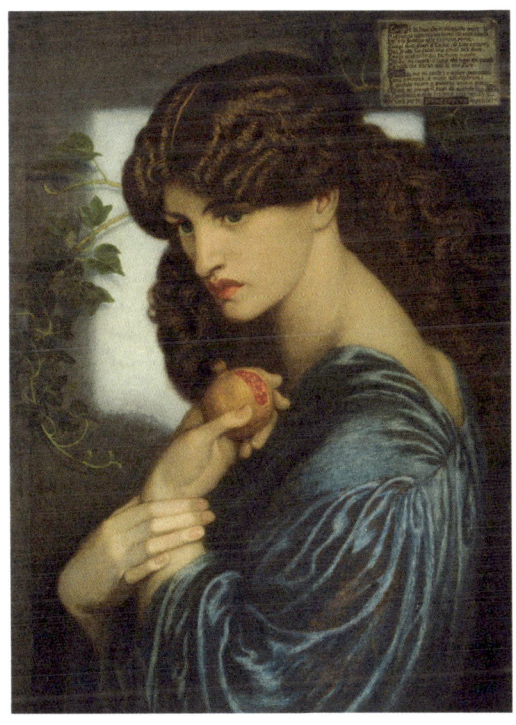

OTHER POMEGRANATE IMAGES
- Botanic Garden of Thutmosis III, Festival Hall, Temple of Amon-Re, Karnak, Egypt, *c.* 1450 BCE.

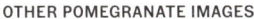

FAMILY Rosaceae

The pear tree is a member of the rose family. Among the most important fruit trees, pears are cultivated worldwide in temperate zones.

The fruit is eaten fresh or canned, although some species are mainly decorative. The common pear (*Pyrus communis*), probably of European origin, has been cultivated since ancient times. The Williams cultivar is the most popular type in America, where it is known as the Bartlett pear.

Pausanias wrote that in Tiryns and Mycenae, the two greatest cities of the Bronze Age Mycenaean civilization, statues of Hera were carved from pear wood. The fruit was sacred to Aphrodite as well as Hera. Pliny called it the 'Aphrodite' pear because the rounded lower form recalled the shape of the female body.

The pear tree is one of many candidates for the Tree of Knowledge in the Garden of Eden. Pears often also appear in images of the Madonna and Child, alluding to redemption and the sweetness of virtue. Crivelli frequently included fruit in his images of this subject; the example opposite features two ripe pears in the upper left-hand corner, and an apple on the right. The cherry on the balustrade is said to symbolize Christ's blood.

OTHER PEAR IMAGES
- Giovanni Bellini, *Madonna col Bambino* (*Madonna and Child*), 1485–*c.* 1487, oil on panel. Bergamo: Accademia Carrara.
- Albrecht Dürer, *Madonna and Child with a Pear*, 1511. Engraving.
- Luis Egidio Meléndez, *Still Life with Melon and Pears*, *c.* 1772, oil on canvas. Boston, MA: Museum of Fine Arts.

⊗ Giorgio Gallesio, *Pera Campana, Pyrus Pompeiana* (Pears), 1817–39.

✻ Carlo Crivelli, *Madonna and Child*, *c.* 1490, tempera on panel. Washington, DC: National Gallery of Art, Kress Collection.

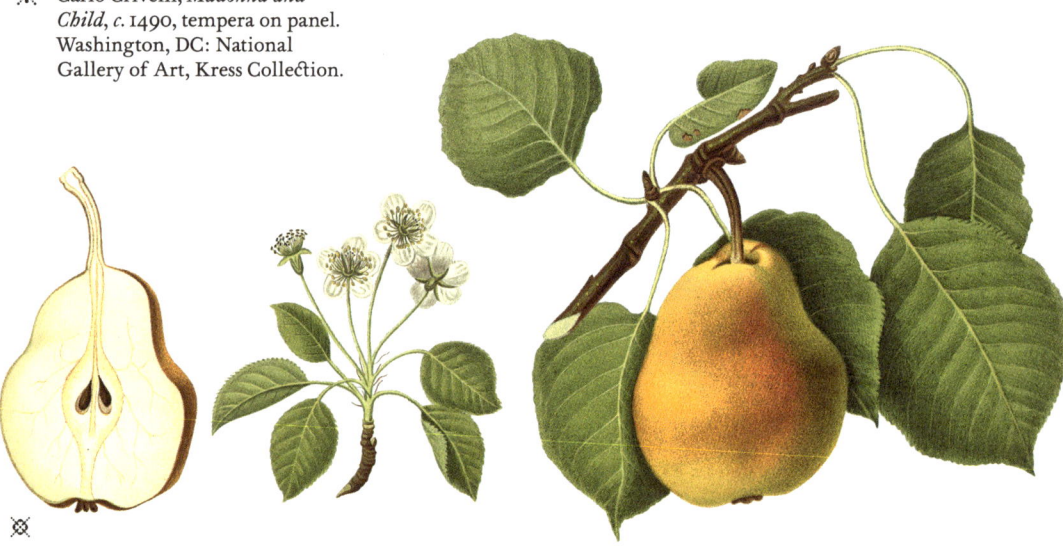

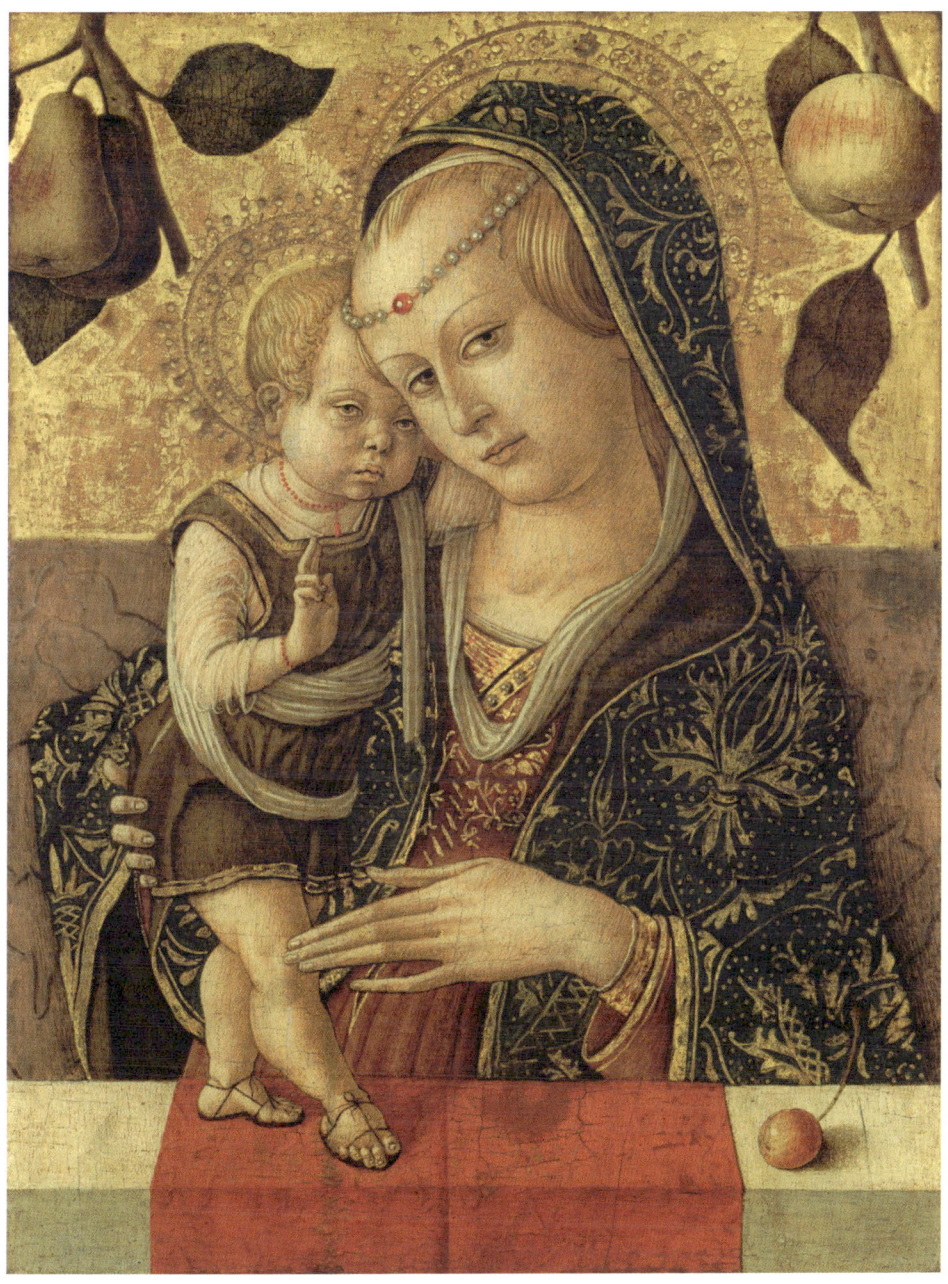

※

FAMILY Brassicaceae

The radish is a vegetable in the mustard family. Thought to have originated in China, radishes have been cultivated for thousands of years.

Medicinally, the radish has antibacterial and antifungal properties, and also helps to clear phlegm from a cold. The Romans linked it with Mars, god of war, and therefore with quarrel and strife – probably in part because it is commonly bright red, though some varieties are different colours. It is also said to be an attribute of wind and weather gods. Counterbalancing this stormy symbolism, the radish was consecrated, traditionally on the day of the Catholic festival of the Chair of St Peter.

The contemporary American artist Jennifer Knaus has created a series of strikingly original portraits reminiscent of both Surrealism and the work of Arcimboldo. Her delicate, detailed paintings depict mostly female figures wearing luscious arrangements of various fruit and vegetables. She bridges portraiture and still life in ways that are mysterious and evocative. In *Radish Head*, as well as the red radishes, there are white flowers in the background, which may be daffodils. Whether the images reflect aspects of the sitter's personality or serve some other symbolic purpose is unclear, but they certainly make remarkable use of plants.

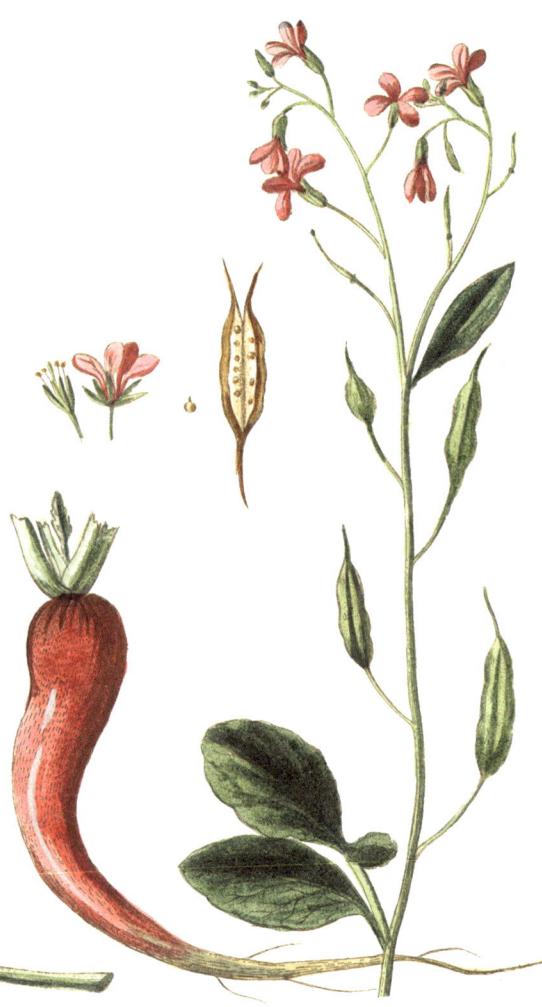

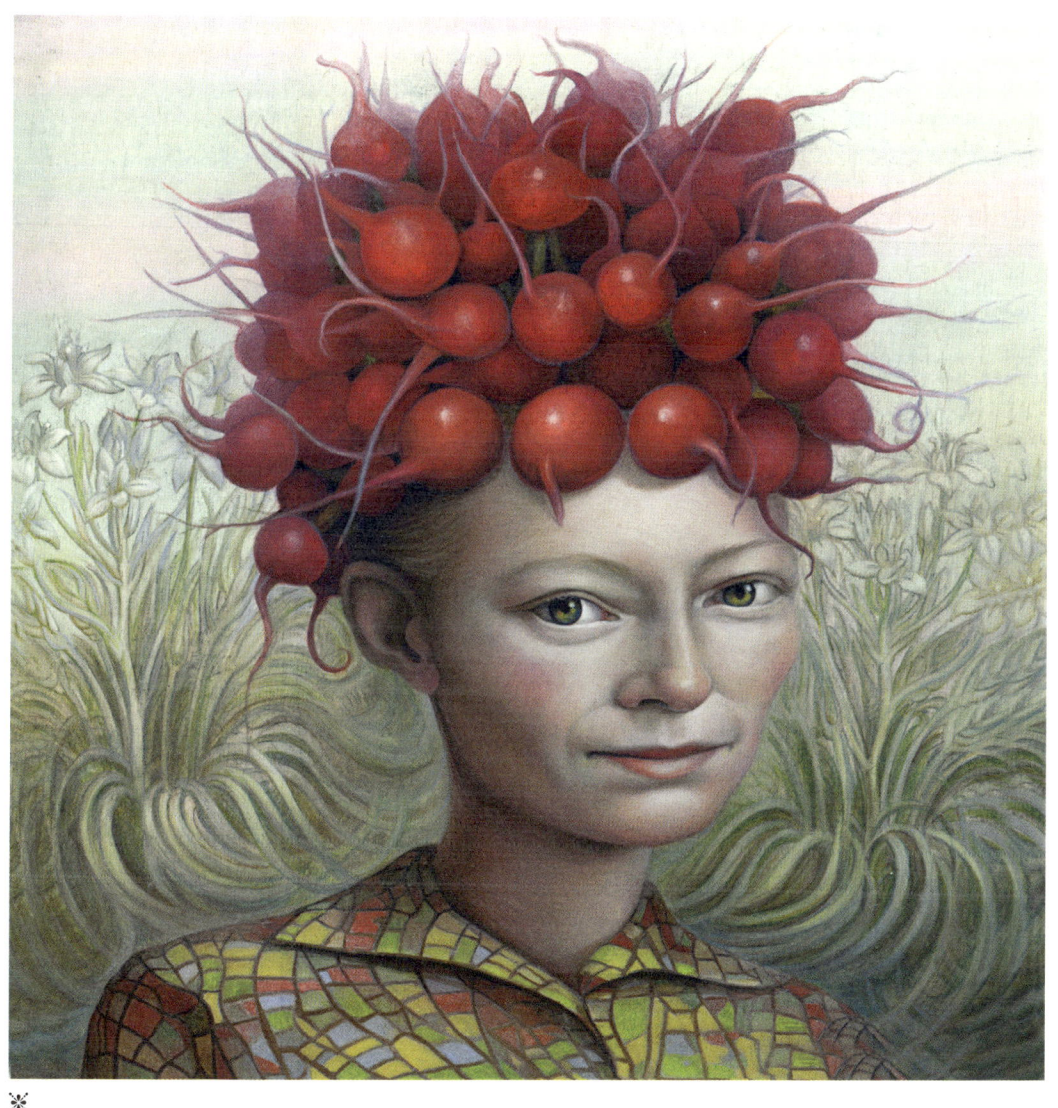

※

⊗ Cesare Ubertini,
Raphanus minor
(radish), 1772–93.

※ Jennifer Knaus,
Radish Head, 2014,
oil on panel.

FAMILY Solanaceae

Technically, the tomato is the berry of a species that originated in South and Central America. It was domesticated by about 500 BCE.

The tomato was first encountered by Europeans when the Spanish conquered the Aztec empire and took the fruit back to Spain, from where it spread during the sixteenth century. Although tomatoes are classified as fruit, they are generally used in the kitchen as vegetables.

In ancient times, the tomato was believed to be an aphrodisiac, and there was some thought that it might be poisonous. It appears in Baroque still lifes, including paintings by Luis Egidio Meléndez. Bartolomé Esteban Murillo's *The Angels' Kitchen*, commissioned by the Franciscans of Seville for the cloister of their monastery, depicts a monastery kitchen and a Franciscan friar in ecstatic prayer. Two angels separate the friar from the kitchen, where celestial cooks prepare food, with one dish featuring tomatoes and squash.

Andy Warhol's *Campbell's Soup Cans* is synonymous with Pop Art and its appropriation of popular and commercial images. The version in the Museum of Modern Art, New York, consists of thirty-two canvases measuring 51 × 41 cm (20 × 16 in.), with an instruction to install them 7.6 cm (3 in.) apart. The canvases resemble mass-produced advertisements, but they are, in fact, hand-painted, with a hand-stamped *fleur-de-lys* pattern on the base of the can. Warhol said he had the soup for lunch for twenty years, like the repeated can images, 'over and over again'.

OTHER TOMATO IMAGES
- Bartolomé Esteban Murillo, *Un miracle du frère Francisco* (*The Miracle of Brother Francisco*; better known as *The Angels' Kitchen*), 1646, oil on canvas. Paris: Musée du Louvre.
- Luis Egidio Meléndez, *Still Life with Cucumbers, Tomatoes and Vessels*, 1774, oil on canvas. Madrid: Museo del Prado.

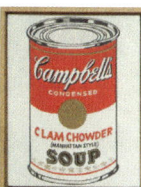 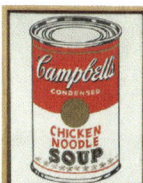 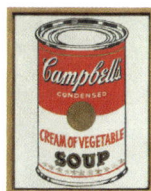 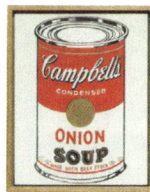 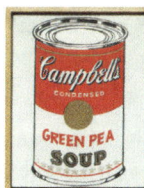 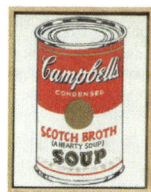

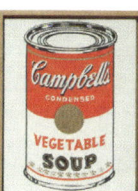 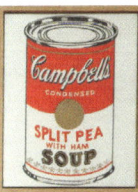 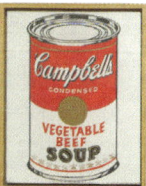 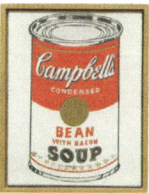 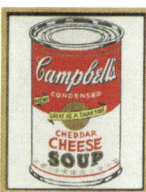 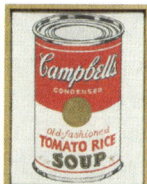

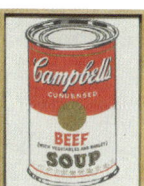 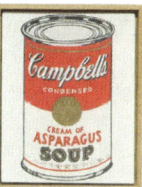 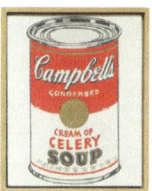 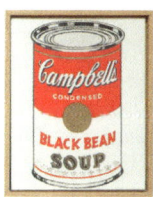 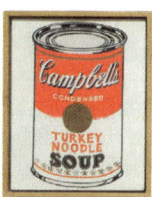 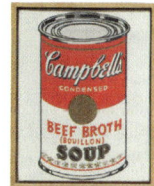

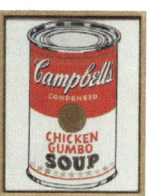 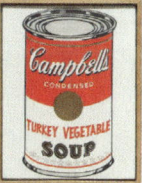 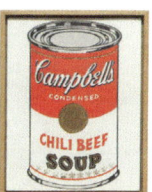 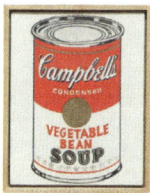 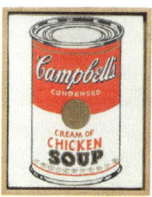 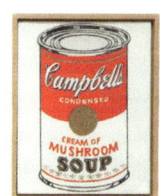

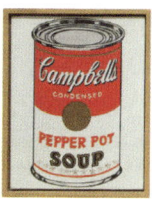 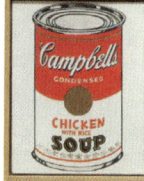 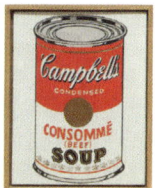 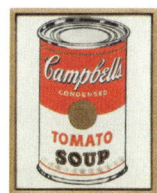 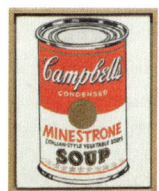 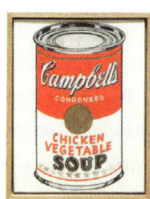

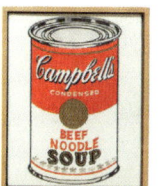 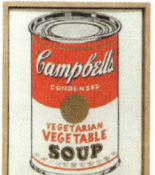

⊗ Pierre Joseph de Pannemaeker, a bunch of tomatoes (*Lycopersicon esculentum*), *c.* 1854.

✳ Andy Warhol, *Campbell's Soup Cans*, 1962, acrylic and enamel paint on canvas. New York: Museum of Modern Art.

✳

FAMILY Solanaceae

Possibly originating in India, the aubergine, brinjal
or eggplant was known in Europe by the thirteenth
century. Its fruits can be white, yellow, violet and rich
purple, and all other parts of the plant are poisonous.

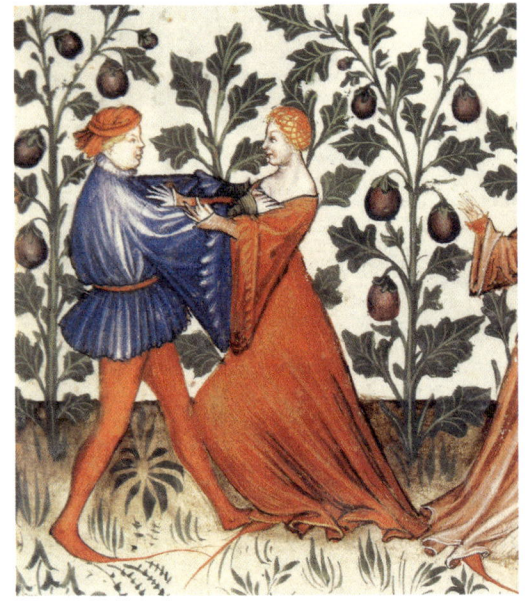

Aubergine has been associated with a number
of health benefits, including stimulation of
the appetite, improved digestion and lower
cholesterol. It has long had sexual connotations,
as a phallic symbol, and since 2010 the aubergine
emoji has been a popular choice for suggestive
messages.

Unknown in the Greco-Roman world, the
aubergine was introduced to Spain in the eighth
century by its Arab rulers. It is mentioned
frequently in medieval and Renaissance
documents, but in the Middle Ages attitudes
towards the fruit were ambiguous, and some
claimed it promoted anger and melancholy,
even insanity. Its aphrodisiac associations
are evident in a miniature from the eleventh-
century health handbook *Tacuinum sanitatis*
(*The Maintenance of Health*), depicting a
screen of plants with globular purple fruit.
An amorous dancing couple feels its effects,
while a single female remonstrates with them.

Renaissance herbalists also attributed
aphrodisiac properties to the aubergine.
It appears in the sixteenth-century festoons
in the Villa Farnesina in Rome; the painter
Giuseppe Arcimboldo depicted them; and in
1601 they were forged into the bronze doors
of Pisa Cathedral. It is found in seventeenth-
century painting, but perhaps the best images
of the aubergine come from the eighteenth-
century heyday of botanical illustration.

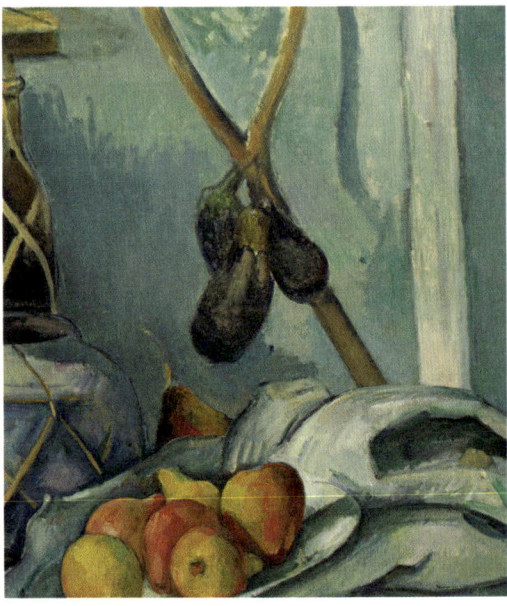

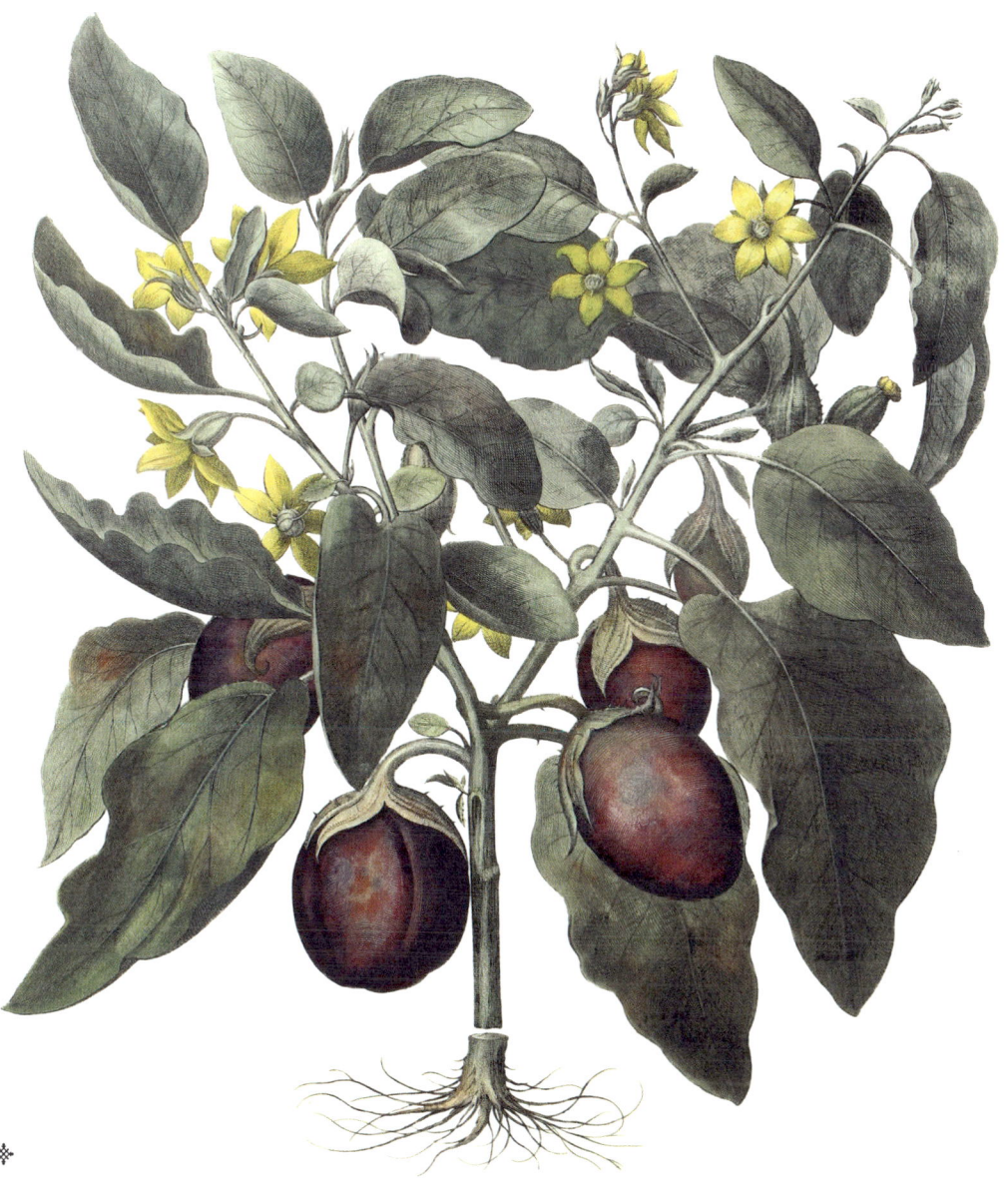

❖

FAMILY Solanaceae

The potato is a tuber in the nightshade family. The wild potato originated in what is now Peru, and was domesticated independently by many different Indigenous groups.

Spanish explorers introduced the potato to Europe in the second half of the sixteenth century, and early in the twenty-first century it became the world's fourth-largest food crop, after corn (maize), wheat and rice. There are now 5,000 different types of potato! As well as being food, potatoes are used to brew alcoholic drinks (most famously vodka). In popular culture, Mr Potato Head, invented in 1949 and marketed by Hasbro in 1952, is a popular toy and the first to be advertised on television. Originally, a real potato was used as the base for eyes, ears and mouth; newer versions are made of plastic.

Like the onion (see pp. 156–57), for centuries the potato was seen as a food of the lower classes. Some nineteenth-century artists, among them Anton Mauve and Jean-François Millet, depicted peasants eating and harvesting potatoes. Probably the most notable such painting is Vincent van Gogh's *The Potato Eaters*, which

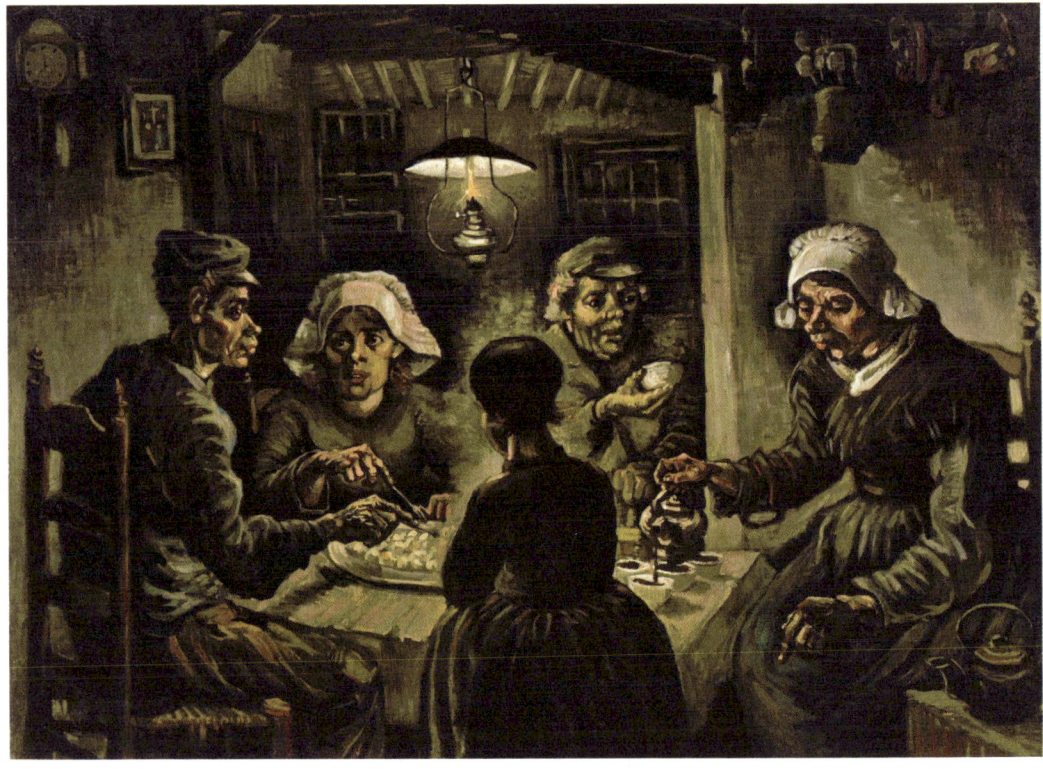

depicts five labourers at a table eating their evening meal. The artist showed the harsh effects of their reality in their coarse, distorted features and bony hands, but nevertheless the meal has a sacramental quality, evoking a sense of endurance and pious gratitude for what little they have. Van Gogh wrote to his brother in 1885:

You see, I really have wanted to make it so that people get the idea that these folk, who are eating their potatoes by the light of their little lamp, have tilled the earth themselves with these hands they are putting in the dish, and so it speaks of manual labour and – that they have thus honestly earned their food... [O]ne would be wrong, to my mind,

to give a peasant painting a certain conventional smoothness. If a peasant painting smells of bacon, smoke, potato steam – fine – that's not unhealthy – if a stable smells of manure – very well, that's what a stable's for – if the field has an odour of ripe wheat or potatoes or – of guano and manure – that's really healthy – particularly for city folk. They get something useful out of paintings like this. But a peasant painting mustn't become perfumed.

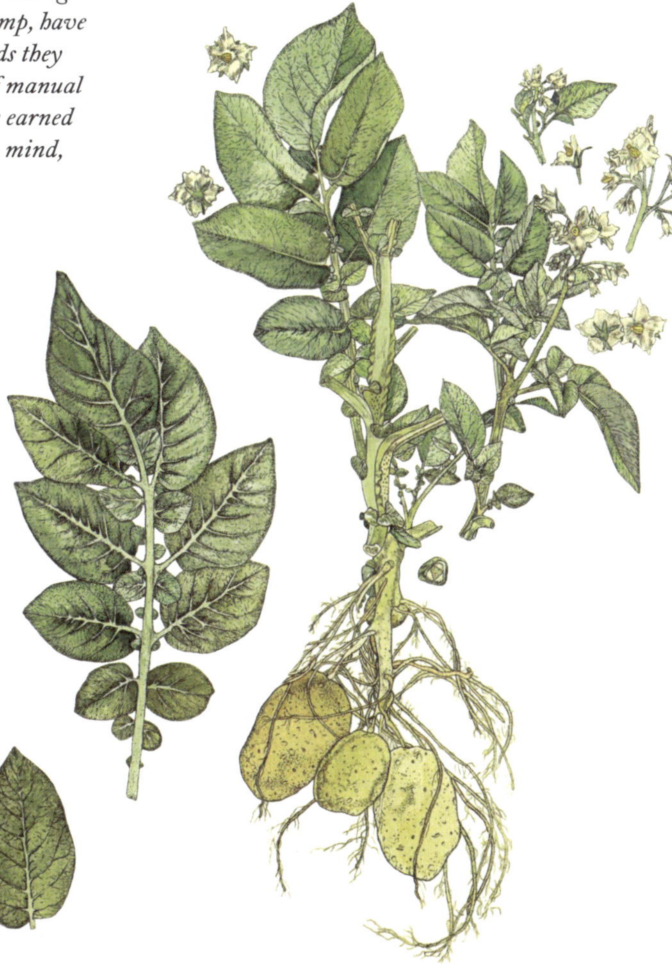

⊗ Vincent van Gogh,
The Potato Eaters,
1885, oil on canvas.
Amsterdam: Van
Gogh Museum.

✳ J. Vreugdenhil,
Solanum tuberosum
(potato), n.d.

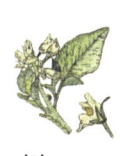
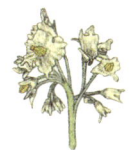
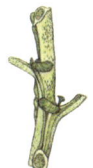

✳

FAMILY Scrophulariaceae

Common mullein (*V. thapsus*) is a herb with a substantial anecdotal history of medicinal use, having been mentioned as early as 64 CE. With worldwide distribution, it is sometimes regarded as a weed.

Mullein stalks can measure between 1.5 and 2 m (5–7 ft) tall and are densely packed with tiny five-petalled flowers. Medicinal products derived from the leaves can alleviate ear pain, coughs and other upper respiratory conditions and inflammation.

In ancient times, the plant was said to be able to drive off demons. From this may come the belief that it provided protection and inner strength. The Romans used dried mullein stalks, dipped in tallow, as torches, and for this reason they called the plant *candelaria*.

Notable appearances in art include Giovanni Bellini's *St Francis in the Desert*, in which the plant grows out of a small, raised garden directly behind St Francis. It appears to be a cultivated plant, and may protect the saint as he undergoes a transformational, supernatural experience, or encourage him to fulfil his destiny. Francis is said to have suffered from a number of maladies, so the mullein may also have served to alleviate his pain.

Writing about Bellini's masterpiece, the art historian James Elkins notes the important roles played by plants. He suggests that Bellini, uncomfortable with depicting supernatural beings, embedded the miracle in the landscape: 'Because nothing is quite what it should be, everything is partly sacred'. The saint has stepped away from his desk and stands barefoot, arms wide, absorbing radiant supernatural light. The Tuscan landscape, frozen in the

moment as the saint receives the transformative stigmata, contains myriad symbolic plants that range from barren to healthy; several are undergoing rejuvenation. These include a laurel tree (symbolizing honour and victory over death, the burning bush[14]) and a grapevine (for the Eucharist and the saint's devotion to Christ). There are also bindweed, daisies (for innocence), two fig trees (redemption), a juniper (chastity), olive, a reed cross and gate, and a Crown of Thorns; James Elkins adds briars, ivy and maidenhair fern. Medicinal plants include orris and mullein. Bellini combines Italian Renaissance macrocosmic spirituality with Northern Renaissance microcosmic naturalism.

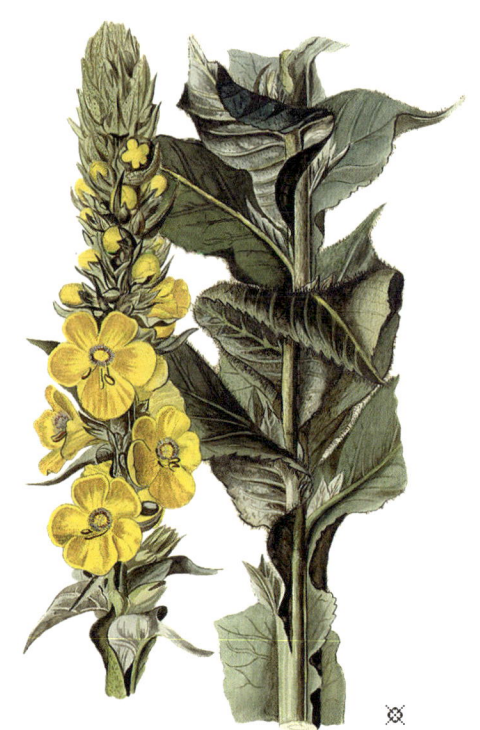

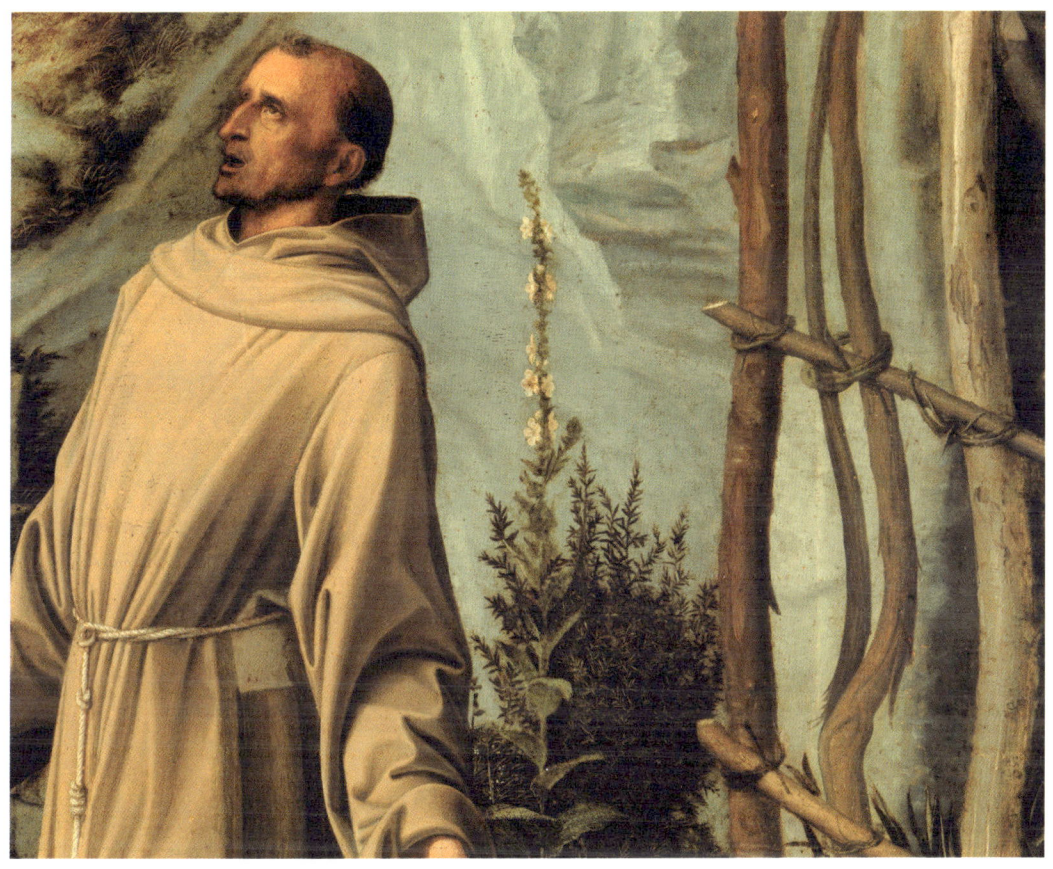

⌗

⌀ *Verbascum thapsus*
(mullein), n.d.

⌗ Giovanni Bellini,
*St Francis in the
Desert* (detail),
c. 1475–80, oil on
panel. New York:
Frick Collection.

OTHER IMAGES OF MULLEIN

- Martin Schongauer, *The Flight into Egypt*,
  c. 1470–75, engraving. Washington, DC:
  National Gallery of Art.
- Caravaggio, *St John the Baptist in the
  Wilderness*, 1604, oil on canvas. Kansas City,
  MO: Nelson-Atkins Museum of Art.
- Gian Lorenzo Bernini, *Fountain of Four
  Rivers*, opened 1677. Rome: Piazza Navona.
  (Depicts thirty-four species associated with
  the rivers' environments.[15])
- W. G. Smith, *Common Mullein*, *c.* 1863,
  lithograph. London: Wellcome Collection.

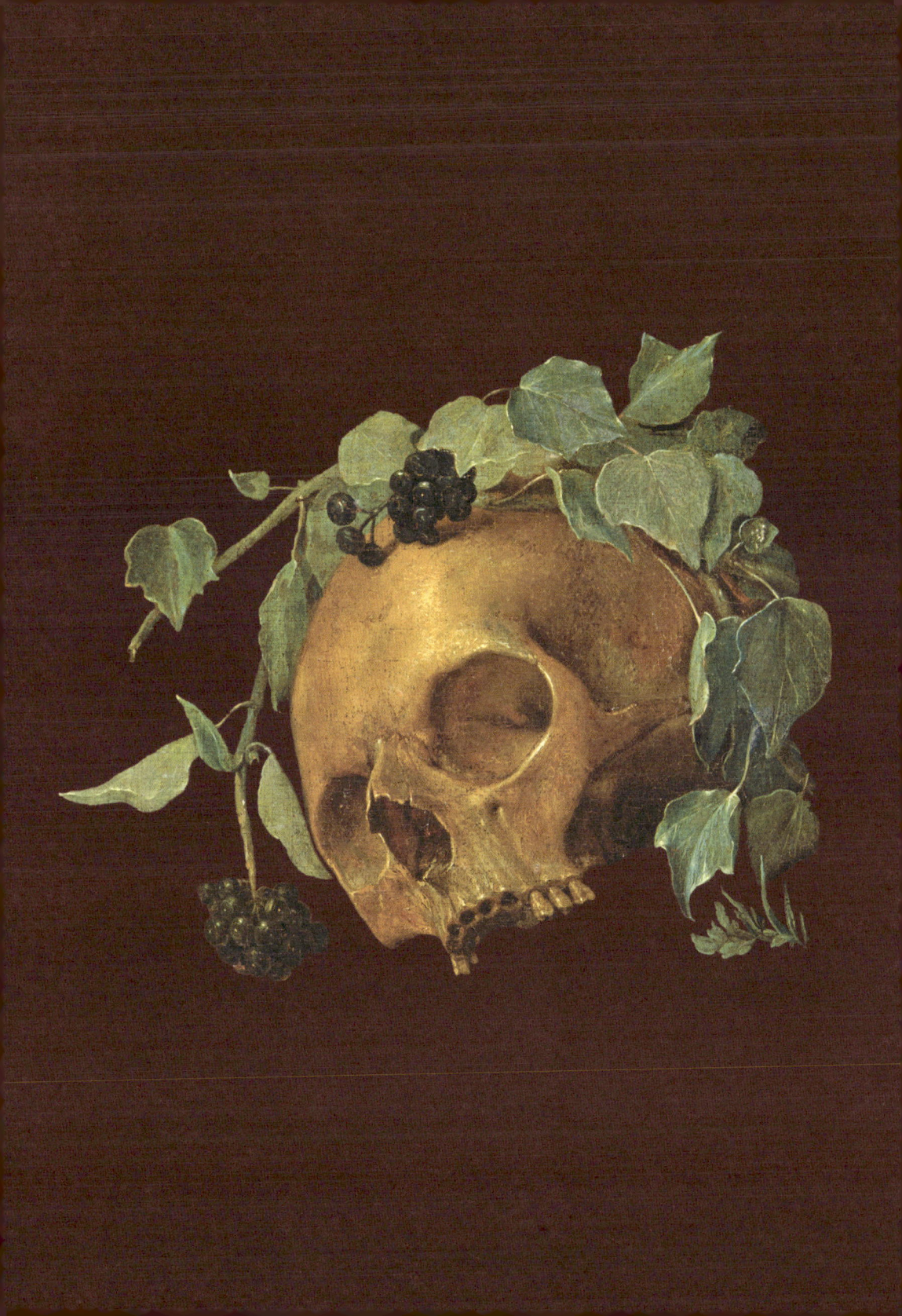

GRAINS, GRASSES & VINES

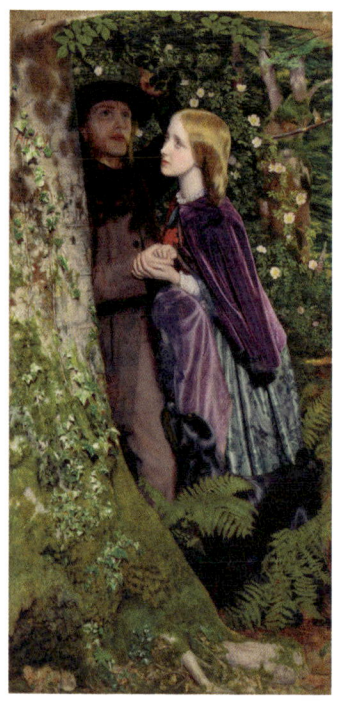

⊗

The grass family includes all the major cereals (including wheat, rice, barley and oats), and most of the grains (corn, rye and millet, among others) as well. Grasses are the most important flowering plants, providing nutrition for both animals and humans, and preventing soil erosion by way of their mat-forming root systems. They are among the largest families of flowering plants, numbering some 10,000 species, and – from evidence of fossilized grass pollen – have been around for at least sixty-six million years. The tallest grass is bamboo, which can grow up to 30 m (100 ft) high.

Vines are plants that require support and climb by tendrils, or twine or creep along the ground. The word 'vine' often refers to the grapevine (pp. 222–23). The prehistoric Mother Goddess was known as 'The Goddess of the Vines', a source of natural creation. Vines in ancient Syria and Judaea were trained on fig trees (pp. 54–57), both plants being symbols of peace and abundance. A golden vine is said to have adorned the eastern wall of the temple in Jerusalem; in 70 CE it was carried off by the Romans and displayed as part of the spoils of war. The Jewish people regarded the vine and the olive (pp. 66–67) as the two Messianic plants, and the vine may actually have been identified with the Tree of Life in Eden. The Jewish Messiah, compared to the vine, became the true symbol of the Chosen People.

The vine functioned as one of the earliest symbols of Christ: 'I am the vine, you [the apostles] are the branches' (John 15:5). Vine paintings ornamented the walls of both pagan and early Christian catacombs. Under Emperor Constantine, the vine became the sole symbol of Christianity. Its symbolism extended to every human soul; God planted the vine, Christ the Messiah visited the vineyard, and his blood redeemed all souls. Cultivated relatively late in Greece, the vine was linked with Dionysus, god of the mysteries of wine, fruitfulness and vegetation, but also madness.

Vines, because of their varying habits, enjoy complex meanings. Their ability to grow and cling signifies strength and energy (using trees, walls or other supports, ivy can reach impressive heights, for instance). Many vines flower and bear fruit, relating them to plenty and resurgence. Vines can also mean friendship, support and intimate companionship (see 'Honeysuckle', pp. 128–29). It is this meaning that perhaps explains the popularity of modern vine tattoo designs.

There are scores of types of vine, and Darwin categorized them by their climbing habits. Some, such as liana and kudzu, are extremely invasive. Many have medical uses. Others – among them bougainvillea, clematis, morning glory, nasturtium, philodendron and wisteria – make excellent garden plants, providing glorious decoration as well as privacy.

⊗ Arthur Hughes, *The Long Engagement*, 1859, oil on canvas. Birmingham, UK: Birmingham Museum & Art Gallery.

※ Hieronymus Bosch, *The Haywain Triptych*, c. 1516, oil on panel. Madrid: Museo del Prado.

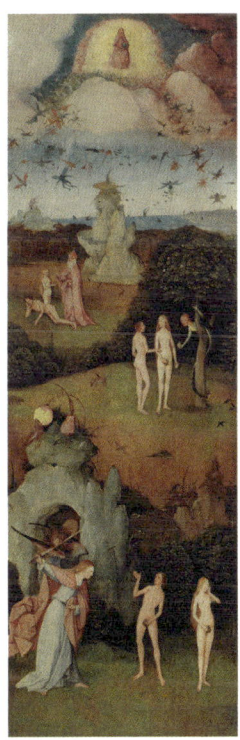
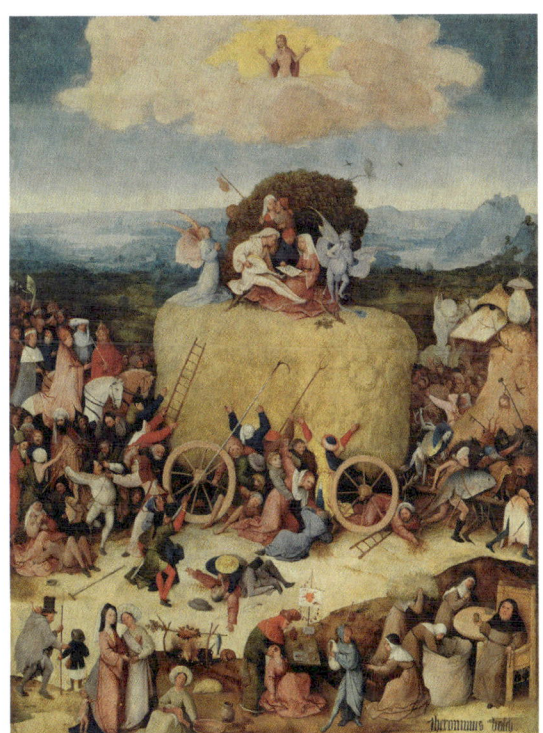
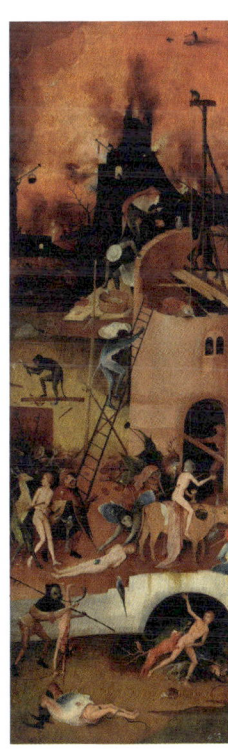

※

FAMILY   Cucurbitaceae

A widely cultivated creeping plant with large leaves and tendrils that enable it to grow on trellises. It has been cultivated for 3,000 years, having originated in India and been introduced elsewhere by the Greeks and Romans.

According to Pliny, Emperor Tiberius ate cucumbers every day in the summer and winter, probably grown in some form of greenhouse. The Romans used cucumbers to treat scorpion bites and bad eyesight, and to repel mice. Women wishing for children sometimes wore cucumbers, which were then discarded by the midwives once the wished-for child was born. In the eighth and early ninth centuries, the Carolingian king Charlemagne's gardens featured cucumbers, and Christopher Columbus introduced the vegetable to the Americas in the late fifteenth century.

   In Christian art, the cucumber often appears in images of the Virgin Mary. A passage in Isaiah prefigures the Immaculate Conception: 'As a hut in a garden of cucumbers, as a besieged city' (1:8), the Virgin, surrounded by sin, remained pure. Carlo Crivelli included a cucumber in his *Madonna and Child*, opposite. The cucumber and several apples dangle from the upper corners, overlapping a folded cloth that hangs behind the Virgin. The Christ Child holds a goldfinch and looks down at a large fly on the balustrade. In this painting, the apples and the fly are symbols of sin and evil, counteracted by the bird and the cucumber, which signify redemption and the soul.

⊗ F. Domingo, *Cucumis sativus* (cucumber), 1877–83.

✳ Carlo Crivelli, *Madonna and Child*, c. 1480, tempera and gold on wood. New York: Metropolitan Museum of Art.

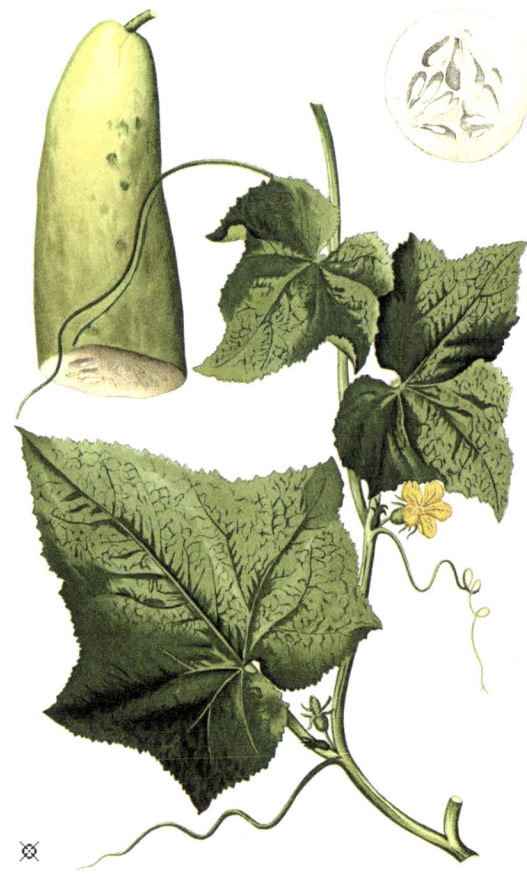

⊗

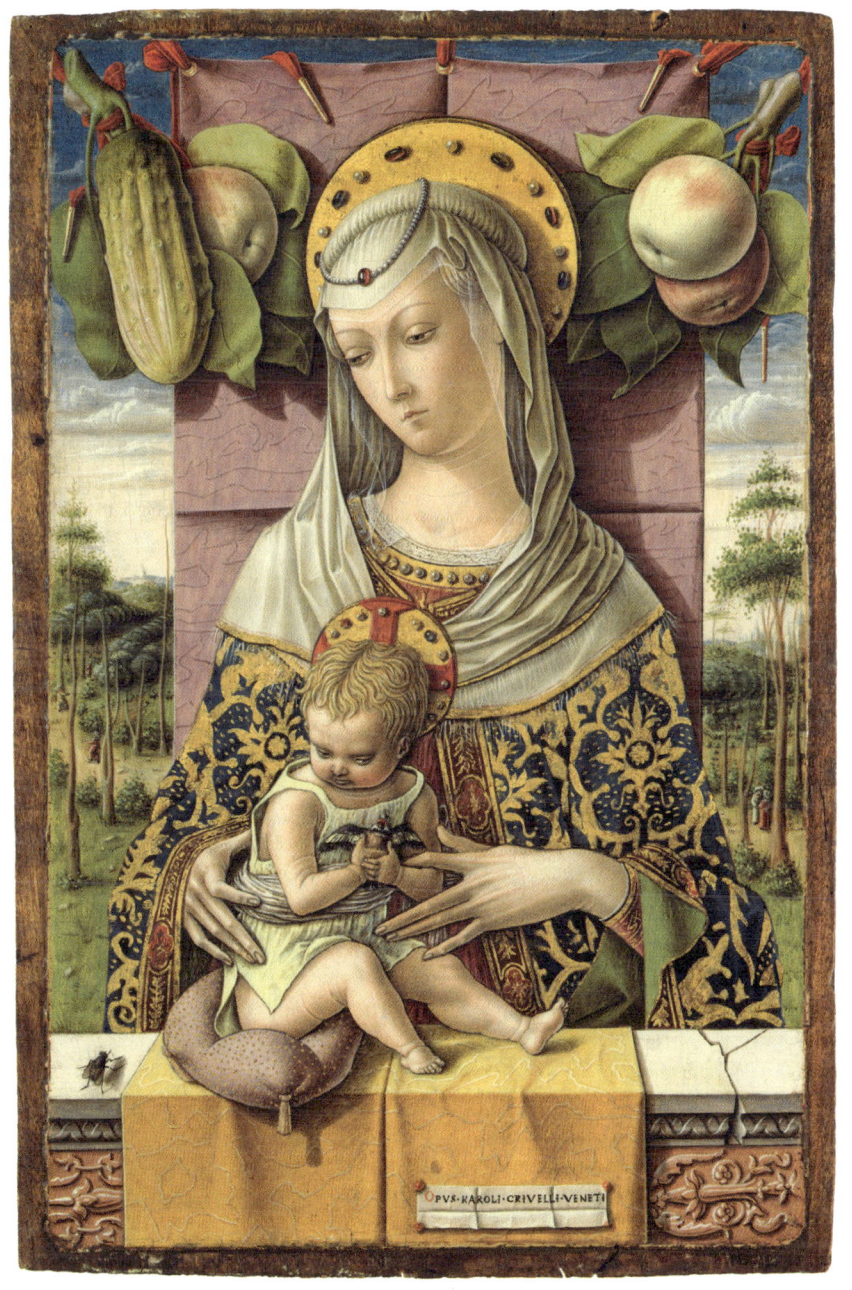

FAMILY Poaceae

Grass is one of the single most important plants in the world, both in the form of natural grasses (grassland) and cultivated grasses, such as corn and wheat.

Grasses appear in all environments, even in Antarctica. This entry refers to what is commonly thought of as grass: grassland or perennials such as Bermuda grass (Cynodon dactylon), bluegrass (Poa species) and fescue (Festuca species), to name just a few.

Grass can represent the idea of a homeland – as in the popular song 'The Green, Green Grass of Home', versions of which were recorded by Elvis Presley, Johnny Cash and Tom Jones – or, when pulled, surrender or conquest of land or territory. In places where it grows prolifically, it has also often been a symbol of usefulness, as a humble common plant. Grass can also signify evanescence, being quick to grow but also to wither and die. 'Under the grass' is a term commonly associated with burial and death.

Grass is tenacious. It is one of the first plants to appear after such natural disasters as floods, wildfires and snowstorms, and many types will grow up through the slightest crack, enlarging fissures in rock or concrete and filling gaps between paving stones.

Albrecht Dürer took great pains to depict the natural world based on careful observation.

His watercolour *Great Piece of Turf* (1503) is generally seen as a study undertaken to help him render plants more realistically. Indeed, the slightly larger-than-life-sized plants are so detailed that they can be identified accurately, and include several kinds of meadowgrass, plantain, speedwell, daisy leaves, hound's tongue and yarrow. The clarity and focus, as well as the scene's detachment from a larger setting, suggest timelessness and a sort of pantheistic perfection.

In Walt Whitman's 'Song of Myself', part of his great *Leaves of Grass* (1855), the poet, asked by a child 'What is the grass?', suggests that grass, like life, is fundamentally unknowable and inexplicable. He guesses at what it might mean, evoking macrocosmically everything in existence. The microcosm is evoked in the following line from Verse 31: 'I believe a leaf of grass is no less than the journey-work of the stars.'

A powerful contemporary example of the regenerative and enduring qualities of grass can be seen in Ansel Adams's photograph of grass sprouting in the crevice of a burned tree in Yosemite Valley. The artists Heather Ackroyd and Dan Harvey, meanwhile, collaborate on works in which they manipulate light to create human–grass hybrids, shown opposite, symbolically looking towards a future of human–plant harmony.

Ackroyd & Harvey, *Mother and Child* (*Heather and Adèle*), 1998, staygreen grass, clay and jute. Commissioned for Santa Barbara Museum of Art, CA.

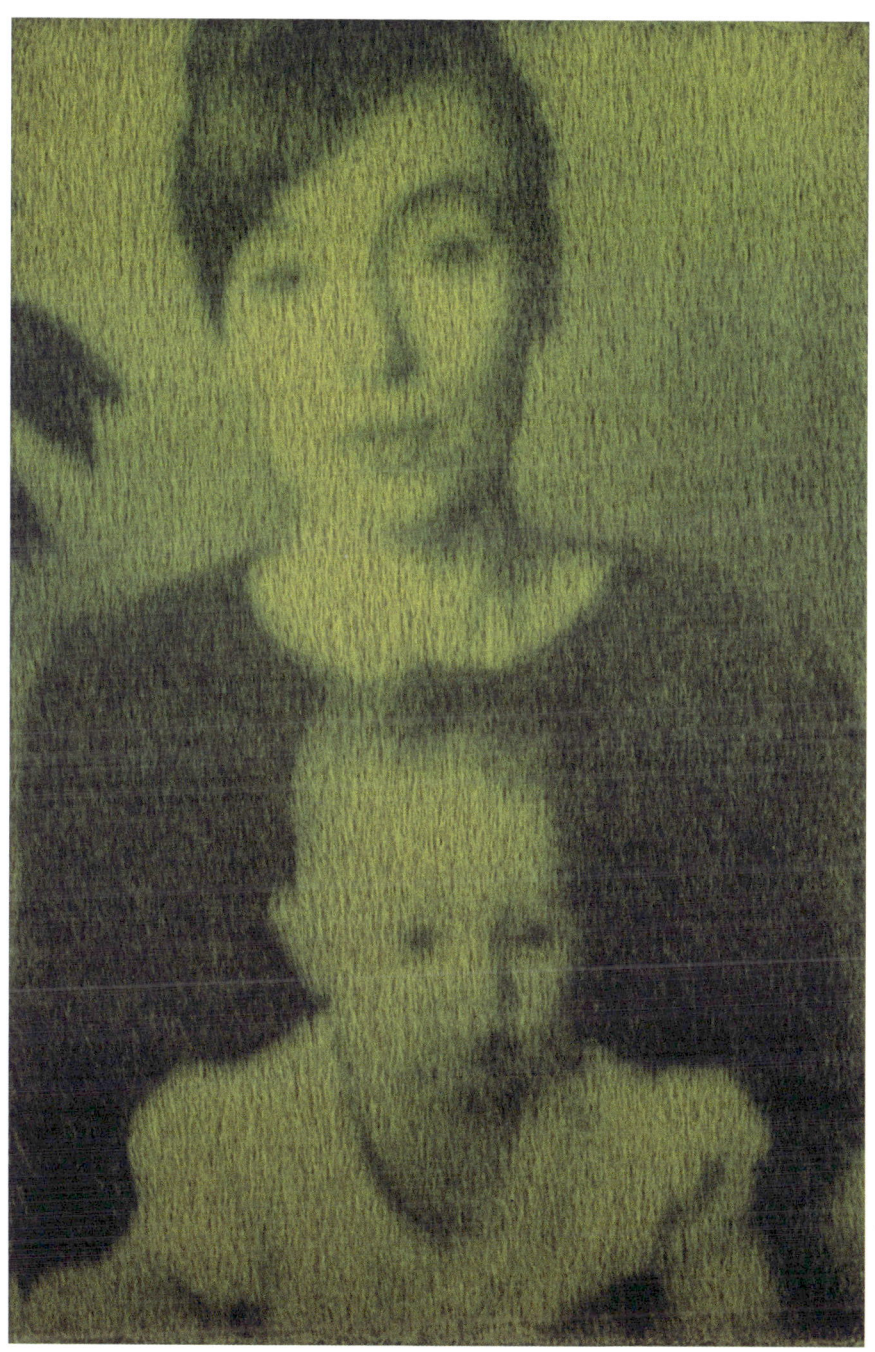

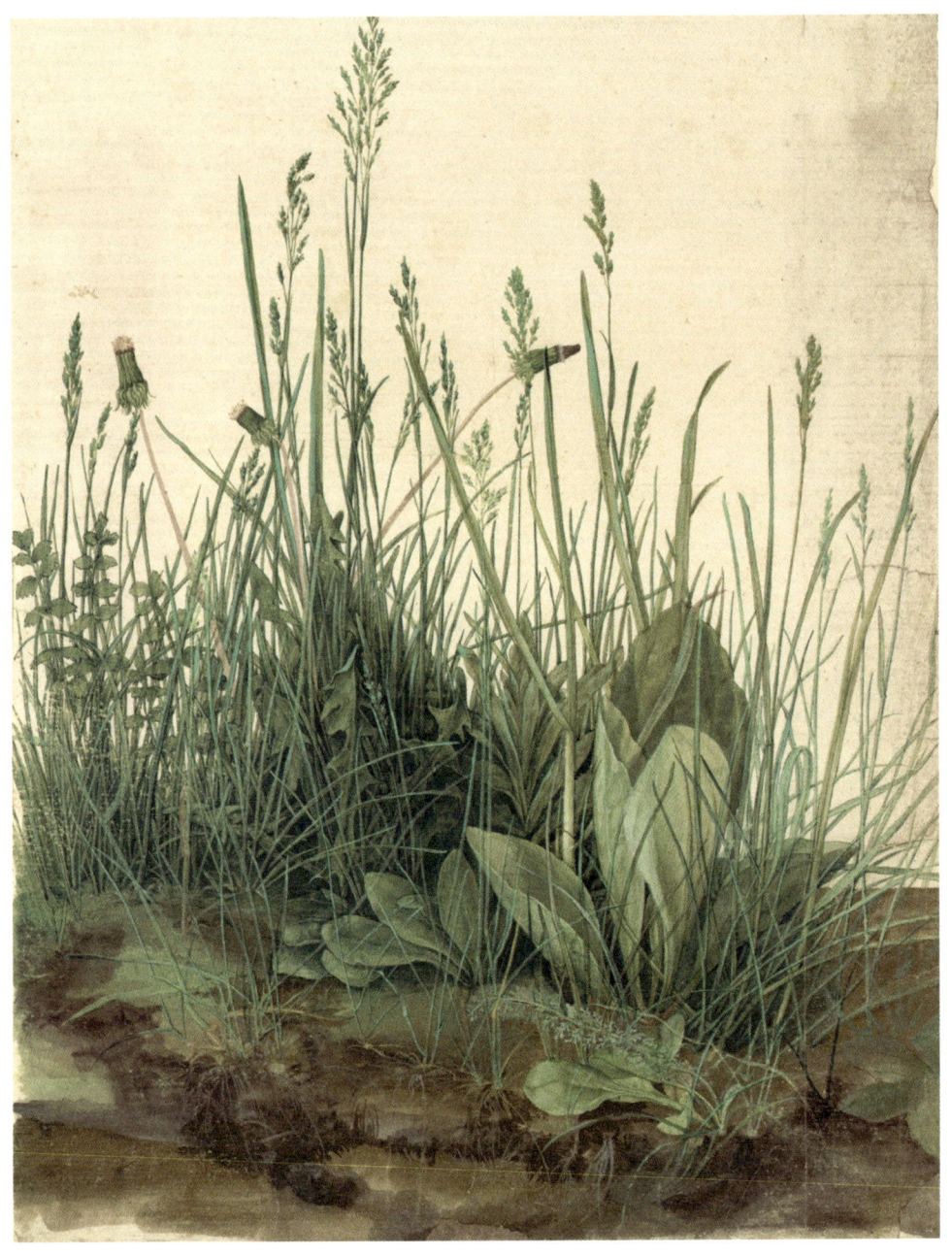

※

GRAINS, GRASSES & VINES

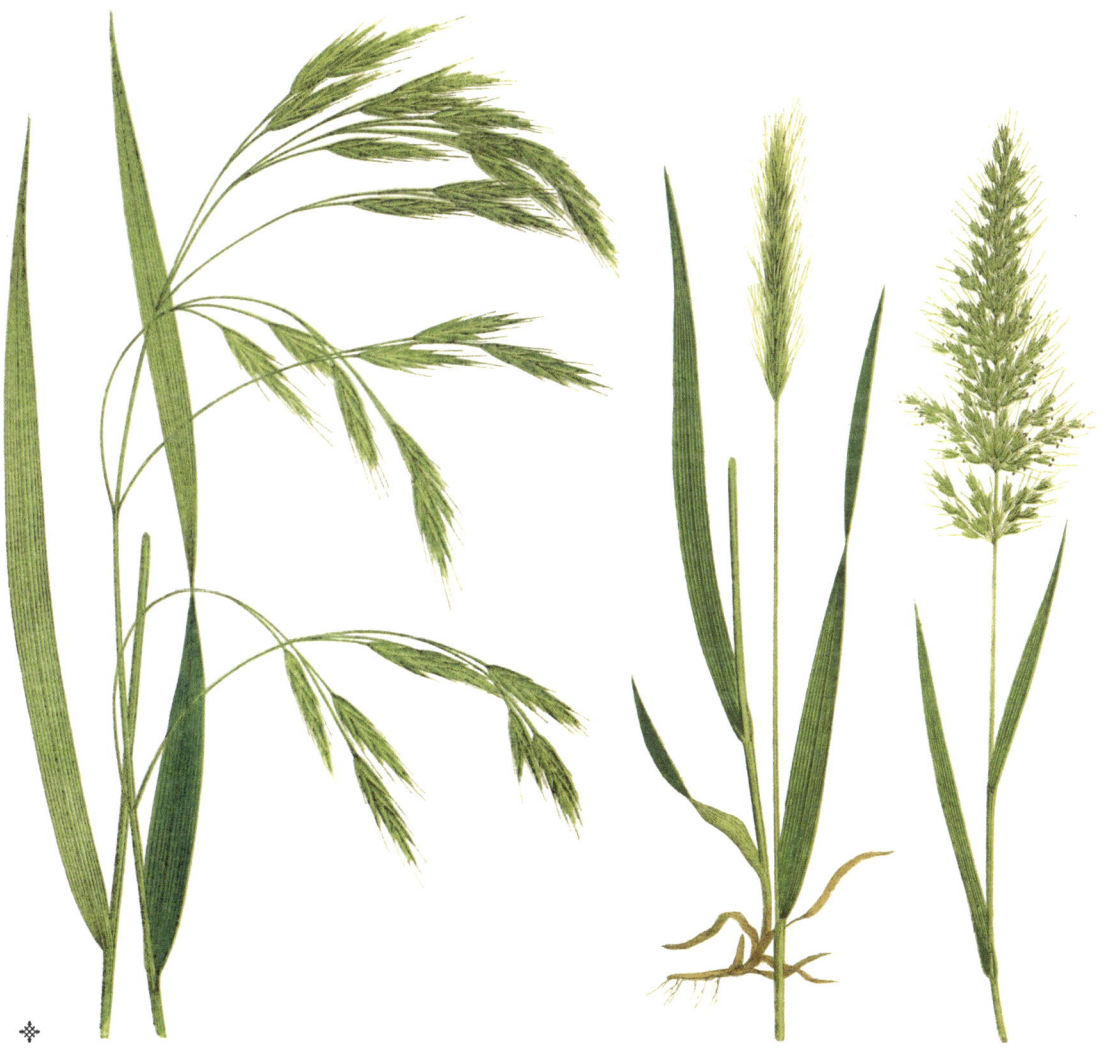

※ Albrecht Dürer, *Great Piece of Turf*, 1503, watercolour and body colour on vellum. Vienna: Albertina.

❖ A. F. Lydon, *Bromus asper, Hordeum sylvaticum and Avena flavescens*, 1858.

FAMILY Araliaceae

Ivy is an evergreen, ground-creeping woody plant native to most of Europe and parts of Africa and Asia. It is now also widespread in North America and Australia. Ivy climbs trees, rocky outcrops and buildings, with a reach of up to 10 m (35 ft).

In ancient Greece, ivy was called *cissos*. According to myth, it was named after the nymph Cissus or Kissos, who danced so energetically at a feast of the gods that she fell dead at Dionysus' feet. Moved, he turned her into the vigorous plant.

When Dionysus, god of vegetation, was born of a union between Zeus and Semele, his cradle was hidden from Hera, queen of the gods', wrath by being covered in ivy. The plant was dedicated to him; his devotees, including the maenads, are often shown wearing or otherwise ornamented with ivy, and even today ivy decorates taverns and wine shops.

The dancing figure illustrated here, from a famous kylix, carries an ivy-covered staff and a leopard, and wears a serpent diadem and a leopard skin. Ivy also adorned images of satyrs and sileni, who, like the followers of Dionysus, enjoyed life's pleasures. The Romans used ivy boiled in wine to alleviate hangovers.

Because of its clinging habit, ivy is associated with loyalty and undying affection. Owing to its trilobed shape, it can also symbolize the Trinity. Green ivy in medieval Christian art often signifies the immortality of the soul after death, and because of its tenacity, it can also represent the passage of time. In Dutch Baroque *vanitas* paintings such as Rachel Ruysch's, illustrated below, where the vine twines around a skull, ivy symbolizes immortality. The plant was a popular motif among Art Nouveau artists and is commonly incorporated into tattoos today.

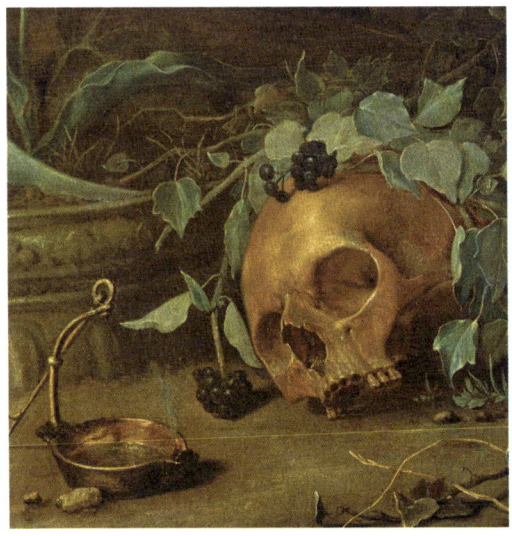

※ Rachel Ruysch (attrib.), *Vanité (Vanity)*, *c.* 1690, oil on canvas. La Fère, France: Museé Jeanne d'Aboville.

※ J.P. Del, *Glechoma hederacea* (ground ivy), 1835.

❖ Maenad with thyrsus ornamented with ivy leaves, Attic white-ground *kylix*, 490–480 BCE, from Vulci. Munich: Staatliche Antikensammlungen.

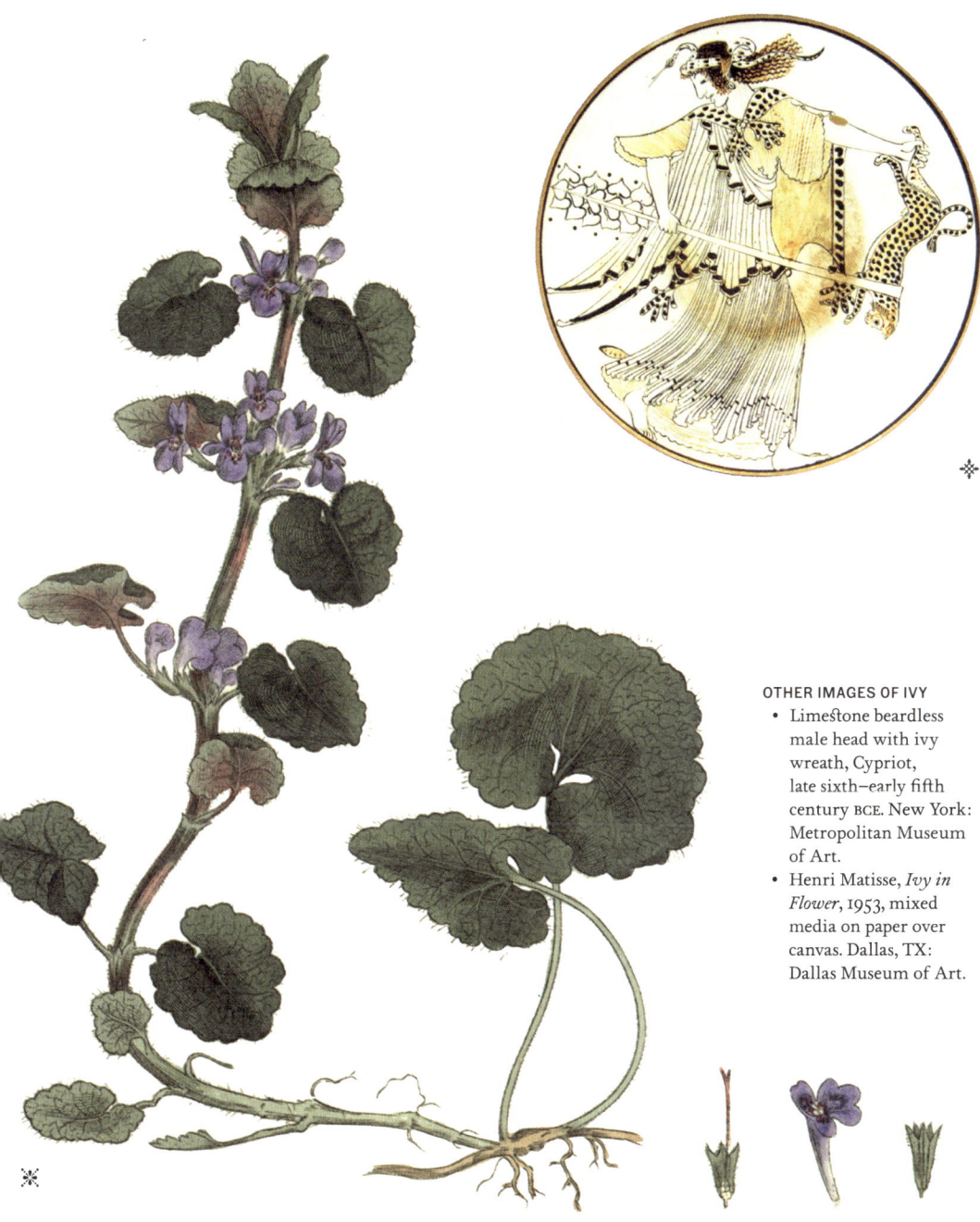

OTHER IMAGES OF IVY

- Limestone beardless male head with ivy wreath, Cypriot, late sixth–early fifth century BCE. New York: Metropolitan Museum of Art.
- Henri Matisse, *Ivy in Flower*, 1953, mixed media on paper over canvas. Dallas, TX: Dallas Museum of Art.

FAMILY Various

Reed is a common name used for several tall, grass-like plants that grow in wetlands. The various families include Poaceae (the grass family), Cyperaceae (sedges), Typhaceae (cattails) and Restionaceae (restiads). Reeds are both flexible and fragile, and have uses as varied as thatching and musical instruments.

The symbolic Egyptian *djed* pillar was made of reeds, and the architectural form of reed-bundle columns may have derived from reed-built homes. The ancient Egyptians called the afterlife the Field of Reeds (A'aru or Iaru) and envisaged it as an agrarian paradise, part of one's eternal journey. Boats were fashioned from reeds in order to travel there. The afterlife duplicated temporal life, but without pain or fear of death. Accompanied by loved ones, the deceased carried out the same activities as they had while alive. The painting of A'aru, below, illustrates one of the spells from the so-called Book of the Dead. In their tomb, the Ancient Egyptian artisan Sennedjem and his wife honour various gods and work at agricultural activities.

Papyrus (*Cyperus papyrus*) and lotus plants are also referred to as reeds, and all played major roles in ancient Egyptian art and architecture. Reed sceptres were borne by some deities; in Egypt, Set – the god of violence, chaos and storms – bore one.

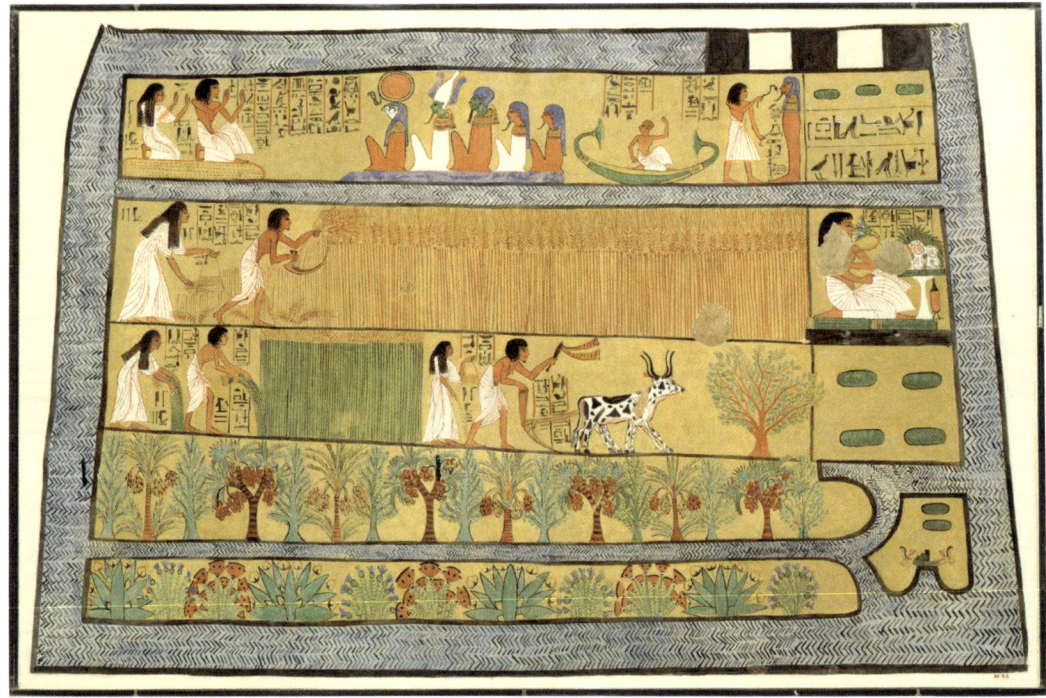

A Greek myth tells of a nymph named Syrinx, who was pursued by Pan and escaped at the river's edge by transforming into reeds. Pan cut the reeds and made his first set of pipes from them.

In the Old Testament, speaking of the coming Messiah, Isaiah wrote: 'A bruised reed He will not break... He will bring forth justice for truth. He will not fail nor be discouraged, till He has established justice in the earth' (42: 3–4). In Christian art, the reed became associated with Christ, and reeds are often woven into the shape of a cross at Easter.

A'aru (The Field of Reeds), Tomb of Sennedjem, Deir-el-Medina, Egypt, *c.* 1200 BCE. Facsimile by Charles K. Wilkinson, 1922. New York: Metropolitan Museum of Art.

Johann Ibmayer, *Arundo donax* (giant reed), 1809.

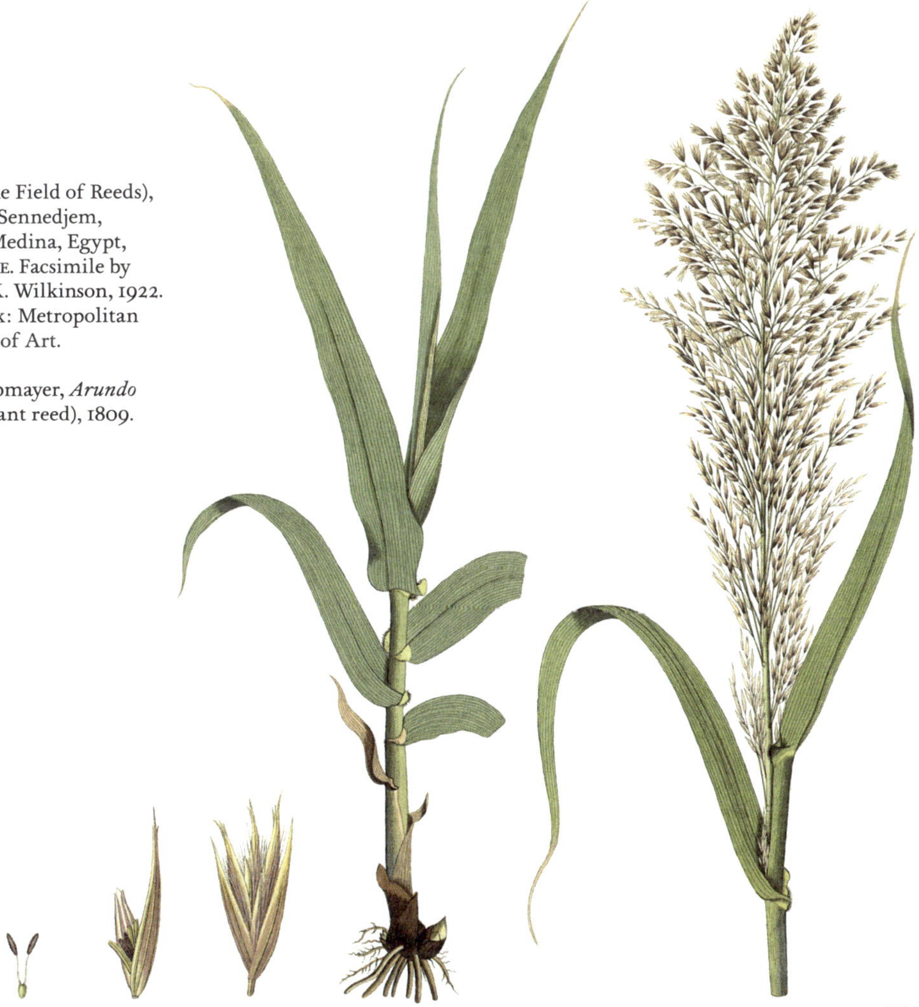

FAMILY Fabaceae

Kudzu is a group of climbing and trailing vines native to parts of Asia and some Pacific islands, where it has been cultivated for centuries and is celebrated for its ability to flourish in even the most depleted soil.

'Kudzu' comes from the plant's Japanese name, *kuzu*, and it has also been known as Japanese arrowroot. Its fibres have been used to make clothing and paper, and it is also used in food and traditional medicine throughout East Asia.

Kudzu was first planted in North America as an ornamental vine, but became widely cultivated and promoted as a soil enhancer and a form of erosion control. It is an invasive species in Europe and North America, and became particularly notorious in the southern United States as the 'vine that ate the South'.

The work of Precious Okoyomon involves transforming spaces into living environments that convey historical or social ideas. *Earthseed*, installed in the Museum für Moderne Kunst, Frankfurt, involved covering the gallery floor with a thick layer of topsoil, in which the artist planted young kudzu vines in the spring.[16] By autumn, the artist's six yarn and lambswool figures had been enveloped by

the vines. Crickets, spiders, butterflies and even snails moved in. Okoyomon's installation drew attention to the resilience of nature – as they put it, 'our entanglement with nature'. Using plant material of this kind serves as a reminder of unintended consequences. As Coco Romack suggests, the artist warns against destroying nature, while celebrating its energy and chaos.

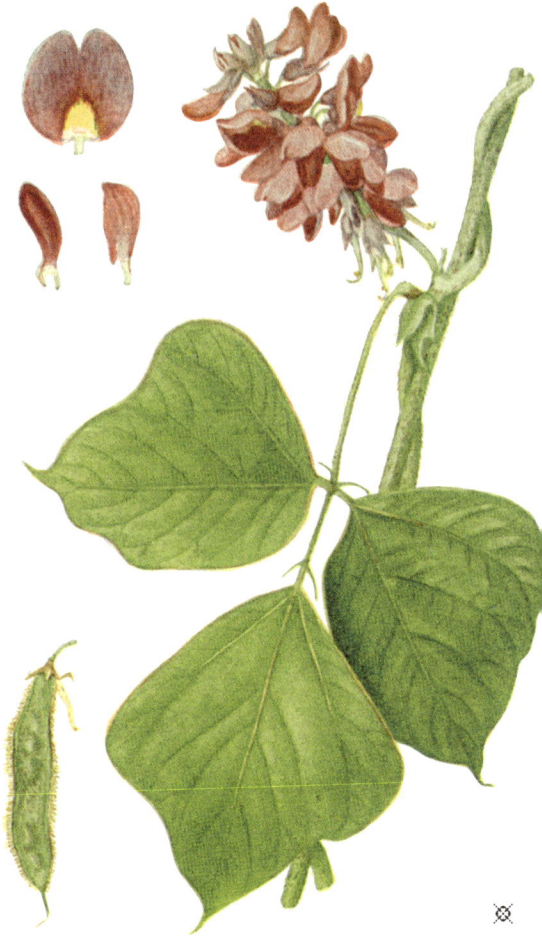

⊗ Mary Emily Eaton, *Pueraria thunbergiana* (kudzu), 1930.

✳ Precious Okoyomon, *Earthseed*, 2020, mixed media. Frankfurt, Germany: Museum für Moderne Kunst.

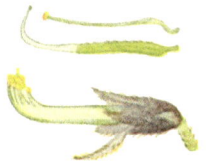

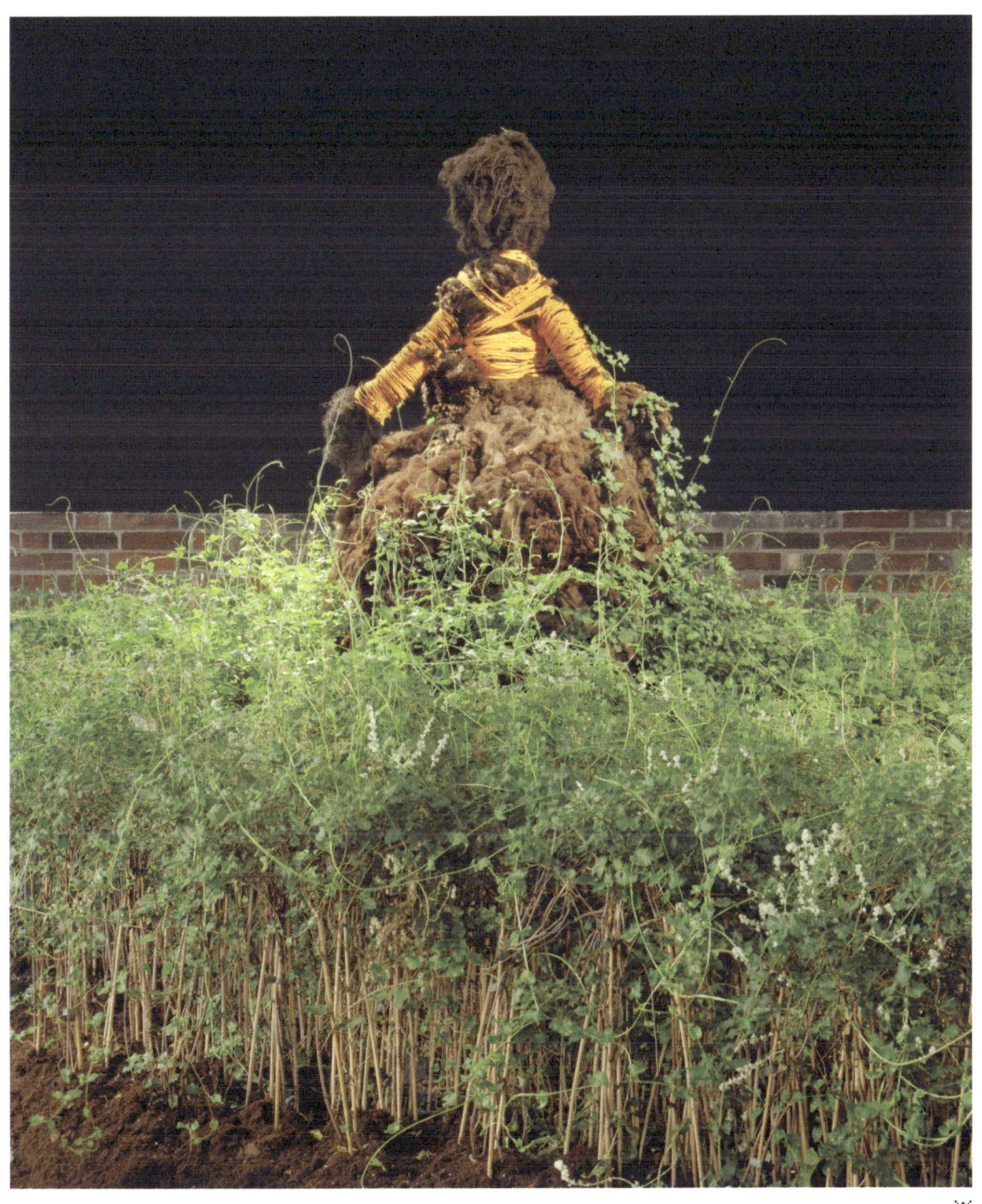

FAMILY Poaceae

Wheat is a grass widely cultivated for its seed, a cereal grain with worldwide distribution and use, and the leading source of vegetable protein globally. Archaeological evidence shows that it was first cultivated in the Levant as early as 9600 BCE.

The Egyptian gods Osiris and Nepra (the god of grain, considered an aspect of Osiris) were both linked with wheat. According to Plutarch, Osiris's main festival began at Abydos with a commemoration of the god's death and planting of wheat on the same day. The Egyptologist Emily Teeter writes that 'Osiris beds' were constructed in the shape of the god, filled with soil and sown with seed; the germinating wheat symbolized Osiris's resurrection from the dead.

In ancient Greece, in the secret rites of the Eleusinian Mysteries, a grain of wheat was displayed to remind the participants of the eternal cycle of life. Wheat is planted, cultivated and finally harvested to provide not only the sustenance of bread but also seed for the next cycle. The origin of wheat was mysterious and therefore regarded as a gift of the gods.

Around the time of Christ, Jewish people made unleavened bread for Passover from both wheat and barley. At the Last Supper, during the Passover meal, Christ broke bread with his disciples and likened it to his body and wine to his blood; they were to consume both in memory of him. Despite considerable variation in both doctrine and practice among later Christians, the Eucharist reflects the ancient symbolism of life's constant renewal and the promise of rebirth brought about by Christ's sacrifice.

A sheaf of wheat appears with other symbolic plants in Hugo van der Goes's Portinari Altarpiece (*c.* 1475, see p. 95). The wheat indicates not only Bethlehem (the word means 'house of bread' in Hebrew), but also the cyclical immortality granted by Christ's death and

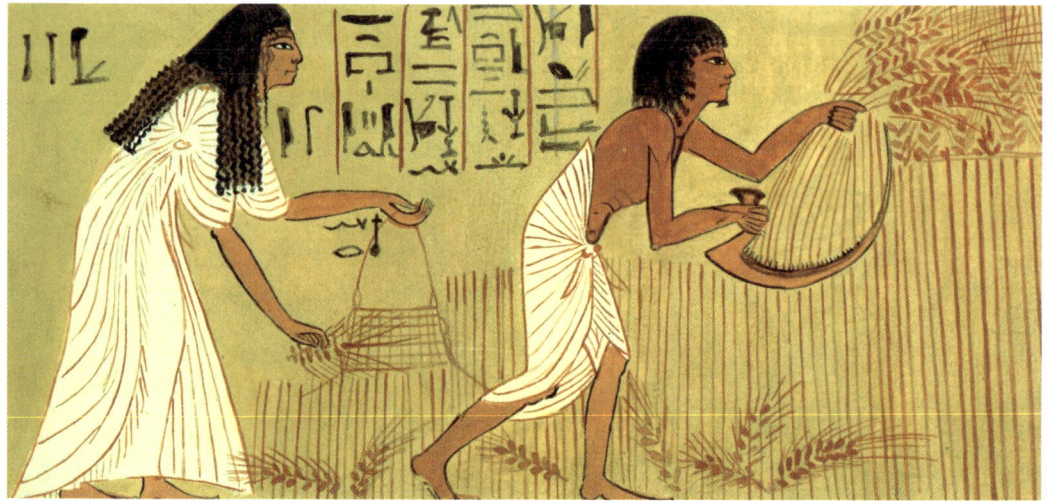

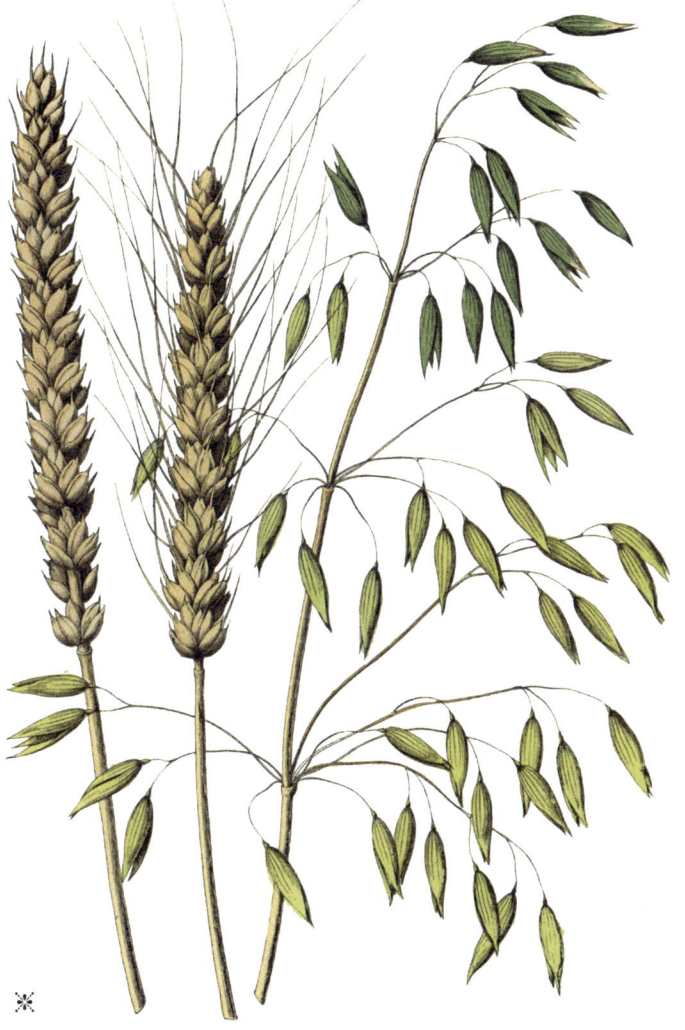

✴

⊗ 'Sennedjem and His Wife
Harvest Wheat in the Fields
of Osiris', Tomb of Sennedjem,
Deir el-Medina, *c.* 1300 BCE.
Tempera facsimile (detail) by
Charles K. Wilkinson, 1922.
New York: Metropolitan
Museum of Art.

✳ Charlotte M. Yonge, *Triticum
aestivum* (wheat and bearded
wheat) and *Avena sativa* (oats),
1858.

OTHER IMAGES OF WHEAT

- Ceres (Demeter) rising from
  the ground with sheaves of
  wheat, Roman, Augustan period
  (27 BCE –14 CE), bas-relief.
- Hieronymus Bosch, centre
  panel of *The Haywain Triptych*,
  c. 1512–15, oil on panel. Madrid:
  Museo del Prado.
- Pieter Bruegel the Elder,
  The Harvesters, 1565, oil on
  wood. New York: Metropolitan
  Museum of Art.

Resurrection. On gravestones, a sheaf of wheat suggests that the individual lived a long life.

Wheat symbolizes plenty and fertility, and has long been an artistic subject. Among the finest depictions is Samuel Palmer's *A Hilly Scene* (*c.* 1826–28), which represents what the Tate website calls 'an ideal image of pastoral contentment'. The enormous flowering horse chestnut (spring) and the ripe autumn wheat may reflect Edmund Spenser's *Faërie Queene* (1596): 'There is continuall spring, and harvest there.'

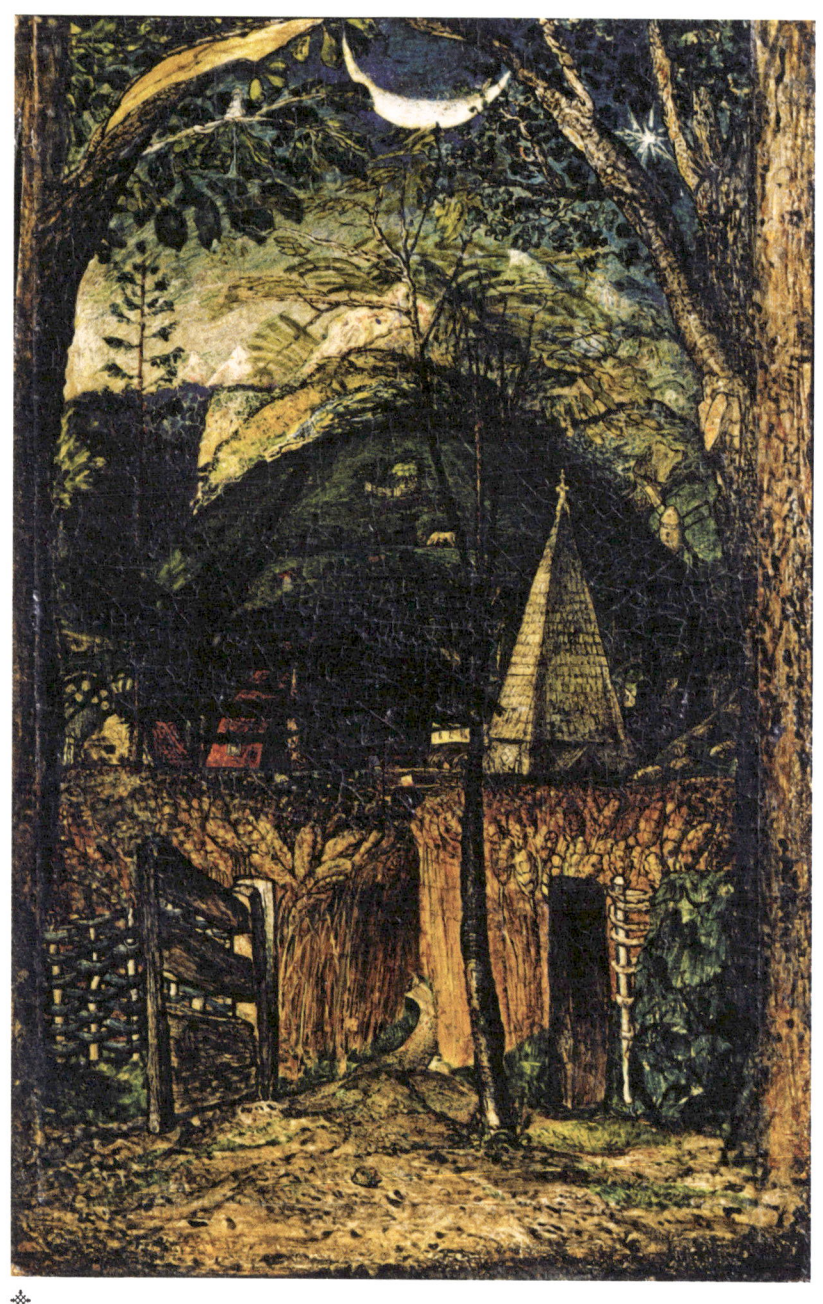

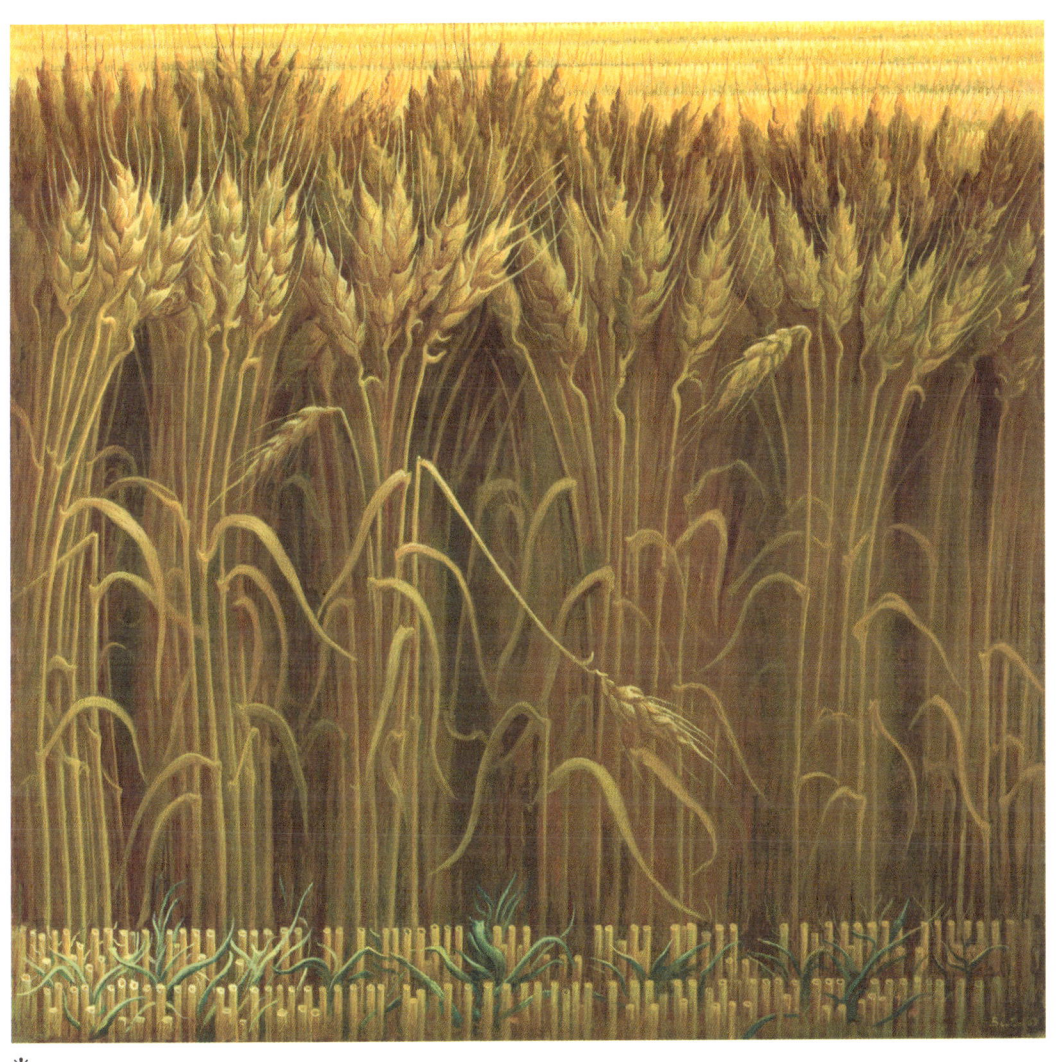

✿ Samuel Palmer, *A Hilly Scene*,
  c. 1826–8, watercolour on paper.
  London: Tate.

✳ Thomas Hart Benton, *Wheat*,
  1967, oil on wood. Washington,
  DC: Smithsonian American
  Art Museum.

FAMILY Vitaceae

Grapes have been cultivated possibly since between 6000 and 4000 BCE, and evidence of wine-making dates back almost as far. Grapevines originated in North Africa and the Levant, and often appear as decorative elements in art and architecture.

Generally, grapes are symbols of wine: intoxication, hospitality (even orgies) and youthfulness. In the ancient world, grapes were an attribute of Dionysus/Bacchus – the god of wine-making, fertility, insanity and religious ecstasy, among other things – and his followers, who sometimes wore grapevine crowns.

In Christian art, grapes symbolize the wine of the Eucharist, transformed into the blood of Christ. By extension, grapes refer to the Last Supper, the Passion and Redemption. The grapevine symbolizes Christ, as in John 15:1: 'I am the true vine.' Late Roman and early Christian art made use of the vine as a proselytizing device, to smooth the transition to Christian symbolic meaning. A wonderful example can be found in a Roman mausoleum. A portrait of Costanza, the daughter of Emperor Constantine (the first Christian ruler), appears in the middle of one of the ambulatory mosaics. Her image is surrounded by twining grapevines, with *putti* harvesting, transporting and stamping the grapes. Some of the same imagery appears on her porphyry sarcophagus, which is decorated with garlands and grapevines, acanthus scrolls and cupids treading grapes.

St Augustine, among other early theologians, compared Christ to a cluster of grapes from the Promised Land, crushed in a press. This interpretation gave rise to the motif of Christ in a wine press, popular in art from about 1100 until the eighteenth century – one of the few medieval Catholic images that is also found in Protestant art.

In Giovanni Bellini's *St Francis in the Desert* (see also 'Mullein', pp. 200–1), grapevines – recalling the Eucharist and Christ's blood – overhang the entrance to the saint's al fresco shelter. This remarkable image suggests oneness with the divine, subtly conveyed through the humble details of the material world.

OTHER IMAGES OF GRAPES AND THE GRAPEVINE

- Roman sarcophagus with garlands, heroes and scenes of sacrifice, 140–50 CE. Rome: Museo Nazionale Romano, Palazzo Massimo.
- Frans Snyders, *Fruit Stall*, 1618–21, oil on canvas. St Petersburg: State Hermitage Museum.
- Henri Matisse, *Vine*, 1958, lithograph.

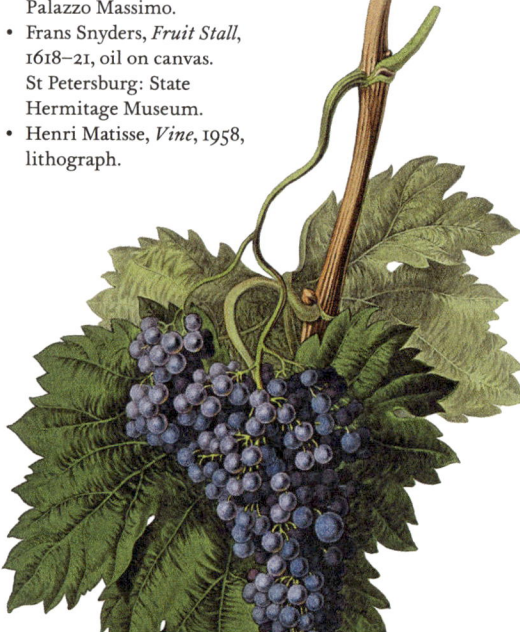

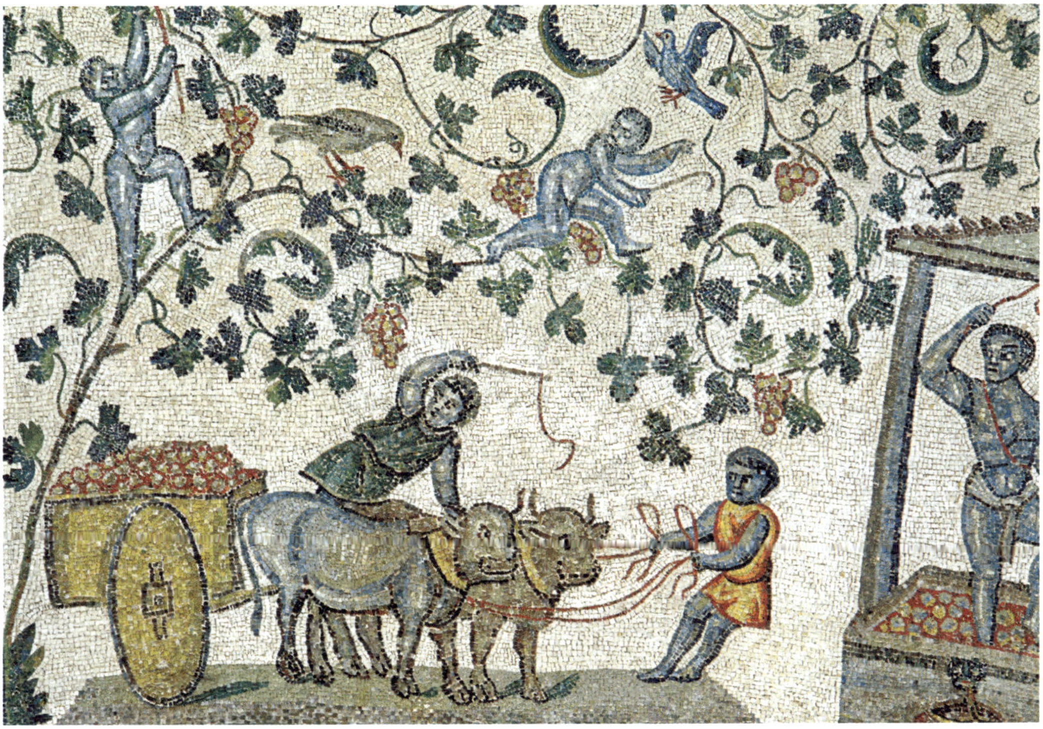

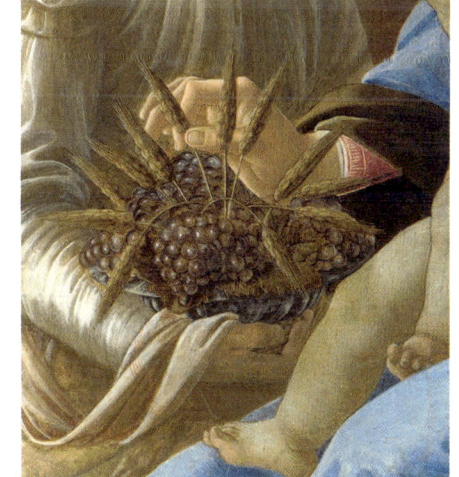

⛾ W. Clark after William Hooker,
Vitis vinifera cv. (Black Corinth
grape): fruiting branch, *c.* 1835.

✳ Cupids harvesting grapes,
detail of ambulatory mosaic,
fourth century. Mausoleum
of Santa Costanza, Rome.

✤ Sandro Botticelli, *Virgin and
Child with an Angel* (detail),
1470–74, tempera on panel.
Boston, MA: Isabella Stewart
Gardner Museum.

FAMILY Poaceae

What we today call corn, and sometimes maize, originated in Mexico and spread throughout the Americas. This tall annual cereal grass was originally domesticated over 9,000 years ago by Indigenous groups in southern Mexico and is now grown worldwide for its ears of starchy seeds, its production outpacing that of all other grains.

As a widespread foodstuff, eaten by humans and animals, corn is often seen as a symbol of prosperity and plenty. It is also used to produce alcoholic drinks; in the US, 40 per cent of all corn production is used for ethanol. In 2009, genetically modified corn made up 85 per cent of the American crop.

In his still lifes, the Dutch Baroque painter Cornelis de Heem depicted many flowers, fruit and vegetables that served as reminders of the beauty, fragility and brevity of life – so-called *vanitas* images. Species that grow in different seasons are shown together in these still lifes, again emphasizing the passage of time, while their rarity is an indication of the wealth and sophistication of his patrons. Corn was a relative newcomer to Europe, having been brought there from the Americas by Christopher Columbus around the turn of the sixteenth century. The earliest depictions come from Renaissance Italy, in the 1510s.

⊠ Otto Wilhelm Thomé, *Zea Mays* (Corn), 1903.

⁂ Grant Wood, *Corn Cob Chandelier for Iowa Corn Room*, 1925–26, copper, iron and paint. Cedar Rapids, IA: Cedar Rapids Museum of Art.

❊ Cornelis de Heem (attrib.), *Fruit and Flowers* (detail), 1662, oil on canvas. London: Victoria and Albert Museum.

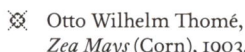
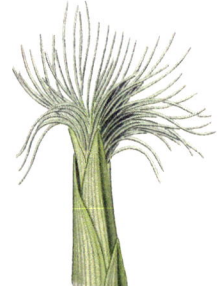
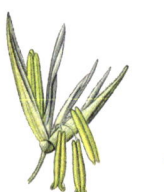
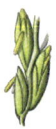

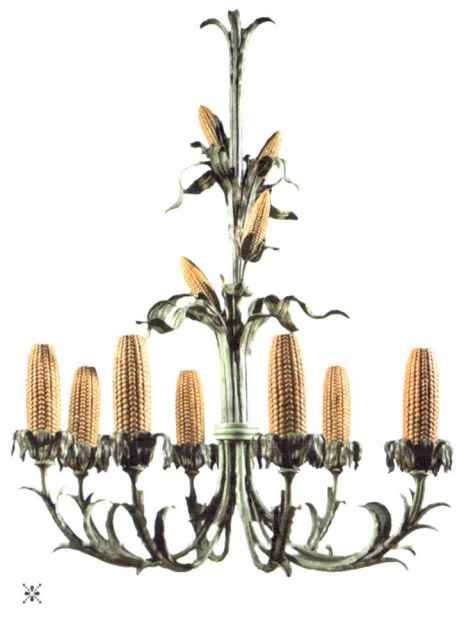

✳

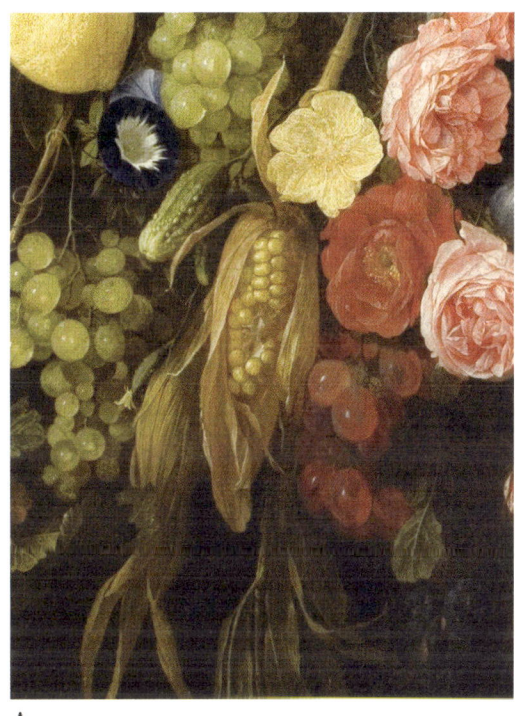

✤

American Regionalist painters, inspired by the landscape of the Midwest, often painted corn. In 1926 Grant Wood created *Corn Room*, a mural commissioned by the hotelier Eugene C. Eppley and consisting of several nearly abstract panels. It was papered over and lost until recently, but is now displayed in the Sioux City Art Center. Wood also created remarkable corn-cob chandeliers for the dining room of the Montrose Hotel in Cedar Rapids, Iowa. Perhaps the whimsy of the chandeliers inspired patrons to order corn on the cob!

Maria Fernanda Cardoso, a Colombian-born artist now practising in Australia, began working with corn as early as 1989. The importance of corn in the Americas consumed her, and while undertaking a Masters degree at Yale she grew corn in as many types and colours as possible, threading together hundreds of dried corncobs to create sculptural coils. These art forms evoke the significance of corn in everyday life in Colombia, and the variety of ways in which they can be used.

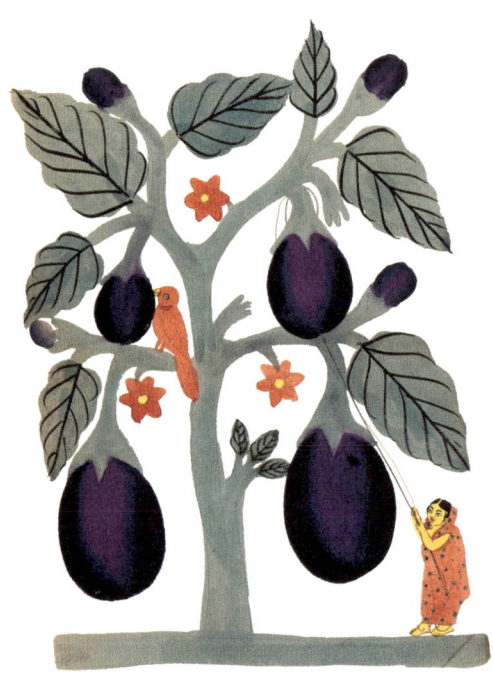

This book would not have been possible without the stellar education I received many years ago, particularly the mentorship of Henri Dorra and Alfred Moir. Additionally, during my years of teaching, my students' interest in symbolism served to encourage me, as did the ongoing support and enthusiasm of my family.

The contributions of the Thames & Hudson 'dream team' – Kate Edwards, Ben Hayes, India Jackson, Lise Seguin, Rosie Fairhead, Aman Phull, Sadie Brookes and Ginny Liggitt – made this the splendid book that it is. The enthusiastic help of the many artists whose work is illustrated is also much appreciated.

GLOSSARY

Agrostology The scientific study of grasses. Also called graminology.

Annual A plant that completes its life cycle in one year, then dies.

Biennial A plant that completes its life cycle in two years, flowering in the second year, then dies.

Botanical nomenclature The naming system of plants, dating as far back as the Greeks. Beginning with Carolus Linnaeus's mid-eighteenth-century binomial organization, the system became more formal, ranking plants from the largest to the smallest groups: kingdom, phylum (or division), class, order, family, genus, species, subspecies. Many plants are also known by common names, which vary according to time and place.

Deciduous A plant that sheds its leaves annually.

Emblem An abstract or representational image that signifies a concept, place or person (such as roses in coats of arms).

Endemic Natural distribution confined to one area. Compare **Native**.

Family See **Botanical nomenclature**

Genus See **Botanical nomenclature**

Graminology See **Agrostology**

Herbaceous Describes a plant that has no woody stem, typically **biennial** or **annual**; also of or relating to herbs and grasses.

Hybrid The offspring of two plants or animals of different varieties.

Keystone species A species that is vital to the health of the surrounding habitat.

Millefiori/millefleur Literally 1,000 flowers. An all-over pattern of small and diverse flowers, popular in weaving and somewhat rare in painting (but see Botticelli's *Primavera*). Medieval manuscripts supply some examples,

and the practice was regarded as passé by the Renaissance.

Native Naturally occurring in one area, but not confined to it. Compare **Endemic**.

Neoplatonic A philosophy that emerged in the third century CE, was linked to Renaissance humanism and continues to the present. It holds that the material world is experienced indirectly through human senses, while the apex, ideal level is known only through mysticism. Time and beauty are implied through ideal forms.

Perennial Describes a plant that grows, irrespective of season, for more than two years.

Species See **Botanical nomenclature**

Taxonomy The grouping or classifying of plants.

Understorey Plant life below the forest canopy.

NOTES

1   This volume focuses on the visual arts. Informative studies of plants in literature include Judith Farr and Louise Carter's *The Gardens of Emily Dickinson*, Cambridge, MA, 2004; and Randy Laist and Jim Horwitz, *Plants and Literature: Essays in Critical Plant Studies*, New York, 2013.

2   Tompkins and Bird's *The Secret Life of Plants* recounts the history of the scientific recognition of plant sentience – a patchy and largely ignored area until the twentieth century.

3   See, for example, Jim Ellis's *Intertwined Histories: Plants in their Social Contexts*, Calgary, 2019; and Gibson.

4   Harrison and Kirkham (12) estimate that some 8,000 tree species are under threat of extinction.

5   See Harrison and Kirkham for an extensive overview of trees, in particular the chapter 'Healers and Killers', 115ff. They also provide a vocabulary for describing important tree characteristics: 'godfather tree' (a tree planted by one generation that doesn't bear fruit until several generations later; 116), 'survivor trees' (those that flourish despite poor environments or other obstacles; 183) and 'keystone species' (trees that are vital to the health of the surrounding habitat; 205).

6   The filbert nut is in fact more elongated than the hazelnut and comes from a different species (Harrison and Kirkham 48).

7   Sources do not identify the girl, although the eye and brow resemble those of Lady Caroline Blackwood (an admired and prolific writer, and Freud's second wife from 1953 to 1959). A close-up by Freud of her right eye, painted in 1950, resurfaced in 2015, having been in a private collection for many years.

8   Harrison and Kirkham suggest that yews were planted near pagan temples because of their symbolic significance, and that the builders of Christian churches used the same grounds and meaning. The writers also list several very old British yews (58ff.).

9   Stephen Buchmann's *The Reason for Flowers* begins with an excellent preface. The book contains everything one might

wish to know about flowers, enhanced by the author's stunning photographs.

10 Incidentally, it is possible that Van Gogh knew of the Wilde caricature, since he pored over British periodicals such as *The Graphic* and the *Illustrated London News* and kept up to date with the art scene. He owned prints from *Punch* as well. These are now in the Van Gogh Museum, including twenty-eight unidentified prints by Sambourne (Jansen et al., Letter 235).

11 One might read *Offices* instead of *Orders*, since the works may reflect the Catholic Church's canonical daily offices that are marked by prayer, which would have been well known to Kiefer.

12 The Metropolitan Museum's text accompanying a woodcut of the same subject suggests that the prone figure may be Robert Fludd, a sixteenth-century English occultist who believed that every plant in the world had its own equivalent star in the firmament.

13 See Gibson's discussion of the water lily and eco-feminism (128–30), and Monet (130f.).

14 Lavin notes that although the burning bush is usually depicted as a bush, Bellini instead depicted a noble laurel, which supposedly had the ability to withstand fire (244). Lavin also explains the desert reference in the painting's title: it refers to an island in the Venice lagoon called Isola di San Francesco del Deserto, where the saint took refuge during a storm (234).

15 Giulia Caneva et al., 'Plant Iconography and Its Message: Realism and Symbolic Message in the Bernini Fountain of the Four Rivers in Rome', *Rendiconti Lincei. Scienze Fisiche e Naturali*, 31 (2020), 1011–26, doi.org/10.1007/s12210020-00946-2. The mullein is associated with the Danube River.

16 Okoyomon obtained the kudzu from Amsterdam. Called 'the vine that ate the South', kudzu was imported to the United States to alleviate soil erosion. Despite good intentions, the project backfired and the plant took over the environment. It is now banned there.

BOOKS AND PERIODICALS

Abella, Alex, *The Total Banana*, New York, 1979
Aloi, Giovanni, ed., *Botanical Speculations*, Newcastle upon Tyne, 2018
——, *Why Look at Plants?*, *Critical Plant Studies*, vol. 5, Leiden, 2019
——, *Lucian Freud: Plant Portraits*, London, 2022
Becker, Udo, ed., *The Continuum Encyclopedia of Symbols*, trans. Lance W. Garmer, London and New York, 1996
Biedermann, Hans, *Dictionary of Symbolism*, trans. James Hulbert, New York, 1992
Bisanz, Rudolf M., *German Romanticism and Philipp Otto Runge: A Study in Nineteenth-Century Art Theory and Iconography*, Ithaca, NY, 1970
Buchmann, Stephen, *The Reason for Flowers: Their History, Culture, Biology, and How They Change Our Lives*, New York, 2015
Caneva, G., et al., 'Plant Iconography and Its Message: Realism and Symbolic Message in the Bernini Fountain of the Four Rivers in Rome', *Rendiconti Lincei Scienze Fisiche e Naturali*, xxxi (2020), pp. 1011–26
Chevalier, Alexandre, Elena Marinova and Leonor Peña-Chocarro, eds, *Plants and People: Choices and Diversity through Time*, Oxford and Philadelphia, 2014
Chevalier, Jean, and Alain Gheerbrant, *The Penguin Dictionary of Symbols*, trans. John Buchanan-Brown, London, 1996 (2nd edn)
Cirlot, J. E., *A Dictionary of Symbols*, Mineola, NY, 2002 (2nd edn)
Dahl, Roald, *James and the Giant Peach*, New York, 1961 (1st edn)
D'Ancona, Mirella Levi, *The Garden of the Renaissance: Botanical Symbolism in Italian Painting*, Florence, 1977
Diffenbaugh, Vanessa, *The Language of Flowers*, London, 2011
Draguet, Michel, *Fernand Khnopff: Portrait of Jeanne Kéfer*, Los Angeles, 2004
Etheredge, Laura, *Egypt*, New York, 2011
Garrard, Mary D., 'The Not-So-Still Lifes of Giovanna Garzoni', in *'The Immensity of the Universe' in the Art of Giovanna Garzoni*, ed. Sheila Barker, Florence, 2020
Gibson, Prudence, *The Plant Contract: Art's Return to Vegetal Life*, Leiden, 2018
Goossen, E. C., *Ellsworth Kelly*, New York, 1973
Greenaway, Kate, *Language of Flowers* [1884], many recent editions
Haig, Elizabeth, *The Floral Symbolism of the Great Masters* [1913], reprinted London, 2018
Hall, James, *Illustrated Dictionary of Symbols in Eastern and Western Art*, New York, 1994
Hansson, Ann-Marie, and Andreas G. Heiss, eds, 'Plants Used in Ritual Offerings and in Festive Contexts', in Chevalier, Marinova and Peña-Chocarro, *Plants and People*, pp. 311–83
Harrison, Christina, and Tony Kirkham, *Remarkable Trees*, London, 2019, reprinted 2020
Hulton, P. H., *Flowers in Art from East and West*, London, 1979
Impelluso, Lucia, *Nature and Its Symbols*, Los Angeles, 2004
Janick, Jules, and Harry S. Paris, 'The Cucurbit Images (1515–1518) of the Villa Farnesina, Rome', *Annals of Botany*, xcvii/2 (February 2006), pp. 165–76, doi: 10.1093/aob/mcj025
Koerner, J. L., *The Moment of Self-Portraiture in German Renaissance Art*, Chicago, 1997
Lehner, Ernest, and Johanna Lehner, *Folklore and Symbolism of Flowers, Plants and Trees* [1960], Eastford, CT, 2012
Mancoff, Debra N., *The Pre-Raphaelite Language of Flowers*, Munich, 2002
Milner, John, *Mondrian*, London, 1995

Olderr, Steven, *Symbolism: A Comprehensive Dictionary*, Jefferson, NC, and London, 2012 (2nd edn)
Porteous, Alexander, *The Forest in Folklore and Mythology* [1928], Mineola, NY, 2002
Saint-Exupéry, Antoine de, *The Little Prince*, New York, 1943
Selznick, Brian, *Big Tree*, New York, 2023
Snider, Tui, *Understanding Cemetery Symbolism: A Field Guide for Historic Graveyards*, n.p., 2017
Sylvester, David, *Magritte: The Silence of the World*, New York, 1992
Taft, Catherine, et al., *Yayoi Kusama*, London, 2017
Tanning, Dorothea, *Another Language of Flowers*, New York, 1998
Tompkins, Peter, and Christopher Bird, *The Secret Life of Plants* [1973], New York, 2002
Torczyner, Harry, *Magritte: Ideas and Images*, New York, 1977
Tresidder, Jack, *Dictionary of Symbols*, San Francisco, 1997
Walker, Barbara, *The Woman's Dictionary of Symbols & Sacred Objects*, San Francisco, 1988
Wilkinson, Charles K., and Marsha Hill, *Egyptian Wall Paintings: The Metropolitan Museum of Art's Collection of Facsimiles*, New York, 1983
Williams, C. A. S., *Outlines of Chinese Symbolism and Art Motifs* [1932], Shanghai, 1976
Wilson, Matthew, *Symbols in Art*, London and New York, 2020
——, *The Hidden Language of Symbols*, London and New York, 2022
Woldbye, Vibeke, ed., *Flowers into Art*, The Hague, 1991
Zohary, Daniel, and Maria Hopf, *Domestication of Plants in the Old World* [1988], Oxford, 2000

ONLINE RESOURCES

'*7,000 Oaks*', Wikipedia, http://wikipedia.org/wiki/7000_Oaks (accessed July 2024)
Alcover-Cateura, Pablo José and Antoni Riera Melis, 'The Presence of Cherries in the Gothic Altarpieces in the Museu Nacional d'Art de Catalunya: A Brief History of Medieval Fruit', 23 April 2020, https://blog.museunacional.cat/en/the-presence-of-cherries-in-the-gothic-altarpieces-in-the-museu-nacional-dart-de-catalunya-a-brief-history-of-medieval-fruit
Anderson, Heather Arndt, 'Celery was the Avocado Toast of the Victorian Era', *Taste*, 23 August 2017, www.tastecooking.com/celery-was-the-avocado-toast-of-the-victorian-era
Art Gallery of Victoria, 'Picturing the Giants: The Changing Landscapes of Emily Carr', *AGGV Magazine*, 1 March 2020, http://emagazine.aggv.ca/picturing-the-giants-the-changing-landscapes-of-emily-carr
Barkham, Patrick, 'Britain's Ancient Yews: Mystical, Magnificent – and Unprotected', *The Guardian*, 28 September 2019, www.theguardian.com/environment/2019/sep/28/britain-ancient-yews-mystical-magnificent-and-unprotected
Bass-Krueger, Maude, 'A Brief History of Food in European Art', Google Arts & Culture, http://artsandculture.google.com/story/tQURN-8DeIXhIg (accessed July 2024)
Blessing, Jennifer, 'Piet Mondrian: Chrysanthemum', Guggenheim, www.guggenheim.org/artwork/2999 (accessed July 2024)
'*Bouquet of Flowers in a Vase*', Denver Art Museum, www.denverartmuseum.org/edu/object/bouquet-flowers-vase (accessed July 2024)
Bowen, Monica, 'Strawberries as an "Earthly Delight"', 9 July 2011, 'Alberti's Window' blog, www.albertis-window.com/2011/07/strawberries-as-an-earthly-delight

British Museum, 'Egyptian Life and Death', www.britishmuseum. org/collection/galleries/egyptian-life-and-death (accessed July 2024)

Brotherton, Barbara, 'Object of the Week: Raven Releasing the Sun', Seattle Art Museum, 2 July 2021, https://samblog.seattleartmuseum.org/2021/07/ raven-releasing-the-sun-george-hunt-jr

Cary, Zulma, 'Top 10 Most Famous Trees in The World', Earth&World, 21 May 2018, www.earthnworld.com/ top-10-most-famous-trees-in-the-world

Chandler, Graham, 'Walnuts and First Forest Farms', AramcoWorld, March/April 2017, www.aramcoworld.com/ articles/march-2017/walnuts-and-the-first-forest-farms

Christie's, 'Paul Nash: The Three', 18 June 2008, www.christies. com/lotfinder/lot/paul-nash-1889-1946-the-three-5097384-details.aspx

Daunay, Marie-Christine, and Jules Janick, 'History and Iconography of Eggplant', Chronica Horticulturae, xlvii/3 (January 2007), pp. 16–22, www.hort.purdue.edu/newcrop/ chronicaeggplant.pdf

Elkins, James, 'Weeping over Bluish Leaves', 2009, www. jameselkins.com/wp-content/uploads/2009/12/Tears-5.pdf

Ewbank, Anne, 'Ancient Greek Funerals Were Decked Out in Celery', 23 October 2018, Atlas Obscura, www.atlasobscura.com/ articles/history-of-funeral-wreaths

'Gardiner's Sign List of Egyptian Hieroglyphs', Egyptian Hieroglyphs, www.egyptianhieroglyphs.net/gardiners-sign-list (accessed July 2024)

Gerry in Art, 'Paul Nash at Tate Britain: Searching for Another Angle of Vision', 'How the Light Gets In' blog, 2016, www.gerryco23.wordpress.com

Gholson, Christien, 'Noise and Silence: The World of Leonora Carrington, Part II: The Alchemical Kitchen', 12 April 2012, www.christiengholson.blogspot.com/2012/04/world-of-leonora-carrington-part-ii.html

Gill, N. S., 'Adonis and Aphrodite: The Story by Ovid from Metamorphoses X', ThoughtCo, 7 April 2019, www.thoughtco. com/adonis-and-aphrodite-111765

Goodeve, Thyrza Nichols, 'Mark Dion: Mourning Is a Legitimate Mode of Thinking', Brooklyn Rail, May 2016, www.brooklynrail. org/2016/05/art/mourning-is-a-legitimate-mode-of-thinking

Gottesman, Sarah, 'A Brief History of Flowers in Western Art', Artsy.net, 1 July 2017, www.artsy.net/article/ artsy-editorial-van-gogh-okeeffe-art-historys-famous-flowers

Gurney, Tom, 'Great Piece of Turf: Albrecht Dürer', History of Art, 19 June 2020, www.thehistoryofart.org/albrecht-durer/ great-piece-of-turf

Hageneder, Fred, 'Yew and Misconceptions in Religious History' (interview), Fred Hageneder's Gateway to the Meaning of Trees in Culture and Consciousness, 2007, www.themeaningoftrees.com/ yew-and-misconceptions-in-religious-history

Harris, Alexandra, 'Top of the Crops: Cabbages in Art', The Guardian, 1 December 2010, www. theguardian.com/artanddesign/2010/dec/01/ alexandra-harris-cabbages-art-first-book-award

'The History of Roses', University of Illinois Extension, www.extension.illinois.edu/roses/history (accessed July 2024)

'Honeysuckle', Ebrary.net, www.ebrary.net/27948/environment/ honeysuckle (accessed July 2024)

'House of the Orchard or of the Floral Cubicles', Pompeii, http://pompeiisites.org/en/archaeological-site/house-of-the-orchard-or-of-the-floral-cubicles (accessed July 2024)

'Interview: Neukom Vivarium, Mark Dion', Art:21, n.d., www.art21.org/read/mark-dion-neukom-vivarium

Jackson, Kitty, 'Symbolism: Honeysuckle in Rubens' Honeysuckle Bower', Artdependence Magazine, 28 February 2019, www.artdependence.com/articles/ symbolism-honeysuckle-in-rubens-honeysuckle-bower

Janick, Jules, 'The Pear in History, Literature, Popular Culture, and Art', Acta Horticulturae, December 2002, www.hort.purdue. edu/newcrop/pearinhistory.pdf

——, 'Fruits and Nuts of the Villa Farnesina', Arnoldia, 2012, www.hort.purdue.edu/newcrop/pdfs/ 70-2_03_villa_farnesina.pdf

——, and Giulia Caneva, 'The First Images of Maize in Europe', Maydica, 1/1 (January 2005), pp. 71–80, www.hort.purdue.edu/newcrop/maize/images_ of_maize.pdf

——, and Anna Whipkey, 'The Fruits and Nuts of the Unicorn Tapestries', Chronica Horticulturae, liv/1 (2014), www.hort. purdue.edu/newcrop/pdfs/unicorn-tapestry-plants.pdf

Jansen, Leo, Hans Luijten and Nienke Bakker, eds, Vincent van Gogh, The Letters, 2009, www.vangoghletters.org

Jobson, Christopher, 'Ash Dome: A Secret Tree Artwork in Wales Planted by David Nash in 1977', Colossal, 9 May 2016, www.thisiscolossal.com/2016/05/ash-dome-david-dash

John Grade Studio, 'Treeline', www.johngrade.com/projects/ treeline (accessed July 2024)

Kargère, Lucretia Goddard, 'Two Sculptures in Deep Conversation at The Met Cloisters', Metropolitan Museum of Art, 22 May 2018, www.metmuseum.org/blogs/collection-insights/2018/ virgin-and-child-sculptures-met-cloisters-heavenly-bodies

Kim, Hae-in, 'The Spiritual Depths of the Feminine Soul in Rossetti's "The Blessed Damozel"', Victorian Web, 2004, www.victorianweb.org/authors/dgr/hikim5.html

Kinver, Mark, 'World Is Home to "60,000 Tree Species"', BBC News, 5 April 2017, www.bbc.co.uk/news/ science-environment-39492977

Knaus, Jennifer, www.jenniferknaus.com

Landmark Trust, 'The Pineapple', www.landmarktrust.org.uk/ search-and-book/properties/pineapple-10726

Laqueur, Thomas W., 'Beneath the Yew Tree's Shade', Paris Review, 31 October 2015, www.theparisreview.org/blog/2015/10/31/ beneath-the-yew-trees-shade

Larkin, Deirda, 'The Medieval Garden Enclosed: The Holly and the Ivy', Metropolitan Museum of Art, 18 December 2008. www.metmuseum.org/articles/medieval-garden-enclosed-holly-and-ivy.

Lavin, Marilyn Aronberg, Jinyu Liu and Adam Gitner, 'The Joy of St Francis: Bellini's Panel at the Frick Collection', Artibus et Historiae, xxviii/56 (2007), pp. 231–56, www.jstor.org/stable/20067174

Lemonedes, Heather, 'Bits of Rainbows', 21 December 2015, Cleveland Art, www.clevelandart.org/articles/bits-rainbows

Linsley, Alice C., 'The Gourd in Biblical Symbolism', 'Biblical Anthropology' blog, 12 December 2015, www.biblicalanthropology.blogspot.com/2015/12/ the-gourd-in-biblical-symbolism.html

Lobell, Jarrett A., 'The Emperor's Orchids', Archaeology, January/February 2013, www.archaeology.org/ issues/january-february-2013/digs-discoveries/ roman-ara-pacis-altar-flowers

McCouat, Philip, 'Perception and Blindness in the 16th Century: Bruegel's The Blind Leading the Blind', Journal of Art in Society, October 2018, www.artinsociety.com/perception-and-blindness-in-the-16th-century.html

McNally, Ross, 'Ash to Ashes: The Vikings' Tree of Life Is under Threat', *Sussex Bylines*, 11 November 2022, www.sussexbylines.co.uk/news/environment/ash-to-ashes-the-vikings-tree-of-life-is-under-threat

'Mark Dion', Lenfest Center for the Arts, Columbia University School of the Arts, October 2021, http://arts.columbia.edu/events/mark-dion

Marks, Tasha, 'Lemons and Lobsters and Cabbages, Oh My! Symbolic Food in Painting', Art UK, 22 April 2020, www.artuk.org/discover/stories/lemons-and-lobsters-and-cabbages-oh-my-symbolic-food-in-painting

Meagher, Jennifer, 'Food and Drink in European Painting, 1400–1800', Metropolitan Museum of Art, May 2009, www.metmuseum.org/toah/hd/food/hd_food.htm

Meier, Allison, 'The Romantic Symbolism of Trees', Hyperallergic, 10 June 2014, www.hyperallergic.com/131541/the-romantic-symbolism-of-trees

Meistere, Una, 'Woodstock, Raves and the Image Recycler', 20 August 2020, Arterritory, www.arterritory.com/en/visual_arts/interviews/25074-woodstock_raves_and_the_image_recycler

Murray, Caroline M., entries in 'Professor Hedgehog's Journal' blog, 'The Artichoke', 16 February 2019, www.professorhedgehogsjournal.uk/2019/02/16/the-artichoke; 'Plant of the Month [Pineapple]: June 2017', 21 June 2017, www.professorhedgehogsjournal.uk/2017/06/21/plant-of-the-month-june-2017

O'Brien, Barbara, 'The Buddha's Robe: An Overview of Robes Worn by Buddhist Monks and Nuns', Learn Religions, 5 April 2023, www.learnreligions.com/the-buddhas-robe-450083

Olszewski, Edward, 'Dionysus's Enigmatic Thyrsus', *Proceedings of the American Philosophical Organization*, clxiii/2 (June 2019), pp. 153–73, www.amphilsoc.org/sites/default/files/2020-03/attachments/Olszewski.pdf

Paris, Harry S., et al., 'First Known Image of *Cucurbita* in Europe, 1503–1508', *Annals of Botany*, xcviii/1 (July 2006), pp. 41–47, www.ncbi.nlm.nih.gov/pmc/articles/PMC2803533

'Paul Nash: *Solstice of the Sunflower*', National Gallery of Canada, www.gallery.ca/collection/artwork/solstice-of-the-sunflower

Phaidon, 'Why Does Yayoi Kusama Love Pumpkins?', 21 March 2018, www.phaidon.com/agenda/art/articles/2018/march/21/why-does-yayoi-kusama-love-pumpkins

Protas, Allison, et al., 'Dictionary of Symbolism', Fantasy and Science Fiction website, University of Michigan, 1997/2001, www.umich.edu/~umfandsf/symbolismproject/symbolism.html

Real, Carol, 'Lene Kilde: The Nutmeg Princess', Art Summit, 9 April 2018, www.art-summit.com/lenekilde

Riggs, Terry, 'Salvador Dalí, *Metamorphosis of Narcissus*', The Tate, 1998, www.tate.org.uk/art/artworks/dali-metamorphosis-of-narcissus-t02343

Romačk, Coco, 'The Artist Who Transforms Galleries into Forests and Fields', *New York Times Style Magazine*, 3 May 2021, www.nytimes.com/2021/05/03/t-magazine/precious-okoyomon-artist-shed.html

Ruiz, Carme, *Salvador Dalí and Science: Beyond a Mere Curiosity*, 2010, Fundació Gala – Salvador Dalí, www.salvador-dali.org/en/research/archives-en-ligne/download-documents/16/salvador-dali-and-science-beyond-a-mere-curiosity

Saffron Walden Museum, 'Saffron', 14 November 2017, www.saffronwaldenmuseum.swmuseumsoc.org.uk/saffron

Dr Samanthi, 'Difference between Pine and Fir', DifferenceBetween.com, 23 August 2011, www.differencebetween.com/difference-between-pine-and-vs-fir

'Samuel Palmer', www.themorgan.org/drawings/item/247415

Sanders, David, 'Introduction to the Tree of Life', The Kabbalah Experience, www.kabbalahexperience.com/introduction-to-the-tree-of-life (accessed July 2024)

Sargent, John Singer, *Carnation, Lily, Lily, Rose*, The Tate, www.tate.org.uk/art/artworks/sargent-carnation-lily-lily-rose-n01615

Schaechter, Moselio (Elio), and Roberto Kolter, 'Small Things Considered' blog, American Society for Microbiology, n.d., http://schaechter.asmblog.org/schaechter/about-small-things-considered.html

'Sennedjem and Iineferti in the Fields of Iaru', Metropolitan Museum, www.metmuseum.org/art/collection/search/548354 (accessed July 2024)

'Sennedjem – TT1', Osirisnet: The Tombs of Ancient Egypt, www.osirisnet.net/tombes/artisans/sennedjem1/e_sennedjem1_01.htm (accessed July 2024)

Sexton, Chrissy, 'Fibonacci Spirals: An Unexpected Twist in Plant Evolution', 16 June 2023, www.earth.com/news/fibonacci-spirals-an-unexpected-twist-in-plant-evolution/

Spanish National Research Council (CSIC), 'A First-ever Find in Egypt: 4,000-year-old Funerary Garden at Tomb Entrance', Science Daily, 4 May 2017, www.sciencedaily.com/releases/2017/05/170504093225.htm

Stańska, Zuzanna, 'Nature in Art: Gustav Klimt's Enchanting Depictions of Trees', 21 June 2024, *Daily Art Magazine*, www.dailyartmagazine.com/gustav-klimt-trees-paintings

Storl, Wolf D., 'A Curious History of Vegetables: Aphrodisiacal and Healing Properties...', Publicism, 2016, http://publicism.info/gardening/curious/7.html

Sullivan, Kerry, 'Wittenham Clumps: Ancient Earthworks Haunted by Gods Long Forgotten', Ancient Origins, 3 October 2016, www.ancient-origins.net/ancient-places-europe/wittenham-clumps-ancient-earthworks-haunted-gods-long-forgotten-006755

'Tower of London Remembers: WWI Centenary Commemorations at the Tower of London', Historic Royal Palaces, www.hrp.org.uk/tower-of-london/history-and-stories/tower-of-london-remembers (accessed July 2024)

'*Treeline*: John Grade', Jordan Schnitzer Museum of Art at PXU, www.pdx.edu/museum-of-art/treeline (accessed March 2024)

'Virgin del Pino', Wikipedia, http://en.wikipedia.org/wiki/Virgen_del_Pino (accessed July 2024)

'What Does a Willow Tree Symbolize?', Reference, 4 August 2015, www.reference.com/article/willow-tree-symbolize

INTERIOR

Dimensions are given in centimetres followed by inches; height precedes width precedes depth, unless otherwise stated.

a = above; b = below
l = left; r = right

Images in the Plant Index are all details taken from images reproduced elsewhere in the book.

Endpapers Front Maria van Oosterwyck, *Bouquet of Flowers in a Vase* (detail), *c.* 1670s. Oil on canvas, 73.7 × 55.9 (29 × 22). Funds by exchange from T. Edward and Tullah Hanley in honor of longtime director, Otto Bach and his wife Cile Bach. Denver Art Museum (1997.219); Dante Gabriel Rossetti, *Beata Beatrix* (detail), *c.* 1864–70. Oil on canvas, 86.4 × 66 (34 ⅛ × 26). Tate, London (N01279). Photo Tate Images; Hilma af Klint, *Tree of Knowledge*, No. 5 (detail), 1913–15. Watercolour, gouache, graphite and ink on paper, 46 × 30 (18 × 11 ⅝). Glenstone Museum, Potomac, Maryland; *The Unicorn Rests in a Garden (from the Unicorn Tapestries)* (detail), 1495–1505. Wool warp with wool, silk, silver, and gilt wefts, overall: 368 × 251.5 (144 ⅞ × 99). Gift of John D. Rockefeller Jr., 1937. The Metropolitan Museum of Art, New York (37.80.6) **Back** René Magritte, *L'Explication* (*The Explanation*) (detail), 1952. Oil on canvas, 46 × 35 (18 ⅛ × 13 ¾). Private Collection. © ADAGP, Paris and DACS, London 2025; Charles Allston Collins, *Convent Thoughts* (detail), 1851. Oil on canvas, 84 × 59 (33 ⅛ × 23 ¼). Bequeathed by Mrs Thomas Combe, 1893. Ashmolean Museum, Oxford (WA1894.10)

1 *The Unicorn Rests in a Garden (from The Unicorn Tapestries)* (detail), 1495–1505. Wool warp with wool, silk, silver, and gilt wefts, overall: 368 × 251.5 (144 ⅞ × 99). Gift of John D. Rockefeller Jr., 1937. The Metropolitan Museum of Art, New York (37.80.6) **2** Francesco del Cossa, *Saint Lucy* (detail), *c.* 1473–74. Tempera on panel, 77.2 × 56 (30 ⅜ × 22 ¹/₁₆). Samuel H. Kress Collection. National Gallery of Art, Washington, D.C. (1939.1.228) **4** Joanne Hill Benedict, *California Palms*, 1999. Watercolour on paper, 35.6 × 25.4 (14 × 10). Private Collection. © Joanne Hill Benedict **6a** Hilma af Klint, *Tree of Knowledge*, No. 1, 1913–15. Watercolour, gouache, graphite, and ink on paper, 46 × 30 (18 × 11 ⅝). Glenstone Museum, Potomac, Maryland **6b** Karl Blossfeldt, *Dipsacus laciniatus*, 1928. Gelatin silver print, 25.9 × 19.8 (10 ³/₁₆ × 7 ¹³/₁₆). J. Paul Getty Museum, Los Angeles (84.XM.142.3) **7a** William Henry Fox Talbot, *Two Plant Specimens*, 1839. Photogenic drawing, 22.1 × 18 (8 ¾ × 7 ⅛). Edward E. Ayer Endowment in memory of Charles L. Hutchinson. Art Institute of Chicago (1972.325) **7b** Tosa Mitsuoki, *Autumn Maples with Poem Slips* (detail), 1670–80. Ink, colours, gold leaf and gold powder on silk, 144 × 286 (56 ¾ × 112 ⅝). Kate S. Buckingham Endowment. Art Institute of Chicago (1977.157) **18** Girolamo dai Libri, *Madonna and Child with Saints* (detail), *c.* 1520. Tempera and oil on canvas, 398.8 × 207 (157 × 81 ½). Fletcher Fund, 1920. The Metropolitan Museum of Art, New York (20.92) **21** H.J. Ruprecht, Trunk and roots of a pine tree cut to show growth rings; microscopic views of wood cells in longitudinal and transverse section and of a root tip. Chromolithograph, 1877. Wellcome Collection, London (27043i) **22** Gustav Klimt, *Tree of Life*, working drawing of the execution of a mosaic frieze for the dining hall of Stoclet House, Brussels. Tracing paper, coloured pencil, gold, pastel, platinum, silver, bronze, gouache, 200 × 102 (78 ¾ × 40 ⅛). MAK, Vienna (MAL 226-4) **23a** Sefirot, *The Great Parchment*, copied by James Hepburn, 1606. Parchment, 108 × 75 (42 ⅝ × 29 ⅝). The Bodleian Library, Oxford (MS Hunt. Add. E) **23b** David Maxim, *Old Man with Young Tree*, 2021. Watercolour on paper, 35.6 × 27.9 (14 × 11). © David Maxim **24** Oluf Olufsen Bagge, *Yggdrasil, The Mundane Tree*, from the *Prose Edda*, 1847 **25a** William Blake, *The Wood of the Self-Murderers: The Harpies and the Suicides*, 1824–27 (from Illustrations to Dante's *Divine Comedy*). Graphite, ink and watercolour on paper, 37.2 × 52.7 (14 ¾ × 20 ¾). Tate, London (N03356). Photo Tate Images **25b** Max Ernst, *The Forest*, 1927–28. Oil on canvas, 96.3 × 129.5 (37 ⅞ × 51). The Solomon R. Guggenheim Foundation Peggy Guggenheim Collection, Venice, 1976 (76.2553.72). © ADAGP, Paris and DACS, London 2025 **26–27** Anselm Kiefer, *Entrance to Paradise*, 2010. Oil, emulsion, acrylic, shellac, thorn bushes, photographs, and lead on canvas in glazed steel frames, 282 × 768 × 35 (111 × 302 ⅜ × 13 ¾). The Broad Art Foundation, Los Angeles. Photo Charles Duprat. © Anselm Kiefer **28** 'Netting Birds, Tomb of Khnumhotep', *c.* 1897–1878 BCE. Facsimile by Nina de Garis Davies. Tempera on paper, 101 × 260 (39 ¾ × 102 ⅜). Rogers Fund, 1933. The Metropolitan Museum of Art, New York (33.8.18) **29** James Watts, after E. D. Smith, *Acacia oxycedrus*, 1827. 203 × 125 (80 × 49 ¼) from Robert Sweet's *Flora Australasica*, James Ridgway, 1827 **30** Wolfgang Meyerpick, after Giorgio Liberale, *Ficus sycomorus*, 1568, from *I discorsi di M. Pietro Andrea Matthioli*, Presso Nicolò Pezzana, 1712. Photo SuperStock/Album/Florilegius/Album Archivo **31** Brian Selznick, *Merwin and Louise*, from *Big Tree*, Scholastic Press, 2023. © 2023 by Brian Selznick. Reprinted by permission of Scholastic Inc. **32a** Antoine de Saint-Exupéry, *The Baobabs*, from Saint-Exupéry's *The Little Prince*, Reynal & Hitchcock, 1943 **32b, 33l** Mme E. Panckoucke and P.J.F. Turpin, *Baobab*, from F.P. Chaumeton, Chamberet et Poiret's *Flore Médicale*, C.L.F. Panckoucke, 1833 **33r** Lith Vayron, Baobab, from Étienne Denisse's *Flore d'Amérique*, Gihaut, 1843–46 **34** Pancrace Bessa, White Birch, from François André Michaux's *The North American Sylva*, C. D'Hautel, 1819 **35** Gustav Klimt, *Birch Forest*, 1903. Oil on canvas, 110.1 × 109.8 (43 ⅜ × 43 ¼). Private Collection **36** Giorgio Gallesio, Spanish chestnut, from Gallesio's *Pomona Italiana*, Niccolò Capurro, 1817–39. The New York Public Library (b13674913) **37** Charles E. Burchfield, *Summer Solstice (In Memory of the American Chestnut Tree)*, 1961–66. Watercolour on paper, 137.2 × 152.4 (54 × 60). Burchfield Penney Art Center at SUNY Buffalo State, Buffalo, New York **38** J.J. or J.F. Haid, after Georg Dionysius Ehret, *Cedrus*, *c.* 1750. Coloured engraving, 45.5 × 29.6 (18 × 11 ¾). Wellcome Collection, London (18377i) **39** John Grade, *Treeline*, 2017. Alaskan yellow cedar and Metasequoia wood, 9.5 × 3.7 × 3 m (31 × 12 × 10 ft.). Karl Miller Center atrium, Portland State University. Courtesy John Grade **40l** William Morris and John Henry Dearle, *The Orchard* (detail), 1890. Tapestry woven in wool, silk and mohair on a cotton warp, 221 × 472 (87 ⅛ × 185 ⅞). Victoria and Albert Museum, London (154-1898) **40r** *Citrus Aurantium*, from David Nathaniel Friedrich Dietrich's *Flora Medica*, August Schmid, 1831 **41** John Everett Millais, *The Bridesmaid*, 1851. Oil on panel, 27.9 × 20.3 (11 × 8). The Fitzwilliam Museum, Cambridge (499*) **42l** *Citrus Limonium*, from Charles Dessalines D' Orbigny's *Dictionnaire Universel d'histoire Naturelle*, MM. Renard, Martinet et cie, 1892 **42r** Antonio da Correggio, *Virgin and Child with the Young St. John the Baptist* (detail), *c.* 1515. Oil on panel, 64.2 × 50.2 (25 ¼ × 19 ¾). Clyde M. Carr Fund. Art Institute of Chicago (1965.688) **43** Maria Margaretha van Os, *Still Life with Lemon and Cut Glass*, 1823–26. Oil on panel, 27 × 23 (10 ¾ × 9 ⅛). Rijksmuseum, Amsterdam (SK-A-1107) **44** *Hemlock* (l) and *fine-leaved water hemlock* (r), from Giorgio Bonelli et al., *Hortus Romanus*, Bouchard et Gravier, 1772–93.

Rare Book Division, The New York Public Library (b14444147)
45 Jacques-Louis David, *The Death of Socrates* (detail), 1787. Oil
on canvas, 129.5 × 196.2 (51 × 77 ¼). Catharine Lorillard Wolfe
Collection, Wolfe Fund, 1931. The Metropolitan Museum of Art,
New York (31.45) **46** George Hunt Jr., *Raven Releasing the Sun*, 1985.
Silkscreen on paper, 50.8 × 38.1 (20 × 15). Gift of R. Bruce and
Mary-Louise Colwell. Seattle Art Museum (2018.29.191). © George
Hunt Jr. **47a** Mark Dion, *Seattle Vivarium*, 2002. Coloured pencil
on paper, 23 × 30.5 (9 × 12). Courtesy the artist and Tanya Bonakdar
Gallery, New York, Los Angeles **47b** Mark Dion, *Neukom Vivarium*,
2006. Mixed media installation, Greenhouse structure length:
24.38 m (80 ft.). Gift of Sally and William Neukom, American
Express Company, Seattle Garden Club, Mark Torrance Foundation
and Committee of 33, in honour of the 75th Anniversary of the
Seattle Art Museum, 2007. Commissioned from the artist by
Seattle Art Museum (funds from donors), 2003. Photo Paul
Macapia. Courtesy the artist and Tanya Bonakdar Gallery,
New York, Los Angeles **48** Andrea Mantegna, centre panel of
San Zeno altarpiece (detail), 1457–60. Tempera on wood, 220 × 115
(86.6 × 45.2). Basilica of San Zeno, Verona **49** Mary Vaux Walcott,
Beaked Hazelnut, 1932. Watercolour on paper, 25.5 × 17.9 (10 × 7).
Gift of the artist. Smithsonian American Art Museum,
Washington, D.C. (1970.355.63) **50l** Evelyn De Morgan, *The Angel
of Death I* (detail), 1880. Oil on canvas, 93 × 112.8 (36 ⅝ × 44 ½).
De Morgan Collection, Barnsley (P_EDM_0021) **50r** Cypress Tree,
from Joseph Miller's *A Curious Herbal*, John Nourse, 1751. George
Arents Collection, The New York Public Library (b10121930)
51 Henri-Edmond Cross, *Coastal View with Cypress Trees*, 1896.
Oil on canvas, 65 × 92 (25 ⅝ × 36 ¼). Musée du Petit Palais, Geneva
52 Pierre Joseph Redouté, *Fagus silvatica*, from M. Duhamel du
Monceau's *Traité des Arbres et Arbustes*, Didot ainé, 1801–19. Rare
Book Division, The New York Public Library (b14485031) **53** Paul
Nash, *The Wood on the Hill (Wittenham Clumps)*, 1912. Pen and ink
drawing, 34 × 33.4 (13 ½ × 13 ¼). Ashmolean Museum, Oxford
(WA2001.60). Photo Ashmolean Museum/Bridgeman Images
55 Roman fresco from House of the Orchard or of the Floral
Cubicles (detail), Pompeii, 1st century. Photo Berk Ozdemir/Alamy
56 Giorgio Gallesio, *Fico Pissaluto*, from Gallesio's *Pomona Italiana*,
Niccolò Capurro, 1817–39. The New York Public Library (b13674913)
57 Lucian Freud, *Girl with a Fig Leaf*, 1947. Etching on paper,
29 × 23.5 (11 ½ × 9 ⅜). Private Collection. © The Lucian Freud
Archive. All Rights Reserved 2025/Bridgeman Images **58** David
Nash, *Ash Dome*, 1977. Closely guarded location, Eryri/Snowdonia,
Wales. Photo, 2009 © Jonty Wilde; Courtesy David Nash **59** Jacob
van Huysum, Flowering ash, 1730. Engraving with watercolour,
37 × 25.5 (14 ⅝ × 10 ⅛). Wellcome Collection, London (20537i)
60 Rebecca Hey, *Holly*, from Hey's *The Spirit of the Woods*,
Longman, Brown, Green, and Longmans, 1837 **61l** Carlton
Alfred Smith, *Christmas Eve* (detail), 1901. Watercolour, 75 × 123
(29.5 × 48.4). Private Collection **61r** *The Unicorn Rests in a Garden
(from The Unicorn Tapestries)* (detail), 1495–1505. Wool warp with
wool, silk, silver, and gilt wefts, overall: 368 × 251.5 (144 ⅞ × 99).
Gift of John D. Rockefeller Jr., 1937. The Metropolitan Museum of
Art, New York (37.80.6) **62, 63l** Pierre Joseph Redouté, *Juniperus
communis, Juniperus oxycedrus*, from M. Duhamel du Monceau's
Traité des Arbres et Arbustes, Didot ainé, 1801–19. Rare Book
Division, The New York Public Library (b14485031) **63r** Emily
Carr, *A Rushing Sea of Undergrowth*, 1935. Oil on canvas, 112.8 × 69
(44 ½ × 27 ¼). Emily Carr Trust. Vancouver Art Gallery
(VAG 42.3.17) **64** Girolamo dai Libri, *Madonna and Child with
Saints*, c. 1520. Tempera and oil on canvas, 398.8 × 207 (157 × 81 ½).
Fletcher Fund, 1920. The Metropolitan Museum of Art, New York
(20.92) **65l** William Clark, Bay laurel, from John Stephenson
and James Morss Churchill's *Medical Botany*, J. Churchill, 1834
65r Lorenzo Lotto, *Venus and Cupid* (detail), 1520. Oil on canvas,

92.4 × 111.4 (36 ⅜ × 43 ⅞). Purchase, Mrs. Charles Wrightsman Gift,
in honor of Marietta Tree, 1986. The Metropolitan Museum of Art,
New York (1986.138) **66l** Benoît Chirat, Olive branch, lithograph
with watercolour, c. 1850. Wellcome Collection, London (27084i)
66r Terracotta skyphos, Greek, mid-5th century BCE. Red-figure,
5.8 × 12.1 × 7.2 (2 ¼ × 4 ¾ × 2 ¹³/₁₆). Rogers Fund, 1941. The
Metropolitan Museum of Art, New York (41.162.100) **67** Vincent
van Gogh, *Olive Trees*, 1889. Oil on canvas, 73.66 × 92.71 (29 × 36 ½).
The William Hood Dunwoody Fund. Minneapolis Institute of
Art (51.7) **68** *Areca catechu*, from Köhler's *Medizinal-Pflanzen*, Fr.
Eugen Köhler, 1890 **69** Francesco del Cossa, *Saint Lucy*, c. 1473–74.
Tempera on panel, 77.2 × 56 (30 ⅜ × 22 ¹/₁₆). Samuel H. Kress
Collection. National Gallery of Art, Washington, D.C. (1939.1.228)
70–71 Caspar David Friedrich, *Winter Landscape*, probably 1811. Oil
on canvas, 32.5 × 45 (12 ⅞ × 17 ¾). The National Gallery, London
(NG6517) **72** *Pinus inops*, 1837, from Aylmer Bourke Lambert's
A Description of the Genus Pinus, George White, 1837. Rare Book
Division, The New York Public Library (b13640523) **74** Giorgio
Gallesio, *Mandorla del Diavolo*, from Gallesio's *Pomona Italiana*,
Niccolò Capurro, 1817–39. Rare Book Division, The New York
Public Library (b13674913) **75** *Christ in Majesty*, from The Speyer
Evangelist, c. 1220. 33.2 × 25.3 (13 ⅛ × 10). Badische Landesbibliothek
(Cod. Bruchsal 1, fol.1v) **76** Vincent van Gogh, *Almond Blossom*,
1890. Oil on canvas, 73.3 × 92.4 (28 ⅞ × 36 ½). Van Gogh Museum,
Amsterdam (Vincent van Gogh Foundation) **78** Pierre Joseph
Redouté, *Quercus robur*, from M. Duhamel du Monceau's *Traité des
Arbres et Arbustes*, Didot ainé, 1801–19. Rare Book Division, The
New York Public Library (b14485031) **79a** Samuel Palmer, *Oak Tree
and Beech, Lullingstone Park*, c. 1828. Pen, ink, graphite, watercolour
and opaque watercolour on paper, 29.6 × 47 (11 ⅝ × 18 ½). The
Morgan Library and Museum, New York (2006.53) **79b** Patricia
Day, *Whispering Oak*, 2023. Pastel on paper, 14 × 21.6 (5.5 in. × 8.5).
Courtesy the artist **80** Joseph Beuys, *7000 Oak Trees*, 1982. documenta
archiv, Kassel. Photo © documenta archiv/Dieter Schwerdtle.
Artwork © DACS 2025 **81** Gold funerary wreath, Rome, 1st–2nd
century. Gold, 31.8 (12 ½). Gift of Mrs. Wallace Phillips, 1957. The
Metropolitan Museum of Art, New York (57.59) **82** Gravestone
with weeping willow, 19th century. St Mary's churchyard,
Rainham, Kent. Photo courtesy Carole Tyrrell **83** Babylon Willow,
n.d. Photo DeAgostini Picture Library/Getty Images **84** Yew
(Ground Hemlock), 1862–69. Lithograph, 9.8 × 5.6 (3 ⅞ × 2 ³/₁₆).
The Jefferson R. Burdick Collection, Gift of Jefferson R. Burdick.
The Metropolitan Museum of Art, New York (Burdick 627, W13.12)
85 Old Yew Trees, North Door of St. Edward's Church, Stow-on-
the-Wold, Gloucestershire, 12th–15th century. The door itself dates
from the 17th or 18th century. Photo SuperStock/David Hall/Loop
Images **86** Thomas S. Sinclair, Thomas's Elm, from Thomas
Nuttall's *The North American Sylva*, J. Dobson, 1842–49 **87** John
Constable, *Study of the Trunk of an Elm Tree*, c. 1821. Oil on paper,
30.6 × 24.8 (12 × 9 ¾). Victoria & Albert Museum, London
(786-1888) **88** Salvador Dalí, *Metamorphosis of Narcissus* (detail),
1937. Oil on canvas, 51.1 × 78.1 (20 ⅛ × 30 ¾). Tate, London (T02343).
Photo Tate Images. © Salvador Dalí, Fundació Gala-Salvador Dalí,
DACS 2025 **90** Sandro Botticelli, *Primavera*, c. 1480. Tempera on
wood, 207 × 319 (81 ½ × 125 ⅝). Uffizi Galleries, Florence (1890 n.
8360) **91a** Jeff Koons, *Puppy*, 1992. Stainless steel, soil and flowering
plants. Guggenheim Museum Bilbao (GBM1997.29). Photo KarSol/
Alamy. Artwork © Jeff Koons **91b** Joseph Stella, *Flowers, Italy*, 1931.
Oil on canvas, 189.8 × 189.8 (74 ¾ × 74 ¾). Gift of Mr. and Mrs.
Jonathan Marshall. Phoenix Art Museum **92** Dorothea Tanning,
Zephirium apochripholiae (Windwort), 1997–98. Oil on canvas,
97 × 130 (38 ¼ × 51 ⅛). © ADAGP, Paris and DACS, London, 2025
93l John William Waterhouse, *The Awakening of Adonis* (detail),
1899. Oil on canvas, 95.9 × 188 (37 ⅞ × 74 ⅛). Private Collection.
Photo The Maas Gallery, London/Bridgeman Images **93r** Johann

Michael Seligmann, *Anemone plant*, *c.* 1768. Engraving with watercolour and gouache. Wellcome Collection, London (20471i) 94l *Aquilegia nikolicii*, from *Curtis's Botanical Magazine* N.9405, 1935 94r Frederick A. Walpole, Columbine, Fisch, Sitka, Alaska, June 26, 1900, from Harriman, et al. *Alaska*. Doubleday, Page, 1901. 95 Hugo van der Goes, *Adoration of the Shepherds* (detail), centre panel of the Portinari altarpiece, 1477–78. Oil on wood, 274 × 652 (107 ⅞ × 256 ¾). Uffizi Galleries, Florence (1890 nn. 3191, 3192, 3193) 96 John Curtis, *Arum italicum*, from John Sims' *Curtis's Botanical Magazine* vol.50, 1823 97 Vincent van Gogh, *Giant Peacock Moth*, 1889. Oil on canvas, 33.5 × 24.5 (13 ¼ × 9 ¾). Van Gogh Museum, Amsterdam (Vincent van Gogh Foundation) 98–99 Sandro Botticelli, *The Birth of Venus*, *c.* 1485. Tempera on canvas, 172.5 × 278.5 (68 × 109 ¾). Uffizi Galleries, Florence (1890 n. 878) 100 Jane Elizabeth Giraud, Daisies, 1846. The New York Public Library (b13501092) 101 Richard Dadd, *The Fairy-Feller's Master-Stroke*, 1855–64. Oil on canvas, 54 × 39.4 (21 ⅜ × 15 ⅝). Tate, London (T00598). Photo Tate Images 102 Albrecht Dürer, *Portrait of the Artist Holding a Thistle* (detail), 1493. Oil on parchment over canvas, 56.5 × 44.5 (22.2 × 17.2). Musée du Louvre, Paris (RF 2382) 103 Alice Carmen Gouvy, *Thistle 215*, 1902. Watercolour on paper, 64 × 45 (25 ¼ × 17 ¾). Rakow Research Library, Corning, NY (88923 1000074694) 104 Piet Mondrian, *Chrysanthemum*, *c.* 1908–9. Crayon on paperboard, 25.4 × 28.6 (10 × 11 ¼). Solomon R. Guggenheim Museum, New York (61.1589) 105 Pieter de Pannemaeker, after Jean Linden, Autumn chrysanthemum hybrids, from Jean Linden's *L'Illustration Horticole*, 1888. Photo Florilegius/Universal Images Group/Getty Images 106, 107b Crocus, coloured etching, *c.* 1812. Wellcome Collection, London (26412i) 107a 'Saffron Gatherers', detail of fresco, *c.* 1500 BCE, Xeste 3, Akrotiri, Santorini 108 James Sowerby, Round-Leaved Cyclamen, from William Curtis' *Botanical Magazine*, vol.1, 1787 109 Moshe Gershuni, *Hai Cyclamen*, 1984. Mixed media on paper, 200 × 140 (78 ¾ × 55 ⅛). Private Collection. © The Moshe Gershuni Art Trust 110l Francisco Goya, *The Marquesa de Pontejos* (detail), *c.* 1786. Oil on canvas, 210.3 × 127 (82 13/16 × 50). Andrew W. Mellon Collection. National Gallery of Art, Washington (1937.1.85) 110r Augusta Withers, *Tree carnation*, from Edward George and Andrew Henderson's *The Illustrated Bouquet*, E.G. Henderson & Son, 1857 111 John Singer Sargent, *Carnation, Lily, Lily, Rose*, 1885–86. Oil on canvas, 174 × 153.7 (68 ⅝ × 60 ⅝). Tate, London (N01615). Photo Tate Images 112 Vincent van Gogh, *Portrait of Dr Paul Gachet*, 1890. Oil on canvas, 68.2 × 57 (26 ⅞ × 22 ½). Musée d'Orsay, Paris (RF1949-16) 113l James Sowerby, *Foxglove*, from William Withering's *An Account of the Foxglove*, M. Swinney, 1785. Wellcome Collection, London (ESTC T55002) 113r Dorothy Cross, *Foxglove*, 2007. Bronze, 70 × 20 × 16 (27 ⅝ × 7 ⅞ × 6 ⅜). Courtesy the artist 114 William Clark, *Sunflower*, from Richard Morris' *Flora Conspicua*, Longman, Rees, Orme, Brown, and Green, 1826 115 Dorothea Tanning, *Eine Kleine Nachtmusik*, 1943. Oil on canvas, 40.7 × 61 (16 ⅛ × 24 ⅛). Tate, London (T07346). Photo Tate Images. © ADAGP, Paris and DACS, London 2025 116 Anselm Kiefer, *Die Orden der Nacht* (*The Orders of the Night*), 1996. Acrylic, emulsion, and shellac on canvas, 356 × 463 (140 ⅛ × 182 ¼). Gift of Richard and Elizabeth Hedreen. Seattle Art Museum (99.85). Photo Prudence Cuming Associates Ltd. © Anselm Kiefer 117 Faith Ringgold, *The Sunflower Quilting Bee at Arles*, 1991. Acrylic on canvas with pieced fabric border, 188 × 203.2 (74 × 80). Private Collection. © 2025 Faith Ringgold/ARS, NY and DACS, London 118 Pierre Joseph Redouté, *Hyacinthus orientalis*, from Redouté's *Choix des Plus Belle Fleurs et des Plus Beaux Fruits*, Panckoucke, 1827. The Minnich Collection, The Ethel Morrison Van Derlip Fund, 1966. Minneapolis Institute of Art (P.18,330) 119 Ellsworth Kelly, *Hyacinth*, 1949. Ink on paper, 41.9 × 30.5 (16 ½ × 12). Private Collection. Image courtesy Ellsworth Kelly Studio. © Ellsworth Kelly Foundation 120 Vincent van Gogh, *Irises*, 1889. Oil on canvas, 74.3 × 94.3 (29 ¼ × 37 ⅛). J. Paul Getty Museum, Los Angeles (90.PA.20) 121 Kazumasa Ogawa, *Iris Kæmpferi*, 1896. Colored collotype, 27.9 × 20.8 (11 × 8 3/16). J. Paul Getty Museum, Los Angeles (84.XB.759.6.7) 122 Pierre Joseph Redouté, *Iris squalens* and *Iris germanica*, from Redouté's *Les Liliacées*, Imprimerie de Didot Jeune, 1805–16. Rare Book Division, The New York Public Library (b10808712) 123 Georgia O'Keeffe, *Black Iris*, 1926. Oil on canvas, 91.4 × 75.9 (36 × 29 ⅞). Alfred Stieglitz Collection, 1969. The Metropolitan Museum of Art, New York (69.278.1). © Georgia O'Keeffe Museum/DACS 2025 124 Simone Martini, *Annunciation with St Margaret and St Ansanus* (detail), 1333. Tempera on wood, 184 × 168 (72 ½ × 66 ¼). Uffizi Galleries, Florence (1890 nos. 451, 452, 453) 125 Charlotte Sowerby, *Lillium speciosum*, from William Robyn's *The Illustrated Bouquet*, E.G. Henderson & Son, 1857. Rare Book Division, The New York Public Library (b14454923) 126 Dante Gabriel Rossetti, *The Blessed Damozel*, 1871–78. Oil on canvas, 136.8 × 96.5 (53 ⅞ × 38). Bequest of Grenville L. Winthrop. Harvard Art Museums/Fogg Museum, Cambridge, MA (1943.202) 127 David Hockney, *Mr and Mrs Clark and Percy*, 1970–71. Acrylic on canvas, 213.4 × 304.8 (84 × 120). Tate, London (T01269). Photo Tate Images. © David Hockney 128l John T. Curran, Tiffany & Co., *Loving Cup*, 1891. Silver gilt, 23.2 × 15.9 (9 ⅛ × 6 ¼). Anonymous Gift, 2010. The Metropolitan Museum of Art, New York (2010.286.1) 128r H. Fletcher, after J. van Huysum, Honeysuckle, 1730. Engraving with watercolour, 37 × 25.5 (14 ⅝ × 10 ⅛). The Wellcome Collection (20536i) 129 Peter Paul Rubens, *Honeysuckle Bower* (detail), *c.* 1609–10. Oil on canvas, 178 × 136.5 (70 ⅛ × 53 ¾). Bavarian State Painting Collections - Alte Pinakothek Munich (334) 130 Salvador Dalí, *Metamorphosis of Narcissus*, 1937. Oil on canvas, 51.1 × 78.1 (20 ⅛ × 30 ¾). Tate, London (T02343). Photo Tate Images. © Salvador Dali, Fundació Gala-Salvador Dalí, DACS 2025 131 Pierre-Joseph Redouté, *Narcissus gouani*, 1827. Hand-coloured stipple engraving, 27.94 × 21.59 (11 × 8 ½). The Minnich Collection The Ethel Morrison Van Derlip Fund, 1966. Minneapolis Institute of Art (P.18,349) 132 Head of Nefertem, 18th Dynasty, 1332–1323 BCE. Wood and paint, 30 (12) high. Egyptian Museum, Cairo (JE 60723) 133 Louis van Houtte, *Nymphaea stellata*, from van Houtte's *Flore des Serres et des Jardins de l'Europe*, Louis van Houtte Éditeur, 1845–80 134 Nakht and family fishing and fowling, *c.* 1400–1370 BCE, facsimile (detail) by Norman de Garis Davies and Lancelot Crane of image from the Tomb of Nakht, east wall, south side of offering chapel, 1908–10. Tempera on paper, 194.3 × 203.8 (76 ½ × 80 ¼). Rogers Fund, 1915. The Metropolitan Museum of Art, New York (15.5.19e) 135 Claude Monet, *Nympheas*, 1897–98. Oil on canvas, 66 × 104.1 (26 × 41). Mrs. Fred Hathaway Bixby Bequest. Los Angeles County Museum of Art (M.62.8.13) 136 Orchids in Low Relief, Ara Pacis Augustae, Rome, 9 BCE. Photo Jean-Pierre Dalbéra 137 John Nugent Fitch, *Cattleya velutina*, 1882–97, from Robert Warner and Benjamin Samuel Williams' *The Orchid Album*, B. S. Williams 138 Roman Sarcophagus with the myth of Selene and Endymion, early 3rd century. Marble, 72.39 (28 ½). Rogers Fund, 1947. The Metropolitan Museum of Art, New York (47.100.4a,b) 139 *Papaver somniferum*, 1887, from Köhler's *Medizinal-Pflanzen*, Fr. Eugen Köhler, 1883–1914 140l Dante Gabriel Rossetti, *Beata Beatrix* (detail), *c.* 1864–70. Oil on canvas, 86.4 × 66 (34 ⅛ × 26). Tate, London (N01279). Photo Tate Images 140r Paolo Veneziano, *Madonna of the Poppy* (detail), *c.* 1325. Oil on panel, 98 × 184 (38 ⅝ × 72 ½). San Pantalon, Venice. Photo Mondadori Portfolio/Getty Images 141 Paul Cummins and Tom Piper, *Blood Swept Lands and Seas of Red*, 2014. Ceramic poppies. Installation at the Tower of London. Photo Zefrog/Alamy 142l John Everett Millais, *Isabella* (detail), 1849. Oil on canvas, 103 × 142.8 (40 ⅝ × 56 ¼). Purchased by the Walker Art Gallery in 1884. Walker Art Gallery, Liverpool (WAG 1637) 142r *Passiflora holosericea*, 1815, from Sydenham

Edwards and James Ridgway's *The Botanical Register*, Printed for James Ridgway, 1815–28 **143** Charles Allston Collins, *Convent Thoughts*, 1851. Oil on canvas, 84 × 59 (33 ⅛ × 23 ¼). Bequeathed by Mrs Thomas Combe, 1893. Ashmolean Museum, Oxford (WA1894.10) **144** Stefan Lochner, *Madonna of the Rose Bower* (detail), *c.* 1440–42. Oil on panel, 50.5 × 40 (20 × 15 ¾). Bequest of F. J. von Herwegh, 1848. Wallraf-Richartz-Museum, Cologne (WRM 0067). Photo DeAgostini/Getty Images **145** Pierre Joseph Redouté, *Rosa Centifoliar*, from Redouté's *Les Roses*, Firmin Didot, 1817–24. The Miriam and Ira D. Wallach Division of Art, Prints and Photographs: Print Collection, The New York Public Library (b13999305) **146** Charles Dessalines D' Orbigny, *Tulipa gesneriana*, from D'Orbigny's *Dictionnaire Universel d'Histoire Naturelle*, MM. Renard, Martinet et Cie., 1849 **147** Maria van Oosterwyck, *Bouquet of Flowers in a Vase*, *c.* 1670s. Oil on canvas, 73.7 × 55.9 (29 × 22). Funds by exchange from T. Edward and Tullah Hanley in honor of longtime director, Otto Bach and his wife Cile Bach. Denver Art Museum (1997.219) **148l** Stefan Lochner, *Virgin with the Violet* (detail), *c.* 1450. Oil and tempera on wood, 121.5 × 102 (47 ⅞ × 40 ¼). Kolumba Museum, Cologne **148r** Ford Madox Brown, *The Convalescent* (*A Portrait of the Artist's Wife*), 1872. Pastel on paper, 46.7 × 44.1 (18 ⅜ × 17 ⅜). Rogers Fund, 1910. The Metropolitan Museum of Art, New York (10.46) **149** Jacques Le Moyne de Morgues, *Violets and red admiral butterfly*, *c.* 1575. Watercolour, 27.3 × 18.7 (10 ¾ × 7 ⅜). Victoria and Albert Museum, London (AM.3267A-1856) **150** J. Vandamme, *Viola tricolor* (1. *Gloire de Bellevue*; 2. *Reine des Panachées*), from Charles Antoine Lemaire's *L'Illustration Horticole*, Imprimerie et lithographie de F. et E. Gyselnyck, 1854 **151a** Vincent van Gogh, *Basket of Pansies*, 1887. Oil on canvas, 46 × 55 (18 ⅛ × 21 ¾). Van Gogh Museum, Amsterdam (Vincent van Gogh Foundation) **151b** British Queen Elizabeth I's embroidered bookbinding, 1544. Bodleian Libraries, University of Oxford. Photo The Picture Art Collection/Alamy **152** Hieronymus Bosch, *The Garden of Earthly Delights* (detail of centre panel), 1490–1500. Oil on oak, 185.8 × 172.5 (73 ¼ × 68). Museo del Prado, Madrid (P002823) **154a** Vincent Van Gogh, *Grapes, Lemons, Pears, and Apples* (detail), 1887. Oil on canvas, 46.5 × 55.2 (18 ¼ × 21 ¾). Gift of Kate L. Brewster. Art Institute of Chicago (1949.215) **154b** Adriaen van Utrecht and Theodoor Rombouts, *An amorous couple with lettuce, artichokes, peas and other vegetables, with a squirrel* (detail), *c.* 1630. Oil on canvas, 148.9 × 129.9 (58 ⅝ × 51 ⅛). Private Collection **155** Paul Cezanne, *Still Life with Skull*, 1890–93. Oil on canvas, 54.3 × 65.4 (21 ⅜ × 25 ¾). The Barnes Foundation, Philadelphia (BF329) **156** Pierre Joseph Redouté, *Allium fragrans*, from Redouté's *Les Liliacées*, Impr. de Didot Jeune, 1805–16. Rare Book Division, The New York Public Library (b10808712) **157** Giuseppe Arcimboldo, *L'Ortolano* (*The Vegetable Gardener*), 1587–90. Oil on panel, 36 × 24 (14 ¼ × 9 ½). Museo Civico Ala Ponzone, Cremona **158l** Sir William Chambers, 'The Dunmore Pineapple', after 1777. Photo Ivan Vdovin/Alamy **158r** Georg Ehret, *Ananas aculeatus*, *c.* 1742, from Georg Ehret and Christoph Trew's *Plantae Selectae*, 1750–73 **159l** Terracotta *pinax* (votive tablet) showing Persephone and Hades enthroned, 500–450 BCE. Museo Archeologico Nazionale di Reggio Calabria (inv. 21016 26.2010) **159r** Cesare Ubertini, Wild celery, from Giorgio Bonelli et al., *Hortus Romanus*, Bouchard et Gravier, 1772–93. Rare Book Division, The New York Public Library (b14444147) **160l** Anselmus Boëtius de Boodt, Cabbage, 1596–1610. Watercolour on paper, 26.6 × 17.7 (10 ½ × 7). Loan from private collection. Rijksmuseum, Amsterdam (RP-T-BR-2017-1-9-61) **160r** Stanley Spencer, *The Dustman or The Lovers* (detail), 1934. Oil on canvas, 115 × 123.5 (45 ⅜ × 48 ⅝). Laing Art Gallery, Newcastle upon Tyne (TWCMS:B7412). Tyne & Wear Archives & Museums/© Estate of Stanley Spencer. All rights reserved 2025/Bridgeman Images **161** Leonora Carrington, *Cabbage*, 1987. Acrylic on canvas, 91.5 × 61 cm. Private collection. © Estate of Leonora Carrington/ARS, NY and DACS, London, 2025 **162** Albrecht Dürer, *St Jerome in his Study* (detail), 1514. Engraving, 24.6 × 18.9 (9 ¹¹⁄₁₆ × 7 ⁷⁄₁₆). Fletcher Fund, 1919. The Metropolitan Museum of Art, New York (19.73.68) **163** Elizabeth Twining, *Cucurbitaceae*, The Gourd Tribe, from Twining's *Illustrations of the Natural Orders of Plants*, Day and Son, 1849–55. 40.6 × 26 (16 × 10 ¼). The Minnich Collection The Ethel Morrison Van Derlip Fund, 1966. Minneapolis Institute of Art (P.18,661) **164l** Giovanni Martini da Udine, fruits, flowers and vegetables, including *Cucurbita maxima*, fresco detail from Loggia of Cupid and Psyche, Villa Farnesina, Rome, 1515–81. Photo Kim Petersen/Alamy **164r** Cesare Ubertini, *Cucurbita aspera Pyriformis*, from Giorgio Bonelli et al., *Hortus Romanus*, Bouchard et Gravier, 1772–93. Rare Book Division, The New York Public Library (b14444147) **165** Yayoi Kusama, *Pumpkin*, 1994, Benesse Art Site Naoshima. Photo Kat Davis/Alamy. © YAYOI KUSAMA **166l** Dancing maenad holding a thyrsus (detail), Roman copy after 5th century BCE Greek original, attributed to Callimachus. White marble, 141 × 79 × 12 (55 ⅝ × 31 ⅛ × 4 ¾). Museo del Prado, Madrid (E000046). Photo SuperStock/Album/Album Archivo **166r** British School, *Mary Tudor and Charles Brandon, 1st Duke of Suffolk* (detail), after 1515. Oil on panel, 41.5 × 44.5 (16 ⅜ × 17 ⅝). National Trust, Anglesey Abbey, Cambridge (NT 515735) **167** Basilius Besler, *Fructus artischochi*, from Besler's *Hortus Eystettensis*, 1613 **168l** Unknown artist (French), 'Fantastic Hairdress with Fruit and Vegetable Motif', 18th century. Watercolour on canvas over board, 43.8 × 55.9 (17 ¼ × 22). Alfred W. Hoyt Collection, Bequest of Rosina H. Hoppin, 1965. The Metropolitan Museum of Art, New York (65.692.8) **168r** Maubert, *Edible roots*, from Aristide Dupuis & Jean-Augustin Barral's *Le Règne Végétal*, T. Morgand, 1864–69. Bibliothèque nationale de France, Paris (S-8442) **169** René Magritte, *L'Explication* (*The Explanation*), 1952. Oil on canvas, 46 × 35 (18 ⅛ by 13 ¾). Private Collection. © ADAGP, Paris and DACS, London 2025 **170** Pieter Bruegel the Elder, *The Blind Leading the Blind*, 1568. Distemper on canvas, 86 × 154 (33 ⅞ × 60 ¾). Museo e Real Bosco di Capodimonte, Naples **171** Cesare Ubertini, *Crithmum maritimum*, from Giorgio Bonelli et al., *Hortus Romanus*, Bouchard et Gravier, 1772–93. Rare Book Division, The New York Public Library (b14444147) **172l** Hieronymus Bosch, *The Garden of Earthly Delights* (detail of centre panel), 1490–1500. Oil on oak, 185.8 × 172.5 (73 ¼ × 68). Museo del Prado, Madrid (P002823) **172r** Upper Rhenish Master, *Madonna in den Erdbeeren* (*Madonna of the Strawberries*), *c.* 1425. Mixed media on spruce wood, 144.5 × 87.5 (57 × 34 ½). Kunstmuseum, Solothurn (AI 32) **173** G. Severeyns, Strawberries, from Charles Morren's *La Belgique Horticole*, La Direction Générale, 1851 **174** Orchard Painter, *Women Gathering Apples*, red-figure column krater, *c.* 460 BCE. Terracotta, 44.1 × 46 (17 ⅜ × 18 ⅛). Rogers Fund, 1907. The Metropolitan Museum of Art, New York (07.286.74) **175** Giorgio Gallesio, *Malus appenninensis*, from Gallesio's *Pomona Italiana*, Niccolò Capurro, 1817–39 **176** René Magritte, *The Son of Man*, 1964. Oil on canvas, 116 × 89 (45 ⅝ × 35). Private Collection. © ADAGP, Paris and DACS, London 2025 **177** Claes Oldenburg and Coosje van Bruggen, *Geometric Apple Core*, 1991. Latex paint, polyurethane and steel 233.7 × 139.7 × 106.7 (92 × 55 × 42). The Doris and Donald Fisher Collection. San Francisco Museum of Modern Art. Photo Bill Jacobson, courtesy Pace Gallery. © The Estate of Claes Oldenburg **178** Berthe Hoola van Nooten, *Musa paradisiaca*, *c.* 1885. Chromolithograph. The Wellcome Collection (16359i) **179** Giorgio de Chirico, *The Uncertainty of the Poet*, 1913. Oil on canvas, 106 × 94 (41 ¾ × 37 ⅛). Tate, London (T04109). Photo Tate Images. © DACS 2025 **180** Lene Kilde, *The Nutmeg Princess*, 2014. Molinere Bay Underwater Sculpture Park, Grenada. Photo © Howard Clarke. Artwork © Lene Kilde **181** *Myristica fragrans Houtt.*, from Köhler's *Medizinal-Pflanzen*, Fr. Eugen Köhler, 1890 **182** Giovanna Garzoni, *Cherries in* *a Dish, a Pod and a Bumblebee*, *c*. 1642–51. Gouache on parchment, 24.5 × 37.5 (9 ¾ × 14 ⅞). Galleria Palatina, Florence **183** Pierre Joseph Redouté, *Cerasus semperflorens*, from M. Duhamel du Monceau's *Traité des Arbres et Arbustes*, Chez Didot ainé, au Louvre..., 1801–19. Rare Book Division, The New York Public Library (b14485031) **184** Giorgio Gallesio, *Persica Magdalena*, from Gallesio's *Pomona Italiana*, Niccolò Capurro, 1817–39. The New York Public Library (b13674913) **185** Jan van Eyck, *The Arnolfini Portrait*, 1434. Oil on oak, 82.2 × 60 (32 ⅜ × 23 ⅝). The National Gallery, London (NG186) **186** Pierre-Auguste Renoir, *Still Life with Peaches*, 1881. Oil on canvas, 53.3 × 64.8 (21 × 25 ½). Bequest of Stephen C. Clark, 1960. The Metropolitan Museum of Art, New York (61.101.12) **187l** Greek vase in the form of a pomegranate, 8th century BCE. Terracotta, 10.2 × 8.3 (4 × 3 ¼). Rogers Fund, 1912. The Metropolitan Museum of Art, New York (12.229.8) **187r** Pierre Joseph Redouté, *Grenadier punica*, from Redouté's *Choix des plus belles fleurs*, Panckoucke, 1827–33 **188** *The Unicorn Rests in a Garden*, Unicorn Tapestries, *c*. 1495–1505. Wool and silk threads, 368 × 251.5 (144 ⅞ × 99). Gift of John D. Rockefeller Jr., 1937. The Metropolitan Museum of Art, New York (37.80.6) **189a** Sandro Botticelli, *Virgin and Child with Angels* (*'Madonna of the Pomegranate'*) (detail), *c*. 1487. Tempera on wood, diameter 143.5 (56 ½). Uffizi Galleries, Florence (1890/1607) **189b** Dante Gabriel Rossetti, *Proserpine* (detail), 1874. Oil paint on canvas, 125.1 × 61 (49 ⅜ × 24 ⅛). Tate, London (N05064). Photo Tate Images **190** Giorgio Gallesio, *Pera Campana, Pyrus Pompeiana*, from Gallesio's *Pomona Italiana*, Niccolò Capurro, 1817–39. The New York Public Library (b13674913) **191** Carlo Crivelli, *Madonna and Child*, *c*. 1490. Tempera on panel, 32.8 × 24.7 (12 ¹⁵⁄₁₆ × 9 ¾). Samuel H. Kress Collection. National Gallery of Art, Washington, D.C. (1939.1.264) **192** Cesare Ubertini, *Raphanus minor*, from Giorgio Bonelli et al., Hortus Romanus, Bouchard et Gravier, 1772–93. Rare Book Division, The New York Public Library (b14444147) **193** Jennifer Knaus, *Radish Head*, 2014. Oil on panel, 30.5 × 30.5 (12 × 12). © Jennifer Knaus **194** Pierre Joseph de Pannemaeker, A bunch of tomatoes, chromolithograph, *c*. 1854. Wellcome Collection, London (28073i) **195** Andy Warhol, *Campbell's Soup Cans*, 1962. Acrylic and enamel paint on canvas, 50.8 × 40.6 (20 × 16) each. The Museum of Modern Art, New York (476.1996.1-32). © 2025 The Andy Warhol Foundation for the Visual Arts, Inc./Licensed by DACS, London **196a** *Melongiana* in Tacuinum Sanitatis (detail), 1385–90. Austrian National Library, Vienna. Photo SuperStock/Album/Prisma/ Album Archivo **196b** Paul Cézanne, *Still Life with a Ginger Jar and Eggplants* (detail), 1893–94. Oil on canvas, 72.4 × 91.4 (28 ½ × 36). Bequest of Stephen C. Clark, 1960. The Metropolitan Museum of Art, New York (61.101.4) **197** Basilius Besler, Aubergine, from Besler's *Hortus Eystettensis*, 1613 **198** Vincent van Gogh, *The Potato Eaters*, 1885. Oil on canvas, 82 × 114 (32 ⅜ × 45). Van Gogh Museum, Amsterdam (Vincent van Gogh Foundation) **199** J. Vreugdenhil, *Solanum tuberosum*, n.d. Coloured lithograph. Naturalis Biodiversity Center, Leiden (L.0939623) **200** *Verbascum thapsus*, n.d. Botanical educational poster, 62.2 × 94 (24 ½ × 37 ⅛). Stichting Academisch Erfgoed, Amsterdam **201** Giovanni Bellini, *St. Francis in the Desert* (detail), *c*. 1475–80. Oil on panel, 124.6 × 142 (49 ¹⁄₁₆ × 55 ⅞). Henry Clay Frick Bequest. The Frick Collection, New York (1915.1.03) **202** Rachel Ruysch (attrib.), *Vanity* (detail), *c*. 1690. Oil on canvas, 70 × 90 (27 ⅝ × 35 ½). Musée Jeanne d'Aboville, La Fère (MJA323). Photo GrandPalaisRmn/Benoît Touchard **204** Arthur Hughes, *The Long Engagement*, 1859. Oil on canvas, 107 × 53.3 (42 ¼ × 21). Birmingham Museums Trust (1902P13) **205** Hieronymus Bosch, *The Haywain Triptych*, *c*. 1516. Oil on panel, 147.1 × 224.3 (58 × 88 ⅜). Museo Del Prado, Madrid (P002052) **206** F. Domingo, *Cucumis sativus*, from Fr. Manuel Blanco's *Flora de Filipinas*, 1877–83 **207** Carlo Crivelli, *Madonna and Child*, *c*. 1480. Tempera and gold on wood, 37.8 × 25.4 (14 ⅞ × 10). The Jules Bache Collection, 1949. The Metropolitan Museum of Art, New York (49.7.5) **209** Ackroyd & Harvey, *Mother and Child (Aka Heather and Adèle)*, 1998, Staygreen grass, clay, jute, 1.2m × 1.8m. Image imprinted on molecular level through process of photographic photosynthesis. Image courtesy of the artists **210** Albrecht Dürer, *Great Piece of Turf*, 1503. Watercolour and body colour on vellum, 40.3 × 31.1 (15 ⅞ × 12 ¼). The Albertina Museum, Vienna **211** A.F. Lydon, *Bromus asper, Hordeum sylvaticum* and *Avena flavescens* from Edward Joseph Lowe's *A Natural History of British Grasses*, Groombridge, 1858 **212** Rachel Ruysch (attrib.), *Vanity* (detail), *c*. 1690. Oil on canvas, 70 × 90 (27 ⅝ × 35 ½). Musée Jeanne d'Aboville, La Fère (MJA323). Photo GrandPalaisRmn/Benoît Touchard **213l** J.P. Del, *Glechoma hederacea*, from William Baxter's *British Phaenogamous Botany*, W. Baxter Botanic Garden, 1835 **213r** Maenad with thyrsus, ornamented with ivy leaves, Attic white-ground *kylix*, Vulci, 490–480 BCE. Staatliche Antikensammlungen, Munich **214** A'aru (The Field of Reeds), Tomb of Sennedjem, Deir-el-Medina, Egypt, *c*. 1200 BCE. Facsimile by Charles K. Wilkinson, 1922. Tempera on paper, 54 × 84.5 (21 ¼ × 33 ¼). Rogers Fund, 1930. The Metropolitan Museum of Art, New York (30.4.2) **215** Johann Ibmayer, *Arundo donax*, from Nicolai Thomae Host's *Icones et Descriptiones Graminum Austriacorum*, A. Schmidt, 1809 **216** Mary Emily Eaton, *Pueraria thunbergiana*, from *Addisonia*, vol.15, New York Botanical Garden, 1930 **217** Precious Okoyomon, *Earthseed*, 2020, mixed media. Exhibition view at the Museum für Moderne Kunst, Frankfurt, 2020. Photo Axel Schneider. © Precious Okoyomon **218** Sennedjem and his wife in the Fields of A'aru (detail), *c*. 1300 BCE. Facsimile by Charles K. Wilkinson, 1922. Tempera on paper, 54 × 84.5 (21 ¼ × 33 ¼). Rogers Fund, 1930. The Metropolitan Museum of Art, New York (30.4.2) **219** Charlotte M. Yonge, *Triticum aestivum* and *Avena sativa*, from Yonge's *The Instructive Picturebook, or Lessons from the Vegetable World*, Edmonston & Douglas, 1858. Photo SuperStock/Album/ Florilegius/Album Archivo **220** Samuel Palmer, *A Hilly Scene*, *c*. 1826–28. Watercolour on paper, 20.6 × 13.7 (8 ⅛ × 5 ½). Tate, London (N05805). Photo Tate Images **221** Thomas Hart Benton, *Wheat*, 1967. Oil on wood, 50.8 × 53.3 (20 × 21). Gift of Mr. and Mrs. James A. Mitchell and museum purchase. Smithsonian American Art Museum, Washington D.C. (1991.55). © 2025 T.H. and R.P. Benton Trusts/Licensed by Artists Rights Society (ARS), New York & DACS, London **222** W. Clark, after William Hooker, *Vitis vinifera cv.*, *c*. 1835. Coloured etching. The Wellcome Collection, London (26391i) **223a** Cupids harvesting grapes, detail of ambulatory mosaic, 4th century. Mausoleum of Santa Costanza, Rome. Photo akg-images/Pirozzi **223b** Sandro Botticelli, *Virgin and Child with an Angel* (detail), 1470–74. Tempera on panel, 85 × 64.5 (33 ⁷⁄₁₆ × 25 ⅜). Isabella Stewart Gardner Museum, Boston (P27w73) **224** Otto Wilhelm Thomé, *Zea Mays*, from Prof. dr. Thomé's *Flora von Deutschland*, Eugen Köhler, 1903 **225l** Grant Wood, *Corn Cob Chandelier for Iowa Corn Room*, 1925–26. Copper, iron and paint, 238.8 × 81.3 × 86.4 (94 × 32 × 34). Gift of John B. Turner II. Cedar Rapids Museum of Art (81.17.3) **225r** Cornelis de Heem (attrib.), *Fruit and Flowers* (detail), 1662. Oil on canvas, 83.1 × 59 (32 ¾ × 23 ¼). Victoria and Albert Museum, London (4641-1858) **226** Indian (Kalighat) School, A woman pulling giant aubergines from a tree, n.d.. Watercolour and pencil on paper, 46.1 × 28.4 (18 ¼ × 11 ¼). The Wellcome Collection, London (26113i)

Hope B. Werness is an Art Historian specializing in non-Western and modern European art. She has taught for over thirty years at California State University, Stanislaus. She is the author of, amongst others *The Continuum Encyclopedia of Native Art* (2000) and *The Encyclopedia of Animal Symbolism in World Art* (2006).

Cover illustration: Leonardo da Vinci, *A Star-of-Bethlehem and Other Plants*, c. 1506–12. London: Royal Collections.

First published in the United Kingdom in 2025 by Thames & Hudson Ltd, 181A High Holborn, London

First published in the United States in 2025 by Timber Press

Timber Press is an imprint of Workman Publishing, a division of Hachette Book Group, Inc. The Timber Press name and logo are registered trademarks of Hachette Book Group, Inc.

Timber Press
Workman Publishing
Hachette Book Group, Inc.
1290 Avenue of the Americas
New York, New York 10104
timberpress.com

Printed and bound in China by C&C Offset Printing Co. Ltd.

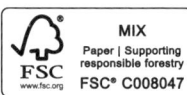

MIX
Paper | Supporting responsible forestry
FSC® C008047
www.fsc.org

The publisher is not responsible for websites (or their content) that are not owned by the publisher.

ISBN 978-1-64326-550-6

A catalog record for this book is available from the Library of Congress.

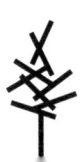

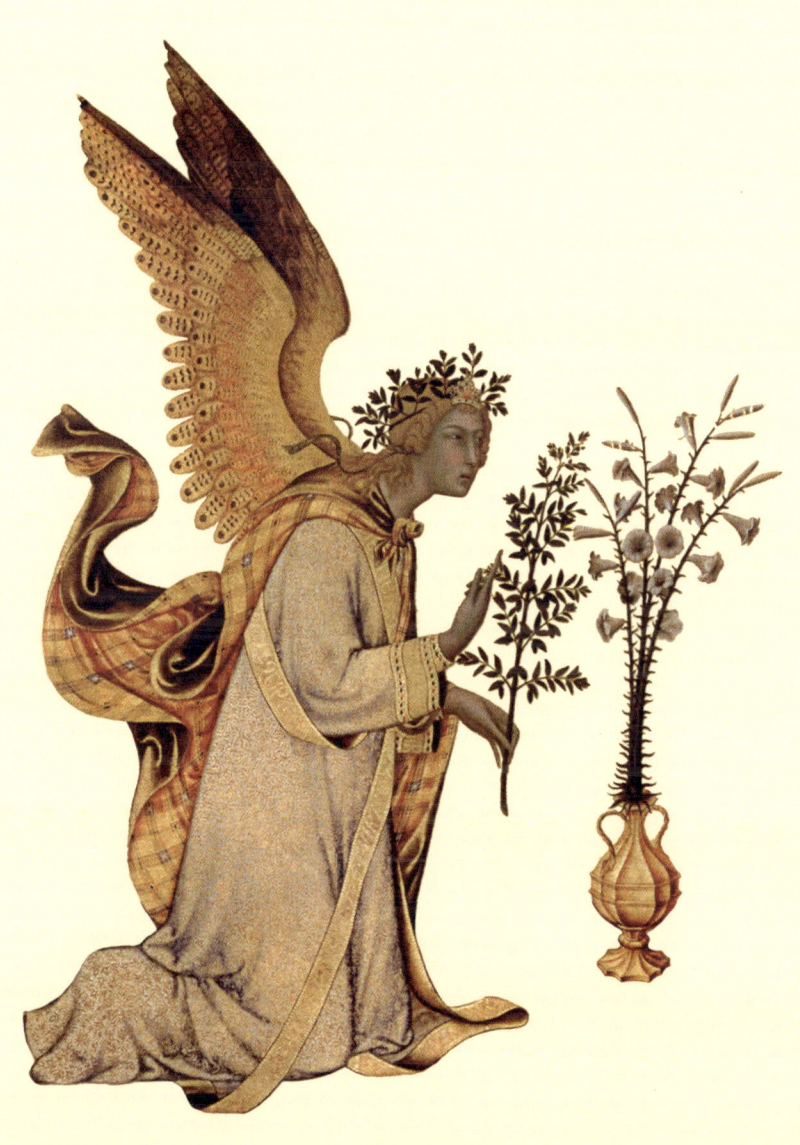

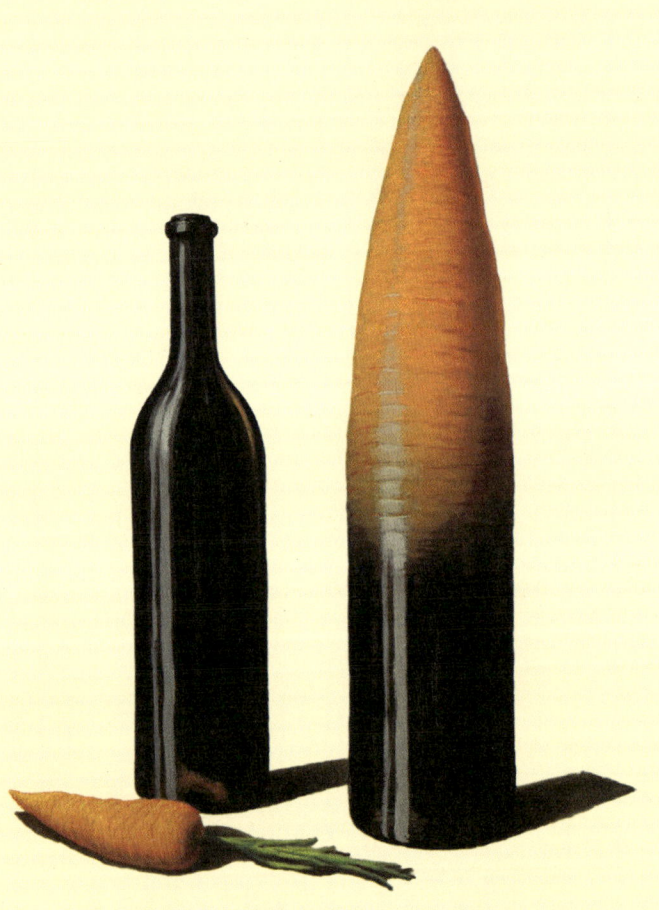